THE DE FACTO SASQUATCH

BEHAVIORAL PATTERNS AND WITNESS ACCOUNTS
BOOK 2

BOBBIE SHORT

HANGAR 1 PUBLISHING

ACKNOWLEDGMENTS

The de Facto Sasquatch is dedicated to my children and grandchildren so that they might know what I knew someday.

Love and heartfelt thanks to Chris for his technical support and believing in me.

Molly Hart Lebherz for her positive encouragement and editing.

M.K.Davis for his help with photos.

Peter Byrne and Peter Guttilla for their generous contributions.

Doug Hajicek, Chuck Prahl, Randy and Ray Brisson, Lloyd Pye, Alex Evans, Mary Lutz Esq., Jon Nichols, Wayne McKinney, Anne Carr, Larry Kaniut, Diane Stocking, Cliff Olson, Doug Tarrant, John Morley, Dr. Henner Fahrenbach, Shannon D. Baker and Chris Reinhardt.

In memory...
Vance Orchard
Rene Dahinden
Rich Grumley
Scott McClean
Archie Buckley
Charlie Edson
Richard Greenwell
Leo Selzer
Henry Moon
Fred Bradshaw

QR EXPERIENCE INSTRUCTIONS

To access this book's bonus multimedia content, open your smartphone's camera and point it at any QR code square found within. Your phone will automatically detect the code and display a prompt. Tap the link that appears to view the content. For the best audio experience, the use of headphones or earbuds is recommended.

CONTENTS

SASQUATCH BEHAVIOR

SASQUATCH
BEHAVIOR

SASQUATCH BEHAVIOR
VOLUME 1

Questions often arise concerning what research might exist concerning Sasquatch behavior. As far as I know, there are no *known* behaviors, only *reported* behaviors; I want to be clear about that distinction.

We can only build on what has been reported by multiple witnesses and draw from that information a picture that shapes what we can say we might know about Sasquatch behavior. Truth is often found in the simplest reports and not in the multiplicity or confusion of twisted particulars. It is probably not wise to make statements about the Sasquatch that might be construed as a universal behavior. Each report is different and describes a different personality unique to that Sasquatch alone.

For me, I find it counterproductive to romanticize reported Sasquatch conduct. I am a conventionalist relying exclusively on what I've personally seen and what the data suggests. I've found it unwise to depend on only one account or one person's take. I lean heavily on records and the statistics in that data. For me, there is nothing more disconcerting than when research members make the choice to spread careless remarks contrary to the data they are supposed to know about.

My own close encounter (as unremarkable as I think it was) gave me the enthusiasm to begin this search nearly thirty years ago. In addition, I've had the good fortune to communicate with thousands of other individuals who came to me through the Bigfootencounters.com website to share what they know and have experienced. Thousands of people who have had experiences to share have written about their encounters with cathartic bliss. Many were relieved to have someone to talk to without the derision, laughter, and ridicule. In gathering the bulk of the data, I have sometimes stood on the shoulders of giants, men much wiser than I am.

I cannot attest to the veracity of these reported behaviors; they are what they are – raw and heartfelt in most cases. Case reports come from all walks of life, from Joe Average types to academics and, of course, professionals and members of various government agencies. I am not here to judge their reports; simply to log the listed behavior for whatever historical significance it may contain for future followers of this mystery.

Most of the previously published data is old, outdated and repetitious – so much so that it adds monotony to the examiner's search for new, up-to-date statistical information on Sasquatch behavior. Much of the previously published data speaks to issues of terrain and witness reactions. Generally, very little behavior is listed in most reports; I'd like to see that change. A great deal of the old published data was about Sasquatch as an ape. We know differently now; tracking the ill-thought-out ape hypothesis was a 45-year distraction committed by those with name recognition who had never seen that which they promoted as an off-shoot of Gigantopithecus. Finding tracks in the wild never replaces a daylight, full-on, face to face with a Sasquatch!

For this purpose, I'm not so much interested in the reactions or feelings of the informant, nor am I interested in naming names. The focus here is primarily on reported behavior patterns and various manners of reported conduct. In almost all reported incidents, the witness reacted with surges of adrenaline and enormous levels of fear.

Some handled the situation well, but most informants (admittedly) did not. It is our nature to fear what we don't understand and cannot control. The overwhelming size of some Sasquatch individuals generally renders the witness to the level of, "this is it, I'm going to die." The level of fear is defined, and perceptions become skewed.

To locate new and unpublished information for *The De Facto Sasquatch,* I poured through old computers, notes, letters, transcripts, and audiotapes with relevant information stored since the 1980s up until today. There were surprising numbers of case reports that were never made public still stored in my old computers whose shelf life had long since passed, and I had forgotten how to work the mega-heavy old Datel computers. Can you imagine today working on an antiquated 8088 (8-bit) running at 8Mhz with 256KB of memory and a 20MB hard disk? Chances are, this current generation can't imagine such an operating system. But it was state of the art for home use in the 1980s.

Today, retrieving data from those relic machines and making any sense of them was challenging. I poured through piles of yellowed Post-it notes, some scribbled incoherently and others written in rich detail...and so my collecting began.

As you read on, nearly thirty years' worth of little-known behavior will become apparent. To be clear, for this volume on Sasquatch behavior, I've omitted most of the extraneous verbiage in the reports that speak to any issue the informant might have felt: his fear, circumstances, and conclusions.

The focus here is strategically placed on whatever message the informant's statement may have contained that reflected specifically on the behavior of the Sasquatch. Where stories are paraphrased, I have not changed the drama or actions of any Sasquatch behavior or cited manners of conduct. Years have passed in some instances, and where I was unable to obtain permissions specific to a case, I've paraphrased the narrative. Where needed, I have changed the names to protect those I could not locate again. If there is a comment, it's my opinion.

Occasionally, I have included excerpts or whole letters that tell a life story or life experience that includes behavior thought to be uncharacteristic. Where those accounts occur, it was done in an effort not to lose sight of the teller's thought-flow. You will notice, too, that with permission, I occasionally include entire emails or interviews to set a scene.

At the beginning of this project, it occurred to me that basic behaviors attributed to the Sasquatch have been, in the past, essentially ignored in favor of the ape bias or alien drama.

The behavior most often recorded would be the wandering of a Sasquatch out onto a road, seemingly oblivious to the dangers of high-speed traffic. I call them road-runner reports; they come from people in cars, vans, trucks, and several 18-wheeler incidents. Road sightings account for most of the numbers in my data, but for this effort, I will mention only a few road-runner accounts to keep repetition to a minimum.

One report came from a driver hauling fuel while working for a major oil company. In 1996, the driver wrote to me about two major highway sightings he had personally witnessed. Both occurred up the Interstate 5 corridor in the northbound lanes through California's beautiful Mt. Shasta County. His report had very little physical detail except its height, which would have placed it in the 9 to 10-foot category – the approximate height of a tractor-trailer's cab. The behavior, however, was something else. The truck driver said this individual strolled out onto the freeway amid tractor-trailers, recreational vehicles, and other general traffic. Brakes squealed, cars fish-tailed, yet the Sasquatch apparently just walked unconcerned amidst the vehicles. We cannot say categorically that all Sasquatch have a high degree of street smarts. Bears aren't that irresponsible; rare are the reports of bears mindlessly sauntering out onto a busy, highly trafficked thoroughfare. Yet, in my data, the most reported cases tend to be sightings from the road.

The informant said the creature walked casually onto the northbound side of traffic, having come out from the pine trees lining the forested freeway in that part of the country. The highway is split in that vicinity into separate lanes. The northbound and southbound traffic is divided by a wide median thick with pine trees, all sides heavily forested. The Sasquatch did not stop and look and was apparently not deterred by the approach of high-beam headlights, horns, and screeching brakes. The Sasquatch strolled smoothly across the trucker's lane, crossing the freeway in just a few steps that he said, "were major steps, it was not leaping but strolling along looking straight ahead. The trucker stated he pulled on the air horn but got no reaction from the strange creature. This behavior is commonly reported in the Lakehead-Lakeshore region of California and all over North America.[1]

The gas hauler in the previous account applied brakes, as did the witness in this next narrative. His reaction was animated and expressive. The story has its origins in West Texas, where the African American trucker became emotionally overwrought during the retelling of his ordeal. Seeing the large hairy primitive amble across the road directly in front of him, he screamed into the telephone, "...Whoa, sweet Jeezus, what do we have here, glory, hallelujah, help me Jeezus, what is this thing I see?" Wildly emotional, the trucker said he was concerned whether or not he would be able to stand on his brakes hard enough to stop the fully loaded 18-wheeler; this was just 3 miles eastbound out of Butterfield, Hudspeth County, Texas, on Highway 62. The informant, Amos Washington, said he had to gear down to allow the loping "barefoot booger" to cross the road, exclaiming that it was "hairy and naked."

Mr. Washington, decidedly upset in the retelling of his experience, remarked that the night was pitch-black outside. He indicated the apparition had better eyesight than he did to negotiate the terrain like it did. I could never decide which was more interesting, the informant or his telling of the event.[2]

A few of the road-runner sightings, however, parlay into additional behaviors like peering into the vehicle, reaching into vehicles, or running along the side of a vehicle, and sometimes facial gestures like smiling or showing teeth and interestingly, in one report, the show of emotion and the acknowledgment of road courtesies.

Steven M. had an unusual road encounter in Jasper County, Missouri. The witness claimed that he saw a "large hairy creature, from head to toes completely covered in long spindly hair," amble down the middle of the two-lane highway that led to his former home in Joplin, Missouri. The creature stood in front of the man's car, perfectly still in the headlights for several minutes. Steven flashed his headlights and tooted the horn with no reaction from the creature; he exclaimed it was almost as if the "Sasquatch was a deaf mute." There are several instances in the data where the hairy man is described acting as if it was mute or deaf and dumb.

The report read, "Suddenly the monster broke into a sprint headed right at the witness's car. The witness stepped on the accelerator and managed to swerve to avoid hitting the beast." He mentioned the car suffered minor front-end damage when he swerved the vehicle off the side of the road. He reported the incident to the local Sheriff, who informed him that there had been several other sightings that same night. In Missouri, the locals call the Sasquatch, Momo.[3]

A retired Federal employee, hunter, and woodsman shared this encounter in 2011 with Stan Huhtala:

> The statement was taken from two ladies who were traveling to work into Lincoln, Montana, because they had to open and get Lambkins Restaurant ready for the morning breakfast crowd. They were driving their car, down the pavement NE of Lincoln, say twenty miles, when a large hairy biped came across in front of the path of their vehicle from the creek below the roadbed on their right and went up an embankment and into the Hagen Creek drainage. I took it that the car was brought to a stop to avoid hitting the creature. The creature was less than five feet in front of their car and in full view through the windshield; it looked in their direction before climbing up the roadside incline. They did not wish to comment, but I finally got one of them to

talk to me about the encounter afterward. I am convinced there are many stories that remain untold. There are many hotspots and these stories, when put together, often broaden the geographic areas, increasing the need for concentrated research efforts down the road. One such, area is between Helena, Montana, and Lincoln Roger's Pass. *

In a separate incident, Stan spoke with a fellow over the phone who'd had a Bigfoot road-runner sighting. The man was traveling down I-80 in California between Sacramento and Reno, Nevada, at 3:00 p.m. when suddenly in front of him was a black Sasquatch crossing multi-lanes of the Interstate Freeway.

Road reports generally lack detail, so the people who see them from inside a moving vehicle are surprised. It's uncommon to get much creature description from an excited informant. Rare are any behavior notations in road sightings.

The next roadside sighting had a vivid description. The behavior shows a lack of interest in the dangers inherent in all busy highways. It was described by Wayne A. M. of Camp Tom Howard, Tennessee, in October of 2004.

Benson County | Hudspeth County | Momo | Sullivan County

---

* Personal correspondence Stan Huhtala, December 30, 2011.

It was broad daylight and we could see clear as day that as we approached, this man was unusually tall and covered about his body with hair - not a thick fur coat, but hair on parts of his body. The guy had no clothes on, had long straggling hair that bounced off his wide shoulders and he walked bizarrely. This guy was going the same way we were going and finally he took a couple of steps and got off the road. Then full stop, turned, looked at us as we drove on by.[4]

A Face Like an Old Warrior

Octavio Ramos of the Albuquerque Examiner documented the encounter. The roadside encounter occurred on March 7, 2011, in Thoreau, New Mexico. According to the witness, he was traveling home in a snowstorm from Gallup to Bluewater when he noticed a figure moving by the road. At first, the witness believed the form to be that of an unusually tall person, but as he got closer, he saw that the creature looked, by its hair, to be more ape-like than human. He estimated the size of it at seven feet tall and over four hundred pounds. The creature was covered with long stands of brown hair over the body, with shorter, grayish hair on its head. It had dark eyes, a pronounced brow, and "a face like an old warrior, both stern and angry in expression." The witness was frightened and elected not to stop because of the mixture of snow and ice on the road, and the size of the creature, which made its way toward his truck. The witness said that the creature did come very close to his vehicle.[5]

It is interesting that the informant described the Sasquatch as ape-like and then contradicted himself by saying, "it had the face of an old warrior," which would be human-like, not ape-like; in many cases, I think the body hair is the confusion.

The Ramos case is one of many that list the behavior of Sasquatch freely moving about in freezing conditions. It is another case where the Sasquatch has been observed walking in snow and ice...barefooted, apparently for long periods of time, according to various reports and snow photographs. Are they oblivious to the pain you and I would normally feel walking barefoot in icy conditions, or are their feet so heavily calloused that they are unable to withstand freezing temperatures?

A Face Like an Old Warrior

Excess Body Heat?

I read a science article that may shed some light on the Sasquatch's ability to withstand extreme cold temperatures.[6] The article suggested that the DNA of the Neanderthal showed markers indicating their body produced excess heat; perhaps Mother Nature's way of warming them in winter. Might this be the case with the Sasquatch? Much has been speculated that perhaps the Sasquatch has this same marker and may account for the ability to walk in snow, teach their children early to walk in snow, and survive winters in such places as Alaska, Northwest Territories, and the arctic reaches of the Yukon and Nunivak, Quebec. We have available in research many photographs of adult footprints in snow, and alongside those tracks, we see tiny 5 and 6 inch tracks identical to those left by the adults.

The Sasquatch cannot be an ape. North America has no fossil record of great apes. Apes are quadrupeds; the Sasquatch is a biped. For me, there was never any logic in thinking of them as upright walking apes.

At the same time, I discovered that all states have strict wildlife certification requirements for any ape held on private or public lands; that includes Florida, where apes are illegal to keep without certificates of state approval, adequate insurance, and strictly regulated facilities and fencing. Steep fines are strictly enforced. Housing an ape is discouraged, especially males, because there is the potential for sudden aggressiveness; fatalities have occurred. State laws require males to be castrated and females the same. Since an escaped ape couldn't reproduce, it more or less rules out a group of feral apes being misidentified as a towering Sasquatch. The news more or less ruled out the Myakka, Florida creature as an ape, relegating it to that of a costumed individual, a more sensible conclusion. I was personally questioned attentively by most agencies when I broached this subject and was admonished that there were no pockets of feral apes in the Carolinas, Georgia, Florida, or Alabama. Florida's wildlife representative also reminded me that a feral ape population would require appropriate vegetation. Palmettos and southern pine trees are not forage for apes. All citrus farms are closely regulated, and the state would know if Florida orange and grapefruit growers were being hassled by any feral apes. Otherwise, Florida has no wild fruit tree orchards available for feral ape forage. The basic dietary requirement for feral ape populations does not exist in Florida or any other southern state.

Another Incident in the Snow

This next case came to me from Quay County, New Mexico:

> My grandfather, Horace, was an engineer for the Rock Island Railroad in the 1900s. In his diary there is an entry that spoke to something unusual. It's in a safety deposit box; my sister has the keys; but I'll try to recall the incident as I think you'll find it interesting. Horace wrote extensively about a winter in 1950, January, I think it was. He guided the freight train north towards Tucumcari, New Mexico, in a "dastardly snow storm." Short of the city he saw through heavy falling snow what he thought at first were Apache Indians wrapped in dark blankets huddled together walking toward the city. Upon closer inspection, there were 6 or 7 upright walking hair covered beings walking along the railroad tracks. He thought them aliens because three years

before this incident there was the big stink in Roswell about an alien flying saucer crash and you know that story. As the locomotive drew passed the bunch, he got a good look and described them as "nothing he had ever seen before." They wore no foot covering or clothes, the blankets were instead thick hair on them and all of them had braided hair down their backs and each walked with arms embraced across the chest against the blowing snow; heads down into the storm. The entry continued with my grandfather saying he was sound of mind and not drunk. I work for Southern Pacific RR and would appreciate anonymity please.[7]

If you fancy the Sasquatch an ape, a point to consider would be that apes are not found in climates where it snows; they live in tropical climates where fruit and edible green vegetation is in abundance year round. Some argue there are macaque snow monkeys in Japan that do live in snowy conditions but they spend the winter sitting in hot springs and they are not great apes; we're not talking lesser monkeys in the case of the Sasquatch.

I don't think I'm painting here with too broad a brush, but if some of these reports are valid, we will, at some point, have to consider the Sasquatch has become a highly successful species. They appear efficient, able to establish themselves and adapt within their environment and to the encroachment of civilized man and modern machinery.

The Sasquatch is like man yet unlike him in that its adaptations are entirely of bodily strength and endurance. The Sasquatch's size and physical strength prove sufficient for its protection and obtaining food without relying on others. With few exceptions, the Sasquatch appears to be entirely a self-sufficient machine that works in concert with its environment to remain covert, all the while functioning as a family unit similar to us but removed from any social interaction.

Beyond finding random tracks for the Sasquatch, research doesn't have much in the way of 'known' behaviors with positive evidence to support the claims. Research essentially is at the mercy of witness interpretations, and anyone will tell you that witness interpretations are often skewed and unreliable. Even my own memories become dim and confused at times.

The flawed perceptions of an informant are often exaggerated by the shock accompanying the visuals involving the strange sight of a Sasquatch and its overwhelming size. I've painstakingly measured all angles of witness interpretation and decided that without anecdotal evidence, research basically has nothing to consider; no clues with which to move forward in deciphering how they maintain life.

DNA may tell us the genetic origins of the Sasquatch, but it will never tell us their rules for living or if they have a moral code. Sometimes, it seems like what's theirs is theirs, and what is ours is also theirs. DNA won't tell us anything about their culture, social structure or how they came to be here. DNA may tell us if they are physically equipped to speak, but it won't tell us if they have been taught a language or what it is like if they have. Do they simply mimic what they overhear?

Still, if only a small percentage of what witnesses tell us is accurate, much might be considered. The only real way to get better accuracy in sighting reports is to polygraph each informant, which is not only unreliable but expensive, time-consuming and not very practical. Not only are reports often faulty, but most of the research participants are keyboard investigators and wholly unprepared to question informants without leading questions. Beyond that, one of the essentials field investigators overlook is the mental health of an informant. Case in point: I worked with a female informant by email for 5½ months daily, unsure that what she told me was happening because there was never any proof, evidence, tracks, or photos. She detailed a family of Sasquatches who often came to her backyard looking for handouts. My exchanges with her moved from email to phone conversations that lasted for hours at a time and often late into the night. So intriguing were her associations with the Sasquatches on her property that I became enthralled in her weekly updates. Frustrations arose from the lack of clear tracks, photographs, or other evidence. Still, she persisted; five months turned into a year, and the communication with her continued until I finally relented to visit her over a weekend. Her home was an eleven-hour drive one way – but I went anyway. She was warm and extremely intelligent, and she taught economics at one of California's prestigious universities; there was no reason not to believe what the woman was telling me. I arrived on a Friday; we talked until two in the morning over a myriad of things. She was genuinely likable and interesting; her Sasquatch descriptions were accurate, detailed, and fascinating. She declared photos were not possible even hidden from inside the house or secreted in her clothing. I could never understand that logic – photos do not threaten, endanger, or give away her secret location; nevertheless, I was prepared with an unseen camera.

Recently widowed, she lived alone on property that backed up to a national forest with all the ingredients for long-term interaction with a Sasquatch family; I admit, I was her captive audience!

We spent all day Saturday in the field, and I actually did find tracks deep in the bush that circled a stagnant pond that was active with dragonflies, tadpoles, and gnats but little else. With the heat, the stench was overwhelming, but it came out of the pond itself, and it was not the odor of some unseen Sasquatch.

At this point, I considered her account merit; there were six 15-inch tracks in all, each with a width of 6.5 inches; all were clearly 5-toed, the right foot with a slight arch, the left flatfooted. Back at her beautiful hillside home and exhausted from the miles we'd walked, we sat on her back deck watching the tree line until well after three in the morning.

Nothing happened, and I turned in for the night.

Sunday morning dawned a gorgeous day. She went to great trouble to fix a breakfast of German sausage and ebelskivers dusted with powdered sugar and coffee; staying at her house was comparable to a weekend stay at a five-star hotel-resort – she was a marvelous hostess and great company – I genuinely like her; she was, to anyone's mind, a credible informant.

We ate on the back deck, and she pointed out where a big male would often come out of the woods and stand motionless, staring at her – watching. I figured with fifteen inch tracks the Sasquatch most likely wouldn't be as big as she demonstrated with her hands; probably a shorter female or older juvenile.

Morning came and went, and I had to consider an eleven-hour drive home. My restlessness was apparent. Suddenly, my informant shouted and pointed to a giant blue spruce not sixty feet from her dining room deck (veranda). Thinking she must mean behind the spruce, I headed out into the yard in the direction she had pointed. But I found nothing and returned back to the porch a bit put-off and suspicious. As I approached the steps, she excitedly pointed in the other direction and announced, "Here they come now. They're curious about you; they want to meet you, I think." Again, turning in that direction, I saw the dog emerging from its dog house, yawning and stretching, and then coming our way. Still, I scanned the area, desperately trying to see what she saw but nothing was there...I mean, absolutely nothing!

Meanwhile, my brain was beginning to reexamine the situation. I found myself there with this marvelously intelligent woman whose company I thoroughly enjoyed. But I said nothing to her as she carried on in her excitement. "You don't seem very interested," she said earnestly.

"I'm very interested, but I can't see what you are seeing," I replied in a rather thoughtless tone. I heard a faint "Oh dear" as she excused herself to run into the house. The woman emerged with a pharmacy prescription bottle. She fumbled to take a pill with her coffee.

Sometimes discretion really is the better part of valor, but holding myself in check that day required some doing! I grew anxious to hit the highway home and made inroads to that end. Then, strangely and as if on cue, her son dropped in for his weekly visit with his widowed mother. During the course of that exchange, I learned his mother was a diagnosed schizophrenic with imaginings and sporadic delusions far beyond my comprehension and training. Without her medication, which I was told she often forgot, she imagined many unusual things including Bigfoot beings canvassing her backyard and visitors from space.

How did I miss the signs? What about the tracks by the pond? A full year of conversing with the informant convinced me of her high intellect and seeming stability. Unfortunately, she had mental health issues, which made for a very long eleven-hour drive back home. It didn't help that she was lonely and seemed to need the mental stimulation that our long conversations brought her. We remain in contact today; her sightings are fewer when she remembers her medication.

Pride aside, as field investigators, we fail miserably at interpreting the merits of a case by conducting telephone interviews/conversations alone. It doesn't matter who you are or how long you've examined evidence in this field. The truth cannot be reasoned by a phone call, no matter how long the call may be.

Another more localized interview in the hills of San Diego County, California, ended quickly when the man answered the door and openly confessed he was hoaxing to see if any Bigfoot people would take the bait. So you never know what you'll encounter. Overall, I think most testimonies are genuine, but who knows? Sometimes, I think the genuineness of a report comes in tiny details the public isn't aware of and I like hearing those from a witness. Small children are especially great with details.

On-site interviews are costly, time-consuming, and long hours away from family. One long-time researcher said of his informant, "he's a really nice guy." Of course, being a nice guy doesn't give his testimony any particular merit. As it turned out, that particular report was fabricated.

I don't know how often I've heard researchers say the report they took was credible, and they based their opinion on the credentials after the informant's name or some impressive affiliation elsewhere? That is a silly way to think; even U.S. Presidents point into the camera lens and lie straight-faced. I like Bill Clinton, but he's a bold-faced liar who preferred to save his ass than tell the truth about Monica Lewinsky; he is no George Washington, although cherry trees may not measure up to an affair in the Oval Office with an intern.

Do not base the merits of a Bigfoot situation on a man's profession or the credentials listed after his name. Hoaxing comes from all manner of personalities. Some of our highly regarded, name-recognition nice guys have fabricated a story or two; hang around long enough, and you hear it all. Thirty years have taught me that deception in this field among the visible, more vocal members would be scandalous if everyone was told.

Interviewing by telephone is convenient, but no way to evaluate the worth of a sighting. I spent a great deal of time with the woman in the cited example, but a greater lesson was learned; not all interviews I've done end up like that one. It was a lesson I didn't expect and chance to think you wouldn't have either!

The only bit of information available to research is an avalanche of 'reported' sightings and encounters. In those accounts, listed behaviors and other manners of conduct tell a story. I like to listen for behavior clues. Every report has a few clues to behaviors once we get past all the talk about terrain and the inherent fear factor that comes with almost every sighting.

The debate over the worth of subjective evidence invariably rages on. Even if only a half-dozen of the reported cases in the database proved true, at least it's something to work with, a starting point worth considering. Data is data, no matter how it's received or how controversial it may be to those who haven't studied the history of this subject. When the data shows additional cases where the same behavior is noted several times, we begin to look at that behavior as a statistic. Statistics then rise to become patterns, and from patterns, we can begin to understand a particular Sasquatch conduct.

In processing the chronology of the case reports to follow, I was surprised at some of the activities and manners of behavior available that few paid attention to. Overwhelmingly, the statistics in *The de facto Sasquatch* demonstrate behavior with a human element; some behaviors show human and ape traits. A few find otherworldly aspects and often where none exist, at least not in my data.

I can honestly say that I have received no full-blown paranormal reports with provable legitimacy in nearly thirty years. A veteran investigator and trusted friend suggested that was because people know my conventional thoughts on the subject. But that isn't entirely true. The data I receive comes from strangers who read my website, Bigfootencounters.com, or newsletter. Initially, they didn't know me or my views or what I thought about the subject. It is rare that I get any inclination from an informant of supernatural activity.

Most informants just want to report what they've seen and heard. Those reports have no melodrama; no strange, out-of-this-world supernatural conduct or behavior listed. My guess is that only those who subscribe to the occult practices and alternate realities are the ones receiving the more inventive and dramatic testimonies. I don't know why that would be, but apparently it is.

Like the people who claim personal relationships with the Sasquatch people (aka habituators), there has never been one shred of evidence provided by abstract theorists that there is a connection between UFOs and Bigfoot. One case report does not constitute a basis for theory unless a string of on-going, verifiable reports follows it.

It's rather peculiar, but the abstract theorists I know tell me they've never seen or encountered a Sasquatch, yet they blame weird feelings on unseen Sasquatches hidden somewhere in the bush...true! What a bum-rap for the Squatch. I don't know what sparks an association between Bigfoot and the paranormal except for the need for attention and drama - the dramatic is much more exciting and sells books.

But if your informant seems deluded on some level, don't recoil. The medical world does NOT regard delusions as a character flaw or personal weakness; not at all. It is a complex chemical imbalance of the brain that causes great imaginings, skewed perceptions, and delusions. The upheaval in our brain's chemical imbalance is often triggered by fear, apprehension, and anxiety. The skewed perception is then greatly enhanced by the use of alcohol and/or the inhalation of illegal herbs (weed), speed, or other controlled substances (hallucinogens). After a while, that person begins to believe in his own delusions; this is how liars beat a polygraph. They believe so strongly in a deluded theory that it isn't lying for them – it's absolutely real. It becomes a futile effort to persuade them otherwise. It is often the same with habituators and shadow readers. They report seeing things relative to Bigfoot that other people cannot see. Many habituators claim long-term relationships with the Sasquatch people only to be made a laughing stock when those claims are investigated and no evidence is recovered.

People do ask me about otherworldly influence, but no report I've received from the masses ever mentioned a credible connection between UFOs, otherworldly influences and the Bigfoot. I received one request in 1998 when a new-to-research woman named Autumn Williams arrived on the scene. She emailed me asking if I knew of a paranormalist who would mentor her; 15 years later, I still have that email. I referred her to Henry Franzoni and heard no more from her until she began the paranormal Bigfoot Underground discussion list; followed by Oregon Bigfoot website.

Many people have witnessed UFOs on some level. I'm no exception. I watched the Phoenix triangle-shaped aircraft cruise silently over Phoenix live in 1997; it was an impressive sight to behold; in fact, for the time, it was stunning! It was a very big deal in the '90s; network television broke from regular programming to follow the strange, silent course the triangle-shaped aircraft took over Phoenix. It was broadcast live over several states. The craft moved so slowly as to almost appear to be hovering...silently. At the time, of course, everyone believed it was a design concept not of this world; "it couldn't be USA engineered," they said, "it was silent." UFO followers might be disappointed to know the airship might be a USA covert test project and not necessarily of alien manufacture after all.

The network announcers covering the live shot from Phoenix never mentioned any relationship between the event and Bigfoot. Dozens of phone calls to nearby Luke Air Force Base recorded their denials that it was on radar. However, I distinctly remember (prior to Desert Storm in August 1990) that the military also vociferously denied the B2 Bomber and the F-17 Stealth fighter that eventually participated in the Gulf War (Desert Storm).

It never occurred to me that the Phoenix spacecraft carried Bigfoot or extraterrestrials or was being flown by visiting grays, little green men, or reptilian beings from another world. Instead, the Phoenix spacecraft had some vague visual similarities to today's Lockheed-Martin's TR3b project. The Phoenix aircraft resembled a remote-controlled aircraft operated much the same as today's remote-controlled drones. Whatever the debate, I'm simply not ready to accept anything quite as melodramatic as Sasquatches arriving in spaceships or being beamed to earth out of the mother ship's windows. The concept imposes a misleading belief... and I think it is a deluded concept.

I sometimes think foreign visitors from another planet are a "maybe thing;" either that or those flying objects are NOT the reverse engineering of alien spacecraft but products of USA secret government aerospace studies. I was reminded by an optical physicist friend in northern California that the nearest star is 24 trillion miles away. He wrote in part:

...there is zero chance of visitation...not finite, not approaching zero but zero chance. There is not even a sniff of anything within light years of known science that would allow for extra-terrestrial visitation.

He was also quick to summarize Erich von Däniken as a con artist. Von Däniken, of course, is the Swiss author best known for his controversial claims about extraterrestrial influences on early human culture in books such as *Chariots of the Gods* published in 1968. Von Däniken is not a scientist by any stretch of the imagination, but he is a successful author. In a parallel instance, a theoretical astrophysicist openly called von Däniken,

> a man who makes his living selling an imaginative product, a concept that popularly sells millions of books annually, a black-belt with words but not a man with any credible extra-terrestrial insight; he is not accurate.

It may be that proponents of the Bigfoot-alien connection are also selling another imaginative product. Many men experience weirdness while in the woods, and they are quick to blame the Sasquatch. I think that an unjust accusation placed unwittingly on the Sasquatch! Instead, they ought to re-evaluate their own mindset and how it is stimulated and apparently controlled by their fear – whether or not they own the fear or are under the influence.

What isn't present in this book are the thousands of email descriptions of unhinged men during an encounter or perceived encounter. Very few reports neglect to describe in detail the fear felt by witnesses. Perceived or imagined – to them, the fear is very real. It skews perceptions. Men have reported wetting their pants, becoming immobile, being frozen, transfixed, weak, sweating profusely, or actually passing out and believing they lost time. It wasn't Bigfoot zapping them with infrasound. It was their own fear colliding with the fight or flight chemicals in the brain. It's time to own those bodily functions.

In another case, a lone UFO reportedly flew over a specific location known for Sasquatch sightings in Hayfork, California. This one event doesn't remotely suggest there is a connection between Squatches and UFO fly-overs any more than it means there is a connection between the airship that flew over Phoenix and the residents of that city – but I wouldn't try to sell that concept to a "UFO-Bigfoot-connection believer." I've heard it said by a self-described "paranormal consultant" that "…following every UFO sighting, there is a slew of Bigfoot sightings." This consultant is apparently ignorant of the facts.[8]

John Green's database does not reflect or support that statement. My data does not support that statement either. There are other well-known database files (most with no search engine capability) that do not reflect or support the ridiculous statement this consultant insists is true, that UFO sightings are followed by "a slew of Bigfoot sightings." That is bloody nonsense and angers me when I hear it. In fact, running numbers on John Green's 4,000 index card file (a copy in my possession) indicate that the opposite is true. In my own database, there are no credible reports with documentation and photos of "a slew of Bigfoot sightings following a given UFO report," not one! This is blatant paranormal propaganda! It amounts to deliberately falsifying information, and those that continue with that premise are spreading misinformation.

Michael Shermer, author of *Why People Believe Weird Things*, and *The Patterns Behind Self-deception*, said:

> …the human tendency to believe strange things – from alien abductions to dowsing rods – boils down to two of the brain's most basic, hard-wired survival skills.

Shermer explains what he calls "pseudo-scientific baloney," what it is, and how self-deception tends to get us into real trouble. Both are excellent seminars and may still be on YouTube.[9]

Eyewitness identification has been the subject of hundreds of studies over the last three decades, showing that human memory and perception can be highly unreliable. For example, of the 273 people freed from prison by way of DNA evidence (via The Innocence Project), three out of four were convicted with false identifications. That is a staggering number of false perceptions and erroneous witness identification errors! Even honest people are capable of perceiving falsely. In his opinion, Chief Justice Stuart Rabner noted in the New York Times, August of 2011, that false witness and witness misidentifications were the leading cause of wrongful convictions and life sentencing across the country,[10] ...what an astounding statistic.

Unsealed Conspiracy Files: Bigfoot

Concerning the veracity of the reports being gathered in various online database efforts, it's worth mentioning here something I heard big game hunter, Bigfoot author-investigator-tracker Peter Byrne say during a television documentary filming. It happened years ago, but Byrne's words were profoundly memorable.

His comments were recorded during a segment on the Sci-Fi Channel, which aired Byrne's statement during an installment of *Sightings*. This particular episode was centered on a nesting site found in Ohio, featuring Dr. W. Henner Fahrenbach, Joedy Cook, and George Clappison.

Talking about his own data acquired during his time with the BRP (Bigfoot Research Project) - Byrne faced the cameras and said: "...out of 3000 bigfoot witness reports, 5 turned out to be legitimate, which leaves a staggering number of misidentifications, wild goose chases and hoaxed reports! I think those numbers may also indicate that witnesses have a great tendency to imagine they see Sasquatch, probably by conscious choice."

How profound; only five genuine reports in 3000? It would make sense to me, though. Reconsidering and reviewing the reports, I can't help but wonder if they are all legitimate. How much do we believe?

Actual Sightings Are Very Rare

While a select few people see Sasquatches all the time (habituator claims), the general rule has always been that sightings are extremely rare. The average person is more apt to find tracks than they are to see a Sasquatch full-on. It is beyond rare that those field people seeking the Sasquatch ever have a full-on daylight sighting. Byrne's quote supports what I've been saying all along, which is that there simply are not enough sasquatches left in the wilderness to support the high volume of witness reports publicized as "credible or class A" by various organizations. There are indications of large numbers of family clans in specific regions, but I don't think the data supports the extraordinarily high numbers often quoted.

Another example is a Canadian resident of Vancouver, British Columbia, who wrote to me, citing a report published by the Paranormal Intelligence Agency. The agency reported that a UFO and a Bigfoot was sighted at Babine Lake on May 16, 2012. The claimant presented a photo of the UFO, but no photo of the Sasquatch that he claimed was seen together with the aircraft. Tracking down the source of that story, I discovered that the Sasquatch at Babine Lake was a wooden replica carving like the one woodcarver Ben Gerow from Terrace, B.C., carved at Burns Lake, British Columbia.[11] Be careful what you read!

Moving on, if research had paid attention to detail, we would have recognized what the data suggested. Little details and small clues indicated Sasquatch was no Gigantopithecus and certainly no new secret hybrid species developed by covert governments.

There are no credible cases documented that I know about of a Sasquatch observed with aliens, UFOs, or expressing special powers. What I find telling is that I've received no such reports in thirty years. It seems like only those who dabble in extraterrestrial concepts receive those reports. That is probably because these things occur in man's mind first. But it makes great drama, and people love melodramatic mystery. Man is quick to blame whatever strangeness happens to them in the rain forest as being generated from some alien concept. The ageless successes of theatrical productions like Star Wars and Star Trek speak to the public's love affair with alien concepts and science fiction stories.

The Sasquatch is certainly no figment of the imagination; the Sasquatch is not science fiction. DNA evidence strongly suggests Sasquatch DOES exist. I've seen them. I am, however, not here to convince anyone of anything; I'm writing *The de Facto Sasquatch* to make public what my data contains. I cannot decide what cases are true or imagined; I'm writing this only to provide the various reported behaviors, hoping it shines a no-nonsense light on the mystery.

There will always be those individuals unwilling to accept new data, new DNA, and what it suggests. Change comes slowly as we will no doubt experience with the new DNA, presumptive for Sasquatch.

However unbelievably exciting to research it may be, DNA will not tell us how the Sasquatch live, how they manage to survive, their rules for living or how their social structure is defined. However, we can cull repeated behaviors that have been reported from the data and see where they take us. Specific behaviors in this book are listed in the index.

I pared down and condensed the accounts in this chapter to allow for documenting manners of conduct. The testimonies were cherry-picked and represent typical cases no matter how rudimentary the listed behavior may be. Unless a researcher actually lives with or grows up around a family of Sasquatch, we will never know how they have so successfully survived living wild in a world gone modern and, in some cases, quite mad.

Many of the stories you'll read in *The de Facto Sasquatch* will seem repetitious, but it's necessary to discuss the numbers of each reported behavior to determine its value and what we can rely on as a probability for actual Sasquatch characters. The life answers are there; we just need to be aware of them.

Included are a few testimonies written by informants. You will notice I often edit out extraneous terrain description and witness reactions to concentrate on whatever Sasquatch behavior I garner from the narrative; let's begin.

Sasquatch Sighting

Sasquatch Sticks Out His Tongue, Touches Witness

Here is an unusual one-of-a-kind report: A representative of the Peabody Museum at Harvard University and one of the great anthropologists of our time, the late Dr. Carlton Coon, a Harvard alumnus, filed an interesting report about a man who lived just below the border in Massachusetts. I neglected to note if that was Connecticut or Rhode Island. You might remember Coon as the American anthropologist who remarked, "…if Africa was the cradle of mankind, it was only an indifferent kindergarten. Europe and Asia were our principle schools." A man way before his time, Dr. Coon's investigation of this Bigfoot case was labor-intensive; his attention to detail is worth noting.

The witness's truck, a converted camper, was parked alongside a wooded glade just off the highway. He and his sons stopped there for the night and went to sleep; the boys in the camper shell behind the front seat and the informant behind the steering wheel. At 11:00 p.m., the man was awakened by the vehicle rocking from side to side and, believing it was a violent earthquake, stepped out the truck and was immediately grasped by a 7-foot tall creature covered with light brown or yellowish hair on the left shoulder. The Sasquatch's right hand pushed the man off the running board of the truck and onto the ground.

The witness said the Sasquatch looked down on him on the ground, and then the big behemoth "stuck his tongue out at the man." Yes, that's how the report read, believe it or not. The man jumped free, of course, and drove off - the Sasquatch in hot pursuit. Both the man and his sons were polygraphed at Dr. Coon's expense and insistence; all three passed the difficult questions. The father had never seen a Sasquatch, but his sons had seen one on television.

Dr. Coon went to the site twice and noted that there were still tracks deeply depressed an inch and a half to two inches below the surface; the rest were covered with pine needles. The pressure exerted with each foot placement into the moist soil was quite noticeable. By comparison, Coon's size 12 shoes left no discernible displacement in the mud; he stared at the ground pondering the implications, his own weight being just short of 300 pounds. It seemed like the Sasquatch deliberately fired the placement of its foot forward in a downward thrust of incredible force. The sheer weight of the creature couldn't impress into the ground that far without exerting force behind it. Coon was unable to equal it. There are any number of recorded cases where trackers cannot equal the force of the Sasquatch foot or the distance between imprints.

In Dr. Coon's filed report, he said his informant's son reported seeing the creature's face peering into his bedroom window at some point after the roadside incident. In the same area, two women reported a blond Sasquatch crouched down in front of a stone wall, but both women refused Dr. Coon's requests for an interview.

What is there to learn from Dr. Coon's testimony? The unusual aspect of the Sasquatch's behavior cited in this case was the sticking out of the tongue and the touching (grabbing) of the vehicle's occupant; both mannerisms were considered highly unusual. Coon's remarks about exerted foot-placement-force are very interesting too.

Concerning the Sasquatch sticking out his tongue, one scientist theorized that the uncivilized "ancient man" lived in small groups or packs. The males, when showing a high degree of mistrust or fear, would stand erect, chest out, exposing his genitals as a threat. The genitals, in some cases, were probably erect; in the wild, it's a show of power and excitement. The great apes use this display usually when in a high state of aggression or alarm.

In modern society, a display of one's genitalia is frowned upon. Showing the tongue (sticking out your tongue) takes the place of showing the genitals. The meaning of the gesture is the same regardless; it is a show of aggression and, to a lesser degree, intimidation. I remember it vividly from 6th-grade boys.

Whatever the reason, Dr. Coon felt it was not aggression but a clumsy way of interacting with a human; I don't know if I agree with his assessment, but whatever you feel about the behavior of the Sasquatch - the end result, of course, terrified the witness.

If the Sasquatch had any intent to harm the man, he could have – no question, but all he did was stick out his tongue, and that in itself is an unreported behavior, but it is intriguing nevertheless. That wasn't the only thing the witness observed. In Dr. Coon's filing, he wrote, "...the animal stank nauseously. He smelled like rotten fish."

Smell and rank odor is a common theme found in many verifiable accounts. Some people's sense of smell is keener than others', and some simply do not take a mental note of any smell, so frightened are they by the sight of a hair-covered giant. In my account, I was within ten feet and smelled nothing, but I should have smelled something given the condition of the Sasquatch's filthy fecal-crusted buttocks, yet I didn't smell anything.

Statistically, Sasquatch odor is only reported in 30% of the cases I've tallied. But apparently, it's reported more often in internet reports than it was in years past. It may be that the reports of odor are exaggerated, parroted, or an outright bit of embellishment. A stench in the air does not mean there is a Sasquatch around, but the internet often influences the thinking of a witness. Since the advent of the internet, it's hard to know what's real and what isn't, and God bless the mighty Google, which none of us can live without but right or wrong, it does influence![*,12]

Grabbing

Another example of the grabbing behavior by a Squatch was made public by Los Angeles law enforcement officer Ken Coon in 1979; Coon described himself as "This old detective bureau commander." On August 27, 1966, three Fontana, California teenagers rushed into the local Sheriff's Station to report an encounter with a giant ape-man. A frantic Jerri Lou Mendenhall, 16, told officers she and her friends were driving slowly along a dirt road north of town when the creature suddenly emerged from the bushes and approached their moving car. The creature reached through the driver's window and grabbed her throat. Near hysterics, Mendenhall put the pedal to the metal and took off straight to the Sheriff's substation, where a group of officers laughed and ridiculed her, saying, "...next, you'll be telling us the creature wore a pink bikini." She then revealed visible scratches on her

---

* Dr. Carleton Coon was among the first of the established scientists to openly discuss the possibility of extant hominids other than our own species. Coon was never very much afraid of controversy; neither did he go out specifically looking for it. His anthropological works range the full gamut from respectable to what some thought to be outrageous. With Sasquatch he followed his normal pattern of studying what was of interest and reporting whatever conclusions he found. In his article, *Why there has to be a Sasquatch,* Coon toyed with various possible views as to Sasquatch's relation to humans and rules out only one – that they represent surviving Neanderthals.

neck and said they had been made when the monster's huge, hairy hand grabbed at her.* While the behavior is rare in the database, Coon elected to believe the informant after examining the witness's neck.

Fat with Discolored Teeth

D. Trull, the Enigma Editor of Parascope.com, retold a story published in The Times and the 1997 Democrat newspapers in Neeses, South Carolina.

The Boy Who Cried Bigfoot

Jackie Hutto, from the small town of Neeses, South Carolina reported that he saw the creature outside his home at midday on July 15. He was inside the house when he heard the family dog barking from inside a dog pen in the back yard. When Jackie went outside to quiet the dog, when he says he saw a large creature tugging at the wire walls of the dog pen. He reported that the animal was about 8 or 8½ feet tall and was covered in black hair, except for its face, chest and knees, where brown skin was visible. The creature bared its large, discolored teeth that were shaped "like baby blocks," and possessed prominent male genitalia. Additionally, in contrast to the popular conception of Bigfoot as a lanky and muscular beast, this creature was described as "really fat."[13]

---

* Retired Police Chief Ken Coon.

Jumping-Leaping Sasquatch Behavior

March 29, 2012; Fremont County, Colorado:

My son Kurt, [38], Grandson [14] and myself [69] were in the mountains going to look for elk and deer sheds. We were about three miles from the road in twelve inches plus of snow trying to walk in on an old logging road. As we went up in elevation the snow became too deep to walk in much further. Then, following the logging road, we went into the heavier timber where the snow was not as deep. As soon as we went in the timber I noticed that something disturbed the snow. There were no other tracks around so I thought a hawk or owl got a rabbit, causing the flurried snow. But looking closer, it looked like there were human five toe prints in the snow. Taking a closer look around, back about 20 feet or so, I noticed more disturbed snow. In that track were perfect footprints of very large feet. The feet were brought together with snow pushed up between the toes and feet as they were brought together to jump again. This was almost unbelievable as the track impressions were 20 feet apart! What could jump/leap that far? Going to the original track there were no more to be seen. We crossed the logging road and there was yet another set of tracks where the creature landed flat footed; spacing between its feet – jumping across the road, which was a 22 foot leap! Snow on the road was about thirty inches deep. We began following the tracks for about a mile or less. The tracks averaged 15 to 18 feet apart as the timber was getting much thicker. By now I knew it was a Bigfoot because of the size of the tracks, about a size 15 to 16. They were not bear or mountain lion tracks. I've been in the mountains all my life and know what makes certain tracks. No animal can jump that far that I know of. Anyway the tracks, distance apart, was very compelling evidence for me. I thought this was the best evidence I have ever heard of. Pictures of Big Foot can be faked; bears, mistaken for big foot or someone in a costume. You can't fake 20 foot jumps in the snow with no other tracks in between.[14]

To further demonstrate the incredible lengths in leaping behavior, in 1992, Lucullus Virgil McWhorter wrote an article about the Sasquatch and "one leg leaping." Here is the reference to the Washington Indians and what they articulated:

There is another tribe of Ste-ye-hah' mah; a tall slender race having but one leg. They live far to the North and are seldom seen. They are the deadly enemy of the Cascade Ste-ye-hah', who are mortally afraid of them. They too, are nocturnal and can cover vast stretches of country in a single night. Their mode of locomotion is supposedly long leaps, since the foot impressions appear at a considerable distance apart. Some Indians contend that these enigmatical beings are possessed of two legs, the same as any other people, and the difference is in the foot alone. Both tracks (impressions) are identical, conforming to the right or the left foot exclusively.[15]

Bigfoot Hunting Turkeys

"Dear Bigfootencounters; I am a Kansas wheat producer. Several years ago I was working the harvest with the usual grain combine when something made a clatter noise. I stopped quickly and climbed out of the cab to see what it was; I was parked in a section of land sandwiched between a run off and a running creek that takes water to the house and feeds our well. After checking the equipment, I went to get back behind the wheel to carry on. It was then I spotted this dark thing making a run across the field about 40 yards in front of me. I climbed up and into the cab and watched this giant man-figure burst out of nowhere and shoot across my field, which was an uncut section of wheat. I did not believe what I was seeing! It was a reddish-brown color with hair over its body, the whole body! I'm thinking, what the...these things are real? It took me several minutes to collect my thoughts. This Bigfoot quickly gathered up two turkeys before they could get airborne and headed for the trees that bordered the creek on the lower section. I never saw anything like that in my life, I'm sober, age 57 and of sound mind. Because of the wheat and corn around here, we've always had excellent turkey hunts but nobody I ever knew had a Bigfoot to deal with. Is it possible that there was only one of them around here? It was early morning (8:15 a.m.) if you need to know, and that was the last I saw of it, maybe lasted a half minute or less. As to its size, I don't have a guess. I raise my hand, this is true. Please do not use my real name or email address; my family is known here, thank you."[16]

Sasquatch Clucking/Gobbling

According to its length, this next bit of correspondence should have been placed under favorite stories. But because it mentions turkey vocalizations, I decided to place it here. The informant was a neighborhood fellow who lived next door to a member of the staff at the Medical School near Paducah, Kentucky. He became very excited when I spoke with him on the phone. Here is the condensed version of his eight-page account.

> We purchased a house/large cabin-type a year ago in an area that backs up to what's known as the Daniel Boone National Forest, Kentucky. The back of my place has a 16 wide x 30 foot wooden deck that cantilevers off the backside of the main house extending out and under tree foliage. It is supported by 6 x 6 wood-beam stanchions that hold up the porch; the deck is 11 feet or so off the ground. On top of that deck there is a 4 foot railing capped on top where the wife puts her plants and several assorted bird feeders. From the railing top to the ground slope is between ten to fifteen feet. The height is important to gauge the height of the Bigfoot.

> On the side of our property there is a narrow three foot wide dirt game trail that goes up into some of the most rugged terrain a man can imagine. It is characterized by rolling mountains, steep grades, deep gullies and sharp overhangs; it is hardwood old growth trees. The forest turns magnificent colors in the fall; that is why we bought the place. A few stories came along with the purchase of the house by way of the real

estate agent. The previous owners told her they kept up the bird feeders and once two bear cubs got up on the deck and tore up the deck furniture pretty good, knocking over the bird bath. There are claw markings on the support beams to verify her account and some claw marks on the railing topper; a few railing slats went missing and were never found. The other tale was about two bears that came up and ate from the bird feeders at night. We've been here a year now and have seen no bears. At the long end of the decking is a staircase that goes down to the ground and meets up with a game trail that takes off into the underbrush that is otherwise too thick to walk through, but on to the story.

I was half-sleeping, half-reading a book when I heard a gobbler calling. What a strange air there was about the place that morning. I sat up and listened. From under this porch where I had been dozing off, there came soft clucking sounds; like turkey hen clucking sounds. In case you don't know, Kentucky, especially Daniel Boone National Forest, brags about having the best turkey hunts in the USA. That's true; we never have to buy Thanksgiving turkeys up here. I relaxed and laid back, and then I heard a loud gobble coming from what sounded like a big ole Tom under the porch and it was answered by another Tom clucking in the trees. The gobbling continued along with intermittent clucking and I thought two things. First, they probably are lunching on spilled bird seed from the porch feeders and two, where did my wife put my scatter gun? I went in the house and took a few minutes to pack shells in my Browning A-5 and hurried back onto the porch but it was quiet again. I laid back on the chaise, the Browning shot gun across my lap and waited, thinking turkey's ain't too bright and maybe he would fly up on the porch to get after the good seeds but time passed, maybe thirty minutes with no clucking sounds and then off in the woods I hear them clucking with an occasional gobble. I figured they moved on, so my enthusiasm diminished some and I fell asleep again.

Freak of Nature

I woke up with the sun beating down on my head, sat upright and figured I'd go into the house for a bite of lunch. No sooner had I got to my feet when straight ahead of me off the porch comes a very loud gobble, I look; I see this crazy thing, this freak of nature standing on the stair case that leads up to the deck. I jumped back startled, reached for the shotgun, aimed quickly and fired, B-O-O-M! The shot tore out a bunch of railing, a flower pot and wood went flying, the birds scattered and so did this freak. The best look I got of it was him leaping off the porch stairs and flying up that dirt path. My hunting buddy comes flying out of the house with a loud "what the hell" and I pointed. Harold saw what I saw as it fled up the game trail. We only saw it for a second and it was gone; I tell you it M-O-V-E-D. We go in the house and talk it over and decide to load up and go look for sign; neither of us thought much about Bigfoot but that is what we seen! Down on the dirt path we discovered tracks of a barefooted man that were 18 inches long, showing 5 toes on the left foot and four toes on the right one (little toe was missing). The tracks went on for a quarter mile and then left the path and went up a steep precipice with sharp rocks that hung over the dirt path. It was the perfect place to ambush deer and, thinking we could get ambushed, thought better of following the tracks any further. We sat down in the shadows and watched until four that afternoon but we never saw anything but squirrels that continually chirped their warning signal that we were in there; you see, squirrels never give up; their danger chirping goes on all night!

One more thing, what we saw was nothing like the Monster Quest television program! This guy was enormous with hair hanging over its face like a sheep dog. We mostly saw its backside, which was covered in short body hair but little detail of anything else. It happened very fast and it was gone. If it wasn't a Bigfoot we saw that day then you folks should know that Kentucky turkeys come haired, not feathered, are ten feet tall and partial to stealing bird seed.[17]

Jackson County, Kentucky

Expressions of Strength

A journalist for the old Pacific Northwest Magazine wrote about a man from Lacey, Washington, who went to the Thurston County Sheriff's Department and stated that a nine-foot creature with long red hair flagged him down as he drove home from a party in the wee hours of the morning. According to the police report, the driver had hardly stopped his small foreign car before the creature walked up to the grill, lifted up the front end, and heaved the vehicle into a roadside ditch.

I don't doubt the capabilities of an angry Sasquatch, but this tale was hard to swallow: a small foreign car after partying 'til the wee hours? If true, it's one of a kind recorded by law enforcement involving a Sasquatch, and it begs the question, where was the breathalyzer test? What I find interesting is the time an informant will take to describe not the Bigfoot but how the informant felt during his encounter. There is almost a cathartic sense of relief to be able to tell someone how it feels to describe any experience with Bigfoot to another person who won't laugh or criticize them.

Witnesses generally tend to spend a great deal of time describing their terror at the sight of a Sasquatch and their inability to control their fear, their general feeling of alarm, and their nervousness. Many informants are so shaken that they go through time with residual effects. Some informants have expressed that they hold deep scars from a traumatic encounter with a Sasquatch, while hunters often retire from hunting after an incident.

My statistics show women tend to give the best physical descriptions of the Sasquatch and less about themselves than male witnesses. Women are more matter-of-fact and less emotional in their descriptions. I would think the opposite true, but in looking through the data, men tend to describe their fear with graphic language and wild gesturing. They express the intense need to leave or run and tell how they dealt with those feelings. Interestingly, most reports are filed by men, and many write that the telling of their experience was therapeutic; in other words, they feel a sense of relief and closure. Very little has changed in descriptions over the centuries. What has changed is the fear level and man's inability to own it.

In the Humboldt County Collection at the Library of Humboldt State College, Arcata, N. California is a small booklet titled *The Hermit of the Siskiyou's* by L.W. Musick. It was published in the office of The Crescent City News, in California, in the year 1896. On pages 79-80 is the following excerpt:

> I do not remember to have seen any reference to the wildman which haunts this part of the country, so I shall allude to him briefly. Not a great while since, Mr. Jack Dover, one of our most trustworthy citizens, while hunting saw an object standing one hundred and fifty yards from him picking berries and tender shoots from the bushes. The thing was of gigantic size – about seven feet high with a bull dog head, short ears and long hair; it was also furnished with a long beard and was free from hair on such parts of its body as is common among men. Its voice was shrill, or soprano and very human like that of a woman in great fear. Mr. Dover could not see its footprints as it was hard soil. He aimed his gun at the animal or whatever it is, several times but because it was so human in appearance, he would not shoot. The range of the curiosity is between Marble Mountain and the vicinity of Happy Camp. A number of people have seen it and all agree in their descriptions except some make it taller than others. It is apparently herbivo-

rous and makes winter quarters in some of the caves of the Marble Mountains.*

Notice the description in Musick's report - northern California field researchers should make note of this article's mention of the Marble Mountain location. Roger Patterson's 1966 Bigfoot sketches also depict a "bulldog head."[18]

Filthy Sasquatch

One of the interesting points in this next 2011 filing is the issue of Bigfoot personal hygiene or lack thereof. Few cases I've looked into mention the condition of the Sasquatch's personal appearance, cleanliness and physical condition. Then I read the Thomas Byers Story in North Carolina. Byers called the creature Knobby, a Rutherford County nickname for Bigfoot.

The Shelby resident spoke with confidence when he described tufts of bushy brown hair and the thick, powerful legs that supported a stocky frame as he watched Knobby come from across a field, walk over a two-lane road, and disappear into the thick woodland that paralleled the road in both directions. "It was the most amazing thing I've ever seen. It looked like it was about 300 pounds and somewhere close to 7-feet tall. It came out of the field and through the briars and bushes onto the roadway," Byers recalled.

Convinced the creature was genuine, he exclaimed excitedly, "I saw its private parts," he said; "it wasn't anybody in a suit or anything like that. It was definitely male." The witness was scarcely fifteen feet away from the Bigfoot. Even from that distance, he noticed a smell like decay, "…it was a hard smell, a cross between road-kill and a skunk." The witness had been out looking for Golden Valley Church Road outside Bostic City in northeastern Rutherford County, not far from the Cleveland County line when the incident with the Sasquatch occurred.

------

* L.W. Musick.

The Cleveland-Rutherford area has a lengthy history of Bigfoot sightings dating back four decades, which the locals personally remember. As a hunter in those hills all his life, Byers heard about Knobby up in those parts, but he didn't ever dream he would see one, and when he did, he told us the hairs on his forearms stood up as Knobby made its way across the road. The literal raising of hair on arms and on the backs of informants are commonly reported.

The indicator that personal hygiene was not important to this North Carolina Sasquatch occurred to me when Byers exclaimed, "...the thing had a dirty butt crease!" This isn't an issue exclusive to the eastern Sasquatch either because I also noticed the same lack of cleanliness in the female I saw in 1985 in northern California. How interesting is it that few reports mention the condition or outward appearance of the Sasquatch when they write up their reports? There are many details I noticed that others never mention.

Byers continued excitedly, "...I could see his private parts here," Byers said, gesturing with his hands towards his crotch; "I could tell it was a male. Then right when it started up the incline and into the thicket, I could see the crack in his butt was very dirty, it had dung hanging off of it; he was filthy," Byers said in his animated way of describing the encounter. The informant and the woman with him described not only the unkempt condition but said the back of the Sasquatch was covered with scratch marks and scars. What the creature lacked in hygiene, however, it made up for in agility. Byers said the Sasquatch scaled a hill on the other side of the road in mere seconds.

It also struck me as unusual but interesting that, like my encounter, this male Byers described made no effort to correct his pathway to avoid the witness. The Bigfoot, again as in my sighting, came within feet of Byers and his female friend, paying no attention to them or making any concerted effort to avoid them. There aren't many reports like this; most Bigfoot duck for cover, hide, and watch. However, reports to the contrary do exist, so we cannot categorically say that ducking for cover is a known behavior; it's only a reported behavior. The Byers case reported deviant behavior to what is generally believed to be.

The media video associated with this report was completely bogus and was made up by the media, not the informant. It served to weaken the importance of other details in the case that Byers could only have known had he seen the real thing, and I think he did. The video, however, was undoubtedly a man in a baggy-leg ape costume; a media reenactment poorly done and misleading.

Still, there were additional witnesses in the Byers case, the woman who was with Byers. The points they both made in cross-examination independent of one another could have only been known had they actually seen a real Sasquatch.

So… my call - I'm convinced the genesis of the initial narrative was true despite the laughable baggy suit video the media played. Sometimes, it pays to simply tell the truth as best you know it and deal with the ridicule and mockery that comes with it. Conversely, the alternative is to suck it up and don't call in the media; they are not known to quote accurately in most cases anyway.[19]

The Arizona Honey Caper

Two beekeepers checking on a colony of bee hives in the back fields of an Arizona citrus growing operation encountered an enormous creature tearing out the honeycomb from bee hive slats/partitions. All the hives were on stilts. Two other hives had been torn open, most of the honeycombs sucked dry, and the debris scattered over a wide area of the citrus grove. Oliver and Manuel Ortega reported the incident to the citrus grower only to find out the grower thought the frequent ransacking of the beehives was due to a black bear, which is not common in the region but not totally unheard of either.

Ortega wouldn't accept the notion of a bear and tried to explain to the owner what he saw; differences in languages left both men frustrated. The beekeeper told me that when he and his son approached the hives, a haired creature jumped up with what they thought was its surprise at being discovered. Ortega and his son were dressed in beekeeper gear and were not armed except for smoke pots to calm the bees.

When the report came to me, I contacted the Mexican laborer. He told me the Bigfoot had honey in its whiskers as well as bees, both alive and dead, and bee's wax that dribbled down the front of his beard and onto his chest; bees were everywhere and frantic. The Bigfoot swatted at the stinging bees but was otherwise seemingly unfazed by them. The witness also said the creature seemed to be eating bees right along with the honey. Arizona has its share of aggressive killer bees, but these hives, according to Ortega, were the domestic strain of bees, which was lucky for the Bigfoot. I couldn't help but wonder if the Bigfoot knew the difference between killer bee hives and domestics. Maybe that these were in man-made hives was the clue. Killer bees usually hive in trees, bushes, and under building structures. Killer bees, that I know of, are not farmed.

If that wasn't unusual enough, then came the fascinating description: "It was very tall with auburn colored hair on its head and deeper red on its body" ...and...wait for it, ... "green eyes. He looked at us with beeeeg green eyes!"

Yes, Ortega was sure the eyes were green in color with blackish-red bushy eyebrows. He was also sure it was no bear. Finishing up this unusual event, Ortega said when the creature stood up, his son became frightened, fell backward, and then ran in terror back to the truck. Ortega felt obligated to protect the property, stood his ground and foolishly shouted at the creature (so he said), but the Bigfoot kept licking torn bits of honeycomb off his fingers, casually eyeing Ortega (seemingly unafraid) the whole time. I didn't fully understand the words in Mexican for "swaying back and forth," but I think that is what he was trying to say. Ortega said he shouted louder and began waving his arms and the smoke can in an attempt to shoo the creature away, but it apparently held its ground and, finally finishing one honeycomb slat, picked up the two remaining and walked into the citrus grove, bees trailing behind. Ortega was dressed in white hooded beekeeper attire, so it is likely that the Sasquatch did not understand there was a human underneath the white garb and netted hood; that seemed to make sense.

Ortega's colorful description was tempered with excitement. I asked if the event was reported to local officials, and he said quite sharply, "no." Apparently, he only told the owner of the citrus grove. I imagine the reason for that was that Ortega was probably working in Arizona illegally. The son, who spoke understandable English, told me his father was a migrant worker in the U.S. from Puebla, Mexico, with no work permit, no papers, no passport, but had a great story to tell his children.[*]

For me, the story was reminiscent of A.A. Milne's classic, "Pooh Bear, Piglet and the Great Honey Pot Caper." Sometimes, I scratch my head, raise my eyebrows, and muse, "You just can't make this stuff up; it's way too cool."

Green eyes: As a side note regarding green-colored eyes, I know of one other account that listed green-colored eyes. In April, 1969, it was reported in *The Sasquatch File*, that an Oroville, California, rabbit hunter named Ed Saville and his friend, Eldon Butler, reported seeing a green-eyed Bigfoot approach them when they used their rabbit-in-distress call. They reported the occurrence to twenty-year-old Jim McClarin, who was, at the time, a student at Humboldt State University in Arcata, California.

Swaying Behavior

It comes as no surprise that there are several stories from New Mexico. This next one was from a resident of Mescalero, who related several ongoing incidents with a Sasquatch. The behavior of the Sasquatch in this report was typical of many such incidents that occur to owners of remote cabin and/or rural trailer homes.

In the remote reaches of Otero County, the hairy humanoid had been

---

[*] Ortega 2002.

seen hanging around off and on for nearly three years. The family noticed a tall dark figure walking the trail below the house, pacing back and forth; sometimes swaying. We hear about swaying behavior quite a bit; it's not an unreported behavior, but we don't know what it means or why they do it. A First Nation friend of mine speculated that the swaying back and forth was a silent signal that, "hey, we be cool, don't be alarmed." He went on to say, "return the signal and then go on about your business."

In this case, however, the Sasquatch would follow them home at a distance, obviously scaring them nearly to death, but over time, they adjusted to it and became used to the idea that the Sasquatch probably meant no harm, or so they hoped. On another occasion, large tracks were found in the snow under their clothesline and the clothes scattered on the ground. One particular day, the Sasquatch walked back and forth and eventually approached the house; the residents went inside to avoid a confrontation. While watching television, they heard sounds coming from the dining room and, upon inspection, found a hairy arm reaching through an open window onto a side table that contained a bowl of fruit. Totally alarmed, they telephoned the local Conservation Office, but nothing more occurred that night. The report came to me in 2004.[20]

Otero County

Years passed, and I heard nothing more about any ongoing activity until 2009. A pair of four-wheeling youngsters descending Crest Trail from Buck Mountain filed a report stating that they were chased by two light-colored hominoid monsters that ran like the wind in pursuit of them for at least a mile and, for the most part, stayed up with their ATVs; the creature never overtook them. The informant, also a resident of Otero County, said one of them screamed a horrifying scream that made the hair on his arms stand up. The two boys apologized for a lack of description, telling me they only wanted to get away and had to watch the trail to stay ahead of them. They noticed that the faces were light-colored and both were haired and bearded. Interestingly, the boys took their father back to the site of the chase, and tracks were found, but they were barely distinguishable.

No Eyeshine

Many stories originate out of Butte County, California. We should not be surprised that this next report comes from the much-loved big game hunter and Bigfoot investigator, Peter Byrne.

The significance of Byrne's short story is the lack of eye shine that we hear so much about. Byrne, one of the great animal trackers of our time, probably knows animal eyes better than anyone. Byrne told this story at one of the Western Bigfoot Society meetings in Portland, Oregon, in the 1990s. He graciously recalled it for this purpose:

> Mr. and Mrs. Robert L Behme of Magalia, California, told me of a curious night meeting with a Sasquatch. On April 16, 1969, at approximately midnight; we were in the car on the road between Paradise and Sterling City, California. The surrounding area was thickly wooded and crossed by deep canyons. As we started around a long curve, our headlights lit up what seemed to be a man in a fur coat crossing the road. During one moment we had a front view when it turned toward the car. After that, it was inserted in darkness. Our impression was that it was high of more than 6-feet [1.80 m] and completely covered with short black hair, which seemed to be marked by either white spots or specks of mud. Its face was white although the details were obscured by darkness. The eyes did not shine in the night-light, as would be the

case with the eyes of an animal. The head was small and finished at a peak at the top. It was heavily built with particularly heavy legs.[21]

Paradise and Sterling City, California

Rubbed Its Eyes, No Eye Reflection

Not realizing in the 1990s the importance research would place on eye shine or the lack of it, I found this next notation in one of my early computers. As with the Byrne account, this next report indicates there was no reflective eye shine in the eyes of the Bigfoot observed late at night by Gary Rutherford.

The informant traveled Highway 40 over Berthoud Pass in the Arapahoe National Forest, Colorado, in 1992. Driving along Highway 40 between Frazer and Winter Park, he encountered a creature he knew immediately was likened to the stories from California in the 1960s. Stunned, Rutherford slowed down and flicked his high beams at what he called, "...an unusual sight." In the lane directly in front of his vehicle was a Bigfoot that appeared to be a dark color looking into the headlights and then shielding his eyes by turning its back on the car. It continued on up Highway 40 in the same direction as Rutherford's vehicle. Twice, the creature stopped, lingered, and then turned to look at the vehicle. Each time, it went on its merry way with no concern whatsoever for Rutherford or the potential danger from moving auto-mobiles on the road. Rutherford indicated that it seemed to have no purpose and was just wandering in the lane ahead of him. After nearly a mile was covered, the Bigfoot slid down an embankment off the side of the road and became lost in the darkness.

Rutherford believed it to be male merely by its great size, but he wasn't sure. My notes indicate that the witness said something about the strange way the creature walked and that the eyes did not reflect eyeshine as would the eyes of a deer. He indicated that the light seemed to bother his eyes; honking the horn at the Bigfoot brought no reaction.[*]

No Eyeshine

Theo Stein, environmental writer for the Denver Post, chronicled many Bigfoot reports in and around the State of Colorado. On January 14, 2001, Theo notes that 2000 was a big year for Bigfoot research, especially in Colorado. While it was a nighttime encounter Theo recorded, his report had no eyeshine.

> In August 2000, two hikers forced by a storm to camp in high wilderness north of Crested Butte emerged with quite a tale. They said they had been shadowed for two nights by at least one Bigfoot that came into their camp and approached their tent.

Drinking From a Well; No Eyeshine

Septuagenarian Edith Andrews wrote in 1995 of an occasional sighting in the woods near her Michigan summer cabin. Sitting on her side porch on a clear moonlit night, Mrs. Andrews watched silently as a family of Bigfoot drank from her well, pulling the wooden bucket up hand over fist and drinking directly from the bucket as had Mrs. Andrews many times before.

In her description of the Big Ones, she mentioned the look on their faces was one of an Eskimo. High set prominent cheekbones with large

---

[*] G. R.

semi-hooked noses with squinty eyes. The freshwater well was stationed ten yards from the cabin's porch; she had an excellent view of them as they drank and often glanced at her. No eyeshine was reported. No aggression was noted, and no words were exchanged with her. The witness noted that there was gibberish uttered between them, which she did not understand, although the gesturing they shared suggested some instructions to the youngster present.

When the drinking from the well was finished, the Bigfoot family quietly left the yard, walking through a small pasture of horses, two alpacas, and their baby cria (cree-ah). The informant said the animals remained calm and unruffled as the Big Ones passed through their field. In those notes, Mrs. Andrews evidently said she believed the haired people came down from the region of the Bering Sea; carrying with them the look in their faces of a cross between the Inuit (Eskimos) and the Aleuts with whom she was quite familiar.

Ancient Hair Reveals Greenland Eskimos' Roots

I regret that I was such a novice in the 1980s that her remarks seemed to be of no importance at the time. Today, however, with remarkable things being done with DNA; Mrs. Andrews' comment regarding the description of the Sasquatch being Eskimo-like is (I think) extraordinary. Ancient DNA findings published in 2008 show that DNA samples taken from existing Eskimo populations around the Arctic show the closest matches, which "came from the Bering Sea region." Some current residents of the southern Aleutian Islands and the Chutchi Peninsula of Siberia carry similar DNA; did the haired ones of that region copulate with the Aleut stock? At this writing we wait for Sasquatch DNA confirmation.[22]

The horses in Mrs. Andrews' pasture remained "unruffled" as the family of Bigfoot passed through it – this behavior is contrary to most other reports filed and, honestly, it makes me wonder if some of the reported behaviors around horses weren't grossly overstated. I have owned horses that went cockamamie nuts over the scent of a simple raccoon that scurried through a riding ring. Some horses are just more easily spooked than others; humans are the same way.

Childhood Encounter Recalls a Gentle Giant

The next report began this way:

> In 1989, my girlfriend came to my house for a sleepover. I lived rurally and up the road from my parent's trailer there was logging - a clear cutting operation where her dad worked. My mom and dad were gone someplace for the evening and we were left alone for a while. There was no TV, we ate spaghetti and went out to play and walk it off. We headed along the road and ended up climbing on the equipment and jumping off the big machines that were left there over the weekend. We fooled around, talked about what children talk about, but it was getting dark and there were no street lights in the woods; when it gets dark, it's like you can't see your hand in front of your face. As we came back into the woods from the clear cut area, for some reason both of us got scared and started holding hands and shivering. My friend thought she saw something and, thinking it was her dad, we began running towards him but instead ran straight into the legs of something that was like the monster under my bed in my childhood nightmares.
>
> It was brownish-black and had fur on its bony looking legs was the best I remember first thinking. I recall holding on to Mary with all I had and screaming; she screamed too. A hand came down on my shoulders and moved us aside with all the gentleness of Shrek; but I

get the willies when I think of that hairy hand touching the back of my shoulder!

The monster man had been standing in the road under the darkness of the trees, and in our young stupidity we ran right into him. I think he moved us aside but maybe he stepped aside and pushed us towards home; I'm not sure how we got around him, only that we did and ran blindly back to our trailer and locked ourselves in my bedroom until my parents got home. This wasn't a young girl's story. I know now that it was a Bigfoot and they are as big as people say. One thing I haven't forgotten was that on top of our screaming, we heard him breathing, so we knew it was real. Thank you for your time.*

Tree-Sitting Behavior

A gentleman from the small community of Mount Cobb, Lackawanna County, Pennsylvania, described tree-sitting behavior by a small juvenile Sasquatch. Tree sitting is not a commonly reported behavior, but there are other reports of a Sasquatch high up in trees, watching and observing quietly.

In this 2011 incident, the witness "Amy" wrote these pertinent words to Lon Strickler's Naturalplane website:

Last week I saw something I cannot explain. It was Thursday November 10th around 10 a.m. when I was in my backyard raking leaves. There is a patch of woods at the back of our property.

My 7-year-old son was playing nearby when he called out to me saying there was a "monkey in the trees." I looked in the direction he was pointing and noticed what looked like a small hairy man sitting in a maple tree watching us. I dropped my rake and walked over toward the tree. The heavy branch was about 10-12 above the ground. This creature was sitting [perched] on it with its legs tucked up like a chim-

---

* Mrs. H. J. Washington State.

panzee - but this was NOT a monkey or ape. It was proportioned like a small man a little under 3-feet in height with thick dark brown hair all over its body. It continued to sit there and quietly watch us. I turned to grab my cellphone, which was in my jacket pocket so I could get a photo but it became alarmed and quickly jumped to an adjacent tree, scampered down and ran upright at a remarkable speed. I was amazed how fast it ran - it disappeared within seconds.

My son told me later that he had a similar sighting this past summer and was sure it was not the same creature. He said the previous creature was larger as he glimpsed it walking through the woods behind our neighbor's barn. I talked to my neighbors this weekend and neither have seen anything but admit that their pets have been alarmed at night, and on one occasion last winter there was distant howling. They assumed it was a coyote or a dog. These creatures seem benign in my opinion but I am curious as to what they are. We are setting out two deer trail cams - one at the edge of our woods and the other in the back of the neighbor's barn.[23]

Possible Juvenile Bigfoot Sightings

Curious Watcher

Many sightings occur when groups are busy doing something that makes enough noise to draw the curious Sasquatch in to see what's going on. There are reports of the Sasquatch watching, with great interest, humans at work. They are sometimes so intent that they forget themselves and wander in close enough that they are spotted. Michael

Acton of Checotah, Macintosh County, Oklahoma, was out building a deer stand that would overlook a shell pit in a deeply wooded area on a section of land not far from Lake Eufaula.

> Darkness was falling and we were about to quit for the day. We carried the scrap wood and tools back to the tractor a short distance away – parked on a gravel road to my house. We were loading scrap wood when I happened to look down the road and there he was, silhouetted against the blue lake just staring at us. Bigfoot! He was probably watching us work. I could see it was covered with hair, head to toe, blowing lightly in the breeze, but his face was too dark to see other features. My brother and I did not hang around to see more; we turned tail and ran. We had to come back later to retrieve the other equipment.[24]

McIntosh County, Near Eufaula, Oklahoma, 1986-87

Georgia residents, Lori and Dusty Chandler, related a story about the time they were having some work done on their house. On the ridge above them was a Sasquatch watching the workers intently. Apparently, our hairy brothers get so wrapped up in what they are watching that they forget themselves and get a bit sloppy about staying hidden. This gave Dusty Chandler a lengthy amount of time to watch the Sasquatch watching the workers; he described the Sasquatch as "The most magnificent creature he had ever seen - like one huge muscle."

Other watchers-from the trees stories came to me years ago; I no longer remember the exact year, probably early 1990, and no doubt came at a time before I got seriously interested in keeping a respectable record of the reports that came my way. Often in the early days, I didn't believe some of the behaviors being reported; all that has changed now.

Coughing and Flatulence

I couldn't believe what I was reading when I read this next report. Get a load of this – Lester Walking Horse reported an unusual happening on the Comanche Grasslands near the panhandle of Oklahoma near the borders of Colorado, Kansas, New Mexico, and Texas.

Paraphrasing his lengthy report, Walking Horse said he was hunting prairie chickens. Inching along, crawling on his belly, he was focused on sneaking up on a clutch of hens. Then the clucking sounds stopped abruptly when someone coughed – but Walking Horse thought he was alone. He was so far out onto the grassland that it surprised him to hear a man coughing. He stayed low to the ground and very still in the tall grass, his shotgun by his side. He listened intently through a buzzing swarm of grasshoppers; sweat trickled from his hairline. The coughing continued sporadically and, suddenly, a shadow was cast over his head. Thinking he was alone, the shadow was disconcerting. Minutes went by, and then a few feet away walked a large man-like figure with hair tangled about his naked legs and feet. Walking Horse was sure the Bigfoot spotted him. He didn't move but lay frozen in the tall grass. The Bigfoot walked on by coughing loudly and passing gas, perhaps oblivious to the presence of anyone around him, including the prairie hens. The report was filed by Edna, Lester's wife, in 2001, but occurred ten years earlier in 1991. She also indicated that her husband said the odor that permeated the air was "unpleasant and burned her husband's nose." Lester found several strands of hair but refused to part with them; the hairs, they said, were sacred and are now braided into the beadwork he wears around his neck. Walking Horse felt the Bigfoot had spared his life.[25]

Sasquatch Waving Arms

In a Pacific Northwest magazine article dated March 1983, there was this blurb:

> Several people traveling in the dome car of a train bound from Vancouver, British Columbia, to Calgary, Alberta, saw a 10-foot apelike creature standing 300-feet from the tracks. Later, one of the witnesses said, "It was waving its arms as if trying to fly.[26]

In another publication, the City Monthly in northern Maine published a blurb that mentioned in part, "…the beast was up on a boulder, waving its arms in the air like a fledgling eagle learning to fly."[27]

Marvin S. wrote a brief note from Pennsylvania Dutch Country in 1995 describing a hairy man's inexplicable behavior. It was yet another case where the Sasquatch was observed waving its arms erratically. For this cause, I'm only interested in the behavior of the Sasquatch.

> …we observed the Bigfoot for one or two minutes; his arms were straight out and he was rotating them in a circular motion. Then he stopped and, spreading his legs wide apart, did the circular arm waving again. We didn't understand what the lesson was but it was a sight to see; we decided to drive on. It was not a guy in a suit.[*]

Bigfoot Mimicry and Strange Sounds

It is generally accepted in the research community that the forest people are great mimickers of animals, birds, and other sounds. There are accounts of diurnal blue jays fracturing the silence of a dark night

----

[*] MES.

with their clicking sounds. Reality is, though, that blue jays are quiet at night. There has to be another explanation for the clicking sounds in the forest at night.

I recorded an account from a family in Coplin, Maine, who told me they heard a boisterous flock of geese flying south totally out of place that far north on a cold and snowy January afternoon in 1996. The geese, they said… "left 13-inch and 8-inch flat, barefooted tracks behind each with five human-like toes." The witness was sure it wasn't a flock of geese but a pair of resident Sasquatch children having fun mimicking the sounds of geese overhead, albeit out of season. The same witness said his St. Bernard limped home with a broken leg a month earlier and that things around the house mysteriously disappeared. Strange noises were heard, and something banged on the house every now and again, but the culprits never showed themselves.

If we rely on the reports (and I often do) – they tell us the Sasquatch, in some cases, are quite able to mimic eagles back and forth; the call of the osprey and other familiar birds in the woods as well as migrating flocks. A case from Richie County, West Virginia, documented in the language chapter of *Growing up with Bigfoot* that the Bigfoot was good at calling in turkeys with a perfect gobble. The Sasquatch are just as likely to scream or howl over valleys to locate others of their kind or, in some instances, induce fear in intruders or passersby.

Interesting Mimicry

Retired Oklahoma State Forestry Service worker Harold Yates, a one-time Honobia (ho-nubby) resident, said in 2005: "I don't know what it is, but something is definitely out there." Yates heard all the local stories and those from his friends who trusted he wouldn't laugh at their accounts. He was deeply puzzled by experiences he had years earlier in 2000 while building a log cabin near Little River, a main waterway that snakes through the Honobia Valley. One day, Yates was cutting planks of wood with his saw; he said the piercing sound of wood colliding with a saw blade could be heard quite a distance. It wasn't long before he heard another saw respond to his. He said that was when he heard the Bigfoot apparently trying to answer him in a deafening sound that mocked his power saw. On another occasion, in the stillness of night, Yates heard large rocks being slammed into the river below his cabin. The crashing sound continued for 40 minutes and unnerved his family. Reflecting, the soft-spoken Yates said, "I don't know what could have made those sounds; the trouble is I don't know anything that can make those noises. I know a bear can't."[28]

Constant Sasquatch Watch Held in Honobia

More Mimicry

Iowan Roger Price listed a series of strange Bigfoot-related events that occurred in his life from 1992 to October 2011. Part of his report contained these descriptive behaviors regarding mimicry by what he perceived was a local Sasquatch:

My wife and I were collecting firewood for the cold night ahead of us. We're deep in the woods approximately 500 yards from camp. As we sat on a fallen log my wife picked up a good sized stick and starts striking the log, just to break the silence. We heard a crack noise close by assuming that a tree fell or a branch broke, which is a common occurrence in this area. However, about 30 seconds later, we heard a tapping sound which seemed to be mimicking my wife's tapping. I passed it off as a woodpecker, but as Cheri kept tapping, so would the other. Three taps, a pause, then two taps. This kept up for about ten minutes. Not thinking much of it, we decided to get back to the wood we had collected earlier. Then the tapping became almost violent, followed by an alarm-like whistling. I was armed with an 1860.44 caliber black powder revolver, which I drew and started in the direction of the racket approximately 50-yards away. As I approached, I saw running at full speed a mass of black-brown hair. With my wife running back to camp to arm herself I slowly followed until the land dropped off to the river. I looked across the river from the top of the bank; I could see where something had evidently climbed out on the opposite side. I stopped my chase at this point. However, to my right, on, as well as under, an eroded part of the bank, I could see a neat pile of twigs and branches, so I went to investigate. I noticed a stack of large carp along with what looked like cleaned roots of some type. We ended up leaving that night due to unexplained noises. The creature I saw was the same creature I saw in '92 and '95. This one was bigger than the last sightings, or it had grown bigger. It had a very large body; his upper chest was very powerful looking. It had little or no neck to speak of...with swinging arms and a bitter smell like dog manure. The creature was 6 to 7 feet tall and possibly weighed about 400 pounds with strides of about 4 feet from the left foot to the right foot.

Roger ends his story with, "what I saw no doubt was Bigfoot."[29]

Iowa Happenings

Mimicking Humans; Building Stick Structures... The Tommy Davis Story

One of the best examples of Sasquatch mimicking humans was uncovered in an investigation by William "Bill" Dranginis in Virginia. I cannot remember a time when Bill wasn't around the Sasquatch community; I know I've turned to him any number of times for help in understanding hairy man behavior; his judgments and honest candor have powerfully influenced me.

Driven by his own sighting, Dranginis is an intelligent no-nonsense straight-shooter who takes a conventional look at research in and around his home State of Virginia. Bill is the inventor of the Eye-gotcha camera, which was designed to be hidden from any detection by forest dwellers, particularly the Sasquatch. Recently, Dranginis generously shared the aspects of a case where the locals were heard imitating Virginia residents, Mr. and Mrs. Tommy Davis. The Davis' letter read like this:

A lot of "stuff" has happened here over the past 3 years so I'll try to compress it somewhat to give you an idea of what's going on and perhaps you can help me understand all of it to a greater degree, particularly the most recent things.

2009/2010 - Small stones began appearing on the center of a trail through our property where I'd walk with my dog.

2010/2011 - Stick structures began to appear. To me they resemble right triangles, equilateral triangles, X's, ovals etc., & tree breaks.

At first there were only a few structures, now there are many dozens of new structures with a large concentration around our house and my Mom's house. During this time, I have learned the following through personal experience.

1. They are very intelligent

2. They are very curious

3. They speak to one another

4. They are not malicious like I first thought

5. They seem to have a sense of humor, one that I would describe as that of a teen-age punk

6. One of them may be much larger than the others and is EXTREMELY strong

7. They seem to be friendly and want to have some kind of social interaction, but on their terms. They will make certain noises over and over until I turn in their direction and loudly acknowledge them, "Hi Foot, how ya doing'? How's the Missus?

Then they stop and are apparently content.

At first we didn't like the idea of Bigfoot being around here, but have gotten used to the idea, and have actually become rather fond of them. 2012 - A few weeks ago, *eye shine*.

Most recently, and the most bizarre, was this:

My wife heard me call her name from the woods one evening when she arrived home from work. At first she thought I was returning from a walk and was offering a greeting. The problem is, I was in the house and when I emerged she was horrified to find that it was indeed not I who had called her name. I have heard of this kind of thing before but of course really know nothing about these creatures, only what I've read and seen/heard for myself. They can imitate my voice and know which one of us is Kathy?

When I first started corresponding with Dranginis, I referred to what was starting to happen around here as "creepy." The name calling is by far the creepiest, so if you could give me some insight as to what it means and what we might expect next, I would greatly appreciate it.[30]

It sounded to me like the local Sasquatch fascinated himself with the Davis family and, for whatever reason, had studied them accurately and long enough to know their names and when they come and go. It's almost like stalking behavior, but I would stop short of declaring the activity a habit. There is no personal one-on-one interaction.

Along those same lines of thought, Anita Fritzenkoetter wrote of her habit of screaming out the backdoor, "DINNER" when it was ready. Her family would come running, wash up at the outside fountain, and then file in for dinner. This was routine for approximately seven years. Then, the day came when she had finished decorating the backyard area for her husband's 54th birthday festivities. At the precise time dinner was usually ready, a "healthy voice" from the forest hollered out, "DINNER." Mrs. Fritzenkoetter believed it was someone invited to the birthday party, but her guests denied responsibility, including her closest neighbors from the adjoining farm.

There was another situation similar to the Davis and Fitzenkoetter households where the couple bought a soccer ball from Toys "R" Us and had fun kicking it around the backyard during summer evenings. When they went into the house for the night, they left the ball on the lawn out back. Within a short while, the two juvenile Sasquatch copied the behavior of the homeowners. Laughter and intense competitive playing could be heard long into the night; a few times the games got very loud when the adult Bigfoot joined in. Eventually, the ball went missing; apparently, the Sasquatch team absconded with the ball, or they kicked it out of the forest. Nobody knew, but it was never found.

Apparently, copying and mimicking humans is a pastime some Sasquatches amuse themselves with, even when you don't suspect they're around – evidently, some of them watch us intently. I've heard that a hiker can pass within feet of a Sasquatch and never be aware he is there. They are apparently that well camouflaged.

Replication, Copy Behavior

Milt R. wrote me in 1999 that he was cutting a load of deadwood for winter's use near Ely, Minnesota, when, at one point, he turned off his machinery only to hear the sound of the machinery whining down again not far from where he was working. Intrigued and curious, the informant moved through the timber to see where this other crank-start chain-saw sound was located, so perfect was the imitation. In his search, he found a pile of broken-end twigs neatly piled on the ground roughly two-feet high, with 16-inch and 12-inch tracks plainly visible around the twig pile.

In discussing this report with the informant, it was easy to see he was impressed with the replication capabilities of the Sasquatch, at least this one. The informant had been witness to a Bigfoot in the same area but had left it alone at the time. "They don't bother me, I don't bother with them." There are several cases reported where birds foreign to certain areas are heard during the night. A meadowlark at two in the morning is odd, as is the nighthawk at midday. But receiving a report of machinery being mimicked; it shouldn't be surprising given the lung power of an 8-foot, 500-pound Bigfoot!

The Big'uns

I found this next story incredibly interesting. In a similar situation, two Sasquatches routinely watched the big screen television from a distance through a bay window near Panther Creek, Arkansas. The resident owners of the house, two elderly brothers, knew they were out there but were too afraid to interact. The youngest of the old folks showed the most concern and apprehension. Remarking about the enormous height of the Bigfoot, he said, "He could whip my ass before God gets the news." The creatures became so attached to the television that when it was switched off for the night, they started howling.

The problem was solved when the homeowners decided to leave the television running all night with the living room drapes open. It was just the trick to stop the howling and get some sleep.

This nightly television concert persisted until the older brother died four years later, and the other brother went to live with his oldest daughter. Presumably, the "Big'uns" were to blame for the extensive damage done to the homestead after the remaining brother moved out. The bay window where the television screen could be seen was shattered, and the flower pots on the porch had been launched against the sides of the house and strewn around the yard. It appears to be a lesson in how NOT to spoil a Sasquatch family. They can be quite destructive when entertainment or treats are removed.[31]

National Buffalo River Wilderness, Arkansas, 2011

Locating Scat (Fecal Deposits)

One of our well-known academics phoned me one night and, during that conversation, told me there could be no Sasquatch. His reasoning was not because there was nobody made available to science but because nobody ever found scat. Understanding that the academic probably paid little attention to the data, I let it slide, but I'm mentioning it here for anyone else who thinks there isn't sufficient scat data presumptive for Sasquatch.

Many notables in research have made scat determinations; Will Duncan and David Mann come to mind. Washington field operatives have photographed and collected fecal deposits. Organizations have recovered and had scat evidence processed. The bulk of those results indicated 'unknown primate', and some even returned from various laboratories as containing the human element, which was, at the time, thought to be human contamination. But surely all of these scat finds

I've read about (even by the most careful men in field research) shouldn't all be chalked up to careless contamination.

There is one fieldman who described Sasquatch scat as identical to moose scat, but only larger pellet size. I don't know what that fellow was looking at but fecal matter from the Sasquatch is tubular, put down in a length of coil, and is generally described to be of massive size; larger than the biggest bear deposit. The diameter of one deposit was measured at just short of three inches and the circular coil was described as large enough to fill the bed of a shovel. Other deposits have been located, not quite that large, but with a similar diameter.

Surprising Deposit

In the fall of 2011, I was conversing with Peter Byrne about his recollections of the old Café in the Hoopa Valley, where some of the early name recognition Bigfoot pioneers used to hang out. He remembered times spent at the Oaks Café located in the 1960s on the Hoopa Indian Reservation. It was owned by two very popular souls in the area at the time, Dorothy and Ernie Alameda. But let me insert Byrne's own words written in his 'signature caps' here to tell the story as he wrote it; knowing the history of the Bluff Creek, California area (as it once was in the sixties) is important:

THE OAKS CAFE WAS LOCATED IN THE HOOPA INDIAN RESERVATION AND WAS OWNED BY ERNIE AND DOROTHY ALAMEDA, GOOD FRIENDS OF MINE FOR MANY YEARS. INDEED I HAD MANY A GOOD BREAKFAST THERE AND MANY A GOOD DINNER WITH ERNIE AND DOROTHY UPSTAIRS ABOVE THE CAFE, AND WHERE THEY LIVED. ERNIE WAS A TOUGH PORTAGEE-AMERICAN FROM OAKLAND. HE SURVIVED THE DEPRESSION BY COLLECTING DRIFTWOOD OFF A WHARF IN OAKLAND, USING A BOAT HOOK TO RETRIEVE IT. HE WOULD BUNDLE THE WOOD AND SELL IT AS FIREWOOD, GOING DOOR-TO-

DOOR THROUGH OAKLAND'S STREETS. ERNIE DIED MANY YEARS AGO WHILE AT A FOOTBALL GAME WITH DOROTHY IN SAN FRANCISCO. HE ACQUIRED WHAT I BELIEVE WAS A BRAIN ANEURISM AND COLLAPSED AND WENT INTO A COMA. HE LASTED ANOTHER THIRTY DAYS AND THEN PASSED AWAY.

DOROTHY WAS A YUROK NATIVE AMERICAN AND WAS ONE OF THE MOST GRACIOUS AND DELIGHTFUL WOMEN I HAVE HAD THE GOOD FORTUNE TO KNOW. AS OF 2007, WHEN I WAS DRIVING UP AND MOVING TO OREGON FROM CALIFORNIA, I VISITED HER. SHE WAS STILL LIVING AND IN REASONABLY GOOD HEALTH ON THE RESERVATION. YOUR PAL PB.

There is always a bit of treasure in my exchanges with Byrne. What a lovely man he is – a true honor and a privilege to know such as he. Here, in his own words, always willing to share a story is the postscript he added after the previous email:

POSTSCRIPT: ERNIE WORKED WITH ME AS A VOLUNTEER ON THE FIRST BIGFOOT PROJECT WHICH, AS YOU KNOW, I RAN FOR TOM SLICK. ONE DAY, DOROTHY, SEEING MY SINCERE INTEREST IN THE BIGFOOT PHENOMENON, TOLD ME A MOST INTERESTING STORY. SHE SAID THAT HER FATHER WAS IN A STREAM BED IN A CREEK GATHERING CRAWDADS IN THE TRINITY MOUNTAINS. HE WAS CROUCHED DOWN ON HIS HANDS AND KNEES WHEN HE SAW A BIGFOOT COME OUT OF THE FOREST A SHORT DISTANCE AWAY. IT SQUATTED DOWN ON A ROCK AND LOOKED AROUND BUT THE BIGFOOT DID NOT SEE HIM. THEN IT DEFACATED IN THE WATER AND, THIS DONE, STOOD UP AND WALKED BACK INTO THE FOREST.*

---

* Peter Byrne, 2010.

This was especially interesting to receive because a similar report came through the website in the mid-nineties that I confess I was hard-pressed to believe. Since I always saw the Sasquatch as human to some degree, I suppose subconsciously it seemed inappropriate to think they used rivers, creeks, and tributaries for their bodily waste. In hindsight, it's a clever way to hide the evidence and no doubt a great reason why so little in the way of scat is ever found. Known to me all these years later, Wesley J. wrote:

> Me and my wife were fishing the Klamath River in late September 1956. She went back up into the bush to relieve herself and then comes this dark figure from up river with another smaller figure. I thought it was a bear but then I caught on quick. It looked like they were looking for something on the water's edge because they gestured. I walked unnoticed up to the trees and told my wife to keep still. We watched for a few minutes and the smaller one began to walk away back the way they came. The big fellow walked into the river, turned toward the trees. He then sets his feet apart, bends over and did a number two job in the Klamath. He hurried off to join the first Bigfoot almost out of sight. Not quite sure what to do, we gathered the tackle & left. *

He could have described a ton more information if only I'd been more judicious. Until Byrne delivered Dorothy Alameda's account, I would have continued to think the Wesley J. story untrue. It never occurred to me that Bigfoot used the Klamath River like a toilet. Was it the same water they drink? I still have to work my way through all those implications. By the way, Toké Mussis is early California's Klamath River Yurok Indian terminology, meaning wild man of the woods.[32]

The story reminded me of when we were walleye fishing one summer at Lake of the Woods, Bob Motlong's old place in Sioux Narrows. That was back before we needed a passport to enter Canada. I was in a 12-foot metal jon-boat with an elder Indian guide who unashamedly stood

---

* Wesley J., August 9, 1995: Gottsville, Siskiyou County, California.

up in front of me, unzipped his pants, and took a leak over the port side gunwale. And then, without missing a beat, he reached down and, cupping his hand, drank from the same water. Maybe that's only disgusting if you are a member of the 'sterile-oriented' nursing corps. I don't know, but I am sometimes guilty of discounting whatever else must take place underwater in the life cycle of the fish and waterfowl. Still, the sight of an 8-foot Sasquatch defecating into a pristine mountain stream is a repugnant thought to such as I, and I dare think to most women.

Strange Choices

There are many indicators that the Sasquatch reasons well. It's probably true with all things in nature that some are smart and others not so bright. With that thought, I mention a filing made in the summer of 2011 that speaks to that behavior.

The report was about ten campers and two adult guides hiking from Mt. Ball in Yoho National Park, British Columbia, to Mt. Assiniboine and then over to Spray Lake Reservoir in Alberta, roughly a 50-mile, ten-day trip. A portion of that trip took the hikers through an area called "Valley of the Rocks," where no fresh water occurs; only stagnant, foul-smelling pools of filthy collected rainwater found in basins of rocky outcroppings.

The unusual portion of this report turned out to be one stagnant pond the hikers came upon 8 miles into the hike in very deep bush. This particular pool was 45- feet across and barely 5 feet deep – it had enormous footprints walking into it and coming out the other side. The tracks were in a single file and very far apart! The tracks got the attention of the group but it seemed very odd that the Sasquatch would walk into such rank, foul smelling, scum encrusted, fly infested water. Trevor, the informant, said the intelligent move would have been to walk around it; there was plenty of walking space, but the lone creature opted to walk through stagnant scum and we were left wondering why?[*]

Crying Behavior

There was a couple at Kirch Flat Campground in Central California. It was the summer of 1992 but I didn't obtain the report until 1999. This is second hand, but it is worth reporting for the unusual crying behavior. To shorten the story and get to the behavior – the witnesses had been hiking all over the area that day. They got back to camp and were in the process of cleaning off the wooden picnic table when they thought they heard crying.

> It wasn't completely dark - looking toward the river they spotted a woman sitting close with her knees pulled up to her face; she was, they said, "loudly bawling her eyes out." They watched for a while wondering if they should intervene. Finally, the witness walked along the trail down to the water and midway she stopped. The crying woman was not dressed like you think - she wasn't dressed at all; I am not lying! Once the woman saw she was discovered, she jumped up on her feet and went toward the river. They told us breasts were visible. The campers described the crying woman as having bodily hair like the commercial "so easy a caveman can do it" all over her body and face. She apparently made no effort to cover herself; showed no modesty.
>
> Then, still crying loudly, she ran off. The next morning the couple went to the next campsite and told their camping neighbors about it. We are those camper neighbors and the story is as told to us that day.[†]

The Robinsky recollection didn't hit my desk until mid-November 1999; I read it to Rene Dahinden one night for lack of anything better to talk about, and his response was literal: "...Dats about an eight on

---

[*] Trev H. Alberta, Canada.
[†] Will Robinsky.

my bullshit meter, Bobbie." And then he laughed and added, "...I don't know." The story was never uploaded to Bigfootencounters because of Rene's criticism.

Small Sasquatch "Crying Like a Baby"

Then, in 2002, my Cincinnati Reds baseball bud, veteran cryptozoologist and creator of *Creature Chronicles*, Ron Schaffner, forwarded me two articles from his extensive collection. One article mentioned the additional behavior of a lone young child crying. The story ran in the Albuquerque Journal. The Bernalillo County, New Mexico Sheriff's Department was skeptical about frequent phone calls concerning the abominable monster. It was covered with hair and had a blank-looking face, reportedly roaming around South Valley "crying like a baby." According to Sheriff Dale Knable and Art Fusco, the small 5-foot tall hair-covered creature wandered through backyards, unclothed and bawling loudly. It scared the children and one woman.[33]

Bernalillo County, New Mexico

More Crying

Sure as I am that the Sasquatch are some form of human, perhaps distant cousins, why was crying a behavior that was hard to accept? Another story that mentioned crying behavior occurred in remote Kezar Falls, Oxford County, Maine. This one morning, a Native American fellow by the name of Curtis was gathering food for his animals in the kitchen when he heard what sounded like a child crying outside. The crying continued and, concerned, Curtis finally went to the front door. Upon opening it, he saw a tall black hair-covered creature standing there. Curtis declared the creature screamed a screech-like vocalization, scaring him half to death! The creature then ran off. He slammed the door because he said he was afraid of the thing... as he called it. The report was simply signed D.R., with a postscript that asked if these beings were legally recognized in any state?[34]

Good question! Obviously, the Park Service Department at the Department of the Interior hasn't shown any level of interest; maybe the approach should be at the State level? Or would the Parks Department withhold Federal monies from State Parks improvement projects if they went against Federal policies? The Department of the Interior (DOI) Parks Services and Forestry Division's policy is that the Sasquatch does not exist. Any effort to suggest otherwise is generally thwarted.

Kezar Falls, Oxford County, Maine

Longest Audio Recording

On July 8, 2012, Californian Ben Hedrick recorded the longest audio vocalization of a Sasquatch I've ever heard, lasting for a surprising twenty minutes of continual screaming. Finally, the non-stop sounds died out, and only one or two screams were heard after that from a greater distance away. Parked by the side of the road, Hedrick recorded a remarkable length of audio from inside his camper window that captured several different Sasquatch apparently communicating with great excitement. A canine of some kind can also be heard. The recording was taped in Clipper Mills, Butte County, California. Posted on YouTube by Bigtoetime; it received something like sixty-five thousand hits by the end of 2012...amazing audio.[35]

Continuous Sasquatch Vocalizations

Strange Use of the Hands

I thought of documenting the use of the hands because hand-gesturing seems to gather interest wherever I turn. Again, Ron Schaffner was a goldmine of information and generously shared a news article from the Akron Beacon published in June of 1980. The curious Sasquatch behavior I noticed in two of the instances was the reaching out of the hands towards the witnesses; one a farmer and the other a legal secretary. It took place in Union County, Ohio; the behavior of the Sasquatch was quite interesting: The 1980 sightings:

June 17: Patrick Poling, a farmer, while cultivating a cornfield saw the creature come out of the woods. "I figured it couldn't hurt me as long as I was on the tractor," he said. "So I gassed the tractor to head it off. That's when it stopped and turned to look at me. It turned around like this." Poling crouched, held his hands at his side and turned his whole body. When facing front, his palms were forward in a curious gesture almost as though in appeal for understanding. When asked about the gesture, Poling glanced in surprise at his hands.

Yeah, he said, the creature held its hands out like this, this is how he stood.

June 24: Mrs. Riegler, a legal secretary, saw the same creature lying on the road, of all places, while she was on her way home from work and said it stood up and held its hands out. Mrs. Riegler was asked what it looked like. She stood up, bent her knees a bit and then held her hands, palms up and out in the same gesture of appeal that Poling had noticed.

June 26: Larry Ramey saw the same creature at the edge of the woods while Ramey was driving a farm tractor.[36]

Each witness illustrated, in words, a man-like creature more than seven feet tall, with a long head of hair, broad shoulders, and a well-proportioned body. The creature, they said, was not exceptionally long-legged or long-armed but built like a very large man. Each witness said the creature moved stiffly and turned its whole body rather than just the upper portion.

Donald Mathys, a neighbor of Poling, made a plaster cast of a footprint found near where Poling sighted the creature. The footprint was about 17-inches long, 7-inches wide, and had only four toes showing; evidently, a digit was missing.

Union County Sheriff's Deputy Mike Powers took a team into the area. The group spent the night there. Deputy Powers told The Beacon Journal Saturday, "We found definite signs that indicate something is there. We have to look into this." Powers said hundreds of people have already driven around looking for the creature. The county's detective said he is concerned that gawkers could pose a threat. Some of them, he said, are armed; his concern was that an over-eager sightseer might shoot someone. Powers added that there was no indication that the creature was dangerous. But he added, he wants no one taking chances and no one shot.[37]

The pleading behavior of the Union County, Ohio, Sasquatch is curious, and the assumption that the Sasquatch was actually pleading may be a matter of opinion. There are many instances of Sasquatches seen drinking from waterways. Some describe them as being face down on their bellies with their mouth in the water, and others indicate the use of their hands to drink from.

Holding Hands

Prior to 2012, I had no sightings or listings from the country of Mexico to the south of the USA. It was just as well because I intended to only use sightings from North America and Canada. But during the month of May, I received an email from Alejandro Alvarez-Nuñez. He described himself as a Mexican firefighter who worked on the Bosque de la Primavera fire that devastated the forest near Guadalajara, Mexico. The fire consumed thousands of hectares of the preserve. On April 26, he was working with a crew of firefighters when they observed two monstrous beings fleeing the fire line position where he and others were clearing hot spots. He described them as covered in dark rumpled hair about the entire body, running upright and holding hands as they fled a falling tree. He thought the two were hiding behind the tree before seeing them running. Alvarez-Nuñez did not know what Bigfoot was called in Guadalajara but described them as "Huge, strange-looking and very odd." The two Bigfoot were approximately seven feet tall, wide-eyed, and looked terrified. He did not notice "creature bulk" or call them giants. He said they looked thin, scraggly, and afraid. They were barefooted, running across burnt fields of smoking ashes.

Four men with him shouted down the line to each other when the two creatures took off running, and in a flash, they were gone.* The translation was as close as I could get; Google helped. Guadalajara has an

____

* Alejandro Alvarez-Nuñez.

enormous deep canyon that is said to be larger than Arizona's great Grand Canyon. Of that area, Ivan Sanderson wrote:

Most of its bottom is choked with forest and there are said to be "people" in there — at least my Yaqui Indian friends told me so. These are said never to come out, to be very big, and to be hairy all over![38]

Abominable Snowman

Draws Water to Its Mouth With Cupped Hand

Then, in May of 2011, a report described this behavior of cupping the hands to drink near a location in Kendall County, Texas. The informant, a Hawaiian gentleman recuperating at a retreat in Texas, wanted no undue publicity for himself but gave permission for this much to be published:

It was Monday, February 22, the time was close to 5:30 pm with scarce clouds and no breeze at all; a beautiful day. I completed my daily journal and decided to venture outside. I headed out past the waterhole to discover the world. I did much walking and venturing that day, finding caves with petroglyph-like ancient drawings of what I recognize now to be of Bigfoot and buffalo that stood on their hind legs chasing elks and deer. There were fossils of big and small reptiles; nobody believed me when I came back one day remarking that I stumbled upon a "bone yard" of fossils.

After walking about twenty minutes, I decided it was best to head on back. There was a slight slope that led up to the waterhole where the foliage was much thicker than where I first started. As I reached the original site, I froze in my pants! I thought what I saw was a bear crouching down and drinking water with its paws. Its back was facing me; it drew water from the pool and raised it to its mouth. I would guess that I was about twenty five to thirty feet away from it. I'm not familiar with wildlife in the bigger USA, but I don't think bears have hands, and they usually stick their whole face in the water and use their tongue to lap water. I stood there not moving then I made an attempt to move quietly behind a shed which had some of its chimney left.

The Bigfoot kept drinking until the horn from our jeep sounded. It was the signal that we all should be heading to the main facility for dinner. The honk got the Bigfoot's attention as it turned its head to the direction of the noise. It was then I had a view of the profile of its head. It had a flat faced, strong protruding forehead with eyes set under it. Cone shaped head and its nose was wide and flat but NOT like a gorilla's. Its lips were large; I did notice that it really looked like a human in many ways. Its hands were huge with its palm lighter than its hair that averaged about three to four inches. Its fingernails were nasty, as well as its toes that accompanied very large feet. It was then I realized my mind still couldn't accept the fact that it was real. When I headed towards the shed, it moved its head slowly (it didn't seem surprised at all) and looked at me straight in the eye.

I now realize that it probably knew I was there but getting a drink of water was its priority. My emotions went from "hyper-drive" to "warp 10" in an instant. I really don't know how long it stared at me, but my feet wouldn't move at all. I was scared; very scared! Finally it stood up. I realized that there are two things that would happen. He'll have me for dinner or simply kill me for the sport, or somehow we could have a decent understanding that I'll just go away.

It was probably about a minute and a half. It turned and looked at me directly, observing me. These are just my after thoughts after all these years had gone by. I'm brown skin. Not black or white.

I remember hearing sounds; it sounded like wood was being used against another. Its hair was not true black but off centered with a reddish color to it, mostly behind its head and down it's center back. It turned its head toward the wood knocking and then looked at me for another thirty seconds. It dropped its shoulders and its gaze was very different from its first. I could feel that it was not going to harm me and everything was going to be alright. Then it turned its head back in the direction of the knocking and walked away. It turned once more to look at me (it must have been about fifty or sixty feet away by then) and simply vanished into the thick brush.

The story had more description than many accounts, and it pretty much matched what I observed except the conical head; but that doesn't mean some don't have pointed heads, although I doubt it; I imagine it was more likely a wad of twisted hair or similar. I wrestled with the concept that the subject in the Patterson film has a conical head. At first glance to the mere observer, she does. But if you've studied the film work done by analyst M.K. Davis, we see that the Patterson subject does NOT have a conical head after all; it is a wad of hair that moves to and fro with each step she takes."[39]

The conical head descriptions came about immediately after launching the Patterson film in 1967. Prior to that event, there tended to be few statistical notations of conical-shaped head reports attributed to the old data. The facts almost suggest witness pre-conditioning - stimuli created by seeing images of "Patty," the subject in the footage attributed to Roger Patterson. The power of suggestion is a mighty tool. It caused a flurry of reports describing conical heads; we see little of that today. As time went on and advancements in film technology grew, we learned much about the Patterson subject we didn't know before. The subject in the Patterson film clip does not have a conical head, sagittal crest, or sloped forehead. Were all those early day assessments describing pointed or conical shaped heads legitimate perceptions? I think not.

Conical Head or Top Knot on the "Patty" Sasquatch?

Booger Bear Was Humming

Lake Barkley, Lyon County, Kentucky, around 1990. Witness testimony involved a senior gentleman who said he was bluegill fishing earlier in the day in extremely hot weather. He found himself cleaning his catch at the edge of a nearby inlet with three ducks quacking away at the water's edge on the opposite side of the pond-like area where the water fed in from a larger stream. Suddenly, the ducks made a loud commotion and flew off.

Looking up from his stringer of bluegill, he saw a frightful sight. Edging itself into the pond, walking upright into waist-deep water, was a booger-bear (Bigfoot). Not making a sound, it brushed away the duckweed with the little finger side of its left hand and, at the same time, cupped the other, scooping up water to its mouth. What I remember most about that incident was that the fisherman said he heard the booger-bear "humming." It was not a recognizable tune, but unmistakably humming to itself, and when I asked if the informant recognized what the booger was humming, he replied he was in too great a state of shock to know. He took his catch, left the area and didn't look back.

Hand Signal?

A 1992-3 habituator in central California noticed hand signals between members of the Sasquatch clan in her area. One in particular was the raising of the palm, which we might consider a stop, don't come any further, signal. Alice M., an acknowledged long-term interactor with the Sasquatch, wasn't sure it meant stop because it was too frequently used between the older members; maybe it has other meanings. What significance is there to the raised palm with fingers pointing upwards? I mention it here because it was the only reference of its kind in my data.

The Desert Sasquatch

On August 6, 1999, Battle Mountain, Nevada, was a raging inferno from multiple range fires. The gist of the story was that a Sasquatch was seriously burned over 45% of its body at some point during the fire. A government employee said he observed the Bigfoot crawling on the ground. Of the 610 firefighters working the wildfire that summer, a few men allegedly captured the Sasquatch and then contacted a local veterinarian, medical physician, and fish and wildlife services who apparently called in the DOI and the BLM.

According to the report, the Sasquatch was tranquilized, administered to, and then removed to an unknown location. All involved were admonished not to talk about the incident, but I don't know who ordered that directive.

The interesting part of the Battle Mountain fire case was that the badly burned Sasquatch apparently tried to communicate with those who administered aid.[40] The attempt at language was ineffective and, apparently, there was no telepathy reported by any of the witnesses.

I wrestled with this account – but if true, it's a one-of-a-kind event. I am not here to convince or judge the merit of this incident, but I don't know the originator of it, and other details seemed lacking. I'm simply reporting the behavior for whatever value may be found in it.

Bigfoot Recovered Injured in Forest Fire

Curious Sasquatch

Continuing with the stories in and around Battle Mountain, Mr. Jordan Williams encountered a very curious Sasquatch. It happened while driving home from his mining work in Crescent Valley, Nevada, through the Sierra Mountains; as the crow flies, not far from Battle Mountain.

Williams was alone in his SUV driving home at the end of the week, which was five hours away. Suddenly, he ran out of gas in the middle of nowhere, approximately seven miles from a gas station. Eventually, his battery drained and died. To make matters worse, when the battery died, the window was down, and there was no way to roll it up. Jordan could not get law enforcement or any other emergency services to respond to his cell phone calls because he was so remote. It couldn't be a worse situation.

Williams found himself stranded on a desolate stretch of high desert highway with the temperatures plummeting down into the low teens; the car temperature registered 17 degrees outside. There are no trees in the desert, only knee-high sagebrush and tumbleweeds, which makes his encounter all the more interesting in that it is usually widely held that the Sasquatch needs timbered forest to exist. Apparently, that isn't true. There are many reports of encounters in desert conditions; the bulk of them registered in the 1970s. Strangely, there have been few reports since the seventies.

But I don't want to stray from Jordan's situation - there is nothing colder than the interior of a car when the temperatures get that low; the seats and the metal inside the car become so cold they burn to the touch. Williams was a southern California man and hadn't been in the area very long, so he was ill-prepared without any kind of proper clothing. All he had was a t-shirt, sweater, and a blanket; not adequate apparel for 17-degree temperatures. It was after eight o'clock at night and darkness found him on the phone with his wife, trying to figure out what to do, but there was no help available.

At those temperatures, hypothermia can begin to set in within 15 minutes, so you can imagine the condition he was in by two o'clock in the morning when something startled him. He glanced up and saw a face looking at him through the car's passenger window. Williams made eye contact for about ten seconds with the strange face of a Bigfoot. The light from his cell phone lit up the face of the creature very well. But suffering extensively from hypothermia after six hours in 17-degree weather, Williams failed to respond coherently. His situation with the Bigfoot; window down, didn't register with him accurately.

At that point, Williams said he knew he was losing it. He lit up a cigarette and looked over at the window again, but now the Bigfoot was gone and it occurred to Jordan that he was possibly hallucinating and imagining the Bigfoot was at his window. He phoned his wife again and told her he was seeing things and needed to get out of there.

Obviously, Williams was experiencing hypothermia but didn't realize it; he was shivering but somehow coping. He then looked up and, over the hood of his car, he saw the Bigfoot again! This time, Jordan got out of the car, looked around, but nothing was there. He even tried to flag down the few cars that past him, but nobody stopped.

Convinced by this point that he was losing his mind, Williams returned to the car, but noticed a shadow cross behind the rear of the vehicle. After seven hours in the freezing temperatures, he gathered himself enough to relax. Visibly exhausted, he managed to fall fitfully asleep. He was jolted awake when the car began to shake. He sat up quickly and saw the Bigfoot looking into the car, then just as fast, the thing ducked back into the darkness again. This time he heard vocalizations coming from the darkness out by the center-divide. He sensed a presence but couldn't make much of it. Then he heard noises, this time coming from the front of the car. Williams described it as a low grumble, a quiet kind of gibberish like Bigfoot was whispering to someone else outside his vehicle.

Williams fought hard to stay awake but thinks he fell asleep again because the next thing he knew, a Highway Patrol Officer was poking at him through the opened window with a flashlight, trying to see if he was alive.

Once home, he explained the ordeal to his wife. Wishing he had tangible evidence that the Bigfoot was really there, they went out to look at the car. Williams found the palm and finger-tipped handprints on the windows of his SUV and took the picture; the palm was HUGE. He wasn't hallucinating after all; a Sasquatch had been visiting him during the night. All things considered, Williams held it together really well; nevertheless, it was a spooky encounter![41]

Sasquatch Encounters Jordan Williams

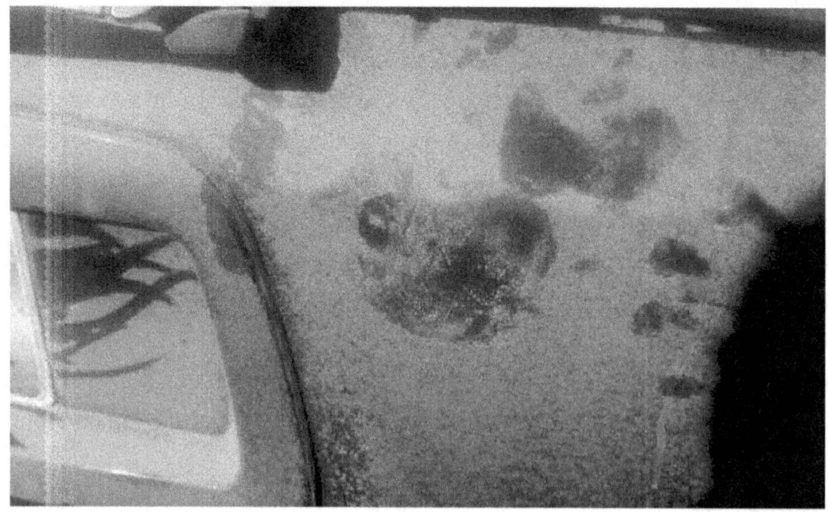

Water Behavior

In twenty-eight years, the diversity in the stories that come in through the website never fails to arouse my interest. There are more sightings and encounters than I ever imagined and it took a few years to discover the little details inherent in the different testimonies. Much can be gleaned from subjective evidence; listed behaviors are far more important than just the numbers of reports...details matter.

There was an interesting account that came from River Forest Park in Cayuga County, New York, in 1996, that involved the use of hands to drink.

A retired couple sightseeing the states in an RV fifth-wheel trailer told me they were sitting with another couple in camp chairs late one summer evening, having a cold beer, when they were startled to see a swimmer looking like he was dog-paddling to shore. The swimmer came up out of the water then, bending over, it turned around and put its face back in the water - presumably to drink, they thought, and then it pinched the water from its nose. I asked if the creature noticed them sitting there, and the observer said, "...if it did, it wasn't apparent to them."

It was only about 15-yards away at this point, our conversation stopped and the four of us stared at it not hardly believing our eyes! Afterwards, it began walking into the tree line using its hands to shed the water from its arms and body; bears don't do that, they shake themselves…but you can't imagine how freaky that was. We folded up our chairs and headed back to the trailer. We left the next day, both of us still thinking it strange what we saw. We didn't think to look for the footprints, but I think there was some on the beach where it came out from the water. It was like a bloody Spielberg moment![42]

Swimming

Apparently, the Sasquatch are excellent swimmers. In 2005, a zoology student described a Sasquatch diving in the Mooselookmeguntic Lake off the Bemis Valley Trail in the State of Maine over a Labor Day Weekend hiking trip. His date that weekend emailed her doubt that it was a Sasquatch because, as she said, "I don't believe in such a thing as Bigfoot, but Jim was sure that it was a Bigfoot that took a header into the Lake." The couple apparently never saw it surface but found partial footprints in the soft soil at the water's edge.[43]

At Mooselookmeguntic Lake

Shadowing Behavior and Rock Attack

I was impressed with the gentleman who wrote the next story because it's a great read and defines the behavior of a Sasquatch very well. I've decided to publish the entire letter as it came to me:

> I am going to tell this story only once, I had never planned on telling it to anyone…ever, but here it goes. My name is Floyd and I am 40-years old with no reason to make up a story like this. There is nothing to gain, nothing to lose, and I really am not trying to scare anyone. My encounter begins while on a fishing trip just south of Nashville, Illinois, at Washington County Lake. It was July 22, 2010; I decided to go cat fishing. I loaded up the boat with all my gear and got to the ramp around 5:30 p.m.
>
> After putting the boat in the water, I headed out for a cove on the northeast side of the lake where the trees shaded the water. I was anchored about 30-feet from the bank enjoying the peace and quiet.
>
> I caught a mess of catfish and decided to fish well into the night as the fish were biting great. Around 11 p.m., something started to stomp around in the woods; I figured it was deer or coons, and I could hear rustling not far from where I was anchored. The thing would make moving noises about every ten minutes. I never really thought much of it and was more into catching fish than worrying about an animal in the bushes. Time passed and I heard a really loud splash that made the sound of a large rock being thrown into the water about twenty feet behind my boat.
>
> At first I thought someone was screwing around with me throwing things in the water. I looked at my watch; it was 1:27 a.m., now the 23rd of July, 2010. After thinking it over I decided it had to be a fish because for someone to be that far back into the woods they had to walk a good distance and I would have noticed their flashlight. Plus, as big as the sound of the splash was, they would have to be Superman to be able to throw a large rock that far out into the water. I continued fishing and never heard any other noises and after a bit forgot all about the splash. When the fishing died down around 3:00 a.m., I packed it up and headed for the dock.

As I was pulling the anchor out I heard a loud noise in the dark of the sandy bank like something was startled when I stood up to pull up the anchors. I figured I spooked a deer bedded down. I was only able to run the "trolling motor" on my boat because the lake had a 10 hp limit and my motor was bigger than 10 horses.

So as I am trolling slowly back to the dock there is that noise again of whatever I spooked moving along the edge of the wood line. This went on for about ¾ of a mile but I could not see what I'd spooked. Now I was about 100 yards from the dock. All around the dock, bait shop and bank there are street lights where the woods begin to thin out. As I reached this area the movement in the woods stopped. Now I was curious as to what the hell animal would be following me like that. I tied off the boat and walked up to the parking lot to get the truck when I heard a grunt sound. I opened the truck door and this thing grunted again so I fired up the truck and shined my headlights towards the area where the grunt came from. To my great surprise I saw a large set of large yellow eyes in the woods looking back at me. I studied them and could see the eyes blink. The eyes were really high in the air, 8-feet or so. Not thinking anything fearful, I backed down the ramp and loaded the boat.

After getting everything buttoned up and ready to head home; I got in the truck and headed up the ramp. I looked for the eyes in the same area but did not see them at that point. Leaving the lake consists of a 20 mph speed limit and a winding road for a number of miles. As I passed the check-in station close to the road I heard a loud bang like something had hit the boat so I stopped and got out to see if I lost something. Everything looked fine, nothing had fallen out, and as far as I could tell nothing, such as a deer, had run into the boat. I climbed back into the truck and before pulling away I heard the noise again like something hitting my boat. I hit the brake lights to light up the boat a bit and looked into the rear view mirror. I saw what looked like a very large man standing next to the boat. I was about to jump out and ask what the hell he was up to when I suddenly got an eerie feeling. My head told me to keep on driving, so I hit the gas with my eyes glued to

· the big black figure with the yellow eyes, then it took off, running towards the truck. It was chasing me! I hit it hard, letting the gravel fly. Then, nearing 35 mph, something hit the truck very hard making it shake violently. Well now, I was done messing around and said piss on the speed limit; I lost it, at what speed, I don't know. But it followed me! When I reached the highway I got out to check the truck and there was, and still is, a nice dent high on the passenger-side bed. I went home, unloaded the boat, grabbed a shotgun, and headed back out there. I crept along those roads until dang near dawn looking for whatever it was that hit and dented my truck but never saw the thing again. I still fish there today but not alone, not anymore.[*]

This guy is a machine! I mean, he's out in the pitch dark of night doing some serious fishing. He's apparently not afraid of anything; he's just trying to get his limit of catfish and get back home. He's got this 8-foot, yellow-eyed Sasquatch shuckin' and jivin' around him, throwing rocks, denting his truck, grunting, chasing, and growling, and the guy just goes about his business, no problem. He made notations of the strange behavior totally oblivious to the size and aggressiveness of the Sasquatch. Do you love this guy or what?

There have been other reports by witnesses who felt they were being followed, but none in my data quite as dramatic. Most men would leave, but Floyd Scott elected to stay and take his time. Apparently, Scott's lack of reaction infuriated the Sasquatch. It is also the first time I've read a report where the Sasquatch deliberately dented a vehicle. The report most assuredly contained strange behavior worthy of notice.

Friends of mine thought maybe the intent was more benign; maybe the Sasquatch only wanted Mr. Scott's stringer of fresh catfish. Opportunistic stealing is a commonly reported behavior - in fact, it falls at the top of the list in their job descriptions. I cannot immediately think of anything moveable that hasn't been reported stolen by the Sasquatch. Apparently, there are no statutes in the Sasquatch book of rules, and

---

[*] Floyd Scott, November 4, 2010.

really, who among us is willing to argue the point with a 900-pound Sasquatch?

Mouth Noises

Mouth noises are occasionally reported, specifically the smacking of the lips together, mouth popping, clicking, whistling, tongue noises, blowing, spitting, wheezing, coughing, sneezing, throat clearing, and choking noises.

California resident Mike Dardanos reasoned that the sound thought to be log rapping may be partly attributed to a nearby Sasquatch making mouth noises or pounding on the chest.

Together, Mike and I theorized that the size of the Sasquatch lung is so huge that it can magnify sound. Dardanos illustrated one of his theories by placing his tongue in the roof of the mouth. By applying suction and then pulling the tongue off the roof of the mouth, he was able to achieve several tones by shaping the lips in unison with hands cupped around the lips (opened or closed) as the tones are emitted. Various popping sounds, that is, baritone emissions from a Sasquatch's giant chest/lung capacity would be much louder. Additional echo sounds can be produced by cupping the hands around the mouth.

In the deep woods, sounds can be distorted yet emanate great distances. It was suggested that the sound could be made with two very large hands slapped together with cupped hands rather than a slapping of the two palms together as in applause. Mike successfully demonstrated the sound of two cupped hands brought together in a forceful manner, and it sounded exactly like wood on wood. Dardanos figured this might be "...an alternative way to regard some of the noises interpreted to be wood on wood communication between the Sasquatch...or not." Knuckle pulling and finger snapping are sounds that campers claim to have heard during the night, supposedly by Bigfoot, since other night creatures don't make those noises.

A proficient Sasquatch trained to run silent and deep undoubtedly has any number of covert sounds and signals in his arsenal, especially if he's been taught that concealment meant life or death. Nobody in the research community has come up with a good reason why they stay removed from society. The hunting season must be a terrifying time of year for them to get through; I can't imagine what that must be like. Statistics tell us that the fall hunting season is when most sightings occur. That might be attributed to the number of hunters out that time of year, and fishermen working the fall salmon run.

Sasquatch and Infrared

When we click the remote control apparatus that turns the television off and on or when we change the channel, the hand-held remote talks to the receiver in the television set. It does this by emitting an infrared signal that human vision cannot see. To some extent, the field trail camera operates the same way. Cameras, for example, the Sony Night Shot, also use an infrared beam. But can anything living wild see or sense infrared? The answer is yes, well, sort of.

Some wild animals may not see complete images. They may just see areas of relative warmth or lack of warmth. Bees see images made up of both lights, which we can see (visible) and light that is redder than we can see (infrared). Their eyes do this for them. Snakes can see heat with specialized organs – distinct pits generally facing forward on either side of the snake's head. But those organs are not eyes, so we figure they sense areas of heat and know when they're getting closer to a source of living warmth like a mouse. This is just a different kind of seeing, as heat IS infrared light.[44]

We humans cannot see infrared, yet in research the question arises: can the Sasquatch see infrared beams generated from field cameras, and is that the reason trail cameras are unsuccessful? When infrared (IR) waves touch a surface, heat energy is released regardless of the surrounding air temperature. The Sasquatch probably does not see infrared, but they might sense the heat from an infrared beam if that beam were hot enough. The IR in a field camera generates very little heat. Wouldn't the Sasquatch need infrared on the order of a small heat lamp to feel infrared heat? There may be other reasons why the Sasquatch seems to avoid camera traps; one being simple street smarts.

Most humans have poor vision in the dark. There are exceptions to the rule for I understand there is a blue-eyed child in China who does his homework in the dark.[45] The consensus tends to be that because the Sasquatch can move easily at night (so we think), they have better vision at night; but do they really? Frustrated by the inability to catch a Sasquatch on field camera traps, speculation at times runs wild off the mark. Whether they see or sense the IR beam remains another one of those much-speculated considerations.

Then again, the reluctance of the Sasquatch to move around camera traps may simply mean that somehow they sense no good comes with the deployment of the metal gadgets strapped to trees in their habitat – similar in some respects to the association with the hunter's rifle. To the Sasquatch, perhaps the camera traps are foreign objects and things out of place in their habitat. Nevertheless, unable to reason why there is little in the way of Bigfoot photographs, men tend to take comfort in wild, if not dramatic, speculation.

I've heard it said (as regards the camera trap) that the Sasquatch has ESP (extrasensory perception) that borders on some supposed alien knowledge of camera mechanics – and they reason that way because it is believed the primitive, wild-living Sasquatch must surely understand the mechanics of the camera. Failing that, for some reason, they see infrared light. There is no way anything living wild understands the modern-day mechanical world...but Bigfoot Research is full of wild imaginings and speculative theater. The wildness in the Sasquatch may not sense anything about trail cameras but intense caution from the intrusion of civilized man; I lean towards that idea.

Recently, a good friend of mine witnessed such behavior in the Sasquatch; we were both amazed. In this instance, a trail cam was set out on a particular property facing a backyard picnic table where a closed ice chest was left out overnight. The camera portrayed a Sasquatch driven by curiosity. It got very close to the field cam, and then it touched the lens; perhaps to see if it would go off and, apparently, it did. Still intensely curious about the ice chest, the loitering Sasquatch couldn't resist it, even though he knew not only where the cameras were but apparently had some idea about the camera. What the Sasquatch did next totally surprised us.

Curiosity about the contents of the ice chest finally caused the Sasquatch to back up into the area where the cameras were deployed. It not only backed up to the ice chest (walked backwards) but also reached out to gingerly touch the ice chest while remaining backwards to the camera; the behavior in the footage was fascinating to watch. Film shows it never opened the chest but apparently wanted to touch it for whatever reason. This, of course, may be an isolated event...or not, but the behavior with the camera present was interesting to watch.

Over time, I've seen photos of tongues licking camera lenses, fingers, palms, and various blurred hairy 'somethings', some of which can be attributed to bears, mainly because there was one photo, in particular, of a tongue licking the lens of a camera that was too long to be a primate tongue. It may be that non-detectable pinhole cameras will be the wave of the future in field observations.

'Cat-Eye' Boy Video Said to Show Chinese Child Who Sees
in Dark

Clacking Sounds

Syl McCoy was U.S. Forestry Service Chief Fire Inspector in Willow Creek back in the 1960s. A tall, soft-spoken man, McCoy was a wealth of information about the early-day Sasquatch. One of the stories attributed to McCoy was about a Forest Service Company truck he provided for California veteran Bigfoot investigator Peter Guttilla to a remote place where tracks had been found and strange sounds heard at night in Humboldt County. At this particular site, Guttilla had what he called his "rock banging" episode. He reasoned that the Sasquatch must bang rocks together as a form of communication, a behavior not well documented previously by any of the old guard in the research community. Guttilla stated that "the click-click, click-clack sounds went on for the better part of an hour one night starting with one area click-clack," and soon he was surrounded by click-clacking rocks that answered his reply click-clacks.

According to Peter, it sounded like a symphony of rock-clacking that would give new meaning to the term "rock music." True story, albeit one of a kind! I often wonder if Peter doesn't secretly take perverse joy in sending gullible me these unusual stories; I am known to be his captive audience.[*]

Teeth Clacking

This next file describes clacking sounds, not the striking of rocks together but the audible sound of teeth clacking together. Previously, I believed the clacking of teeth as it was described to me could only be attributed to grizzlies or the warning of a black bear sow protecting her cubs; they would huff and clack teeth together when threatened.

Now, of course, three decades later, I stepped back and thought about the larger picture. In 1989, Simon Kajne was in Idaho hunting with two other men, camped on a high ridge, preparing dinner. Kajne said they

---

[*] Peter Guttilla, 1996.

threw on some sausage and fried up some potatoes. Hungry, they sat around the fire and began to clean their plates. A distinct tooth-clacking sound was heard, and like anyone familiar with bears, all three men thought big grizzly! Alert now and tense, Kajne said they scanned around the darkened perimeter of their campsite but saw no bear, yet the clacking continued intermittently. Each man reached for their rifle and, removing the safety, stood back to back, waiting for the grizzly to come charging out of the darkened forest towards them. The teeth clacking of a grizzly bear is generally thought to be a warning! There were several moments of silence – but then the clacking noise grew louder and more distinct. Kajne told me the sound was unmistakably the powerful clashing of upper and lower teeth. Sometimes, it came from high up in the trees somewhere, and other times, it seemed to be coming from the ground. What unnerved them was the loudness of the clacking. It came louder than the crackling from their campfire.

Then it stopped, and there were no more sounds until two hours later when the men were huddling down in a tent contemplating some measure of sleep. At that point Kajne said large rocks flew into their campsite. It was then they realized bears don't throw rocks; a familiar realization by field researchers. One of the men, by then with frayed nerves, screamed, "...knock it off, we have enough fire power here to blow you away!" And with that, the younger of the men fired off a couple of rounds into the trees, ending the incident. Nothing more happened that night or the night that followed.

Don't you find the behavior of the Sasquatch to be thought-provoking, as compared to the verbal threat issued by the hunter? At least the intimidation technique stopped it. Did the Sasquatch understand? I only know that it wasn't the hunter's imagination at work because they found two sets of footprints circling their campsite; a set of 18-inch tracks and another half that size.

In hindsight, the clacking of teeth may have been a hunger noise and the want of some of the meat the men cooked for dinner that night. Sausage and bacon smell delicious in the night air around a campsite.

If not that, I don't know the reason for the teeth-clacking behavior. It isn't often reported. Other such mouth sounds may be recorded in other databases; this was the only one in my files describing teeth clacking.

The "Whistle Man" Pee'd

I pulled another odd report from a 2001 folder, where Alicia Bancroft's children were playing in the backyard of their rural mountain home not far from Phoenicia, Ulster County, New York.

Responding to a terrible stench coming through the open kitchen window, Mrs. Bancroft was met at the backdoor by her children, breathless from running across the open yard screaming, "…the whistle man is back, Mommy." Then, out of the mouth of the youngest, 4-year-old Dillon, announced, "…and he pee'd himself, I saw him." Dede, the older child, described a man with "messy hair came into the yard and gave her a daisy." When she screamed, "the man with the messy hair wet on himself and ran away." This event was one of several that occurred when the family was in the backyard, though none were as interesting as what Mrs. Bancroft's children had to say. The other behavior Miss Dede described was that the man with messy hair "danced a jig like his feet were on fire." That is hard to visualize, but it made me smile. Alarmed, the Bancroft family has since moved back to a smaller town north of Poughkeepsie, New York.[*]

Whistling and Whistle Sounds

Whistling is apparently a common theme among the Sasquatch. Campers returning from a week's vacation at Catherine's Landing in Hot Springs, Arkansas, reported a bad odor and "whistling" from opposite areas of their RV at 3:00 a.m. The 1996 informant said the figure was large, but it was too dark outside to describe detail.[†]

---

[*] The Bancroft story, 2001.
[†] Signed only as butcherboy1532.

Apparently, the Sasquatch can whistle with all the flexibility anyone might imagine. I once asked an ape theorist if apes whistled? You can imagine his answer.

Whistling Described

Therapist Matt Huey had an experience in 1997 that just won't go away. In August 2011, Matt wrote, "I had an experience in De Soto County, Mississippi, several years ago; it was after 11:00 p.m. at night when I heard a long, loud [sustained] whistle that caused my old Boston terrier dog to bark. When I heard it, I thought it was a person but it was much longer and sustained for a longer period of time than a person might manage. I've been searching for answers to it for years." Huey lives on ten acres that are densely wooded; the sustained whistle came from this area.[*]

Peter Guttilla Recalls Whistling

One of the most generous, no-nonsense Sasquatch investigators from the old days is California-based Peter Guttilla. I met Peter as his Bigfoot tracking career began winding down in 1996, and at this writing, we've remained friends for seventeen years despite differences of opinion regarding the Sasquatch. Of the friends I trust and count on the five fingers of my right land, Guttilla is among those five. Peter is a friend of many, including Terry Albright and Tom Muzila. Other friends have passed on now, like Bobbie Ann Slate and her husband Vince Gironda, Rich Grumley of the CBRO, and bad-boy Erik Beckjord, who was, interestingly enough, a staunch side-kick friend of Canadian author John Green. Beckjord bragged about invitations to Green's home and dinners with the Green family.

Guttilla remembered a much younger Peter Byrne in the 1970s and Syl McCoy, to name but a few. He preferred working closely with martial

---

[*]   Matt J. Huey.

arts expert, Tom Muzila and Terry Albright. Guttilla did fieldwork in the early years with anthropologists Dr. Connie Cameron, and Sally Page Sheppard-Wolford. His annual trips into the Bluff Creek region brought him into contact with Rene Dahinden and others. There were, of course, others, but at the time I started inquiring, their names began to fade from Peter's memory. Peter goes way back, but the best part of Peter was and still is the trust you feel with him, his ability to allow for differences; a rare, honest, forthright friend you could always count on; I still feel a warm kinship.

Guttilla doesn't put up with the Bigfoot nonsense; he's Sicilian, after all. He would just as soon leave a dead horse's head in the bed of a hoaxer than to put up with the baloney. Peter sees right through the deceivers, the self-promoters, and the deception inherent in Sasquatchery. As it turned out, he was the only one of a couple of investigators with some authority on the desert Bigfoot; Ron Morehead was the other. Recently, Guttilla sent me this offering that refers to the desert community of Borrego Springs, California. Peter wrote: "Here's an interesting little pluck from *The Abominable Sandman of the Borrego,* written by Major Victor Stoyanow...

The Screaming Giant of Tuolumne County

"I've often wondered just who that Frank Cox was..." Peter wrote. The mysteries of the desert are many. A dancing skeleton with a light in its ribcage cavorted through Borrego long ago, which I believe was finally found to consist of a giant tumble-weed that had picked up a phosphorescent mineral along its route. And then there was a creature that Frank Cox killed years ago near Dead-man's Hole in the vicinity of Warner's Hot Springs. According to accounts in the San Diego Union-Tribune, it had a head rather small, large buck teeth like a carnivorous animal, muscular arms, enormous feet 24-inches long, weighed about 400 pounds, and was a cross between a man and some carnivorous animal, probably a bear. And then since the first of this year, there have been positive sightings of the screaming giant of Tuolumne County that terrorized residents of Pinecrest a year ago. A pilot observed a 10-foot man from the air, and Sheriff's Deputy Albert Miller investigated huge footprints and observed that they were about six feet apart and not bear tracks.[*]

Whistle, Whistling

Peter and I remain in close contact; in fact, I asked him if he had anything in his arsenal that he might share about whistles or whistling Sasquatches. To my surprise, he did, and I will attempt to quote some of what he told me here.

Patterson Site Photo © Peter Guttilla, California.

Yes. I have heard strange whistles on a few occasions, always at night, once from a spot on the woods not more than a hundred yards away. This was during one of my early day campouts on the Patterson sand-

---

[*] Peter Guttilla.

bar. I was with Tom Muzila when we heard a deep whistle, long and drawn out; there were footfalls heard and both Tom and I dashed after it only to find ourselves stumbling around in the dark. At the time, the Patterson sandbar was wider than 100 yards across and strewn with rocks and pebbles. At night, it was black as pitch.[*]

Peter continued,

There was another time we heard whistles in Oregon and another incident of whistling northwest of Happy Camp, California. Of course these were many years ago. One of those times I remember because Bobbie Ann Slate was with me...egad, that had to be 1973 in an isolated area of San Bernardino County. We heard whistles, light and airy, moving toward us in a remote canyon called Big Rock Creek located on the eastern slopes of the San Gabriel Mountains. I whistled back and the whistler responded. It got closer and closer and I stood my ground. I whistled again and didn't move; the heavy footfalls came closer. The strange thing was the whistling almost sounded like a melody of some kind...not quite, but almost. I took a chance and spoke, asking the whistler to come closer, no harm in the offing. At that point the whistling stopped, the footfalls moved away and that was it. Though the soil there was cement hard, nevertheless the next morning there were marks showing a foot roughly 18-inches long.[†]

A History of Whistling Behavior

There are whistle notations made in previously published accounts, this one from Janet Bord's 1977 Bigfoot Casebook.

A Spearfish, South Dakota, mother and her three daughters saw two Sasquatches in 1977 in a cornfield eating corn. One was roughly 8-feet tall, black, and the other smaller with a brownish red body and black

---

[*] 100-yards = the length of a USA football field.
[†] Peter Guttilla, 2011.

face. The report says "they whistled" but there were no further nota-tions in the brief blurb.

While the curious behavior of the Bigfoot was 'whistling,' the prox-imity of the Bigfoot to a cornfield does not go unnoticed. The history there is very long, and the data shows them being seen in and around unharvested crops, in particular sweetcorn, alfalfa, peanuts, potatoes, and yams. There are also reports of whole rows of onions being uprooted and the entire fruit yield of one apple or avocado tree simply gone; both the ripened and unripe.

While reading Ronald A. Beck's story of his father, Fred Beck's 1924 account with those famous ape men on Mt. St. Helens, I noticed whistling in chapter one, which he (Ron Beck) titles, *The Attack*. In the fourth paragraph, Beck writes:

> We had been hearing noises in the evening for about a week. We heard a shrill, peculiar whistling each evening. We would hear it coming from one ridge and then hear an answering whistling from another ridge. We also heard a sound which I could best describe as a boom-ing, thumping, just like something was hitting itself on its chest.[46]

Several dozen old letters were stacked in a basket by my desktop computer in the office. It was there that I uncovered a letter written in the late 1990s from a widowed lady who had only signed herself as Janneen. She wrote to say she heard whistling start-up every evening about the time the eleven o'clock news came over local television channels. "Nearby whistling," she wrote, "was often echoed or returned from across the valley adjacent to their small house just off the Angeles Crest Highway in Los Angeles County's Angeles National Forest."

According to her note, it often lasted several hours and included forlorn, wailing cries, which she equated as being "like a person in pain." She never saw the whistlers, which came always after dark, but two of her grandchildren did. One late summer night, after eating outside, the grandchildren embarked on the ritual of spitting watermelon seeds. It is a contest to see who can spit seeds the farthest from a line drawn in the dirt. The contest was followed by hearty romps about the backyard with their yellow lab puppy, Striker. "The sounds of children at play ceased," she wrote, "when the children came in the back door breathlessly exclaiming there was a furry man watching them from outside the gate. They stopped playing," she continued, "noticing him when he whistled either at them or in reply to them."

The squealing noise small children make while at play seems to be an attractant to any nearby Sasquatch. There are instances recorded where they stand and watch the playful activities. But so intent on watching the children at play, the Sasquatch often forget themselves and are noticed when they step too far out into open spaces.

Car Peeping

A Marine named Jim Campbell from South Carolina was trying to get home on leave. He was driving through the Great Smokey Mountains of South Carolina when he felt sleepy. Campbell pulled off on a mountain-top observation-looking point, locked the doors of his vehicle, sprawled out on the front seat, and closed his eyes to fall sleep. He doesn't remember how long he slept but the feeling of being watched awakened him. Sitting up, he observed a 7-8 foot Sasquatch staring at him through the front windshield.

A Marine's Encounter with Bigfoot in the North Carolina Mountains

Campbell said that when he sat up behind the steering wheel, the Sasquatch moved off and walked away like a man does. The Marine drove off but apparently never forgot the incident.[47]

Sasquatch and the Elk Hunters

Great story! The next entry is about the interaction between a few elk hunters, Sasquatch, and a trophy elk too heavy to muscle out of the wilderness without help. The story amazingly speaks to the issue of Sasquatch understanding and their willingness to participate in generous help with those who have shown kindness to them. These specific behaviors are not often recorded but are heart-warming to read in this true story, which builds to a surprise ending originating in Apache Junction, Arizona.

Titled the *B.J. Thompson Story*, it was investigated and reported to anthropologist and avid Bigfoot researcher Dr. Wilson. G. Wheatcroft, Ph.D. He graciously permitted for it to be published in toto here. The events described happened in March 1992 and again during elk hunting season in July 1994.

First Bigfoot Experience

These events happened in the Blue Mountains of the State of Washington. The nearest city was Walla Walla. Pop Sumerlin (Wes) was a friend of mine. He is now deceased. Pop was a grandson of Chief Joseph of the Nez Pierce Indian tribe, famous in the 1800s. Pop was an expert hunting guide. Once, he showed me photographs of giant footprints in the woods. They looked human to me. What I mean is that one footprint was in front of the other, like humans walk. Right away, I guessed that they were Bigfoot footprints. Pop did not overly explain things; he let you learn for yourself. At that time, although I had only known Pop for two days, he decided to take me into the Blue Mountains with him. He told me that he had never before taken a white man into the mountains for the purpose of seeing the Bigfoot.

Here's what happened: We took a horse trailer with us, with two horses inside. When we got to the right area according to him, we then saddled the horses and went in further on horseback. Pop was very experienced. We rode on horseback for five hours. It was wilderness. We rode for maybe six miles. Then we stopped and tethered the horses. We had arrived at a flattened-out area where there was a simple sleeping lean-to. On a tree at this campsite, there were hoists for pulling a deer or elk up onto the tree for skinning purposes. We dumped our gear and got a fire going. Then we began hiking on foot for about 1½ hours. There was snow on the ground at this time of year. We started seeing Bigfoot tracks in the 3-inches of snow. The tracks were huge, 18-inches long. We also saw some thick deposits of grey-colored Bigfoot hairs stuck to the bushes along the pathway. At the end of our hike of about an hour and a half, we entered a clearing about 40-feet in diameter. Pop took 4-peanut butter and jelly sand-wiches out of his bag and put them on wax paper in the middle of the clearing, as an offering. He then swept some snow off of the rocks, and we sat in the shade there to wait. We sat quietly for about 45 minutes. Then we could hear rustling sounds in the pine trees and bushes. Then suddenly, two Bigfoot came out of the trees across from us, walking 8-feet into the clearing in front of us.

One of the Bigfoot was 9-feet tall, and the other was 8-feet tall. Their fur or hair was grayish brown. They were very hairy, but surprisingly, they had human-looking faces. They had wider mouths and somewhat flatter noses than humans have. Their cheeks were clear of hair. Above their eyebrow ridges, these Bigfoot had a low hairline. Their heads were dome-shaped. The two Bigfoot just stood there for about 10 minutes, staring at us, while we were staring at them. No words were spoken. I had the feeling that they would have stayed longer, if I (a new person) had not been there. But Pop did not say this to me. Who knows? I had a feeling that they knew of our presence well before we got to the clearing. Pop felt that the Bigfoots were humans of some kind! He was, perhaps, actually more friendly towards the Bigfoots than he was towards whites! This was kind of an American Indian thing with him. He felt that the Bigfoots were American Indian blood beings.

After about 10 minutes of standing in the middle of the clearing, the Bigfoots backed up, and then disappeared behind the trees. Then we also left. I assumed that they would come soon to retrieve the sandwiches that we left in the clearing for them. The shorter Bigfoot seemed younger to me. Initially, when they first arrived, the shorter one made a move as if he was going to come get the sandwiches. But the bigger, seemingly older Bigfoot made a grunting noise, at which point the younger Bigfoot stopped advancing towards the sandwiches. Then, as I said, they both just stood there looking at us. Their arms are long so that their hands were at the level of their knees. They also had long legs, and really massive shoulders. When they backed up into the trees, Pop also got up and touched my shoulder. Then we turned and left the way we came. On the way hiking to this clearing, we had avoided stepping on the Bigfoot footprints, but on the way back we weren't so careful, because we had no plaster of Paris with us, so we couldn't make footprint-casts.

We had hiked in just to see the Bigfoot, so after riding our horses back to the horse trailer, we put them into the trailer and left the area.

The Second Bigfoot Experience

In July of 1994, I again hooked up with Pop Summerland. He asked me to help him because he was taking a hunting party of six men to hunt elk up in the same forests of the Blue Mountains of Washington State. He was such a good hunting guide that he guaranteed that each paying hunter in the party would be able to shoot an elk! He asked me to help out; I was to look after the camp, do the cooking, and so forth. We all assembled together. There were six paying hunters. Pop provided everything except the guns and ammunition as part of his package deal. We pulled two, four-horse trailers for a total of eight horses. When we arrived at the hunting area with the same lean-to I described before, at first, all of the hunters wanted to go off in two, 3-man parties, on horseback. The lean-to was about 15-feet long, and about 2-feet tall in the back. But by the time we had arrived there on the first day, there was no time to start hunting. So, the first night after our arrival, the men cleaned their guns and we cooked some grub. I also corralled the horses.

Elk Hunting, Day 1:

On the first day of hunting, we left at 5:30 a.m.; all eight of us on foot because if we took the horses, it would scare the elk we were hunting. This is what Pop said. As a guide, I went with three of the hunters, and Pop went separately with the other three men. Pop had made one dozen peanut butter and jelly sandwiches. That first day, out of the six hunters, three of the men shot one elk each. I tell you, Pop was really good; that's why he guaranteed that each hunter would shoot an elk on the hunting trip! These three elk were not too big, but satisfactory. Out in the forest, we field-dressed them, (this involved de-gutting them, and so forth, and quartering them) and we hiked back to camp to get the horses to use them as pack horses, and loaded the meat and hides on the horses. Deep in the forest, Pop left twelve sandwiches on a log. When we returned that night, we cooked and ate some steaks from the elk. Elk meat is better than venison! The field-dressing of the elk was crude, just enough to get the game meat back to camp.

Elk Hunting, Day 2:

On the second day of hunting, the three men who had each killed an elk the day before did not go with us because the rule was: one elk per person as a condition of the group-hunting license. That is, one tag for one elk. On the second day, one man was sick, and he decided to stay in the camp. Therefore, four of us went hunting—two hunters and two guides, on foot, carrying guns. One of the two hunters shot an elk that day. Out in the forest, we noticed that the sandwiches were gone from the log where Pop had left them the day before, including the wax paper. Pop then left another six butter and jelly sandwiches on the same log. We field-dressed the elk that had been killed that day, went to get the horses, and then packed the meat back. As we were returning to our camp, we spotted some giant tracks of a huge bull elk. This was only about one-half mile from our camp.

Let me make a note about field dressing: this involves cutting the animal into quarters, or halves in certain cases, then removing the tongue and liver and keeping the hide. All the meat is wrapped in burlap, and brought by horseback to the camp, where each of the men put their meat on ice in various coolers we had with us. Therefore, at the end of the second day, three of the hunters left with four elk cut up into meat, preserved on ice in the coolers, because they had killed their legal limit. One of the hunters decided to stay in the camp, so now there were three hunters and two guides.

Elk Hunting, Day 3:

On the third day of actual hunting (the 4th day of our trip, though), we left camp at dawn at about 5 a.m., right after breakfast. The hunters who had not shot an elk wanted to bag that large bull whose big tracks we had seen the day before. The man who was sick the day before also still needed to bag an elk. Right as we left, at only about 150 yards from the camp, a 500 pound elk stepped out of the bushes and the man who had been sick pulled his rifle, and shot it. The two hunters then field-dressed the elk and loaded it on the horses that they retrieved from the nearby camp. They took it the short way to their truck to put on ice.

So now, this left only one hunter and us two guides to continue the hunt. We wanted to track and to shoot that giant bull elk! So, we continued the hunt on foot. Pop had about twenty peanut butter and jelly sandwiches with him. Every hundred yards or so, Pop would put two or three of these sandwiches on a rock, or log, while we were tracking the footprints of the big elk. We travelled about 4 miles from Camp at that time. Then I spotted the giant bull elk. It was really huge;

probably 1400 pounds! The remaining hunter shot and killed it. It was so heavy that the three of us couldn't even turn it over! We had our skinning knives with us. So we merely de-gutted it on the spot. It was too far to drag the carcass back to camp, so we decided to walk back and the next day to get the horses, and then drag it behind the horses. But while we were talking, the hunter reconsidered. He decided he wanted to have this specimen mounted, which would include the head, rack of antlers, and shoulders. So after some discussion, we decided to leave the giant elk right there, and to deal with it in the morning. Pop then placed the rest of his peanut butter and jelly sandwiches right next to the giant elk. We walked back to camp. I cooked dinner for us. The hunter who had shot the big elk was so excited with his trophy that he ran back to camp by himself. On our way back to the camp, Pop and I were talking. We noticed that the peanut butter and jelly sandwiches we had left here and there along the trail had been taken. While we were hiking, I could see some Bigfoot stalking us, but staying well hidden. I could just see parts of them lurking in the bushes. They were quite stealthy. At the camp, the two hunters were drinking and celebrating. They were very happy.

Hunting Trip, Day 4 – Our Surprise:

On the fourth day we got up real early, maybe 4 a.m., to make breakfast. It was still dark. By the time we had made breakfast, it was just dawn. Our task was to saddle up the four horses, to return to where we left the giant bull elk, to field-dress it, and then bring the butchered meat back to camp. But when I went over to the horses, right there near where the horses were tied up, was the giant bull elk lying on its back! Boy was I surprised! Nearby, I saw some large-sized Bigfoot tracks. I was mystified, but happy. Pop smiled when I showed him the bull elk and the tracks. Obviously, the Bigfoot had retrieved the huge carcass for us during the night. We waited for the sun to come up and searched the area to see if there were any other Bigfoot tracks nearby. Further out, we did see somewhat smaller Bigfoot tracks, which we presumed had been left by companions of the larger Bigfoot. I want to point out that there were no drag marks. This means that probably two Bigfoot had carried this giant elk carcass at least 4 miles to our camp during the night. This was amazing to me.

An hour later, Pop and I woke up the hunter who had killed that big bull elk the day before. We told him that his elk was right there, near the horses, but we would have to pull it up onto the tree, with the block and tackle Pop had fixed to the tree, in order to dress and quarter the elk, and remove the meat. We did not tell any of the hunters that Bigfoots had transported it, because this was something between Pop and me, and we had not told any of the hunters that Bigfoot even lived there. Pop said fairly strongly that we should not tell the hunters about the Bigfoot. As to the sandwiches Pop left out in the forest on logs and rocks, we had explained to the hunters that we were leaving the food for the birds and wild creatures, as well as to mark our trail. That had all been reasonable to everyone hunting, the days before.

So the hunters dressed and quartered the giant elk. They butchered it in such a way so that the antlers, neck, and head could be stuffed and mounted by a taxidermist. After this, they put all the meat on ice. It was a really heavy load of meat! The hunters were thrilled. Since they had each gotten an elk, as guaranteed by Pop, like the other hunters, they now left to go home. Pop and I were there for an extra night. There was a table there at the hunting camp to eat on near the lean-to. We set out bananas, peanut butter and jelly sandwiches, and apples on the table, as an offering gift to the Bigfoots. We had hoped to see them come and get the food at night, but we fell asleep.

Hunting Trip, Day 5 – Departure:

Early the fifth morning (actually the sixth day we were out, since we had driven the first day), all the fruit and sandwiches were gone. Obviously, the Bigfoots had come in the night and taken our offerings. Pop insisted that we scratch out the Bigfoot footprints nearby, and by the horses, so no one else would know that there were Bigfoot living in the area, in case hikers might come across Pop's hunting camp. So we dragged some branches over the Bigfoot footprints. Pop felt strongly he should protect their territorial rights. He had a lot of respect for the Bigfoot. He thought of them as a special kind of people.

We cleaned the camp, put the horses in the horse trailers, and left the camp in good order. This was Pop's camp. He depended on it for part of his living. He was really good at what he did. He is deceased now; and I remember him as a good man.

A few days later, we heard that the hunter who had shot the giant bull elk got 1000 pounds of meat from the animal, not counting the head or the weight of the bones. This means that the Bigfoots had probably carried at least 1300 pounds of elk for us, for over 4-miles, as a return favor for us giving them the peanut butter and jelly sandwiches.

Back in Walla Walla, Washington, I asked Pop if he had actually left the sandwiches for the Bigfoot and not for the birds and animals as he had explained to the hunters. I hadn't directly asked him this before. Pop then told me about an experience that he once had after leaving sandwiches for the Bigfoot. Apparently, when hunting alone, he killed and then field-dressed a large elk. Because of weight considerations, he was only able to take one-half of the butchered elk with him on his own horse. The other half of the dressed elk he left right there in the forest. It was also a rough area of forest and rocks to ride in by horse-back. Surprisingly, the next morning, he discovered that the other half of the dressed elk, which he had left in the remote forest, had been delivered to him during the night, by the Bigfoot, near to where he was sleeping. So with this prior experience in mind, he figured that on this trip, by again making an offering of sandwiches, he might get some help from these forest beings. Pop told me: "I knew that the Bigfoots were following us in the forest, and watching us all the time. They stay real well hidden; but I saw them. For several days this was happening. I knew it, but I didn't say anything; I definitely did not want the hunters to know. Not at all! So, I was just hoping for any help the Bigfoot could give us with getting the elk back to our camp, if in fact we needed their help. And as it happened, we did need help.

And they came through for me. This is what happened, just like I have said. [*,48]

Bigfoot Encounters of B.J. Thompson

Stalking and Shadowing

The Sasquatch in the elk hunter story had benevolent intent, and it made great reading. Unfortunately, that same behavior is not universal among all Sasquatch. One thing I can guarantee... you may not be a great deal wiser in the behaviors of the Sasquatch from reading this book, but you will be a great deal older.

A man named Gale filed an interesting report with no date about a Sasquatch that shadowed a rancher. I suspect Mr. Gale was the rancher, but he never said, and he told the story as if it was someone else. He was also great at dodging direct questions. In fact, we laughed about it, but he never admitted the story was his own; so I write this not knowing who the rancher was.

---

[*] Permission to publish this story was generously provided by Dr. Wilson Wheatcroft, October 6, 2011. Dr. Wheatcroft is a retired cultural anthropologist, who in his twenties undertook extensive Ph.D. field work in the jungles of Papua New Guinea, near the Irian Jaya border with the Tifalmin Tribe. He received his Master's Degree and Doctoral Degree from the University of Chicago. Dr. Wheatcroft taught college in the State University of New York system for 12 years, ending in 1984. His many interests include entomology, alchemy, and other subjects; but he keeps abreast of the study on the orang pendek and Sasquatch. We are grateful for his interest. The story is also posted by Tom Shirley on the Bigfoot Reference Guide Forum April 2008.

The main character in his story was a hardened ranch-raised good ole boy who hunted, farmed, fished, camped, and did hard work all his life. He wasn't afraid of anything in the wilderness that framed his mountain homestead. The fellow ran a small herd of cattle on his place, and one morning, he discovered a dead cow lying in the pasture. Figuring there was a killer about his place, he wanted to quickly dispose of the carcass so predators and scavengers wouldn't be attracted down onto the property from the surrounding mountains. In the past, he had his share of grizzly and mountain lion problems.

He fired up his tractor with the intent to scoop up the carcass of the cow and take it on up the hill into a remote area a good distance away from the ranch; it was a densely wooded area with briars, brambles, tall sugar pine, and wild berry fields. Upon reaching the site, the rancher suddenly felt like he was being watched. The feeling of being watched is a commonly reported feeling informants relate in their testimonies. Undeterred by his sense of uneasiness, he looked around briefly, and then continued to finish the burial process and be done with it.

At some point, the rancher got off his Nor Trac to quickly relieve himself. He shut down the tractor and listened to the wind in the pines, an eerie sound against the mountain's quiet. The rancher hopped back on the tractor, and that's when a golf-ball-sized rock came flying in and landed near him. Undisturbed, the rancher swung the tractor around and headed home. That's when another rock was thrown at him, this rock actually hitting him between the shoulder and neck. His first reaction was that somehow kids were on the property, and now his jittery apprehension turned to irritation. Who would be this far out into the mountains?

Looking towards the trajectory of the incoming rock, the rancher thought he saw the figure of a man in the trees. He also thought the guy was lucky he didn't get shot because the rancher had his 30.30 Winchester with him. Gale said it didn't take long before the man realized by its size that it wasn't an ordinary man and that he was red-haired in color. This, he determined, was no ordinary man. Its size was intimidating, and that was the reason he was anxious to move on. The road home seemed long and snaked around down the hills and back to the ranch. The entire time, Gale said the rancher was able to observe the creature shadowing him along the tree line. Coming around a curve in the road, he was able to see the creature standing not more than thirty yards away from his moving tractor. It was simply standing there, apparently waiting for him at each point and making no effort to stay concealed. I found it rather unsettling when he told me that, especially because the rancher was alone on that road, a great distance from the ranch.

The rancher continued on toward home, stopping only to fill in and level off a rut in the road that had washed out in the trail from a recent rain. At times, he was able to get a good look at the creature when it stood out in the open. It wore no clothing and was covered in short black hair except its chest, which was broad and bare. The hair on its head was black, shiny, and it cascaded down over his shoulders in twisted braids; his beard was short and gray. By its genitalia, the figure was male, its face oval and expressionless.

The figure appeared to watch him with great interest. "Watching" is a commonly reported Sasquatch behavior, especially around heavy road or logging equipment, or children playing. But the usual report states they watch from a distance and are usually semi-hidden from view. In this case, the Sasquatch showed himself in what appeared to be a deliberate move.

At one point, thinking to scare it off, the informant slowed down the tractor, steered it to face the watcher then raised and lowered the bucket while inching forward toward the creature. But the haired one was undeterred and became increasingly brazen but cautious, backing up or side-stepping any advance from the tractor.

The creature raced on ahead, meeting the rancher at every blind point on the trail home. Gale said the rancher kept his 30.30 close and ran his fingers down to release the safety. I would like to think the Sasquatch was probably playing some kind of chase game with him, but the aggressive behavior was unsettling. Finally, hitting the straight-away, he gunned the tractor, and that's when he no longer saw the creature stalking him. Relieved for the moment, he told his wife. That night, he went outside where the dog was going nuts, and he took off running towards the pasture. The rancher apparently knew the creature was around, and within a few minutes, the dog returned whimpering, nearly tripping the rancher as it cowered beneath his legs. The behavior of the rancher's dog is also commonly reported.

Approximately fifty yards away stood the creature, not moving, frozen in place, staring at him and the dog. They stared at one another for some minutes, and then the creature walked casually away back towards the area where it had been encountered earlier in the day. The behavior the rancher described is not all that unusual as reports go. Stalking and shadowing are commonly reported occurrences, and again, the Sasquatch made no effort to conceal itself, as many of them stay out in the open. In this case, however, it almost seemed like the Sasquatch was in some way challenging the rancher. Perhaps he wanted the remains of the cow the rancher sought to bury. General research cannot categorically say that the Sasquatch duck for cover all the time - some do, some don't.

The narrative was paraphrased from a telephone call and several months' worth of email exchanges with members of the family.

What we can take from this account and those like it is that the Sasquatch are intensely curious about us - at least, we can say some are. If the rancher had thought to wave at the stalker or in some way acknowledge his presence, some sort of communication might have developed. The trouble is that most informants are so overwhelmed by the appearance and threatening size of the male Sasquatch (as they should be) that intimidation and fear take over, which is a natural response.

Upon reading the Gale story, Bigfoot enthusiast Lee Chen pointed out that I may have the intent of the Sasquatch wrong. Chen charged me with romanticizing the Sasquatch and suggested that the intent of the hairy man may have been malice from the beginning. Maybe Chen has a point. It also may have been the result of the informant urinating in plain sight of the Sasquatch as the following accounts often suggest. There are narratives in the data that indicate relieving oneself in the forest is insulting to any watchful eye of the Sasquatch, and perhaps there is something to that thought which research hasn't entertained. In the Snelgrove Lake, Canada account, Doug Hajicek also mentions that the Sasquatches in that story urinated on top of their urination deposits. This does lend itself to being seen as a challenge by the Squatch, perhaps an insult.

Urinating in the Forest and Sasquatch Reaction

I have upwards of four or more reports of men out camping, fishing, or doing what people do in the forest being confronted during, before, or after urination. In the process of camping, men frequently relieve themselves near a tree line or on river banks. Apparently, urinating is frowned upon by the Sasquatch establishment – or some reports seem to suggest. Again, ethnologist Lee Chen suggested walking toward a tree line to urinate may be like throwing down a gauntlet; an open challenge to the Sasquatch...an in-your-face challenge. The data suggests that in most cases, the Sasquatch will respond or voice his displeasure by growling, yelling, screaming, huffing, or throwing things.

One such case happened at the Mottet Campgrounds in the Wenaha-Tuccannon Wilderness, Oregon. In this case, the Bigfoot voiced his displeasure by screaming.[49] Another incident, almost identical in description, occurred at night at a campground in the Huron National Forest, Michigan. Fly-fishermen, working the middle fork of Idaho's Salmon River, reported through a Vance Orchard's contributor that they were greatly alarmed when a large male escorted his family away from the river after one of them urinated into the river.[50]

One of the scariest reports happened to a camper while relieving himself in the Big Timber region in Montana's Boulder River area. The nearest town was Cardwell, Jefferson County, Montana. Sixty-year-old

Timothian J. Revis stepped into the darkened forest to relieve himself out of the sight of his fellow campers. In mid-stream, not twenty-five feet further in front of him, a Sasquatch stepped out from behind a tree and "screamed a deep chest crushing yell!" Revis admitted the creature was so close, and so frightened him, that he stood half paralyzed, unable to move, unable to breathe adequately. "The yell was so terrifying I thought sure I was a dead man!" Revis ran back to camp wild-eyed and with his fly still wide open. Apparently, everyone on that fishing trip heard the scream and said, "the scream was indescribably terrifying in tone, every hair on my body stood straight up, it was deafening!"

Umatilla National Forest

Urinating and Using Bear Spray

When I got into word searching my files using the keyword 'urination,' the data showed many unexpected encounters by fishermen and hunters while going off into the woods to relieve themselves. The next file involved two hikers climbing the Crow Mountain Trail in Park County, Montana; the year was 2007. The two stopped to rest, eat trail mix, and 'water up' at the point where Mill Creek transects the trail. One of them walked over to the creek to urinate against a tree and was startled to see in the trees a male, female, and juvenile Bigfoot looking at him from several yards away. He called to his trail-mate who also saw them. The largest of the trio made low-volume grumbles and gestured in a way the informants interpreted to mean, "go away, don't come any further." Concerned by the size of the male, the hiker then backed up to the other side of Mill Creek to his backpack to retrieve a container of UDAP grizzly bear deterrent; both hikers were unarmed. The report stated the male advanced toward them with his arms waving wildly. In a quick retreat, he gave a quick burst of bear spray, which stopped the creature in his tracks. Then, believing the Sasquatch was defending his family, the two hikers left the area and warned an approaching couple about the incident.

The two hikers felt they were being followed all the way back to the forest service area, where they reported the incident to disbelieving officials.[51]

During my conversations with the hikers, they each gave a physical description of the Sasquatch male, but there was nothing unusual in their remarks other than the thickness of the hair that covered the large male. What I felt was more interesting was the behavior of the US Forestry Officials who talked down to them in their words, "like we had gone stark raving mad." I encouraged them to write the Department of the Interior to file a complaint. They did and never received a reply. Not surprisingly, the hikers told me they were not asked to fill out a report form.

Park County, Montana 2007

In a separate account, Rob Janis cited another incident. His camping experience included night screaming in Butte County, California. The entrance gates to the mountain were locked, and the trails marked impassable. Janis and his wife had just come down off the mountain and knew there were no downed trees or other obstructions on that route up the mountain. Nevertheless, the forestry closed the gates – apparently, they knew something about the area Janis didn't.

Shadowing, Stalking Behavior

The Feather River near Laporte and Quincy in Plumas County, California, 1988. What's a hiking-fishing trip without a bit of drama? Sean Fries tells it in his own words.

I had a close encounter in June 1988 on the North-Fork of California's great Feather River in Plumas County, in a very isolated area. It takes three days to hike in and four days to hike out; there is no foot traffic in this area. My two dogs and I hiked to this spot in the North Fork of the Yuba and Feather Rivers; a place called Middle Fork. I found a spot near a tree line so I could tie my food up in a tree to keep the wildlife out of it.

Settling in, I made camp and cooked a few trout I caught earlier. I was getting tired and decided to turn in; the fire was now just about out, smoldering a little so I didn't put any water on it, I just climbed into my tent and laid down on top of my bedroll. The dogs ran loose outside the tent, sometimes in the tent with me. They never strayed far from me. I dozed off to the sounds of crickets chirping. Then, suddenly, I woke up with a start, something wasn't right – it was quiet, no crickets, and my dogs came running inside the tent shaking. My dogs are usually very aggressive, though not mean. They would bark at anything that came around. I was scared and alarmed, so I grabbed my rifle and pistol along with a flashlight and stepped outside the tent but couldn't see anything. I had that sensation of being watched. I grabbed some more firewood and threw it on the embers left from the dinner fire. Then I clearly heard some very heavy footsteps right behind me in the trees. There was also a very strange odor almost like a cross between a skunk and something dead. This thing circled my campsite all night long. At first light I packed up and started out and this creature followed me almost the entire day. I could hear him, smell him, and even saw the creature through the woods about 75 yards distance. It paralleled me as if to make sure I was leaving its territory. I never shot at it with my rifle because I don't believe in killing things for sport. I have never gone back to that place.[52]

Yuba and Feather River, 1988

Shadowing a Forest Service Employee

The following incident happened in the mid-1960s between Willits and Fort Bragg, in Mendocino County, California. It struck me as unusual in that it happened to a U.S. Forestry employee at a time when they still spoke openly about such things. The story was filed on Kyle Mizokami's old website in the late 1990s.

I was walking a couple of miles through the woods to pick up our Division of Forestry Surveyor's truck. It was twilight when this occurred. What was really frightening were the stories going around about Bigfoot at the time. The noise of the vegetation and small trees popping like twigs is scary when you know what kind of strength it takes to do that in bush so thick a tractor would stall. But the Bigfoot just followed me for a while; there was a herd of deer in a meadow and birds were singing. There wasn't a feeling of menace or foreboding during most of my walk. In fact, other than the temporary fright, it was almost tranquil and soothing, because nothing seemed alarmed. I never have known a bear to move like that and I have never seen or heard anything like that before or since. I smelled no odor and no sounds were uttered. I was working for the Division of Forestry for the State of California, surveying in Jackson State Forest at the time.[53]

Fort Bragg, California | Bigfoot Ruined My Sex Life

Loitering

According to an article in The Willits News, in a remote area near Fort Bragg, Robert Hatfield reported seeing a Bigfoot standing head and shoulders above a six-foot-high fence. Later, Mr. Hatfield rounded the corner of his house and walked head first right into the creature. He was knocked to the ground and then scrambled in terror to the house on his hands and knees. A neighbor tried to close the door to prevent the creature from getting inside the house. Hatfield reported the Bigfoot incident to officials. It ran off, leaving a large muddy handprint measuring eleven inches on the front door.[54]

Bigfoot Sighting on Highway 101, Willets

Special Forces Vet Hears Primal Scream

Willits, California resident and former anthropology student Heather Gonzales wrote to me on November 1, 2009, regarding the following case she heard second hand. I'm not a fan of second-hand accounts and for that reason, I label them as such, though some contain interesting Bigfoot behavior, and behavior is what we need to compile. The first reminds us of how they scream their displeasure. The second brief also talks about loitering.

> I know a hunter who was formerly special forces in Vietnam and afraid of nothing. One night, at Cherry Creek, something was next to his camper loitering outside. It let out a loud primal scream, like it wanted him to know he was not happy with the camper being there, or him! My friend said he was so shocked and paralyzed by the sound and what could make that sound that he had his rifle in his hands lying next to him at the ready. Whatever it was, he said you could easily tell it had a huge lung capacity to make that yell.[55]

Rob Janis, who manufactures a popular fishing lure, was told a story by his First Nation fishing guide. During the night, as Janis slept in his tent, they were visited by more than one Sasquatch. Peeking from his tent, the outfitter told Janis that he saw two of them hanging around the boat, touching it, as well as the rope around the boulder where it was moored for the night. The guide told Janis that the two were gesturing, signing by hand back and forth, and making deep tones. When Janis asked if his guide thought the two Sasquatch were actually talking, the guide told him he didn't know. He wasn't sure and heard no audible language – just a grunt as if in acknowledgment. Before the two Sasquatch went into the tree line, they fingered and inspected the fishing net, the rods, and easily opened the guide's tackle box; no problem. Apparently, great interest was shown in the fishing gear by the two Sasquatch. I wouldn't think that unusual behavior.

The Sasquatch Medicine Man

This next filing proved informative and I was intrigued by what I learned. An informant named Glenn was fishing and camping not far from Lake Pinecrest in Tuolumne County, northeast of Sonora on Highway 108 towards the end of 2002. Paring down his letter to the specific behavior of the Sasquatch, the informant described hearing a noise. He turned and watched an auburn-colored Sasquatch tearing off leaves from a bush and then rubbing them all over his body.

The informant agreed to meet me the next summer. Summer came as summers do; I met the man, and we were able to locate the same plant. We took a stem and a handful of leaves to a local nursery. They identified the plant as a type of Yerba Santa. A little research taught us the plant had unusual medicinal properties. When the leaves are crushed and applied, it speeds the healing of open sores, sore muscles and arthritic conditions. Perhaps the Sasquatch was suffering from one of those maladies. The early Indians made a tea of Yerba Santa, and rather than drink the horrible tasting brew, they inhaled its steam. That Glenn was able to observe the Sasquatch in the process of rubbing handfuls of the Yerba Santa plant on its body told me the Sasquatch is well versed in plant identification and the plant's specific healing properties.

Interesting?

Medicinal Plant Use

From California to the far reaches of Canada, the Sasquatch has been reported to have used various forms of plant life. In 1974, a salal plant picker reported seeing a brown-colored Sasquatch stripping buds off a second-growth hemlock sapling in the forests near Qualicum Beach; a town in the Regional District of Nanaimo, British Columbia, Canada. I found the use of hemlock strange in that hemlock is toxic, and sheep, cattle, swine, horses, and other domestic animals are poisoned by eating small amounts of the green or dried plant. It is also extremely poisonous to humans.[56] Possibly, the witness misidentified the tree or, as my perceptive editor suggested, "...attempted suicide?"

Another Sasquatch was observed by two young men pulling up roots and eating them at Skutz Falls on the Cowichan River on Vancouver Island in 1975. The Victoria Times reported in 1975 that a Sasquatch chased three youths on Humpback Road near Goldstream, also on Vancouver Island. The creature was reportedly eight feet tall with a white spot on one leg. It was otherwise a reddish-brown color. Colwood Royal Canadian Mounted Police (RCMP) investigated the sighting.[57]

A chase report was emailed to me from a beer salesman traveling north on Western Avenue, north of the Trans-Canada Highway 11 between Cochrane and Lillabelle Lake, Ontario, Canada, in mid-August. He said he was near to dozing off when...

> The black thing came out of nowhere and flashed across the road in the blink of an eye. I thought I was hallucinating for sure, and then I looked to my side mirror after I passed it and there it was! The damn thing was running alongside my trailer AND IT WAS ALMOST KEEPING UP with my speed of 45 mph. A southbound vehicle breezed by me blowing its horn, so I guessed it was real after all and I wasn't road blind that day.

Poison Hemlock

Flashing across a highway is a commonly reported behavior. Keeping chase with a vehicle is reminiscent of Lee Majors in the television series *Six Million Dollar Man*. Chasing behavior is not common, but it has been reported.

Sasquatch with Ducks, a Club and Sticks

Richard Stolz, formerly of Luxton, Vancouver Island, Canada, reported in 1988 seeing the same Sasquatch with a white blaze on one leg carrying two ducks by the neck in one hand and a large club in the other. According to Stolz's report, the Sasquatch crossed Sooke Road, climbed up the embankment, and disappeared in the trees.[58]

Throwing Stick Behavior

Canadian researchers focused their attention on Peawanuck early in June, 2001, when Sam Nanokeesic, an employee at the medical station, was struck by a 16 inch (40 cm) stick while driving his ATV on an empty road to the airport outside of town. A foul odor at one end of the stick made him curious. Inspection of the woods nearby revealed tracks that were approximately 17.5 inches (45 cm) all over the place. Nanokeesic said.

> We saw where it had been standing behind trees near the road and more footprints leading away from the area in a straight line, crossing the end of the runway, heading towards the rock cliffs a few kilometres away. It must have thrown the stick at me thinking I was too close, trying to scare me off. It worked.

"This is not friendly terrain to be walking in," said Fletcher "Red" Mack, waving away swarms of black flies. "It's obviously very large and heavy, more than 485 pounds (220 kilograms), judging by the depth of the prints, and it appears to have a gait of six and a half feet (2.1 metres). The prints were still better than two inches deep in lichen and hard moss, after three weeks."[59]

In 1992, Henry Don also reported a secondhand story from the Strathcona Provincial Park region of Vancouver Island, British Columbia, Canada. Mr. Don said he and his cousin were towing a boat down Muchalat Drive and Gold River Highway when they saw an eight-foot tall, gray-colored Sasquatch cross the road. "It was carrying an enormous club in its left hand. It was no tree branch, it was a fashioned club," Don warned. "He looked intent, as if he was hunting something."[60]

In September of 1967, two girls were walking on a beach on the east coast of Vancouver Island when they encountered a wet, seven-foot, reddish-brown Sasquatch. It held a stick in one hand and three or four ducks in the other. After a few seconds of staring back and forth, both the Sasquatch and the girls fled in opposite directions.[61]

There are many reports where the hairy man stops to stare, but we don't know if he is assessing the situation, if he is startled by human appearance, or just plain curious. It occurs to me that we are, perhaps, as strange a sight to them as they are to us.

The Standard | Too Bizarre for Science

Fishing with Rocks...Staying Warm Under Leaves

As a mother, I didn't quite know what to think about the story up next. It had all the trappings of tabloid fodder, headlines and all; but it wasn't that way. It was reported to the Park District in 1953, long before much was known about Bigfoot; the term Bigfoot was not in use at the time. The story may be old, but worth mentioning because it lists a behavior I had not heard before – Bigfoot fishing with rocks and stones. It also mentioned how the Sasquatch stays warm under piles of leaves. The story was published in *Today in Bigfoot History* in the 1970s.

Headline: Riverside State Park, Washington, Bigfoot took my kids!

Mary Jane Tuttle reported a horrific story to the Spokane County Park Rangers on her way out of the Riverside State Park in Washington. Tuttle told the Rangers she and her three children had arrived at the park for an afternoon picnic on Friday. Sometime after they finished their sandwiches and lemon squares, a large hairy man emerged from the woods. In one massive sweep, the hairy man scooped up her three children – ages 4, 6 and 10 – turned and ran back into the woods! Tuttle spent the next night and day frantically following the sounds of her children. Convinced they were being tortured and eaten, she was frantic but on the morning of Sunday, May 25, 1953 the three children emerged from the bushes, completely unharmed. They quite candidly reported having a very nice time with a wild man, who taught them to fish with rocks and how to stay warm under leaf piles.[62]

Bigfoot Done Take My Keds!

Mother Sasquatch to the Rescue

In 2013, David Weverka told a story on Internet Radio to Chuck Prahl and Stacy Hostetler about a time when he was six years old. While camping with his parents in Central Oregon, little Weverka became lost a mile away from his parents' campsite, and it got dark quickly. Scared, cold, and very alone, he started crying. It wasn't long before Weverka said he heard a rustling in the trees where a hairy woman took him by the hand and led him back to his campsite, or at least close enough for them to hear Dave's mother calling for him. He recalls the Bigfoot's hand was quite rough and hairy, but not much more other than she even hoisted him by the arm, up and over a flowing creek. The youngster told his parents he was lost and was brought back to camp by a monkey. Since the child was into *Curious George*, it made sense to the parents.[63]

David Weverka

The Power of the Thrown Rock

I like to frame it this way: A good baseball pitcher can throw a fastball at well over 90 mph (a few can throw a baseball over 103 mph). That is enough force to cause serious injury or even death to any human at close range with or without headgear protection. Granted, throwing a ball at that velocity is a feat that only a select few physically gifted men are capable of bestowing. Now imagine and apply this talent to the strength of a Sasquatch. I don't think it is unreasonable to assume that an average-sized Sasquatch could easily throw a stone at speeds high enough to stun a deer or fish in a creek, making it easier to retrieve. To illustrate the power of a stone thrown by a Sasquatch, let's consider the next testimony from a Haida woman.

The Gogiet Stones a Doe to Death

A woman living somewhere near Terrace, British Columbia, in 1985 is the source of this next documented behavior of a Sasquatch accurately launching a stone that took down a deer – killing it. The woman was living over on the QCI (Queen Charlotte Islands) in a cabin by the Honna River. A neighbor came by one afternoon to tell her of a strange event he had just been witness to. Her gentleman friend had been fly-fishing further along the Honna River when a very tame deer (doe) came out from the woods near him to drink from the river. He stopped his fly-casting and stood quite still to admire the gracefulness of the deer. Suddenly, a rock flew out from the trees, striking the deer in the head and knocking it down. This was immediately followed by a very tall, hair-covered Gogiet that came down, threw the deer over its shoulder, and dashed hurriedly back into the darkness of the woods. After that, there was no pleasure in fishing. The informant hurried away, not wanting to stick around the place with a rock-chucker who was that accurate. The informant said this was the first time she had heard of the Gogiet being on the island. But considering the many stories we hear about what great swimmers the primitives are, it is not surprising that they also hunt on the islands. According to this lady, the local native people speak quite openly about them.[64]

A quick mention of something another Haida woman told me in 1996 was about a hairy pre-teen Gogiet girl who played with her daughter and taught her how to weave mats from pine needles. After the mats were sufficiently large, any sharp pointed needles were pointed downward into the mat and secured with pine sap. After the mats were washed in the creek and allowed to dry, they were sprinkled with sandy creek wash to keep the sap from sticking to their body hair. Fascinating!

Gogiet is local QCI Haida for Sasquatch. Curious about the possibility of language among some Sasquatch in the 1990s, I asked if there was verbal communication between her daughter and the young Gogiet girl. Apparently, there was only a string of two or three words which were not easily understood. The two girls worked well together, mostly by hand illustrations, insistent pushing, humming, and soft mouth noises.[65]

Northern British Columbia

Hiding Under a Pile of Leaves

Here is another "leaf-pile-related" story. Bob Titmus allegedly told this story to Larry Battson; Battson picks it up here:

Titmus was deep in the backcountry of Bluff Creek by himself one afternoon; at the time he was certain there was a Sasquatch or Sasquatches very close by the evidence he was finding. He was so involved and so focused that he lost track of the time and the sun was starting to go down. The density of the forest overcame him. He recognized it was practically dark and much too late to get back to the main campsite for the night, and it became clear that Titmus was going to stay put and spend the night alone in the mountains. Trying to find his way out in the darkness would be foolish if not dangerous. Nights can be quite cold in that wilderness and he was not wearing enough clothing to just lie in the woods and try to sleep, so he began to dig a pit to sleep in. After he finished digging his bed he laid in it and started covering himself with a thick layer of leaves, branches, and pine needles. After he finished the only part of him still exposed was a small area around his face. He was quite comfortable, sufficiently warm enough, and had no problem going to sleep.

Titmus guessed the time was probably about 1:00 a.m., when he was startled awake by the sound of something moving through the forest nearby, and it seemed from the sounds to be heading in his direction. He could hear the sound of heavy footsteps crashing methodically through the forest brush, breaking limbs etcetera. At first he thought it was a bear but it wasn't long before he realized it was too noisy for a bear. It came closer and closer… then it stopped. Titmus could hear the thing breathing, not just breathing but also sniffing the air like it was trying to pick up a scent, and now he realized that it had indeed picked up his scent but could not figure out where he was. With just his face exposed, Titmus was very well concealed from what he came to understand had to be a Sasquatch.

All of a sudden, it started screaming, breaking branches and throwing rocks in his direction. Titmus held very still, very quiet. The Sasquatch started moving around, pacing back and forth through the forest continuing to scream, bellow and throw vegetation and other debris. Titmus related that this behavior persisted until about an hour before daybreak. Then, as the sun began to rise and light trickled through the forest canopy, the creature went away and the forest fell silent again. He pulled himself out of his make-shift leaf bed in the ground and started to look around investigating the entire area. He walked in the direction of where the ruckus had come from and could not believe his eyes. It looked like a bulldozer had gone through the forest. Saplings had been pulled out from the ground, larger trees pushed over, broken or snapped in two. There were branches covered with hair and the ground was littered with footprints. It was no bear.[*]

Sasquatch Leaves Rock on Hood

In March of 1999, a man reported a strange occurrence in northern California. He was driving up Interstate 5 to visit a friend in Oregon, and around 10:00 p.m., he exited the highway to see if he could find a

---

[*] Larry Battson.

place to get some dinner. When he couldn't find a restaurant, he decided to pull onto the side of the road and make do with some snacks he had in the car. After he ate, he dozed off but was awakened by a loud thump. He got out of the vehicle to investigate and found a good-sized rock on the hood of his car. He got back behind the wheel and started up the car. In the beam of the headlights, he saw a tall creature covered in thick, dark hair. The creature watched him for a minute, turned around in the road, and walked slowly off into the woods. Undoubtedly, the great stone on the hood of his car was a message of some importance to the Sasquatch. Certainly, a stone that size could have been launched easily through the windshield.[66]

Bigfoot: The Pacific Northwest's Claim to Cryptid Fame

Sasquatch and Dogs

After reviewing the data on my old computers, at first, it almost seemed like the Sasquatch had little tolerance for domestic dogs, such as their snarling, barking, heel nipping, and leg biting. The information that came in to me in the late '80s ranged from slamming dogs by their hind legs up against tree trunks to quiet them down to a Bigfoot running playfully with feral dogs and coyotes. But there was one in my files that spoke to a New Hampshire Sasquatch that actually saved a dog's life.

Sasquatch Saves Dog From Drowning

Ed Parsons wrote an interesting piece for the *Conway Daily Sun* that I've never forgotten. In fact, the story had a fascinating aspect. Parson's friend, Peter Samuelson, at the time 72-years old, had at one time been prospecting in the Ossipee Range. Samuelson had many stories with their origins in the White Mountains and encouraged Parsons to write about them, including one about a Sasquatch sighting in mid-summer 1979. Parson's picks up the Sasquatch encounter from there:

> Samuelson, his dog Kat, and his girlfriend Holly Swaffield, then of Wolfeboro, New Hampshire, were out prospecting in the Ossipee Range. They drove in the Gilman Valley Road, parked at the gate, and continued up the old road past the Tamworth/Ossipee town line. Then they cut into the woods on the right and headed west up Bald Mountain. Bald Mountain is taller than Mount Whittier and is located just south of it. From its open ledges, you can look directly below to Connor Pond, located center of the range.
>
> "We bushwhacked in two miles, up to the ledges on Bald," Samuelson said. "The area contains a lot of Conway granite and we were looking for contact zones, edges where two types of rock meet. Along these zones, it is possible to dig for pockets of beryl or topaz crystals."

As the trees opened up before them and Connor Pond became visible far below to their left, they saw a strange sight about 100 yards ahead on the ledges.

> It was a small structure yet made of big stones stacked on each other. The roof was flat and made of thatched hemlock bows. There was an opening, like a rustic doorway. We saw a giant man-like creature inside, about seven feet high, with its back to us. It was totally covered with tangled gray hair about three inches long.

In the same instant this all became visible to them, Kat began growling intensely and the creature started to make loud noises indicating it was upset. "I can't describe the noise," said Samuelson. "Anyway, Holly freaked and we all felt threatened. We high-tailed it out of there immediately, in the direction we had come. Only later, part way down the mountain, did we pause and ask yourselves, 'What did we see?'"

They both carried cameras, but in the urgency to leave, they never thought of taking a picture. Over the next few days, they told various acquaintances of their experience. Asked how these people reacted, Samuelson said with a smile, "You know how." Holly excitedly called him a few months later and said she had been to the Wolfeboro Library and found a fascinating story.

Apparently, during a midwinter thaw in the 1890s, a person in a cabin on the shore of Connor Pond, located in the center of the Ossipee Range, saw an amazing thing. A dog had wandered out onto the thawing pond. It fell through the ice and was floundering vainly for a long time to get out. Suddenly, a large hairy human-like creature came out the woods from the direction of Bald Mountain, reached out long arms and rescued the dog, then immediately disappeared back in the woods from the direction it first appeared.

That old story added a little continuity to their experience, no matter how unbelievable. Still, it took Samuelson a year to get his courage and curiosity up enough to return alone to the site of their mysterious and alarming encounter on Bald Mountain. Holly wouldn't go with him. As he walked out onto the ledges, he was struck again, this time because there was absolutely no sign of the structure they had seen the year before. He picked over the area thoroughly, looking for the slightest dent in the ledges where the big stones might have rested, stones that would normally take two or three people to move, but there was nothing.[67]

Any dog rescue story is a feel-good story. That a Sasquatch rescued this drowning dog speaks volumes about the behavior of that particular individual. Great story, loved it.

Hiking: Myth Versus Reality of Sasquatch in the Ossipee Range

Dog Killing

Not all Sasquatch are as kindhearted. Many reports describe the Sasquatch chasing dogs that were later found with their necks broken or dead by some other means.

One story described a dog lodged between branches some 14 feet high up in a pinion pine tree. Another dog impaled atop a rural ten-foot-tall signpost. Glen Payne of Pettis County, Missouri, heard from his cousin Martin Burford that coon hunters chased a hairy being that was killing his sheep and goats. It killed all dogs that tangled with it. As far back as October of 1947, Payne reportedly chased the creature with his "hog dogs" and saw in flashlights a giant hairy man-shaped thing running ahead of his dogs. In the end, it killed the dogs and, in the process, overturned his jeep.[68]

San Antonio, Texas researcher Rick Tullos recently added to this discussion:

> I know a guy who raises beagles and one of the "Hairy friends" threw his favorite beagle over a tree limb and hung the beagle by his leash. Whoever thinks that these varmints are just giant fluffy fur balls has

got another thing coming. These animals will kill your favorite pet or domestic critter and lay it out in such a way as to let you know that they did it and there is nothing you can do about it! They are mean, ugly and nasty... and those are their good qualities. [*]

Older Reports From the State of Missouri

More Animal Killings (Dogs)

A Boonville, Warrick County, Indiana fisherman by the name of Ralph Duff reported to police that his dog was torn to shreds in an encounter with a screaming hairy beast. Mrs. Duff said she heard terrifying howls late at night and saw a towering beast much larger than a bear running away. Duff believes the monster lives in one of the caves along the Ohio River and decided to set out a number of bear traps, but apparently, nothing came of them. [69]

For many years, a story circulated in research about dogs being swung by their heels into trees to quiet them during Bigfoot tracking pursuits. As stories go on, these events become embellished to the degree that one could hardly believe them. If we believe all the accounts that include dog killings or the unexplained disappearance of dogs – the list would be too long to publish!

To track down the source of the unbelievable story about dogs being bashed up against trees, I found the probable basis for the gruesome,

____

[*] Rick Tullos, San Antonio, Texas.

well-worn dog-killing stories in old newspaper files. This one, dated October 19, 1958, is somewhat grisly. Strangely, Bigfoot attack stories seem to be the most sought-after and Googled tales.

The Sasquatch-dog-killing probably speaks to Bigfoot's frustration at being hunted; in this case, during the road construction and bridge building years in Bluff Creek during the 1950s and '60s. The headline in the Humboldt Times Standard read:

New Bluff Creek Mystery puzzles Indians: 4 dogs found ripped to pieces...

An Indian who works near the Humboldt-Del Norte County line believes he may have discovered signs of a Big Foot temper fit, a Eureka man told The Humboldt Times yesterday. Harold C. Goodwin, 66, said Curtis Mitchell, an Indian who works for him discovered the mutilated bodies of four dogs last Sunday evening. He told me they "looked like they'd been ripped apart," Goodwin said at his home just off the Elk River Road about 5-miles south of Eureka. "The bodies were still warm." The Indian told Goodwin that all of the dogs had been torn apart and one of them had apparently been slammed against a tree. No footprints were found and Goodwin said the Indian "didn't stick around" to investigate, not after finding the dog's bodies.

Goodwin, a superintendent for Sharp Construction Company has been working in the Bluff Creek area on a concrete bridge about two miles south of the county line for the past four weeks. A Humboldt County resident, Goodwin said he "used to think the big footprints were just a joke" but now he's convinced there is some sort of human creature wandering through the northern California wilderness. "I think it's the straight goods." He added an eerie note to the speculation about the Big Foot: "...the fellow who owned those dogs might be laying up there some place too!

The construction worker said the discovery of the dead dogs changed the mind of many a skeptic working in the area. "This," he said, "is when all of us old-timers start to believe." Goodwin said he had sometimes been staying on the job over the weekends because it was such a long drive back to Eureka. "I think I'll be coming home from now on though," he added firmly.[70]

I can't be sure this newspaper article was the genesis of the dog-killing stories, but the article was old enough to have fanned the flames of the rumor even if it wasn't the source.

In 2010, Mr. Dewey Haupe, formerly of Hat Creek, California, contacted me through the website. He was the driver-operator of an F-12 road grader during the road construction and bridge-building era through Bluff Creek. In the course of that exchange, which included a lengthy interview on what he knows about the famous Bluff Creek film, Ivan Marx, Bob Titmus, Eric Beckjord, and Mr. Haupe assured me that at least two of those dogs killed were very expensive specialized bear-hunting dogs belonging to Ivan Marx. Haupe occasionally hunted bears with Curtis Mitchell and Ivan Marx of Burney, California, and Bob Titmus, who lived in Weaverville at the time, along with several other men from that region like Ernie Alameda of Hoopa.

There was a silent bounty on bears by the construction and logging industries. Haupe, back in the 1950s, said the Six River Park region was "thick with bears, big ones that caused quite a problem for the loggers, bridge construction crews and road cutters." Haupe said, "I shot 'em, Titmus skinned 'em, and we made a purdy good dollar a bear that away and split it. That was a lot of money in those days."

Later, another hunter joined them, who had just acquired some expensive bear dogs from Walt Disney's animal trainer, Mr. Ivan Marx. That bear hunter's name was Larry McGowan. McGowan acquired Bob Gimlin's 30.06 Bluff Creek rifle through Ivan Marx, and the story behind that exchange is in another book. Dewey Haupe got his job operating the road grader in 1967 with Sharp Construction by way of a solid recommendation from his bear-hunting buddies, Bob Titmus and Ivan Marx. Some of Ivan Marx's trained animals were sold in the five-figure range, which was huge money in the 1950s and 1960s.

There are many stories of dogs cowering or whimpering at the feet of their owners when the scent of the Sasquatch was present, and nearly as many cases where expensive tracking dogs refuse to go on scent by sitting down and having to be dragged back to their truck kennels. Reportedly, they were ferocious dogs that chased and treed bears during a hunt or would take off after bears that ventured onto the dog's territory. Some of these were Ivan Marx's specialty-trained dogs. The stories I've received involving dogs are many, and a few end up with sad outcomes like this next Coos County, New Hampshire report.

Sounds Like a Bear Yarn

The Homer Story

I loved this thought-provoking account, which boggled my mind and simultaneously creeped me out. See what you think about the *Homer story*.

Margaret "Maggie" Kjeldsen contacted me in 2002 with an interesting story. Mrs. Kjeldsen supplemented her income by baking for a big city baker. This day, she was preparing orders for the coming holiday. She paused in the kitchen to feed Homer, her friendly 4-year-old yellow lab mix. She routinely took his prepared meal to the back porch and called for Homer. This day, however, she called again and again, but no Homer. He was known for chasing the local rabbits, so she went back into the house. Then, finished in the kitchen for the night, Mrs. Kjeldsen went again out back, and noting his untouched meal, she called Homer in again for his evening dog food, scraps, and fresh water.

This time, she called several times, H-O-M-E-RRRR; but the wayward dog did not come running home as usual. She phoned her nearest neighbor, who lived in a cabin three miles to the south, to ask if they had seen Homer; they hadn't. Figuring Homer would come home during the night, Mrs. Kjeldsen left his evening meal on the back stoop and retired for the night.

Sunday morning dawned, and both the dog's dishes were missing. The baker-woman hopped into her vehicle and drove in the direction of the lake toward the road's dead end. She hollered out the driver's window for HOMER along the way, but no Homer. Pulling up at the dead end in the road, now some 2 miles further from home, she parked, got out of the car, and called for the dog some more. Silence. By now, Mrs. Kjeldsen's concern for Homer was growing. She crossed the road and headed down the steep path towards the lake where they often went together to toss a ball - it wasn't like the dog not to wander back home at night. He usually hung around the house, occasionally chasing a rabbit, but he was docile and never this far away from home without his owner.

Down at the lake, the witness continued calling "HOMER" quite loudly. She told me she became quite nervous for no apparent reason and, after looking around, headed back up the incline to her car, all the while still calling for HOMER.

I became increasingly apprehensive and, as I reached the road again, I stopped to gather myself and call one more time. But before I could get my breath, I heard a distant voice call Homer's name with all the same intonations I had in my voice. I couldn't believe my ears! Who was calling my dog? I was at this point a few miles from my nearest neighbor, chills ran up my back and my hair stood on end. Maybe I'm hearing things - so I called out again and listened. In a few minutes a distant voice called, "H-0-M-E-R!" The caller sounded just like me, except it had more basso profundo than my voice tone, but had similar intonations and rolled the 'R' in Homer's name just like I did. It scared me because it was no echo I imagined! Someone called my dog and it sounded just like me. I walked briskly over to the car and called out, "who is there?" The voice replied, "Homer," again with all the same inflections I made in calling my dog. It was the creepiest thing you can imagine. I sat in the car and waited, calling, "Hello? Hello? Is anybody there?" But the caller never answered. I waited in the car nearly fifteen minutes and then left making my way down the road, randomly calling for Homer out the driver's window. That was 3 months ago - Homer never came home. I don't know what is in the woods around here, but in the days that followed I continued to put out Homer's dog dishes, dry food mixed with table scraps and water, and each time I hoped he would return home. The dishes were always gone and I never found those either. Yesterday I nailed down an aluminum pie plate to the porch and put the usual dog food and scraps out minus the water. This morning the food was gone and the aluminum pie plate was torn off and scattered in pieces around the back yard. Those people I've told say I have a bear around here. But do bears mimic me calling for Homer? Others think it might be a raccoon but can a raccoon speak?[71]

Tossing a Dog

According to local Colorado law enforcement in the San Luis Valley, during the last week of December 1993 and the first half of January 1994, there were seven sightings of Bigfoot recorded within a seven square mile area of northernmost New Mexico and a portion of the San Luis Valley in Colorado.

These encounters include a trucker spotting and reporting a large, hairy creature seen near the highway, a sighting of an extremely rare white Bigfoot, another sighting of a Sasquatch that appeared to be stalking a herd of elk, and lastly, an encounter with a large two-footed creature that ran right by a ranch house and allegedly tossed a dog over a 6-foot high fence.[72]

The next situation was probably the worst report that ever came my way, and I quite frankly wish it hadn't. In this 1999 situation, a woman asking for anonymity provided evidence that she and her oldest son had discovered a family dog with a tree branch staked through its mid-section. It was skewered so high up off the ground that the son required a ladder to bring the pit bull's body down for burial. They lived so remote that the only logic they came up with was that it was the work of an angry Bigfoot. What else does that?

Whoever did the heinous deed, the perpetrator actually impaled the dog on a dead branch. I saw the photo. The dog was at least twelve feet off the ground and again as many feet high as she was tall. This is not the behavior of a passive Sasquatch; the mental image made me shiver. Why skewer a dog that high up in a tree if not to leave a sign with some degree of drama? If it was a Sasquatch, I'm not sure why it went to so much trouble unless it was a show of strength and purpose, or perhaps just plain anger. I don't have permission to publish the woman's name, state, or photo; it is suffice to say it happened in the Midwest and you wouldn't want to see the photo anyway!

Jessica W. filed a report where she said she encountered a smallish bear while hiking on Ape Island, British Columbia, Canada. "Suddenly the bear reared up and, looking behind itself, ran off like it had been shot out of a canon." At the same time, she noticed what had to be an 8-9-foot Sasquatch watching her. She estimated his weight at 800 lbs. Frightened over her wildlife encounter, Jessica stopped two passing trail walkers and asked to walk back with them. The two men figured the Sasquatch was what scared off the little bear. They hurriedly left the area and reported the encounter.[*]

In 2007, another case was reported of a dark colored humanoid in the Enchanted Forest near Tofino on the northwestern side of Vancouver Island, British Columbia. The informant noted that "...when it was

---

[*] Rob Janis.

upright, it looked human but when it crouched down, it resembles a big black dog."

The Mysterious San Luis Valley Bigfoot, 1996

A Gruesome Find (Dead Cat)

A Beaufort County, South Carolina woman reported her cat was killed one morning. It was found hanging from the clothesline with the line twisted tightly around its neck - twice! The investigator said the plastic-coated line was strung between the main house and the garage approximately six feet off the ground over a grass-lined yard where quilting fabrics were hung out to dry. "There is no way that cat got up there by itself." The family said there were occasions when they saw a hairy man crossing the property but thought he was a vagrant living off somewhere in a cave.[*]

Wild Man Calls Cabin Owner

Wayne County, Pennsylvania:

> We thought we should tell someone about the unusual occurrences at our cabin property in the Poconos north of Hawley. We inherited the property from my husband's parents when they passed within weeks of each other. They had told us about a wild man my father-in-law called

---

[*] Rob Janis, 1995.

"Pocono Buck," but we hardly believed any of it until we took posses-sion of the cabin and stayed there for ourselves in 2006. "Pops" described Buck like a hair-covered wild person but broader through the chest and shoulders. His arms had no hair, and he told us hair went mostly down the Buck's backside. That is all we knew. Buck did not show himself to us, but we hoped.

There has been whistling in the night. I should say that we are the only cabin on this side of the mountain, so we didn't know what was whistling unless it was Buck. My father-in-law apparently fed Buck for years but we didn't know what he left out for the creature. What do you feed a wild man? We tried a lot of different vegetables and fruit but he never took any of it. Then in the summer of 2007, we were sitting on the porch one evening watching the sky, stars, and so forth. The crickets were chirping and the frogs were croaking; a really beau-tiful night. Just as we were about to turn in, we got up and, heading toward the screen-door, there was a very loud baritone voice that called, "AAAAbram." We were shocked. In the darkness, we never saw what called for Abraham but we think it was Buck. By the way, Abraham was my father-in-law's name. Spooky, I know! He had been dead a year by that time but the wild man must have missed my husband's father as we did, of course. It is now 2008 and we are here again in the Poconos with a bit of success, as we found your advice to feed apples and corn worked. He does take them and he does take pears. Where we put out the apples, bites were taken out but not eaten whole, and Buck consistently left two twigs in the shape of an "X" and one time a "T." The bites are large mouth-size, not raccoon-size. We don't know the meaning but the last time he only took one ear of corn and left nothing in the way of a stick sign. For several days nothing was taken and then we left Buck some summer squash. He showed up and took all four of them. He does not show himself to us and he does not call for Abraham anymore; he only did that once and we both heard it, you couldn't mistake it. His whistles always come around 2:00 a.m. in the morning. We will keep you posted.*

In 2010, I received an update on this situation in the Poconos. The Sasquatch, "Buck," has not been seen since 2009.

The Tim Peeler Encounter

Many of us will not forget Casar, North Carolina resident Tim Peeler's 2010 encounter with a Sasquatch standing over his chained-up dog. Peeler is the fellow who "rough-talked" and poked at the hairy beast with his walking stick. The walking stick, of course, was to become known as a "get-stick." Mr. Peeler rough-talked the Sasquatch, poked at it while urging it up the trail, shouting, "Get, get, go on, get now, go on." Peeler was insistent in getting the ten-foot giant to leave his terrified dogs alone.[73]

In retrospect, during a hard-to-get interview in late August 2011, Tim Peeler said he didn't like to talk about that day anymore. But he noted that the mercantile stores in Casar churn out "ol Knobby" t-shirts by the dozens and "get-sticks" like the one Tim Peeler used to ward off the ten-foot behemoth that messed with his dog.

I do not have any firsthand accounts where a witness actually saw a Bigfoot eating dogs – but the interest in Peeler's chained-up dog was certainly a unique Bigfoot behavior in that it came brazenly right up to the Peeler homestead in broad daylight and checked out his dogs. Casar is in Cleveland County, North Carolina, and it was those authorities Peeler notified saying, "...it looked like a giant ape with a man's face and I was afraid to kill it." Sasquatch sightings are widespread throughout that region, some of them documented by law enforcement, including Mr. Peeler's account.

Peeler's Bigfoot may have been sizing up his dog as an easy meal

---

* Mitzi, Pennsylvania, 2008.

ticket, which reminded me of a similar story written up after a shaggy-haired Bigfoot was seen carrying a dog under its arm in Louisiana, Pike County, Missouri. Little notice is given to Missouri, but that State has a very long history of hair-covered giants, some of them brazen and unafraid of the local citizenry. It is said that the eastern Bigfoot, particularly the Missouri Momo, is less intimidated by humans and often makes no effort to conceal itself. The description of the Momo is generally the same as those seen in the Pacific Northwest.

Mr. Peeler's use of the "get-stick" to shoo and poke at the Bigfoot to get him to move away from the dog in daylight hours was noteworthy behavior and not at all the behavior we've come to expect of the Bigfoot.

Research has long held that hair-giants generally move about after dark and sleep part of the daylight hours; this is no longer the case. It occurred to me some years ago that the Sasquatch probably rest or sleep whenever they feel the need, night or day. There are many reports of the Sasquatch being active during the daylight hours, but there are just as many case testimonials of them moving about in the dark of night.

Tim Peeler's Bigfoot

It is also held that they bed down at night; some making nests to sleep in while others have been observed sleeping on the hard ground with no bedding, around logging piles of stripped timber, and another old report of one sleeping out in the open on a sandbar, which is most unbelievable but not if you understand that the location was nearly 4 to 5 miles into the deep forest where people never go. A favorite sleeping place is under or nearby stacks of logs awaiting removal by logging machinery. I'm not sure why that would be the case, but I heard that first from Dahinden, and then in various other places following his untimely death.

Dogs, Disemboweled Animals

Ft. Bragg, Mendocino County, California: The witness heard a crashing sound coming towards his tent one night, close enough that he became seriously alarmed. The man's two dogs were in hot pursuit of something huge running through the woods, snapping and crashing through the underbrush. The fellow wrote:

I suspected that whatever was moving that quickly and violently through the woods was trying to elude the dogs. I think this whole event lasted about 30 seconds and then the crashing stopped. It was then the next scariest thing happened. The dogs barked a few more times and then made that sound dogs make when they're hurt or injured. After that, I did't hear a single thing except the loud white noise that fear made inside my head. I never saw my dogs again. The last strange thing I would share with you from the last twenty-two years of my life is 12-miles east of Fort Bragg. In the woods is the frequent discovery of disemboweled animals. Disemboweled! The rest of the animal intact. It's strange, but we've discovered several.[74]

Fort Bragg, Mendocino County, California

Sasquatch Stays Out in the Open

Mendocino County, California has a very long history of casual sightings of Sasquatch people. Tye Mayer's sighting in June of 1998 on Masonite Road is another incident where the Sasquatch did not duck for cover. If we read deeper into the data, many sightings occur where they do not run for cover – but instead hang around momentarily out in the open observing us. It is an unusual behavior when we stop to think they prefer being concealed.

Mr. Mayer wrote:

> This happened near a wooded area not far from Ukiah, California. Ukiah is located in Mendocino County north of Santa Rosa between Willits and Healdsburg along US Highway 101 on the banks of the Russian River near Clear Lake and the Pacific Ocean. The creature was hair covered and somewhere around 8-feet tall; its color was brownish grey. It didn't seem at all threatening but he did smell similar to that of a goat. It made no vocal noises and didn't seem afraid. The Bigfoot stayed within 30-feet of us, just staring in our direction. It, or he, stayed until it apparently lost interest in me and then it walked back into the trees. It made changing my tire memorable.[75]

Mendocino County, California

Sasquatch Killing, Fighting Dogs

Browsing through the late Ramona Clark Hibner's data, I see she had a Florida witness who stated she saw a Bigfoot fighting with dogs; May 1977. Most of these brief reports give the impression that Bigfoot is intolerant of dogs. There was a single case file of a 7-foot Sasquatch that killed a bulldog - allegedly with one blow, which was cited in John Green's 1978 book, *Sasquatch, the Apes among Us*. It occurred in Colfax, Washington in October of 1891. It's another very old report but one worth mentioning.

In 1926, the McCurtain County, Oklahoma Sunday Gazette of July 9, 1978, page 16, recorded a statement by two hunters who saw a man-like beast kill their dog near the Mountain Fork River.

Then, in 1947, several Pine Ridge, Christian County, Missouri hunters reported a Bigfoot killed some of their stock; sheep and goats. When they hunted the beast, it killed their dogs and overthrew the hunter's jeep. But again, these are very old reports, and nothing like that is currently being registered, at least not in my data. Still, the history of the Sasquatch and its association with dogs is reportedly both good and bad.

Dogs: Three "Whatever Was in the Woods," Stories

First story: Dogs and it whistles like meadowlark…

A typist for the county, Mrs. Morgan, was walking her two dogs up a trailhead in Stephens State Forest, Lucas County, Iowa, when her two Dobermans began barking earnestly at a dark part of the white pine forest. Concerned that a cougar was prowling about, Mrs. Morgan turned to head the dogs back down the trail, fearing that the dogs would tangle with a big cat. Then Mrs. Morgan explained that something strange occurred. She said whatever was in the woods whistled like a "meadowlark bird" only louder, and it persisted for several seconds, then stopped. The dogs "went crazy and pulled hard on the leash, it was difficult to keep control of them; they kept looking toward a very dark part of the trees." Then she described a return whistle also sounding like a meadowlark coming from the opposite side of the path. This is when she began to panic. The dogs stopped barking and cowed around her legs; whining. Mrs. Morgan turned and ran back down the pathway to the parking area. The event left her "drained and in fear" of whatever was in the woods that caused her dogs to act like that, insisting those whistles were too deep to be a meadowlark and her Dobermans had never barked at meadowlarks before.[76]

Sasquatch Frustration with Hound Dogs on Scent

Second "Whatever was in the woods" story:

In a letter from long-time Bigfoot enthusiast Fred Bradshaw dated Tue, 6 Mar, 2001, was another story regarding incidents with dogs.

> I interviewed two bear hunters in the fall of 1987 that used several hound dogs that would easily track and tree bears and yes, Bobbie, these dogs actually would track a Sasquatch this one time in the Capital Forest. Allan Smith of Melone, Grays Harbor, Washington was out with a second hunter. They live a mile apart from each other there in Melone. This one trip Smith told me about, he had kenneled five hounds in the back of his truck for a bear hunt. Let loose, the dogs lost no time catching scent and ran off after it. In a few minutes (if you know hound hunting) the hounds "sounded" just like they did on any bear hunt when they got its scent or treed the animal. The dogs were in the woods about 100 yards from Smith's truck sounding as if they'd treed this bear! But quickly Smith and the second hunter heard the hounds cry out like something hurt them – they yelped horribly. The men became alarmed when two dogs came back and jumped inside his truck; one was hurt.
>
> All went quiet as Allan and the other hunter (I forget his name, Bill, I think it was) walked into woods headed toward where they last heard the dogs on scent, yelping and howling. Approaching the scene

cautiously, they found one dog dead and another so badly messed up that he had to put it down. Searching with rifles cocked now, they came upon a very large barefoot track shaped similarly to a man's, only larger. There was a trail of these tracks on the ground and the air smelled foul. Smith found hair of something he couldn't identify; it was black to brown in color. Back at the truck, caring for the hounds and grieving for the lost ones, they decided to return the next day to continue tracking whatever killed his hound dogs.

The next morning Smith buried his dogs and found more of these large human-like prints. This time he had only one dog with him and it pulled at its leash headed forward at whatever did the damage, but Smith kept him on leash. He found more large footprints that were measured bigger than any man he knew. The shoeless tracks were all around the area of the woods where the dead dogs were found the day before but whatever made the tracks wandered off into deeper woods where forest litter ended the search for the killer.[*]

More Dogs

Third and last "Whatever was in the woods" story…

George Wise was hunting up Pete's Creek Trail on a decrepit logging road near Donkey Creek in the fall of 1986. That would be the Wynoochee River area in Grays Harbor County, Washington. Mr. That day, Wise had with him two very expensive dogs that were seasoned bear trackers. The dogs, nose to the ground, trailed off down the old logging road as fast as they could run to gather scent.

Wise followed and could hear them barking quite a ways off. Soon, only one of his dogs returned and wouldn't leave his side. Wise took off to look for the other canine and located him a quarter mile down the road. He was dead. Wise was shocked. It happened so fast. He wasn't prepared for anything like this. Approximately two hundred feet

---

[*]   The late Fred Bradshaw, AKA "Tracker3".

further down the same road, he saw two people walking and looking back over their shoulder at him. Wise hurried along, trying to catch up with the couple in an effort to find out if or why they killed his dog. Wise got about eighty feet from the couple, and as they turned slightly, he realized these were not ordinary people but strange-looking "things" with dark hair all over their bodies. They were not clothed. Wise stopped and stood there watching the "things" walk on (upright like him, not bear-like at all) and off the road into the woods. From the woods, he heard whistling.*

Thoughts About Sasquatch Eyes

I recently had to have my reading glasses upgraded to a thicker Coke bottle type lens, and during that exam, my optometrist looked deeply into the iris of my eyes with his pinch-nosed glasses and handheld spotlight. After studying the mechanics of my eyes he remarked, "so that's what a Sasquatch looks like"...we both laughed. After thirty minutes of lecturing me about how my eyes have suffered the ravages of time from years of close computer work, he handed me a newspaper article he'd been saving for that visit. The tattered 2005 article was about an encounter with a Sasquatch on Highway 199 in Del Norte County, northern California; its headline read, *Trucker sees Bigfoot.*

42-year old Travis Cover from Brookings, Oregon, told an Oregon Curry Coast Pilot reporter that he was driving in his truck around 5:00 a.m. It was still dark outside when he reached down for his lunch. When Cover looked back up, there before his eyes stood "a big hairy monster standing next to a yellow road sign. It raised its arm to block the beam from my headlights. I've never seen anything like it."

My optometrist kept the article because he thought it would interest me, and it did. He believed the behavior of the Sasquatch protecting his eyes was nothing short of human behavior. He further suggested that

---

* George Wise. Wise lived at the time off north 101 on Youmans Road in Hoquiam, Washington.

the eyes of the Sasquatch were probably much like ours, with all the same strengths and weaknesses when it comes to the glare of bright headlights. Bigfoot research has speculated much about eye glow, the color, and glare of their eyes. Little has been discussed about eye sensitivity to light, but I know I shield my eyes from bright lights.[77]

As humans, we can appreciate the reaction of the Bigfoot. It differed from the optometrist's previously held thought that the Sasquatch may have specialized predator vision. If these giants are human and have a degree of specialized vision, that is, some uncomplicated deviation from our human eye that makes moving around and hunting at night easier than what we are equipped for - then perhaps, like all things living wild, it's more about adaptation than any specialization of the eye's anatomy. Familiarization and adaptations make us different yet the same in many respects.

Shielding Its Eyes, Its Breasts Showed

In 1993, a resident of Miller County, Missouri, in the region of Lake of the Ozarks, not far from Osage Beach, reported:

I got a fairly good look at the creature as it crossed the road in front of me. When I hit my high beams it stopped like a deer frozen in headlights. It threw its left arm up in front of its face as to shield its eyes from the bright light. That's when I noticed the breasts and hairy armpit; it was a female. It was covered with long reddish/brown hair that looked matted, like a wet shaggy dog is the only way I can describe it. Her face had the visage of a woman of the age – say 35ish. I can only guess the height but it didn't seem that tall, maybe 5-6 feet. I noticed not only the non-hairy breasts but the arm that was up shielding its eyes had no hair on the underarm or palm. I could see its skin that was light in color, not dark like a chimpanzee. I guessed that it was a female because of its breasts and line-backer butt. I wasn't the only one to see it. Other cars were pulling over and slowing down to look at her. This one car put down his driver's side window and yelled at it, then pulling up alongside me, said something like, "get a load of that, will ya?" That guy didn't know what he was looking at. To avoid ridicule, I only told relatives.[*]

George Goode of Pocahontas County, West Virginia, also mentioned seeing a Sasquatch shield its eyes when he wrote me in 2003. "I quickly got another charged light and you could see that it was humanoid with dark brown to black hair on its arms and body. It raised its arm to shield its eyes and then in just a flash it ran over a football length field and out of sight. This thing was enormous. When it ran off it used both limbs to run."[†]

In October of 2011, Jon Nichols in Vancouver, Washington, graciously passed along an original copy of Roger Patterson's 1966 book, *Do Abominable Snowmen of America Really Exist?* I noticed on pages 167-9 that Patterson investigated a local Yakima report that included shielding of the eyes and the behavior of peering into the driver's side window at the occupant. While we might think these are unimportant behaviors – they are indicative of human behavior, curiosity, and the Sasquatch's often reported ability to run easily alongside vehicles in transit. Again, we see another mention of human sensitivity to bright lights at night. Here is what Patterson filed:

> When I returned from my latest pre-expedition, much to my surprise I received a phone call which related an amazing story of a high school boy here in my home town who had come face to face with a gigantic creature west of Yakima. I checked his story thoroughly by interviewing the boy and his father and mother, and it seemed to me an outstanding straightforward account.

> Ken Pettijohn was returning home late at night September 19, 1966. As he rounded a bend in the road his light shone on what he thought was a huge man covered with silvery white hair standing in the middle

---

[*] A. Lovgren.

[†] George Goode.

of the road. There was a drizzling rain falling and when Ken saw this creature, he slammed on his brakes and stopped about three feet short of the figure. The creature held his arm up over his eyes to shield them from the bright lights. In the meantime, Ken's car engine stopped because of the suddenness with which he applied his brakes. The creature then walked around the back of the car to the window where Ken was sitting desperately trying to start his engine. The creature stooped down and peered in at Ken. The sensation Ken felt was one of horror and he was greatly relieved when the engine started and he could get away from there. When he looked in his rearview mirror as he drove away, he could see the creature's silhouette as lightning lit up the sky. His description of the giant coincided completely with those of previous sightings, even though he did not know of this book or other sightings. I feel that in Ken Pettijohn's stepping forward and telling his bold story, it may help bring out other stories of incidents by those with similar experiences.[78]

To end the reports about shielding of the eyes, long-time enthusiast Cliff Kopas briefly mentioned facial shielding in his article *Sasquatch, Fact or Myth?* published in the British Columbia Digest in 1963. "The Bella Coola Indians had a dance called the *Boqs dance*, which portrayed the Sasquatch shielding his face from the squirting of seawater from the clams." The terms Boq and Snanaik are the descriptive words used by the Bella Coola and several other Pacific Northwest Indians in coastal northern British Columbia, Canada, Washington, Oregon, and California. In some areas, the term Boq is used interchangeably with the term Sasquatch.

From native descriptions, the Boq resembles man more than the Salish Sasquatch. The Boq is said to have somewhat of a neck; the feet, hands, and the region around the eyes seem, according to various accounts, distinctly human.[*]

The 'bush man' walks upright like the Indian but with a slight lean

---

[*] Wayne Suttles.

forward at the upper torso. It has a huge barrel chest and massive shoulders from which its arms seem to simply dangle from the sockets. The Natives associate the hair on the torso in the same manner as the grizzly bear's hair and, in places, is just as thick. Other bushmen are so sparsely haired as not to tell the difference between them and civilized man. A few First Nation people believe the Boq is a spirit animal, but wolves, wapiti, eagles, killer whales, the bison, and the buffalo are spirit animals, too. Do we think them any less real?

Speaking of Boqs, several sightings were featured on BCTV's 6 o'clock news on November 13, 2002. The television anchor stated that there had been several sightings of Sasquatch-like beings by people traveling on the highway between Port Alberni and Tofino, as well as near Long Beach on Vancouver Island. A large dark-haired creature with yellowish-orange eyes, walking on two legs, was seen by two Vancouver Island men. Two brothers named Ito, visiting from Japan, were hitching a ride on a freight train into Port Alberni when they spotted a large creature below the Rogers Creek trestle.[*]

In a separate report, two Nuxalt anglers, while fishing about 30 yards offshore, said they saw two Boqs either playing or after something on the rocky shoreline in the same general area of Long Beach. Neither man wanted to give their names, but the report came in separately before the BCTV evening news made it public. The men described the Boqs as large-shouldered, shiny black in color, and covered with thick hair, though not as long as the bears of that region on the mainland side, and said, "you know, they looked like all Boqs look, covered with a length of hair." They said one of the creatures was watching them while the other scrambled about the rocks after something they couldn't make out. Both creatures were wet in appearance and made no effort to leave but stayed out in the open, going about whatever Boqs do. After watching the activity for some minutes, the informants reportedly left the area "out of respect for the Boqs" but were too astonished to do any more fishing and returned home. A grand-daugh-

____

[*] Ken Kristian.

ter, Alissa, emailed me about the incident, saying that her "Pops" was quite surprised to have seen the creatures.[79]

We are beginning a time in research where more reports are coming in about the Sasquatch staying out in the open, giving informants more observable time to note various behaviors.

Long Beach, Vancouver Island

Fred Bradshaw

I've written a lot about Fred Bradshaw as he was one of the really colorful characters involved in research in the early days. He lived one mile south of Elma, Grays Harbor County, Washington, just off Highway 12 south in the heart of Bigfoot country. Once he discovered the internet, he unloaded a life's worth of encounters with the Sasquatch and led many a novice to their first sighting. His stories of his brushes with the Sasquatch people both amazed and baffled those of us who listened to him. Fred was very active in the Washington field and easily located all manner of Sasquatch tracks in and around where he lived, ranging from 14 inches in length by 6 inches at the ball of the foot and 4 inches at the heel. The stride was measured at 43-inches. There were additional tracks in the range of 17-inches in length that had a stride length of 52-inches and more.

Bradshaw told stories of the Sasquatch rocking his small trailer side to side and hearing them vocalize at night. The rocking back and forth of trailers, all manner of vehicles, and truck toppers is an often reported behavior. Bradshaw never lost the enthusiasm for locating the big folks and seemed genuinely interested in relating their behaviors to anyone within earshot. I remember an email from his sister, and I believe she said he died of a massive heart attack out in the field while hunting. It was what he loved to do.

Gesturing, Arguing?

Outdoorsman-hunter Peter Ray Williams reported traveling northbound on Colorado 96 past Wetmore en route to Florence when he blew a right rear tire. He pulled over to change it just a few yards short of the right (east) turn to CR-389. It was about 7:50 p.m.

Williams stated that as he was putting on the spare and dumping the blown tire in the truck bed, something caught his attention up the road to his right. "I looked up and was shocked to see two Bigfoot looking creatures crossing the road from east to west in about 3-4 steps and disappear into an open field in setting sun on the other side." He swears he heard them talking in a frantic kind of nattering. "I looked up because I thought what I was hearing was men arguing. Just that quickly, they were there walking across the road. I heard these sounds —maybe talking angrily—then they were gone."

Williams figures they were fleeing northward or northeastward from the fire line, or were confused or displaced. He described them as black, one taller than the other, and the bigger one wasn't looking where it was going but at the other Bigfoot with arms straight down at his sides, and the other one was gesturing, not wildly, just gesturing with its hands about something.

"Maybe," he speculated, "they were arguing, but carried on their merry way like people do. It was wild seeing my first Bigfoot sighting. I don't know if they were male or female because as fast as my eyes adjusted to seeing them, they were gone. Man they moved, but they weren't running! We saw a couple of deer cross road 96 earlier. There was a wildfire burning in the distance, somewhere towards the east."

William's stepdaughter, Leslie Ann Marshall, was also a witness to the event, but she was inside the truck cab, caring for a baby. In a telephone interview, Mrs. Marshall said she thought they were both taller than 8-feet in height and that they must both be males. She didn't hear any sounds from them, she wasn't outside the truck, but she did hear Pete yelling at her to look at the Bigfeet crossing the road. "I already saw them by the time Dad started yelling at me," she said, "I saw them coming but thought I was seeing things. Yeah, this is like not a real happening. Who would believe this? They were both big males, I mean, like two BIG dudes."[80]

Pueblo County Sighting

Firefighters Report Sioux Lookout Tracks After Fire

It was mid-July, 1996, and it was a hot day. It had rained for a few days earlier so the forest fire had cooled enough for crews to take action against it. The fire was designated Sioux Lookout Fire #70, located in the forest about one mile north of the kilometer 74 marker on Vermillion River Road, north of Sioux Lookout, Ontario, Canada. Sioux Lookout is a town about 400 km northwest of Thunder Bay, Ontario, and is visible on most world maps. The sighting was on the north side of a large lake called Lac Seul. The logging road turns off the highway 27 miles northwest of Sioux Lookout and then continues straight north. There are signs every kilometer showing the distance. Kilometer 74 is about 2 kilometers before the Root River, which should also show up on a detailed map of the area. Several of my co-workers and I were patrolling for smudges and looking for smoke and any other burning material needing to be extinguished when we came across huge footprints in the middle of nowhere. One footprint in particular that was encased in mud was huge. We took a few pictures of it and even had a tape measure to determine its length.[*]

There wasn't much detail in the Aaron McGill footprint find, and nothing related to Sasquatch behavior other than tracks found in the aftermath of what must have been a devastating forest fire. But in 1996, when McGill sent in the notice, research was hungry for any case that mentioned Bigfoot and forest fires, so I mentioned it here for the many questions that come in each fire season.

A more interesting story begins with another forestry fire lookout tower, this time in the Estacada region of Clackamas County, Oregon. The lengthy story was beautifully written by Vanessa Voorhis and published in the Estacada News, October 1, 2008. In her words:

> While hiking the snowy banks of the Clackamas River one January afternoon in 1969, Millie Kiggins, her husband and their friend, Art Schneider, found something that would thrust the Kigginses and the quiet wilderness surrounding Estacada into an international spotlight.
>
> We went to look at a Forest Service cabin up above Squaw Lake on the way to Cold Springs about 20 miles from Estacada. They were going to sell them, and we wanted to look at them. We started out late, and we were in about three feet of snow. There was a gate, and we couldn't get through. So we started to walk, and it looked like somebody had already gotten through, because there were tracks in the snow.
>
> They noticed the large size of the tracks and their depth, which were 18 inches. Whatever had made them was heavy, because ours were a couple inches deep. It had to have been walking on two feet and its

---

[*] Aaron McGill, November 26, 1996.

stride was 67 inches. The path of the tracks was in a straight line, too straight to be manmade. The hikers followed the imprints for about a quarter mile before realizing it was late and decided to turn back.

Before leaving, Kiggins documented their discovery and contacted the U.S. Forest Service. They said it was a snowshoe rabbit. I have no idea what it was, but if it was a rabbit, it would have to be a big one to make footprints that large. I told him if it was a snowshoe rabbit they had better look out, because it's big enough to eat them.

Back at home on their farm on the outskirts of Estacada, the Kigginses began to experience a series of Bigfoot-like phenomena. He was around here for a year. We found footprints all over the farm. Once, they led to a five-foot fence and continued on the other side uninterrupted as if he stepped right over it. Sometimes we would smell him. Smelled like a bad nursing home. We heard loud screams and grunts all at once lasting 10 or 15 seconds. It could be heard miles away. The hair on the back of your neck would stand up. It spooked the cattle.

A U.S. Forest Service employee, not wishing to be identified, said she has never taken a single Bigfoot report in the 12 years she's worked at the desk of the Clackamas River Ranger District office. "We don't have a book or piece of paper that states sightings at all," she said. She refused comment further for fear she would "get in trouble again."[81]

True perhaps, but a strange remark by the forestry official; deny, deny.

Bigfoot Lore Alive in Estacada Area

Sasquatch and RVs

This next report is second-hand and relates a situation where a vehicle was violently rocked back and forth; this time, it wasn't a travel trailer. The behavior is interesting and will be familiar to those who regularly review these data submissions. In each case, the mischievous Sasquatch was easily run off by the men in the RV, and there was no apparent drama in the aftermath.

Are they looking for attention or trying to scare off the campers? Some feel they're just having a bit of ill-behaved fun. I've heard them called tricksters, but I don't think I'd find it too amusing if I was parked in an RV alone at night.

> A few years ago, I was visiting friends in Campbell River on Vancouver Island. A friend of mine, Ted Storey, used to live there. He took me fishing on a lake in the mountains, and told me about a fishing trip in that area and what happened to him. It seems they returned to their RV after fishing and had a few beers. It was dark when someone or some 'thing' tried to push their RV over. One of the men hurried outside and saw a large thing like a person run off, leaving a bad smell. They did not want to report it because the authorities would say it was their imagination. I heard that later footprints were cast. *

Sasquatch and Trucks

Along those lines, Patrick T. wrote in late August 2011 that he had a strange incident while fishing the Pecos River near Loving, Eddy County, New Mexico.

> One night while sleeping in my pickup truck I was awakened by the truck being shaken, rocked back and forth. I had to work up the nerve to rise and look out but I didn't see anything. Later, in the course of

---

* Orville Parker (2012).

another fishing trip to the Pecos River, I heard a loud splash in the river where I was fishing (something thrown into the Pecos) and then all went quiet. I keep a revolver close now.

It would seem the stories, complete with the same Sasquatch behavior, are told over and over throughout Sasquatch history. Rock throwing, vehicle shaking, and camper rocking are consistently reported as typical conduct by errant Sasquatches.

Aerospace engineer Dr. Jim Karl of Santa Monica, California, reminded me in the summer of 2011 of a story Fred Bradshaw told him about seeing a Sasquatch cross the road in front of his truck. It looked into the truck's front window and, according to Bradshaw, had a smile on its face. Bradshaw may have misinterpreted it; it could have simply been a show of teeth – aggression.

These are the little known details about Sasquatch life that would be interesting if we had more information about their culture and rules for living. Dr. Karl wrote,

> ...he [Bradshaw] was one of the most friendly, generous men I met along the way. Bradshaw had genuine love for his friends, a peach of a guy in my book.

> On June 16, 2001, Bradshaw sent me a message. It read, "...about 8:30 p.m., while out with George Karras's group in one of my research areas near Ft. Lewis Army Base (Pierce County, Washington), I saw a white sasquatch and brought it to the attention of the others in the group. What I saw was from mid-chest up to the head, and you're right, they stand out like a lighthouse. This animal was so white it didn't look real; black face, about seven feet tall from what I could see; it was a mind blowing day!

On Saturday, June 30, that same year, Fred wrote that he was smiled at again. It was a wide smile showing teeth – this time near the backside of the Ft. Lewis Army Base in civilian territory. But the creature was not white. This time, Bradshaw was smiled at by a big dark-colored Sasquatch – so dark that the only details visible happened to be his white teeth. Many of Bradshaw's stories, including vocalizations, were directed at him; it was almost like they recognized him and didn't care who he brought along with him. Crazy and unusual behavior.

Stone Throwing

The Greenwell report from the Six Rivers Project noted three incidents of throwing various objects - logs on two occasions and rocks on another. Noting that bears and other wildlife do not throw things, the late ISC Secretariat Richard Greenwell said in his time that he interpreted the behavior as a mark of "primate intimidation." Throwing objects is not new, but it is an old, reliable behavior that has happened to many people in the field. The Sasquatch's intent can only be speculated on, but it's obvious it was not to harm. If harm was the objective, they certainly have the power to inflict any manner of injury and destruction. It is said they hunt effectively with stones to bring down prey. I imagine the Sasquatch and other primitive men were proficient at stone-throwing.

Playing From a Hidden Spot

One such incident involved the family of Wes and Natalie (Pee Wee) Sumerlin when they camped out for several days at a favorite spot called Timothy Meadows, also in the State of Washington. While enjoying such an outing, the youngsters of the family were playing in the open field with a soccer ball when it suddenly careened off the designated field area and into the brush at the edge of the clearing. Straight away, the ball became airborne out of the darkness of the timber-lined field and back onto the playing field. This happened once more, according to former game warden Mr. Bill Laughery. Recalling the incident, Laughery said no humans were in the bush at the time. Adult or juveniles – the behavior was a playful one, and the Sumerlin family enjoyed the hairy man's participation.[82]

Belly Crawling

Stories that mention being watched from hidden spots often involve Bigfoot watching children play. There was a report, and perhaps it was by David Holly, at the time associated with the Texoma (Texas) Bigfoot Research team, who wrote that he had observed the Sasquatch crawling towards him on its stomach. Holly found it rather unsettling to have a creature that size crawling towards him in high grass; it was huge, and he only saw it momentarily as he turned to a fellow researcher to answer his question. The remark was posted publicly on January 13, 2002, on the old red and black network54.com forum. Evidently, Holly had observed a Sasquatch belly crawling once before, also using embankments to "squat" behind while observing him.

There were reports on that same forum by individuals who witnessed the Sasquatch hunkered down and then crawling around on hands and knees in an effort to observe human interactions without being discovered.

Carol B. watched a reddish-black Bigfoot crawl toward her home from a second-story bedroom window in the fall of 2011. It occurred in broad daylight and was described as crawling like a horned toad lizard. "Its hair was matted and dirty." Its focus was on two pet goats romping in the yard with her children. The Bigfoot fled when the witness's husband went out into the yard.[*]

Crawling is a behavior not often reported.

Screamer Watches Children at Play

Dana Richardson, a resident of Fairfield Center, Maine, shared this 2005 sighting:

---

[*] CAB.

My family were gathered to celebrate a birthday. Eight of my nieces and nephews, ages from 6 to 9, were in the back yard playing when suddenly all the children started screaming and came running into the porch area. I could tell by the screaming that something had terrified them. I ran out onto the porch to see what was going on. My oldest nephew, aged 9, told me that a big black man was watching them from the edge of the woods. I knew that he was telling the truth because his voice was shaking and all my nieces were crying.

My two brothers and I ran outside to see who was watching them. I noticed that my parents dog, Buffy, a chow and golden retriever mix was watching something. Her tail was down and all her hair was standing up. I ran to the woods where she was watching and called her to follow, but she wouldn't come with me. I could hear something moving very fast away from me through the brush about 100-yards away. My two brothers and I split up and searched the area but did not find anyone. I did find where it ran through the brush but that's all.

The following weekend, my oldest brother and two daughters were at my parents' for a visit. I showed up about two in the afternoon and walked into the house. About five minutes later both of my nieces ran into the house screaming. They both stated that they saw a big man watching them from the edge of the woods. I grabbed a gun and had my oldest niece show me where he was standing. I asked my niece to describe what he was wearing. She said he was all black and very tall. I searched the area for about two hours and didn't find anything or see anyone.

Then another time, August it was, I spent the night at my parents again. A loud vocalization woke me. Then it vocalized again; I've never heard anything like it before. I was able to record its vocalization. I played it to several people and was not able to identify what made it. Somewhere, I have the recording. That fall, two of my friends were in the same section of woods hunting rabbits. David and Tex were separated by about 100 yards. The hunt ended suddenly when David saw something that really scared him. Later that day, Tex called to tell me that David saw Bigfoot and he refuses to go in the woods again. I don't know what to make of it. I didn't know that there were any reports of any sightings in Maine nor the northeast. In fact I am very skeptical about its existence. The woods in this area are very thick and have a large amount of rabbits, turkeys and deer. Coyotes and some moose are occasionally seen.*

In the 1980s, it was very rare to receive a report mentioning strange screaming, howls and such, and I don't recall ever hearing anyone say a Sasquatch growled. There was only the more famous Puyallup extended moaning-like howl that seems lost to any notice these days. Currently, however, screams, howling, and growling of all things seem to be trending like the Road Runner reports. In fact, looking at the data, all manner of vocalizations are trending right up there as the most commonly reported occurrence.

Patterson-Gimlin Footage

In the 1990s, the most reported Sasquatch feature was the conical head; the "pointy" head, "the dunce cap look." Those reports suddenly stopped when Mississippi film analyst M.K. Davis produced a continuum of stabilized slow-motion frames from the film attributed to Roger Patterson, which showed the supposed conical head moving to and fro with each step the creature took. As it turned out, what was previously thought to be a cone-shaped skull was a top-knot of hair

---

* D. Richardson.

that moved back and forth with each step the film's subject took as she advanced up the creek bed. There never was a conical head. Funny how that film influenced physical descriptions BEFORE Davis stabilized the footage.[83]

Bigfoot Steals Deer Kill From Hunter

A gunsmith named Ed Sizemore from Yadin County, North Carolina, sent in his memory of a childhood event that involved something capable of easily stepping over a 5-strand barbed wire fence like it was nothing. During childhood summers, Sizemore and another friend named Patrick spent time playing in a fort they'd built up in the loft of an old hay barn where they could see in most directions the landscape including a farm pond and rolling cow pastures that were fenced with 5-strand barbed wire to keep cattle from straying into the woods. His letter picks it up here:

> While in this barn loft playing one day, we looked across the pasture and saw a very hairy beast on all fours drinking water from our farm pond. This amazed us, as there were no cattle or horses in the pasture the whole time. At first we just thought it was somebody's cow in need of water, as the summer was very hot. My friend went to get a pair of binoculars to see what it was, but before he could leave the thing stood up on its hind legs and walked back towards the woods. It was tall and a dark brown, almost black-like creature; I would say about 8-foot after it stood up. It stepped over a 5-strand barbed wire fence like it was nothing. I didn't go looking for tracks; I was scared stiff after we heard the screeching that sounded almost like fingernails on a chalkboard. We never told anybody about this – not until recently when I heard about a hunter tracking in the same area. He claimed that he shot a deer, but before he could find it he heard, in his words, "the damnedest scariest screeching he had ever heard in his entire life." When he got to the kill site something had dragged his deer off and he wasn't about to go looking for it. I've told my wife about it as well as a friend by the name of Durant Haire. I don't know the deer hunter's

name. I'm also a gunsmith and I hang out in another gun shop when I'm not working. He was relating the deer-kill story to a man there, and I was listening in...[84]

When I started the rock throwing project, it was to search the database for only those reports that spoke to the issues regarding known Sasquatch behavior patterns, specifically the art of throwing things; rocks, pinecones, boulders, machinery, and other equipment. The data shows that the Sasquatch will throw just about anything available, and for whatever reason. There tends to be an alternative attention-getter that various Bigfoot will use: banging on houses, cabins and campers, as well as window peeping.

Getting back to this rock-throwing behavior; it can have many meanings. Rock throwing can be done in an effort to gain attention, ward off, defend, or frighten someone away. It may also carry a message that the rock-thrower intends to do in the trespasser, even if the unconscious trespasser knows he is trespassing. Boulder pushing and boulder heaving; rock and dirt slides will no doubt convince even the most strong-willed individual that he's not wanted in a given area. If that doesn't work, a robust scream that rattles your chest is often employed.

There is no real way to know the intent behind the rock-throwing behavior; we can only record the behavior and benefit from the statistics. There are cases in the database of the Sasquatch using rocks to down a bird or nail a rabbit on the run. Another instance was filed where the informant saw a Sasquatch launch a rock side-arm that downed a small Texas deer, described similar to throwing a discus. Less lethal, of course, is the pine cone, but few are the pine cone throwing reports. It may be that the rock-throwing areas are stocked with piles of stones where there are no stones naturally. Mounds of stones have been found in odd locations; piles of pine needles, pine cones, and stones are curiously found.

Minor Aggression; Pine Cones Thrown

Bigfoot enthusiast John Mionczynski had a rather frightening encounter during an outing in the Wind River Mountains of Wyoming in 1972 whilst at a base camp for a government-sponsored study on big horn sheep. All alone that night, he was awakened by what appeared to be a large hand pressing on the top of his six-foot-high tent. Thinking it was perhaps a bear, he quickly realized it had stubby fingers and a distinctive thumb; a primate hand, not a bear! During a radio interview, Mionczynski told his audience that he could hear breathing at a rate of six breaths a minute, and then the unthinkable happened. The Sasquatch collapsed the tent around him and then ran off into the dog-hair pines and the protective darkness of the trees. Mionczynski kept watch during the night by his campfire while the creature moved around, intermittently throwing pine cones at him for long hours into the night.

Mionczynski worked around the clock studying Sasquatch, spending summers assessing possible habitat and food sources, setting camera traps, and trying to snare DNA. He collected plaster casts of big foot-prints from across the West, the largest being 18-inches in length and 8-inches across. Except for the size, it looked human. By anyone's standard, that's an incredibly large foot; it's not at all ape-like, nor is the behavior.

A wildlife biologist specializing in Big Horn Sheep and grizzly bear studies, Mionczynski once, while working for Wyoming Game and Fish, took hair and skin samples to an agency's lab for analysis. An irate superior threatened to have him fired if Mionczynski's name was ever publicly associated with this Bigfoot thing. What an interesting position for the fish and game officer to maintain.

Nevertheless, Mionczynski worked quietly after that and kept any interest in the existence of the Sasquatch to himself.[85] The behavior Mionczynski reported is the only one of its kind that I've heard, and it speaks to minor aggression or perhaps irritation with his presence.

Special Guest John Mionczynski | MN.B.R.T. Radio with
John Mionczynski | A Biologist Revered and Ridiculed

Old Stories Remembered

Bill Wells in Sacramento, California, posted this to a discussion list.

In his 1971 book, *The European Discovery of America*, Samuel Eliot Morison wrote in few words about "The 550-AD Voyage of St. Brendan" into the Atlantic Ocean. In quoting St. Brendan's journal, Morison wrote:

> At a rocky, fire-scarred island with neither trees nor grass, a horrid sub-human, hairy creature rushed down to the shore and hurled at our ship a red hot mass of lava or slag, which fell hissing into the sea. "Let's get out of here," said Brendan. They made sail and plied their oars just in time to escape a crowd of similar monsters who threw more hot stuff at them.

It was later speculated that the island may have been Tenerife according to Brendan's map and chart depictions of the pre-Columbian era. But the story left me wondering what manner of beast hurls red hot chunks of slag or lava rock and why were they hot; volcanic or otherwise?*

There is a long history of Sasquatches throwing various objects. For instance, as far back in our history as 1840, we have the journal writ-

---

* Bill Wells, Sacto, California.

ings of the Reverend Elkanah Walker. He described the devils having a strong, intolerable smell, whistling in the night, and he also recorded them throwing stones at the people's lodgings. Not all encounters with the devils were as peaceful.

According to Wenatchee Valley College historian, John Brown, Reverend Elkanah Walker listed some interesting behaviors known rather early in the history of the North American Sasquatch. Walker's letter to the American Board of Commissioners for Foreign Missions from F0rt Colville, Washington, was included. Part of that text is interesting to historians:

> I suppose you will beat with me [sic] if I trouble you with a little of their [the Spokane Indians] superstition, which recently came to my knowledge. They believe in the existence of a race of giants which inhabit a certain mountain off to the west of us. This mountain is covered with perpetual snow. They inhabit its top. They may be classed with Goldsmith's nocturnal class, as they cannot see in the daytime. They hunt and do all their work in the night. They are men stealers. They come to the people's lodgings in the night when the people are asleep and put them under their skins and to their place of abode without even waking.

> They frequently come in the night, steal their salmon from the nets and eat them raw. If the people are away they always know when they are coming very near by their strong smell, which is most intolerable. It is not uncommon for them to come in the night and give three whistles. Then the stones will begin to hit the houses. The people are troubled with their nocturnal visits.[86]

Isn't it interesting what the Reverend Walker said about the race of giants not being able to see well in daylight? There were several behavior traits common to the Sasquatch that research apparently overlooked or summarily ignored. I don't know which...but it was interesting to me to read the commonality between what Walker observed twenty years prior to the Civil War and what we continue to see reported relevant to these strange people today.

Ivan Sanderson recorded an incident of rocks being hurled at Alexander Caulfield Anderson, a well-known explorer and an executive of the Hudson's Bay Company, who was doing a survey of the newly opened territory while seeking a feasible trade route for his company. Anderson reported "hairy humanoids hurled rocks down upon him and his surveying party from more than one slope" in 1864, some 24 years after the Walker notation.[87]

Most acts of aggression appear in old reports such as those abbreviated and published in the *Bigfoot Casebook* by Janet and Colin Bord. Fewer acts of aggression are being reported today. For all its bravado, modern man will generally cut and run in unabashed fear from a Sasquatch. It is wise not to test the will of the Sasquatch. The data suggests they are (at best) unpredictable.

Witness perception, of course, is largely responsible for how the report is filed. Aggression may not have been the intent of the Sasquatch in this next incident; it may have been a playful accident.

Many will remember the much written about Christine van Acker case. It occurred in Monroe, Michigan, in 1965 and made several local newspapers. Seventeen-year-old Christine Van Acker and her mother were driving on a dark country road on August 11, 1965, when a giant, hairy man who appeared to be at least seven feet tall and completely covered with black hair stepped out in front of their car. The girl hit the brakes, causing the car to stall. As she frantically tried to restart the engine, the creature reached inside the car with a long, hairy arm and hit her in the face, giving her a bruised and blackened eye. The girl and her mother managed to escape and went to the local police, where they told their horrifying story. The next day, newspapers carried a photo of Christine Van Acker's black eye and a harrowing tale of her account.[88] If the behavior was accurately assessed; it's hard to figure out what motivated the Sasquatch to behave in that manner; but can we say they are unpredictable? Yes, by anyone's portrayal.

The Spokane Indians, 1975 | Bigfoot Prowls the Midwest |
Bigfoot Resurfaces in Wisconsin

Hostile Intent?

I found the conduct of the Sasquatch in this Rip Lyttle report interesting. Two teenagers in Bridgeville, California (I'm guessing the year was 1994), claimed they were investigating a cave partially hidden under a waterfall.

Suddenly, they were bombarded by dozens of rocks flying and landing just feet from them. They thought it was some human doing it and ended up hunting the culprit but were unsuccessful. Long-time investigator Rip Lyttle broke the story back in the day by showing up at the waterfall two hours after the incident. Rip found several rocks situated at the top of the falls, probably waiting to be hurled some 60-70 feet below. In a nearby cave situated in a rock formation was a bed of leaves that Rip said he measured at eight feet long by three feet wide. Exploring the surrounding area, Lyttle figured the Sasquatch was trying to scare the boys away from his cave; he determined they were unhurt. Several tracks were found in the area, along with a doe with a broken neck. Twin fawns were seen close by. Nature is sometimes brutal.[89]

These are all well-established stories that began my research, familiar to almost anyone who bones up on this stuff, but what of the newer rock-throwing stories? The most expressive story that involved stone-throwing was the Snelgrove Lake case.

The Laughing Sasquatch

Two brothers, Jeff & Jason McKenna, while deer hunting near the Mad River in Trinity County, California, began feeling strangely uncomfortable. The informant, a bodybuilder from the East Coast was aware of Sasquatch stories. He and his brother, formerly with Boston law enforcement, never actually saw the culprit on this hunting trip, but the event included behavior typical of the hairy man. Jason wrote:

> ...I began to feel uneasy. A large rock, probably weighing in the neighborhood of 30 pounds, was hurled by something in the creek in front of me, making a huge crashing sound. The creek bed was only about 15 yards away; then complete silence. At first we thought the rock fell from the sky but Jeff said he thought it was hurled from the trees. It could have been a bear, but I never heard of one throwing boulders! I listened, but all I could hear was the ripple of the creek and wind in the pines. It was unnerving so we broke camp and took off to hunt elsewhere. As we left the area, I swear we could hear laughter. We saw no other hunters the whole trip, I'm not hearing things because Jeff heard the damn thing laughing the same time I did. To be sure, we stopped, turned around and listened intently. It sounded like a man laughing. [*]

Rocks Whistled Through the Trees

Then, in Wabash County, Indiana, in 1979, there was this notation in the data that Wildlife educator Larry Battson emailed me many years ago:

> As they listened they could hear it moving from the camp and down through the woods to the edge of the river. Then they could hear the sound of rocks being thrown from the river towards them. The rocks whistled through the tree branches and landed very close to their tent. Both men clambered from the tent and stood in the center of the camp,

---

[*] McKenna (1990s).

back to back. Then they heard the sound of whatever it was heading back to their camp. It began circling the camp just far away enough they could not get a good look at it until it moved close towards them. They were not prepared for what they saw. It was at least 8 feet tall, black in color and walked with a speed they could not believe.[90]

Rock Throwing Sasquatch Terrorizes Camping Fisherman

Rock Throwing, Vocalizations, Baby Crying

The most recent sightings, which included vocalizations, rock throwing, baby crying, crashing around, and a tree falling, came from multiple witnesses enjoying a Fourth of July holiday in Morgan County, Ohio. The witnesses described the Bigfoot's behavior as their "Ohio Grassman Encounter." Here is their report as it was filed in 2012.

My Husband and I just spent July 3rd through the 7th camping in southeastern Ohio at private lake, which we prefer not to name. On the night of July 4th around 11:30 p.m., we were on the private lake, which borders the west side of a stretch of power lines. One of our friends in a kayak smelled a strong musk-skunk odor from the west side of the lake. The wind was blowing to the east. At the same time, we heard crashing branches like something running through the woods over on the east side of camp on the other side of the power lines.

She brought the kayak back to shore and then her boyfriend went out to the deepest end of the lake. All the sudden a huge rock about the size of a full grown German shepherd flew across the road, which runs all the way around the lake, over the bank, over the grass line and into the lake! This was approximately 20 yards from the kayak. Then our friends antagonized it and it threw another one just as big. It landed a lot closer, within 10 yards of his kayak. The three of us on the bank were approximately 100 yards from the creature, and our friend in the kayak was about 30 yards. We all saw the creature. He was peeking out from behind a tree. He rocked his body back and forth from one side of the tree to the other. Then he moved to the water line and back. At that point my husband set off three bottle rockets thinking it would scare the Bigfoot off. He then loaded his 12-gauge shot gun. He didn't want to harm or make it mad, just didn't want it to get any closer.

The creature stood only 4½ to 5 feet tall with no neck. He looked very thin in the chest, broad shoulders and glowing dark yellow eyes in the flashlight; he was light brown. We had our really bright Mag-lite with new batteries pointing right at him. We thought we heard sounds from another Bigfoot to the south of us possibly calling the smaller creature with a WHOOOP sound! Then we lost sight of the Bigfoot. The whole time we were there, before, after and during our stay at the lake, we heard a baby crying, a woman screaming and even heavy breathing at different times. My Husband also heard strange whistles, whooping sounds and even a tree falling over in the woods on the other side of the lake. We all heard that. We were all so excited from our encounter that we stayed up until daylight. In years past, at this same camp, we've heard things and smelled things, but never had the encounter we had this year. WHAT A RUSH! My husband believes they use the power lines as a trail. We truly believe there was more than one Bigfoot around our camp this year. It's changed the way we think about going into the woods for the rest of our lives.*

---

* Sally and Neil de la Fuentes (2012).

Rocks Pelt a Camper's Tent

Betsy Ann Marshall-Downes told a story she remembered as a young bride when she went with her new husband and brother on a deer hunting trip. Betty recounted the story for me, saying she stayed behind in camp after the men left and slept in. Emerging from her tent mid-morning after "something woke her up," she was alone deep in the woods. For company, she hung up a radio on a branch and played music loudly as she cooked breakfast, all the while feeling odd, like something was watching her. She continued with her day.

Finally, her feelings of uneasiness sent her to the tent to load the rifle her brother left behind, and it was then the first rock hit the tent. Terrified, she huddled down on the tent floor for a very long time, wondering what it was or if it was her imagination.

She nervously listened to the sounds around her tent for hours and finally mustered the courage and cried out to whoever was out there to "knock it off, I have a gun." To her surprise, the rocks stopped, but she did not come out of the tent until she heard her husband's voice after he'd finished hunting.

They didn't believe her until they saw the rocks that littered the ground around their tent. There were rocks in the frying pan and good-sized rocks in the fire pit. There were more pages to that story that added color, but the behavior of rock-throwing is logged for this purpose. [*]

Bigfoot enthusiast, Jenice Blevins, reported her family being harassed by a Sasquatch on the Merced River near Bagby in Mariposa County, California. It threw rocks at the family camper in the middle of the night, which angered her father to the degree that he got up, went outside, and angrily fired his gun skyward into the night air. The rock-throwing stopped.

A similar incident happened to the John Kramer family camping in a

------

[*] The Marshall-Downes Story (1996).

small travel trailer at South Fourche Campground, Perry County, near Hollis, Arkansas, in the summer of 2001.

It was midweek and we were the only RV around that night. We saw nobody during the day. That evening, my son and I harmonized country songs for several hours. My wife videotaped the best of it for our parents who couldn't be with us that trip. It was close to midnight by the time we put stuff away and turned in. I was just about asleep when rocks started hitting the camper. At first I thought it was hail. I had no gun, no means of protection so we stuck it out. The pebbles and larger stones continued intermittently until well after two o'clock." The next day they found a set of 15-inch barefoot tracks around their fire pit. [*]

Rock Throwing and Screams in the Distance

A Sasquatch was dubbed by the informant as "Mr. Peepers," because he watched the young couple getting it on in their favorite necking spot off Lake Aldwell, Washington State. On Wednesday 4th July 2001, the Sasquatch made himself known by tossing pebbles at the couple. Thinking it was the girl's brother "messing with us," the couple returned fire with larger rocks and saw a dark figure, which was a description of an adult Sasquatch, depart the scene. Later, they heard screams in the distance. They reported the incident to the authorities in Port Angeles, who appeared disinterested. [†]

Anger or Entertainment?

Berry Creek in Butte County, California:

In the summer of 2001, a county surveyor emailed my old website, California Sightings List, to report watching a Bigfoot heaving creek

---

[*] John Tinsley Kramer story (2001).

[†] L.M. (2001).

rocks over his head and into the creek with enormous force. The stones quickly became larger boulders, and finally, the Bigfoot went over and lifted a dead tree out of the shallow water where it apparently fell and hurled it into a deeper part of a pond adjacent to the running creek. After a few more rocks were thrown, the Bigfoot apparently became bored with the exercise, walked off into the heavy timber, and disappeared from the surveyor's sight. Nervous, the surveyor asked for a transfer and I never heard from him again.

Stories that reflect rock throwing are almost as many in my data as road-runner crossings and those types sightings.

Washing Their Food

An intriguing behavior was mentioned in a 112-year-old report out of the Campbell River area off Vancouver Island in BC. The informant, Michael King, was recorded saying he saw a Sasquatch at the river's edge methodically washing roots in the water and placing them in neat piles. I have a special interest in reports like this as they tend not to be influenced by any pre-conditioning of the mind or by the media images, the Internet, or Google searches. As I began to search this subject, I found that there were many reports of hairy folks eating unwashed food and even roadkill.

What does the washing of vegetables suggest to us? It suggests prudence and wisdom in properly caring and preserving food items. Or it might be the preference for clean raw vegetables? Could be, but there are instances in the data where the Sasquatch has been seen eating roots and shoots right out of the ground with no food preparation whatsoever. Conversely, one logged report from Keno Hill in the Yukon Territories, Canada,[91] saw a Sasquatch sitting on the ground picking the bones of a dead elk. That was their perception, but it might have been that the Sasquatch was picking at the grubs and maggots under the carcass. It might be that cleanliness, as it pertains to food, is a taught behavior present in only some tribal groupings.

Hungrier, perhaps others eat what is available, dead, dirty, rotten, or not.

Some sources have told me they've seen Sasquatches running off with their deer and elk kills – the suggestion is that the meat is either taken back to others who are waiting or it's eaten raw in transit; few reports tell us what is done with the fresh kills. I do not have a case where we are able to learn how meat is consumed. Before the Internet really started humming, discussion groups tossed the idea back and forth that the Sasquatch only ate the liver from fresh kills, but there was little evidence to support it then or now.

Keno Hill, Yukon Territory

Use of Fire?

It has been speculated that if the primitive Sasquatch actually did kidnap Indian maidens and children in the past, those women indeed knew how to use fire. Held against their will, Indian women must have used fire for warmth or to cook in the presence of their captors. We don't know about the hairy man's ability to withstand the cold, but there are limits to how much those kidnapped Native American women could handle cold temperatures and inclement weather. Kidnapped women, children, and young boys require the warmth of a fire.

There is evidence that Indian women also used tobacco; to smoke, it required fire. They smoked salmon and venison, which also required fire. One can easily deduce that fire in some limited form is probably used in very remote reaches and in underground caves, lava tubes, and tunnels. I had to rethink previous notions that the Sasquatch were so wild that they were, like bears and cougars, possibly afraid of fire, though I'm sure now that they've mastered the use of it; at least on some level. I don't know how they could survive a Yukon winter without it, and if they bartered with the Indians once upon a time, then yes, they knew about fire.

I was not surprised to read about modern-day fire usage as recorded by Dr. Ed Fusch and his work among the Colville Indians. In September of 1985, he interviewed a Nespelem, Okanogan County, Washington woman who gave great insight into the behavior of the Skanicum; the tribal name for Sasquatch.

Among the many details she cited for Dr. Fusch were the following:

1. Skanicum was very vengeful – to harm one of them meant the Indians would no longer be safe. Even in the face of Skanicum kidnapping an Indian maiden, they could only follow at a distance.
2. Skanicum's primary diet consisted of roots. Primarily roots of the Thule or cat-tail plant, which they gathered, dried and stored. This is evidence of food caching.
3. Skanicum built fire using flint stone and often thought nothing of stealing hides from the Nespelem, which they used for bedding and to cover cave entrances.[92]

Dr. Fusch also cited by name the still-living descendants of Skanicum-Indian women. Why those offspring have not had their DNA evaluated is beyond me. Many of them are in advanced age and should have their DNA sequenced.

I probably learned more about behavior from Dr. Fusch's little self-published book, *The Stick Indians of the Colvilles, the Interaction of Large Bipedal Hominids with American Indians* than any previous book. Use of fire is also mentioned in the chapter on Native American and First Nation sightings.

Lewis and Clark Expedition

To illustrate how the Sasquatch was perceived in times gone by – here is an excerpt from the Journals of the Lewis and Clark Expedition:

August 20, 1805, Meriwether Lewis:

> In order to get to his relations, the first seven days we should be obliged to climb over steep and rocky mountains where we could find no game to kill nor anything to eat but roots such as a fierce and war like nation lived on whom he called the broken moccasins or moccasins with holes, and said inhabited those mountains and lived like the bear of other countries among the rocks and fed on roots or the flesh of such horses as they could take or steal from those who passed through their country.

The above mentioned entry was clarified in a secondary journal of the explorer William Clark on the same date. The phrase "moccasins with holes" was meant to be understood as "people who wear no moccasins." They lived in caves and were closer in kin to bears than people. They were considered war-like as they stayed to themselves and defended their rocky crags with fierce determination. The neighboring tribes feared them to the utmost and called them "the old ones" or "spirit beings of the mountains." In another reference they described the hairy ones as "men who lived like the bear."

The Indians of the 1800s were never quoted calling them animals or ape-like. The ape description came about with the influx of the European settlers. References to apes and ape-like descriptions are a white man's portrayal. The North American Indians would have no way of knowing anything about apes or what they looked like. To my knowledge, North America has no fossil record of apes.

NO RED EYES: Another interesting notation in my files is that I can find no credible published text where the early North American Aboriginals ever described a Sasquatch as having red eyes, an odor, or supernatural power. Descriptions of red eyes, or eyes that projected red, was a H-U-G-E trend during the 1970s, and then that particular description trailed off dramatically and is rarely reported today.

The popular image of the Sasquatch as raw meat eaters has been backed by only secondary evidence until now. There are instances where the use of fire has been recorded. But that doesn't mean all clans use fire; more likely, some do, others don't. It may only mean they are smarter in where they build fires to eliminate detection.

Along the lines of fire usage, it is interesting to note that the same was said of the Neanderthal people – that is, that they ate their meat raw. Even if the Sasquatch is found to be totally removed from the Neanderthal genome, we can still make primitive man comparisons on how the two were able to live wild with some success and survive winter conditions. New research shows:

> Neanderthals cooked and ate plants and vegetables, a new study of Neanderthal remains revealed. Research studies in the U.S. found grains of cooked plant matter in the teeth of Neanderthal remains.[93]

If the primitive Neanderthals cooked, I see no reason to think the Sasquatch couldn't use fire for warmth and cook meat, too. Again, I stress some do. Some don't because we have the 46-year-old Glen Thomas report of a Bigfoot family observed eating squirrels out from under a rock pile while they were still warm and in hibernation. A male, female, and young Sasquatch were observed searching a boulder pile, sniffing under rocks, and eventually locating seven hibernation rodents. The report read that the adults ate three rodents apiece (raw, still warm) and gave the youngster only one. Oregon field investigator James A. "Jim" Hewkin investigated the Glen Thomas story on-site with Jack Sullivan and Rip Lyttle. Joe Beelart wrote about it in his Bigfoot Journal.[94] All told, it was a fascinating story.

Just because we haven't uncovered evidence of continual fire use doesn't mean they don't use it. Some believe that field researchers are not working high enough altitude-wise. A new thought is that the Sasquatch might be holed up in the rocky crags of the highest elevations, and that is where field men should focus the hunt for remnant fire debris – if there is any to be found.

There are other theories that the Sasquatch live underground in some months of the year and they do use fire; it would explain how they eked out life in winter months in such as the Alaska, Yukon, the Northwest Territories, and the Arctic tundra where winter tracks have been found. But then there are those in research who insist the Sasquatch travel south in winter from such places even though we have winter tracks discovered year after year in ice and snow.

The earliest evidence of controlled fire was dated at around 300,000 years BC. Excavations dating from approximately 790,000 years ago suggest that H. erectus not only controlled fire but could ignite fires – if Homo erectus and the Neanderthals mastered fire[90] why not Sasquatch? Fire was probably first acquired by a lightning-caused blaze, then used as torchlight in dark caves and eventually to the warmth of cave fires for lighting and cooking.[91] Those individuals who think fire is beyond the mental acuity of the Sasquatch apparently cling to the old, "Sasquatch is a relic ape premise." But if the preliminary DNA, presumptive for Sasquatch holds up, and I'm confident that it will, then whatever early survival skills the ancients had certainly holds true. For me, it makes great sense they use fire.

Humans build campfires for cooking, for the light they provide, and to keep predators away. Animals only approach a fire within certain perimeters. The early settlers used fire to warm rocks to sleep on under a layer of dirt to keep from freezing. Fire is only used by those who can control the fear of building it and the emotions that correspond with working with live burning flames.

Neanderthals Cooked and Ate Vegetables | The Glen
Thomas Sighting | Sasquatch Investigations in the Pacific
Northwest

The Smokeless Dakota Fire

In my associations with Henry Moon, one of my guides into the Six Rivers Wilderness areas, I learned amazing things. Moon's Lakota teachings showed me how to build a "Dakota fire hole." It is a system of two side-by-side holes dug in the ground in such a way to start a fire beneath the earth, beneath ground levels, that creates a no-billowing-smoke fire. It is completely smokeless, passers-by won't see spiraling smoke, so it is an excellent way to build a fire if the need is to remain undetected. Moon's ancient Lakota people used the Dakota way of building a fire, so why not Sasquatch?

There is another reason for building the Dakota fire; it is an absolute must in high-wind areas to keep from setting the forest on fire. It is also the best way to cook in a cave to warm the area without choking on smoke in an enclosed area. If the Dakota fire is built correctly, there is no smoke. Each night on my trip with Moon, he would dig two post-hole-sized recesses side by side in the ground. He then created a short tunnel connecting them at the bottom, so the left fire could draw air through the right hole. The right hole is kept open and undisturbed as a draft-ventilator for the fire built in the left hole. The holes were about 14 inches deep side by side. Since the fire is below ground, it doesn't spark or make gray or black smoke - if it does, check the size of the air intake on the bottom - adjusting the connecting tunnel to either draw less air or more air to reach the desired effect. It takes a little practice, but it works. In the 1990s, of course, there were no YouTube instructional videos, but today, video lessons on how to build a smokeless fire are listed on YouTube.

When I heard that the Dakota fire was used in caves that kept the occupants warm yet not choking on the smoke, I asked Moon if he thought the Sasquatch people used fire. He glanced up with a look on his face that made me feel really stupid and answered, "of course they use fire, who do you think taught my people?"

"Why don't we ever locate tell-tale signs of their fires?" I asked. Moon responded, "…because their fires are below ground, when finished with the fire, they refill the fire hole back up with dirt, cover the remnants of the Dakota holes with leaf litter and nobody knows the fire was ever there." What he said made sense, but still wrestling with the idea, I asked, "what about cave fires?"

Then Moon told me, "you'll never find a fire pit in a cave; the white man doesn't scout deep enough into the cave. The hairy man lives deep, very deep in lava tubes and very deep caves that drip with water."

I still thought maybe a well-lit occupied cave might reveal black soot on the ceiling. But a fire built below ground, supposedly using the Dakota way to be smokeless, may not leave soot. Moon then said, "the Sasquatch never leaves things laying around; that is white man's sign, not the red man!"[*]

Once you learn how to build a smoke-free fire, it's a really slick trick, though I never quite got the hang of it. Once in four tries, I got it smokeless, and that was with Moon's assistance.

I have no case records to draw from that suggest Sasquatches cook their food except those documented by Dr. Ed Fusch in his work with the Spokane Indians. Yet there are many of us in research who have

---

[*]   Henry Moon (1997).

taken notice of the accounts where Native American and First Nation Canadian women have been reported, captured, and held for indeterminate amounts of time. Surely, those Native women knew how to use fire; the record is pretty clear on that issue. Captive women knew how to preserve meat by smoking it, which required fire or long periods of warm sunshine to dry it. See J.W. Burns account in the Sightings on Indian Reservations chapter.

None of these kidnapping capers by a Sasquatch mention whether or not the captive women used fire while in captivity, yet I strongly suspect they did do a fair amount of cooking. Staying warm and warding off predators would be the primary reason for fire use. It makes sense they did.

Who is more expert than Indian women at smoking salmon and venison for preservation and storage in winter months? Native Americans and First Nations people were proficient at herbal poultices, mustard-plaster, and the brewing of herbal concoctions in tea. Each required boiling water, and thus fire.

The making of bannock bread* cached and stored for the leaner winter months also required fire.

Looking back on ancient times, who taught who to use fire? The concept of fire use by Sasquatch is a hotly debated topic on discussion lists even today, and it's hard to think of it when the idea of Bigfoot as an ape clouds any other source of information.

Running with Coyotes

Apache County, Arizona, was the 2001 setting for a report from a land

---

* Bannock or bannock bread was traditionally a large, round, loaf-like bread that required baking. It was usually made from whole or ground barley, acorn, wheat, or oat, often combined with elk or moose lard and laced with local berries that varied according to region. Earliest records show it was baked over heated stones in open fires and cached for winter use.

surveyor working in the north of that county when he heard close-by a pack of coyotes yapping their heads off.

The yapping came from under an overhang where he set his transit up to measure a specific area. Breaking for lunch, the surveyor wandered over to the area where the yapping had been loudest and was startled to see a tall reddish-black haired Bigfoot tearing apart a jackrabbit, tossing parts of it out to a pack of hungry coyotes. He described the creature as having a thick brow-ridge but a body like a man, stout, well built. He was covered in hair with cockleburs, pine gum and pine needles. The Bigfoot realized he was being observed when the surveyor dropped his metal lunch bucket. The creature looked at him, turned, and walked off with the coyotes giving chase. That story ranked right up there with the other strange happenings.

Four years prior to the Apache County filing, a Bigfoot coyote report was posted on one of the discussion lists. A man with the screen name "Hoganomics" posted a sighting that occurred south of Seguin, Texas, not far from Meadow Lake. Guadalupe County is not particularly noted for Bigfoot reports, but this one was interesting in that this "Hoganomics" person said the creature was eastbound across Loch Lane, heading into the morning sun towards the Meadow Lake region. The Bigfoot, he said, was accompanied by no less than six coyotes; two leading the way and the rest tagging along behind the Bigfoot. A silhouette against the blinding sun, the informant could not give descriptive details of the Bigfoot other than it was big and the coyotes seemed to be adult size (he clarified that they sounded like coyotes, but some could have been dogs trailing after the Bigfoot). The witness believed that the Sasquatch would catch, kill deer, and leave the carcass behind for the coyotes to keep them from nosily trailing behind him.

A more recent report that included coyotes came from Thomas Matuski in California. Here is a portion of that case file:

I had a strange encounter in Southern California back in 1991. I had never heard of a Bigfoot story from that area so me and my two friends decided to keep it to ourselves. I was looking at your site and saw that there were two other encounters in the area where ours took place. It would have been in the area of Barton Flats, off Highway 26 near Big Bear Mountain in San Bernardino County. I want to be clear - we didn't see the creature. We heard two legs walking in front of our tent from about 200 feet, or 6 or 7 yards away, along with more than a dozen coyotes. This thing sounded like it had a long stride to it and was very heavy in weight. My business partner, myself, and one employee lay paralyzed from the fear of not having anyone to help us and no means of defending ourselves. I had never heard of a Bigfoot traveling with coyotes before, until I met a man from the Puyallup, Washington area that said he had seen one in his area growing up that traveled with coyotes. This took me aback a bit, as I had not told him of our story and had only known him for a short time. With coyotes sniffing at our tent and a large creature in front of the camp site, you can imagine our state of mind.[*]

Chehalis Sounds Identified as Coyotes

The next entry is important because many screams or lengthy howls attributed to the Sasquatch may have roots in the vocalization of energized and excited coyote packs. The other suspect is the timber wolf. Alone in the dark at night, unarmed and frightened to death, the sounds we hear are often misinterpreted. Fear heavily influences how we perceive noises and how our brain decodes auditory messages. The last notation concerning coyotes and the noisy vocalizations attributed to the Sasquatch people came from Gerry Matthews and Thomas Steenburg on April 5, 2006.

Steenburg and Matthews were out on the Chehalis Harrison River flats area early one morning doing follow-up investigative work on possible

---

[*] Thomas Matuski (2011).

Sasquatch activity in the immediate area. At 9:30 a.m. while exploring along the edge of the bush-line, both men were astounded to hear the familiar cries called the "Chehalis Sounds" emanating from a pair of coyotes.

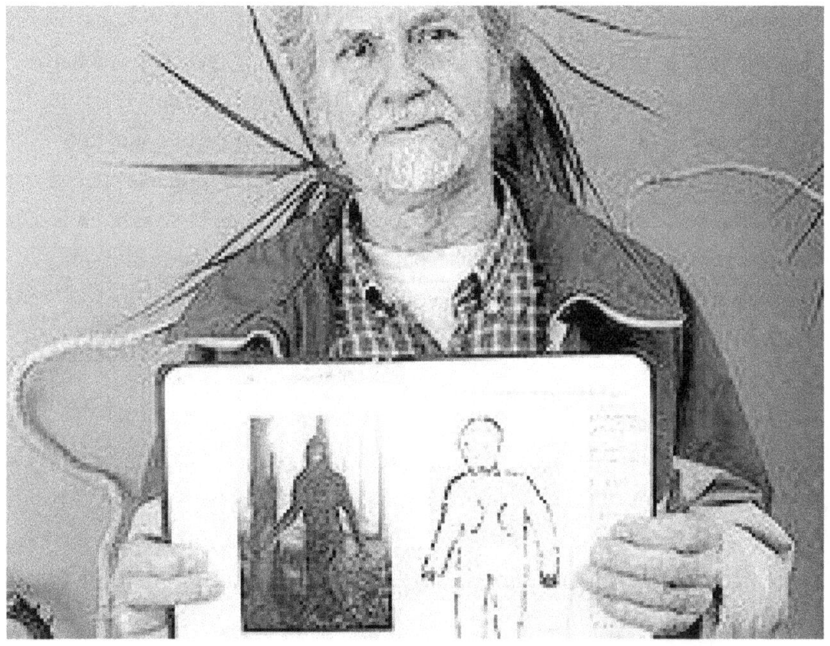

Nobody was more surprised and disappointed by what we witnessed on the flats yesterday than Gerry and me. I have lived with coyotes around all my life and during that time I never heard one utter a sound like what we saw and heard April 5th, 2006, 09:30 a.m.

It appears to be a rarely heard sound which the animals use to locate each other over distances. When the second coyote appeared, the one making the sounds changed back to the more familiar yip type call I have heard a thousand times before. We both watched as the two animals ran along the edge of the flats around the trailer park and headed toward the main road which was about half a mile to the west of our position. The sounds which Gerry and I heard were what our witnesses recorded and the same sounds which have had folks in the campground nervous of walking outside at night. The same sounds which are so similar to other alleged Sasquatch recordings made over the last 30 years from the Klamath River in Northern California to southwest B.C. Now, this does not mean that Sasquatch are not around in this area, of course. Coyotes are not an explanation to the many sighting reports and footprint findings in this heart of Sasquatch country since the coming of the white man and they may not account for the entire strange animal cries heard around here over the years. It just gave us an answer to the particular sounds which have come to be known as the 'Chehalis recordings', which at the same time has put the similar recordings over the last 30 years into question. But research is research and when the evidence points to an answer other than the Sasquatch, we must just accept the facts and carry on with the quest.*

Brazen Confrontation: Adult

Swan River Winnipeg man Archie Motkaluk waited fifty-one years to talk about his 1960 face-to-face encounter with a Sasquatch. Archie went to visit his parent's farm near Renwer, Manitoba (south east of Swan River). While he was there, Motkaluk took a team of horses, pulling a sleigh to chop some wood three miles into the bush in the back of his parent's farm. Pulling from his stored, handwritten notes and sketches, Motkaluk said the female stood a mere eight feet away from him in the deep bush where he had been chopping deadfall for firewood. With horse and sled tied to a nearby bush, axe in hand, Mr. Motkaluk busied himself chopping wood when suddenly, across a clearing, he saw what he described as a "man" coming towards him. Eventually, he realized it was a Sasquatch, and a female, who brazenly confronted Motkaluk in a manner that left him paralyzed with fear and frozen in place. The behavior of the brazen female is quite unusual but not unheard of in the data. Confrontations are usually recorded as males, not females; her manner of conduct is most unusual. The

---

* Thomas Steenburg (2006).

tendency is for them to walk off into the thick brush and be gone on their way. Eventually, this one did.[95]

Manitoba has a long history of Sasquatch sightings documented as far back as the 1700s, but none of the witnesses were actually confronted within eight feet by a female Sasquatch.

Winnipeg Man Claims Sasquatch Sightings

Oldest Publications Referring to the Sasquatch

Referring to the creature in Lake of the Woods, Manitoba, Canada: The London Times January 4, 1784:

> There is lately arrived in France from America, a wild man, who was caught in the woods 200 miles back from Lake of the Woods by a party of Indians. They had seen him several times but he was so swift of foot that they could by no means get up with him. He is near seven feet high, covered with hair but has little appearance of understanding and is remarkably sullen and subdued. When he was taken, half a bear was found lying by him whom he had just killed.

The article is interesting in that not much has changed in physical description in the nearly 230 years that have passed. What is different is that the Sasquatch was apparently easily subdued, which is a dramatic notion to contemplate in today's research. We don't seem to be able to photograph them well, much less capture one of them. There are endless discussions on camera avoidance and blurred photographs, some of which boggle the mind. The best descriptions are from the recollections of men who have shot and killed them from a distance; those surpass even the best photographic offerings. The odd part is that while photographing them seems to elude the best woodsman, finding and photographing their spoor and footprints works quite well.

Other area sightings of the Sasquatch occurred near Easterville in 1968 and 1970, one of them reported by the local school's principal. More recently, the residents of the remote community of Norway House were thrilled about a two-minute, 49-second piece of videotape shot by ferry operator Bobby Clarke in April of 2005. Vancouver author Christopher L. Murphy thought Clarke's Norway House a highly credible sighting, albeit distant. Murphy remarked that there were thirty-five other sightings listed in Manitoba. The most recent sighting occurred in March of 2007 near Peguis, Manitoba.[96]

Zoologist Doubts Bigfoot Claim

Brazen Confrontation Behavior: Children

Dr. Henner Fahrenbach shared a report he investigated in Grays Harbor County, Washington. The interesting behavior in his report was a sort of chase/following/shadowing of two young boys. Kirk and Kelly arrived back in their hometown of Satsop late at night after attending a baseball game. They were walking along East Satsop Road in the vicinity of Stevens Road when they heard a noise behind them in the dark. At first, they thought the figure was a road sign, but they took off running anyway, and the road sign followed them, keeping up with them but not overtaking the boys. The two scared youngsters hurtled the first split-rail fence that lined the yard of the only house before their own. They breathlessly pounded on the door, screaming for help; a woman answered, recognized the boys as neighbors, and let them in. The boys excitedly told the woman that something was after them. The woman exclaimed, "oh, there are no such things as monsters," as she stepped out onto her porch. Dr. Fahrenbach said in his email that by this time the Sasquatch had stepped over the split-rail fence and was standing in the woman's yard. She exclaimed, "OH GOD, THERE IS!" and bolted back into the house and slammed the door.

Teens Returning From Baseball Game Were Chased by
Bigfoot

Apparently, the Sasquatch followed the boys down the road and into the woman's yard with intent of some kind or another. In fact, it came within twelve feet of the front door. Looking out the front door window, they said the Sasquatch stayed in the yard, briefly looked around, and then stepped back over the fence and walked across the road. Another neighbor, Wayne Moore, subsequently found footprints that measured 17 inches in length, 8 inches wide at the ball, and 4 inches at the heel. He tracked the footprints down river where it apparently entered the water.[97] It's hard to know what the Bigfoot had in mind for those two boys, but its behavior was worrisome and certainly brazen even after they entered the house.

Exacting Revenge

In 1990, the family of 54-year-old Colette Brooshaun summered at their Lake Pepin cottage in the Old Frontenac District near Red Wing, Minnesota.

One warm afternoon, she set a portable radio on the railing and then stretched out on a cot in the shady part of the sunny porch to doze and listen to music. She was awakened by something gently massaging her foot. Sitting up, she described being startled seeing a large 8-foot tall red-haired Cee-ha-tonka* pulling/massaging on her ankles and leg. Unable to fight off the creature, Brooshaun said she kicked and screamed for help. The men came rushing out from the cabin, causing the creature to "bellow a horrific sound that vibrated in our chests." The woman's husband, Jacques, fired a 12-gauge shotgun in the face of the monster, and it fell backward. His shot hit it upwards through the upper neck, under the chin, nearly decapitating the creature.

The original email was extremely graphic and disturbing. The report indicated that the men hurriedly buried the monster alongside a wooden bridge and stacked a cord of wood over the grave. The incident was over.

The following summer, upon returning to the cottage, the Brooshaun's discovered the woodpile strewn about the property and the grave dug up. The support beams to the wooden back porch were on the ground, and the wood-shingled canopy was severely drooping over the remaining stanchion that supported the porch roofing. The screen door

---

* The term, Cee-ha-tonka translates as 'the big man' in Red Wing, Minnesota, where there are four Dakota Sioux communities; one is in Prairie Island, near Red Wing, MN. That region also has seven Anishinaabe Reservations plus Chippewa and Ojibwe people.

According to Jim Anderson of the Republican Eagle in Red Wing, there is a modern-day, account of a Native American named Running Wolf who was sitting in his living room at 9:30 p.m. when his dogs began barking. Looking through the window, Running Wolf saw a big shadow/man-like shape. He thought someone was messing with his car. When he went out to check, he found two 18-inch human-like footprints in his driveway. One became obscured in harder soil, but the other had five distinct toes. The footprints belonged to the Sasquatch-like Cee-ha-tonka; "the man with big feet."

was torn off and thrown twenty feet from the porch. A family friend, Nor Le Ferrette, who was along on that trip, said there were 19-inch footprints around the yard. He felt they were being watched, was deeply uncomfortable, and suggested the family leave. They have not been back.

Le Ferrette hired a construction crew to repair the cabin. After two days on the job, the carpenters quit and told Le Ferrette to hire someone else. This time, Le Ferrette hired a roofer/carpenter from Hastings, Minnesota, to finish the job and put them up in the cabin over a holiday weekend so they wouldn't have to travel to and from Hastings. Le Ferrette stayed with the workers and kept his shotgun within reach until the job was completed – the men were paid and on their way. Le Ferrette closed the cabin for the season, including also the main breaker box before putting antifreeze in the drain pipes. Finished, he drove to St. Paul for the Christmas holiday. Ten days later, the fire department phoned to inform the family that the cabin had burned to the ground. The only thing left standing was the wooden bridge where the Bigfoot had been laid to rest under a cord of firewood earlier that year.

It should probably be noted that if the above story was a case of exacting revenge for wrongful death on Bigfoot kinfolk, the Bigfoot was certainly fully capable and had unusual knowledge. Little was understood about that fire because the cabin was built five and a quarter miles off the beaten path behind locked road/property gates. There were no neighbors or river access. With the house shut down for the winter months, it was impossible to determine how arson could have occurred. The Bigfoot must have known how to either set fires, or carry fire to the cabin from somewhere else. It was a puzzling story. [*]

Cee-Ha-Tonka Rites of Passage

There is a Sioux legend about the Cee-ha-tonka that dates back to the

---

[*] Leslie Each.

Franciscan priests in the 1600s, which says they have a test to pass going into adulthood, and they must jump in front of a hairless man on the trail and wave their hands wildly in front of the human's face. If the hairless human runs off frightened, the Cee-ha-tonka then becomes a man. If not, he must try again until they succeed – it is the male Cee-ha-tonka's rite of passage. According to the legend, when the Cee-ha-tonka giants become men, they leave their mother and father and strike out on their own to find a woman and start a family. Sometimes, they steal Indian maidens and carry them to distant places in the mountains, other times they steal children to raise as their own.[*]

Apparently, there are no rules pertaining to kidnapping in the social structure of the Sasquatch. What's theirs is theirs; what is ours is also theirs. Some of them have learned, however, that the hairless man will quickly stop unacceptable behavior with a rifle. It's clear a large percentage of them understand the hunter's rifle. The Sasquatch does not regard boundaries, borders, or ownerships unless they are their own. I think it wrong to romanticize the Sasquatch; they are a walking mass of power if you're not armed. I am not in favor of shooting them, but I will defend me and mine, and I do understand those who do likewise.

Live Like Wild Dogs

A woman from another Sioux community, Leslie Each, said these "people of hair live like wild dogs in the mountain escarpments and are fiercely protective of their family and the areas surrounding their dwellings. Often the juveniles will shadow humans or sometimes give chase. It is a game the people of hair play with humans – it gives them pleasure to chase and scare off the white man."[†]

I told Leslie that their scare tactics work quite well and is a very effec-

---

[*] Leslie Each.
[†] Leslie Each, personal correspondence.

tive game. To which Leslie added, "...even the grizzly is smart enough to run from them."

Breaking and Entering

Here is a story describing a totally unanticipated behavior and a home-owner's worst nightmare. This story is the only account of its kind that speaks to daring behavior by a Sasquatch who broke in and helped himself to the family's moose meat dinner. I imagine hunger drives them to do such things in settings like this one, so far north in what must be polar bear country. Here is that account:

The story was told to me by my brother-in-law who is Métis. The Métis are Canadian Aboriginals descended from mixed European and First Nations parentage. My brother-in-law's mother, Isabelle, is roughly 75 years old. Nobody knows her age for sure because she was born deep in the bush in Northern Saskatchewan not far from the Northwest Territory line. Isabelle cannot read or write and is not worldly; she was 12-years old before she even saw an automobile. She does, however, have one of the best stories about Bigfoot I have ever heard told.

She says one night when she was a little girl, her very large family were settled into their tiny shack. She described a huge hairy man who suddenly threw open the door and came inside. Immediately, the entire family ran into the corner of the room and huddled under blankets scared to death. They sat there like that while the Sasquatch helped himself to the moose meat, eating all of it and then he left. She said that to this day, she can still hear its teeth gnashing away as it ate the meat, a horrifying sound. You have to understand that she still has no idea what a Bigfoot is to this day. To her, it's just a scary incident of her childhood. The next day, her father went to the nearest RCMP post [Royal Canadian Mounted Police] and brought back the "redcoats" as she calls them. They checked out all around the cabin, found footprints and told them that they should move and not come back because they figured that whatever it was would come back. They moved that day and never lived in the deep bush again.[98]

Bigfoot Breaks Into House and Accosts Homeowner: The "Boone County Yowler"

In 1995, I received an old newspaper item. The Kentucky Post published a 1980 piece headlined *Night time Yowlers Reported in Boone County*.

> The Jones family encountered a 4-foot tall, flat-faced, broad shouldered creature covered with black hair, thought to most probably be a young male. It shook their door and caused much alarm. It was accosted by the man of the house and each time it ran away making its escape by jumping into the nearby Ohio River. Police investigations revealed nothing other than the area had a long history of Bigfoot sightings.[99]

There appears to be a history of infrequent breaking and entering homes, cabins, and an occasional tent. If not out of curiosity, the intent perceived by the witness is deliberate; perhaps motivated by extreme hunger. The behavior of jiggling doorknobs, screen doors and unzipping campers' tents is not new. Over time, other authors have recorded such behavior.

Attempted Break-in

There was an old Seattle Times article by Don Hannula that Warren Thompson of the Bay Area Group sent me in 2001. It was dated November 15, 1975, and concerned the breaking into a home on the Lummi Nation Indian Reserve in Whatcom County, Washington State.

The story has been featured prominently on television documentaries and in newspaper accounts where in the ancient Lummi language, Ts'emekwes is the tribal name for a Sasquatch-like life form. Modern members of the Lummi Nation use Boq, Bukwis, and Bigfoot as the term for hairy life forms. I fully intended to place the report in the Native American section of this book but instead elected to place it here because of the attempted "breaking and entering" behavior outlined in the narrative.

On the night of October 23, 1975, Lummi Police Sgt. Ken Cooper was called to the residence of 78-year-old Emma Smith. She reported a Bigfoot attempting to break into her home. Terrorized, she had fled. Sgt. Cooper found the plastic on a storm door torn and the door's wooden frame splintered. In addition, Sgt. Cooper found boards torn from a nearby smokehouse but he could not find the creature, nor any sign of a person. He returned to the residence around 2:30 a.m. shining the spotlight from his patrol car into the woods. He found a group of seven people already there with their own spotlights set directly on a huge seven-and-a-half foot (2.3m) tall "hair creature"— a bigfoot. Cooper aimed his 12-gauge shotgun at the creature but, concerned that it could be a human in a costume, yelled, "if there's somebody just fooling around you better knock it off because we have weapons." The creature just crouched down (crouching down is a frequently reported behavior). As Sgt. Ken Cooper stepped forward, the creature lowered himself even further until only his head was showing above the brush. For 20 minutes, Sgt. Cooper and the other people stared down the crouching "hairy creature" until they heard noises in the brush to their right and then they believed there were more of the big creatures lurking just out of flashlight range. At that point, Cooper decided it was time to leave the scene and ushered everyone away.

The next morning around dawn Cooper returned to the area and found bare footprints in the frost-covered ground. He measured the footprints. They were 18-inches (45 cm) long and 7-inches (17 cm) wide. Over the coming weeks, the Lummi Tribal Police received over 100 reports of sightings of Bigfoot creatures. Sgt. Cooper saw the Bigfoot two more times shortly after his first initial encounter.

This particular Sasquatch clan had the potential for being dangerous. They were blamed for the deaths of three dogs and a ghastly neck wound on a horse that required 16 stitches. "There are no people on the road at night now," Cooper told reporters and most of those people did not believe the first reports. When they saw the Sasquatch's footprints or heard it scream then they changed their minds.

Sgt. Cooper said so many people were foolishly out chasing the Sasquatch with guns and such that the Lummi Tribal Council voted to outlaw shooting the creature. We get reports every other day.[100]

Now It's Sasquatch vs. the Indians

Unfriendly Behavior

In Pennsylvania, May 1988, at approximately 11 p.m., while preparing to do some "lantern fishing" at a place called Sleepy Hollow, where the bridge goes across the Loyalhanna Creek, a man saw a large, strange, foul-smelling creature that he said would make an extra-large gorilla "look like a small chimpanzee." The witness said he was about to light his lantern when he "heard a scuffling racket on the hillside in the woods about 25-feet away."

In the beam of his "three-cell spotlight" the creature appeared to have red-brown hair and large fiery eyes that glowed orange like the eyes of a bear. Convinced the creature was approaching him in an unfriendly manner, the man ran to his car and left, but not before seeing the creature in the headlights. The witness was a hunter-tracker with 50-years of live trap experience. He said it definitely wasn't a bear or gorilla. Ligonier is located in Westmoreland County southwest of Johnstown between Greensburg and Laughlin Town along US Highway 30 near Laurel Mountain State Park in Pennsylvania.[101]

Ligonier, Westmoreland County, Pennsylvania

Sad and Nonaggressive

The intrigue of a description sometimes says more about the informant than the Sasquatch. Charles Justin Hall of Jackson County, West Virginia, wrote me in March of 2000. Hall wrote that he'd been hunting when, in his tree stand 30-feet off the ground, he caught a glimpse of Bigfoot.

I was becoming bored when something began rustling leaves. What I saw was three deer followed by a large humanoid around 7-feet tall, hair covered except for the face. It had a sunken nose, reddish brown eyes with yellowish teeth and a stocky build. Why do I know these details? I put my Golden Eagle Scope up on my gun at a distance of about 100-yards and frankly was about to squeeze the trigger when I got a very good look at this thing. What stopped me from shooting it was the creature looked sad and nonaggressive. Ordinarily that wouldn't stop me, but I was scared like hell. It wasn't until I yelled as loud as I could to take off your mask or I'm going to shoot that I realized what it was; but the creature just looked at me and growled. I watched him through my rifle's scope the whole time...nearly paralyzed with fear. At the same time, the Bigfoot turned and bolted. It ran extremely fast for its size.[102]

In January 2012, The Rt Rev'd Aaron Melhorn read Hall's account and wrote the following:

Re: Charles Justin Hall's story: I went to the Roane Jackson Tech School in '81 & '82 - the school is in Frozen Camp. I can attest to the fact that there is something out there because I heard screams while at the school that I've never heard before. I have spent time in the West Virginia woods. I cannot identify the screams.[*]

Jackson County Hunting Incident

Sasquatch Cripple-Foot Frolicking

Mike Lowery, a writer for Yahoo, reported an amazing account describing how he and a companion traced and examined Sasquatch tracks made by two adult Bigfoot and one juvenile found near La Queva Creek, Glorieta, New Mexico. The juvenile tracks were reported to be 10 x 4 and were splayed, reminiscent of the baby Sasquatch snow tracks found in British Columbia by Randy and Ray Brisson in 2009. Lowery said one adult track measured 17 x 6, 3-inches deep in the mud. The other adult track was only 14 x 5, with the right foot imprint showing "severe heel trauma and was curved inward,

----

[*] E. A. Melhorn, Ripley, West Virginia.

sickle-like." The shape of that track presented itself consistently over the range they examined.

Three interesting points are clear in this report. One is the 17-inch track, its size, and the fact that it sunk three inches deep, which suggests its mammoth size. Second, the cripple foot described is a stark reminder of the 1,089 cripple Bossburg, Washington, tracks of 1969, which was covered in Don Hunter and Rene Dahinden's *Sasquatch*.[103]

Finally, the determination that the three distinctly different sets of tracks suggested "playing and frolicking" made this report unique and a previously unreported family behavior – at least in my files. Here is a portion of that reference published in June 2011:

> Five distinct areas of grouping were found, two behind large trees, one behind an earthen embankment, and one in a brushy ravine. The individual leaving the largest prints was consistently separated from the other apparent adult and juvenile in these groupings by about twenty feet and consistently in a forward position, uphill from the other two. In two distinct, open areas, evidence of "playing" or "frolicking" was evidenced by the confused nature and large number of prints left by the apparent juvenile member of the group. In these areas, slipping and sliding is apparent in the distortion of the prints. In these groupings, the smaller apparent adult was positioned in a stationary position facing the large grouping of "frolic" prints left by the apparent juvenile. The larger apparent adult left prints facing away from the other two individuals approximately twenty to thirty feet away and uphill from this group.
>
> No conclusions can be drawn from the evidence in the form of footprint trails through the woods of the Sangre De Christo Mountains in Northern New Mexico other than something heavy with huge humanlike bare feet left prints over a large area in the vicinity of La Queva Creek in Glorieta, New Mexico. No evidence seems to exist in the logs of the New Mexico State Police even though numerous residents of the area related that two State Police cars were parked by the side of the

La Queva Creek Road for several hours on or about the afternoon of June 10th in the same area as the author and his companion found the series of footprints described here.[104]

The Bossburg, Washington (Cripple) Tracks | Sasquatch Family Group Footprints Reported and Examined in Northern New Mexico

Facial Expressions of Another Cripple Noted

Sasquatch Hand and Foot Casts from the same creature 18 miles NE of Walla Walla by Roger Thornton January 29, 1992. The hand is 12 inches wide X 10 inches long and the footprint was 6 inches wide X 14.5 inches long.

I think of all the people attracted to this subject that have come and gone, I miss Vance Orchard the most. His research had a profound effect on me in many ways, and he was a magnificent human being. The octogenarian had an amazing knack for tracking down some of the best stories in and around the Blue Mountains of Washington State, and he shared them freely.

This next story happened closer to Dixie, Washington, down Highway 12, some ten miles east of Walla Walla. For some reason, I didn't record the month or day, but the year Vance sent me his copy and published this story was 2001.

Vance wrote the story himself after the interview; his narrative began like this:

A most unique interview was done the other day when my friend and former game warden Bill Laughery and I met up with the man who had a long, long look at a Sasquatch; up close. The distance separating man and beast was close enough that features and expressions on the Bigfoot's face were plain for the observer. Laughery heard of the man's encounter and convinced him to tell his story. Convincing the man to meet us on the Black-Snake Ridge Road was not easy but he finally consented. "But no name please," the man insisted, recounting some of the ridicule he had received when a story of his encounter leaked to his "buddies."

So, we've gone along with that and he suggested the nickname of "Jack the Logger." What Jack had to say about the Bigfoot he met on the mountain road with a truckload of logs makes for one of the better Bigfoot stories I've recorded.

For Jack, his trip that afternoon off the mountain, heading towards Dixie, was to prove the highlight of some 45 years trucking logs. Jack probably knows more about Black Snake and Biscuit Ridges than most people. He said he makes two or three trips per day when he's hauling logs and this accounts for many days when he has to put on chains at the top, and take them off when he drove below the snowline.

Jack first spotted the Bigfoot on an open slope some three fourths of a mile away, but at the time he didn't realize what the moving object was. Jack says he estimated about where on the road he would likely cross its path. "All that time, I'm wondering what kind of animal it was," he said. "It never entered my mind that it was going to be a Bigfoot." As his rig came into the curve at the end of a long grade in the road, the two met, with only about 40-45 yards separating them.

"As I got there and saw him," Jack said, "I stopped my truck and shut off the motor. He was standing there in a heavy, tufted grassy area, just standing and looking at me. We both eyeballed each other real good. I was close enough I could see his facial expressions … he didn't look like an ape in the face, more like man features but hairy in the face. I would say he had a nose but not much else. The skin was black and his hair color was like this (and he pulls a smoky-blue ski hat out from his truck cab). He was about this color and had gray hairs showing like an old dog will get around his nose. Anyway, while he was standing there, the expression on his face changed three or four times. That led me to believe that man may not be the only animal that has reasoning. This old boy was thinking and every time he'd go to a different train of thought, his expression would change."

Bill asked if Jack could see its eyes.

"I wasn't really interested in that," Jack said.

"I was looking at the width of his shoulders and his height, wondering what the hell was going to happen."

"How wide was the Bigfoot?"

"He was a good yard or more through the shoulders and I've had people tell me how a Bigfoot is about eight foot tall … well, this dude was taller than eight feet and closer to nine feet tall. When you're that close it's no problem to figure out how big it was. And, he never made any effort to run from me. He never acted like he was scared … I sure know he wasn't scared of ME … not a bit! Then he turned and walked along this way (Jack demonstrated a limping gait) like something was wrong with one leg, like he had an old injury or someone had shot him. Then he stopped, turned, and looked at me for another full minute before he left; didn't run … he just walked over to the edge of the brush that dropped off steeply into the Dry Creek north fork. There was no getting around it, this wasn't any man-made object or a man dressed up, there isn't a man in this county big enough to wear that suit."

Jack said this sighting was his first Bigfoot encounter, although several years before he saw something that he thought was a bear standing up… and always thought it was a Bigfoot but could find no sign.

"But this time, it's different… absolutely no doubt about it. I would pull $50 out of my own pocket though, if one of you guys could have been there with me." Jack told us more about his initial reluctance to come forth with a report of what he'd encountered nearly two years ago.

"I didn't know whether to say anything to anyone about this … you know? If I'd gone downtown and told the guys I saw a Bigfoot, they'd laugh me clear out of the place. I told my wife about it and she kind of had her doubts about it for a while, but she knew I wasn't going to come in with some kind of cock-and-bull story to take a ridiculing over.

"But, I don't really care what people think … I just didn't talk about it, except with someone who has seen a Bigfoot or is a serious believer. They can believe what they want, but I'm the one who knows what I saw … they can say there is no such thing but they don't have anything to back that up and I do. This thing was the closest to a real human than anything I've seen on television or real life… his body is proportioned more to a human than anything I've ever seen. He's not like an ape. This dude walked like a man and somehow acts like a man. He walked like he was crippled in the right leg or foot. I'll tell you this much, too; I've never seen anything like it, before or since. He's a one-of-a-kind for me!"

So, the interview ended that sunny day on Blacksnake Ridge in the Blue Mountains of Washington State. Jack climbed into the cab of his log truck and headed into the timber country for his second trip of the day. As he stepped into the cab, I heard him shout back to us. "Keep your eyes open, kids. At least there are two of you … you can back up each other's stories."[105]

A Long, Long Look at a Bigfoot!

Chasing Cars and a Motorbike

Al Hodgson told this story regarding a chasing behavior in the mountains north of Bluff Creek, Humboldt County, California, on videotape and later through email.

While on a hunting trip, a Willow Creek resident was sitting on an old log landing, high up on a mountaintop, where she could get a full view of the winding switch-back road where they were camped. She was sitting in her lawn chair, watching down the road when from around the bend coming up the road towards her was her son on his motorbike, and it was running full out. Running behind his motorbike was a juvenile Bigfoot giving chase until he got close to the woman, and then it apparently veered off into the bush.

The woman didn't say how close the Bigfoot got to the motorbike, but it came close enough to her to see the features on the creature's face. When her son reached camp, she asked him if he wasn't afraid of the Bigfoot chasing him up the hill, and the kid didn't even know the Bigfoot was behind him. Later, they found Bigfoot tracks. Al Hodgson said he suspected the Sasquatch was a juvenile and just having fun. This behavior is consistent with Sasquatches chasing kids on bicycles, not really trying to catch them but just having good-natured fun.[106]

At one time, it seemed like I'd spent a lifetime burning up the desert roads between Southern California and Dallas, Texas. I've never been one to drive the desert highway at posted speeds. I figure the desert is the desert, and the best way to get through the monotonous drive is to get across it as fast as my car will go; not always healthy, but it's the way I made the crossings.

In the course of those trips, I met a Highway Patrolman who, for whatever reason, always seemed to be lurking in the desert of Arizona no matter the time of day I drove through or in what car. I could always count on him saying, "Oh geez, not you again," and I would echo the same line back at him. We laughed, but I always got a ticket for speeding; it doesn't speak well for talking my way out of delicate situations, or maybe it was because I called him Phantom of the Highway that irritated him – so much for my crime record.

In the course of one of those desert trips, and at 109 degrees Fahrenheit that day, the highway patrolman told me about an incident he had overheard in 1992. One of his co-workers stopped a frantic woman in a white cowgirl hat driving erratically on a Moped near Flagstaff, Arizona. He hit the lights, pulled her over, and found the woman near hysterics. She told him she was running away from an apparition with the likeness of a hairy man; she claimed the beast chased her and twice pushed the back end of her Moped sideways before veering off the road and into the trees. Noting how disturbed she was, he sat with her for an indeterminate length of time and finally agreed to follow her home, staying behind her until she pulled into her garage. In the course of that exchange with the woman, she told him the creature towered over her moped and that he glided along effortlessly, and yes, she passed a breathalyzer test.

The fascinating part of that story to me was how fast the Sasquatch was running. I am told that Mopeds and some motor scooters generally run wide open at 30mph or less; apparently, the speed is factory-set on the Mopeds. If the hairy man she talked about was keeping up with her, he must have been doing roughly 30mph, and that is the only reference I've heard as to how fast the Sasquatch might be able to run. Deer have been clocked running full out at 40 miles per hour; able to jump 9-foot fences, and swim 13 miles in a given hour. The great apes, on average, run full out at speeds of 20-24mph on all fours, but I dislike comparing to the great apes since the physical anatomy is different between humans and non-human primates.

Bluff Creak, Humboldt County, California

Bowlegged Bigfoot Chases Truck

This 2007 story involved a woman named Evelyn and her 15-year-old daughter who happened to be driving home after picking up pizza for dinner. Both women were shocked out of their minds when a Bigfoot covered with black hair ran across the road between Hardy and Ravenden in Sharp County, Arkansas.

The creature squatted down, and when the vehicle neared the creature, it made eye contact with the ladies in the car. The creature then jumped up, and either gave chase or ran alongside her truck.

> I was concerned it would jump in my truck bed, but it didn't - instead it turned, swerved off and left the road. It was not an adult but a short Bigfoot and it was bowlegged. [107]

Arkansas isn't the only state to report a bowlegged Sasquatch. Eleven years earlier, a "light-colored" Sasquatch was seen crossing the Nehalem Highway, Route 202 in Clatsop County, Oregon, in 1996. I tucked the report away and literally forgot about it because I didn't believe it all those years ago. Amazing how one's thinking changes over time. I have vague recollections of another bowlegged Bigfoot report from Ohio, but I was unable to locate the source.

County Road 60 in the Bankhead National Forest was the sighting of another bowlegged juvenile Sasquatch reported in 1996 by a maintenance man named Orville from Haleyville, Alabama. "That feller just come out like a bar was on its tail then commences to run across the road and hurls himself over the railing and into the creek; that was that."

Witness Sees Bowlegged Bigfoot Run Alongside Her Truck

Bigfoot Chasing Logging Truck

Prince George, B.C., Canadian Bigfoot investigator, the late Leo Selzer, had a chase story that occurred only twelve miles from where he lived.

Back about 15 years ago, a logging truck driver was coming out of the bush with a full load of fresh-cut logs. The road was fine gravel and a bit rough so he was driving slowly. At about 25-30mph something caught the driver's attention in his side-door mirror. He couldn't believe what he was looking at so he stuck his head out the open window and clearly saw a seven foot-plus tall Sasquatch running alongside his truck close to the driver's door. When their eyes met, the

Sasquatch veered off the road and into the bush.*

Leo Selzer passed away suddenly on May 23, 2012. Research lost a dedicated Bigfoot devotee that day and his untimely death shocked us all. Leo freely shared his personal experience tracking the Sasquatch of Prince George, British Columbia, and we spent many hours brainstorming Bigfoot behavior. I'll miss Leo and those conversations.

Chases Snowmobile

Snowmobile riders in 2001 reported Bigfoot tracks in the snow after they doubled back to the safety of The Lodge in Pitkin County, Colorado. The Bigfoot tracks eerily followed the snowmobile treads and then swerved off into the big timber where snow was too deep to follow, the trail unknown. The length of the snowmobile measured 72-inches, and the distance between the barefooted tracks in the snow was just short of that measurement. The fresh tracks were the length of a four-cup thermos bottle, which was what they used to measure it.

None of the trail riders saw what made the tracks, but all of them noted that the track-maker was heavy enough to hard-pack the inside of the track imprint. All the tracks were barefooted with 5 toes, "…the maker of the tracks was not wearing shoes, boots or snow shoes. Whatever it was, it had TOES!"

Normally, a line of Sasquatch tracks is reported to be straight, not off-set left-right, left-right like our footprints would be. In this case, however, the report states that the pathway or trail of the Bigfoot had off-set imprints. I thought that was atypical because there are few other reports of "off-set" Sasquatch tracks, especially in snow. It may be important to remember this report for the value of the "off-set, left-right" track imprint with stride lengths just under the length of a 72" snowmobile. Much notice has been given to the frequently photographed straight line of tracks, which never made much sense to

---

* Leo Selzer, (2012).

me considering the biomechanics of human mobility, and I do believe the Sasquatch is human.

Chases Quad-Runner

The same sort of situation occurred in the Big Horn Mountains of Wyoming in 2005. Peter Williams gained a report from his brother-in-law, whose wrangler/ranch foreman was out riding and repairing barbed-wire fencing on a quad-runner. Doubling back over a rise, he saw a dun-colored Bigfoot chasing after him, and it was quickly gaining ground. Without a rifle, the wrangler had no choice but to ride off in the opposite direction as fast as he could. According to Williams, the Bigfoot chased after the Kawasaki quad runner all the way to the river at a dead run (approximately two miles) before it changed direction, fleeing into the woods on the western slope. In a follow-up,

Williams said the ranch foreman no longer goes out mending fences without his rifle.[*]

I didn't have a photo of a dun-colored Sasquatch, of course, - as unusual as this color sounds, but I did have access to a file photo from the Bureau of Land Management of a dun-colored stallion; strange coloring for a Sasquatch; if indeed the witness was correct in his assessment.

Sasquatches, it seems, play games with our vehicles, and again, we are apparently, at times, a source of amusement and entertainment for them. I have moments when I wonder if this 'chase behavior' isn't more a ritual, perhaps a rite of passage for Sasquatches coming of age.

12-Foot Tall Bigfoot Gives Chase

Forty-year veteran Bigfoot investigator Peter Guttilla sent me a yellowed article published in the Post-Register, Idaho Falls, Idaho. It reported a most unusual encounter with Bigfoot by two men from Jackson Hole, Teton County, Wyoming, in 1980. Robert Goodrich and Glen Towner excitedly reported to representatives of the Jackson Hole Police Department that they were chased off Snow King Mountain by a Bigfoot-like creature that was (according to the witness report) a full twelve feet tall with long dark hair and "arms that hung to the ground."

The report said the two men were trying to visit a friend at his lean-to on the mountain when the encounter occurred. There was concern for their friend because he had not been seen for 1½ weeks so they decided to check on him around three o'clock in the morning, but when the pair of would-be rescuers got to within a few yards of their friend's lean-to, they met up with the 12-foot Bigfoot instead. The report stated that the creature breathed heavily and made a moaning kind of growl. They described the creature as having a "face as big as a stop sign" and said the twelve-foot beast "was hunchbacked."

---

[*]   Peter Williams (2005).

The two men turned and ran, and the Bigfoot followed in hot pursuit. The last time they saw the creature, it was standing under the street light near the Ramada Snow King Inn in Jackson. Police determined neither man had been drinking and the report made no mention of the fate of the man in the lean-to.[108]

Other chases: There are several more listings in the data describing a Sasquatch chasing after various things, including people, cars, and recreational vehicles, for unknown reasons. It almost seems like the Sasquatch gets some sort of perverse pleasure out of chasing and bluff-charging, or whatever behavior scares the wits out of us.

Two Men Report Seeing Huge Hairy Creature

Arm Waving

In 2009, two men hunting bullfrogs were reportedly chased off a sandbar by a Sasquatch at the mouth of the Endless Brook that runs from Lake St. Catherine, Vermont. Other witnesses to the incident watching from the shore described the creature as "enormous and wildly waving its arms in a circular motion... yelling like Tarzan of the Jungle." Hearing of the incident, the owner of a rural café went to the site and poured two castings of a left and right footprint that measured 16-inches from toe to heel. According to the café owner, the area is rich with giant bullfrogs the locals enjoy eating marinated in garlic and lemon juice. It was supposed that the "big people" also enjoyed eating frog legs.

Readers may be surprised to learn there is a very long history of Sasquatch sightings in Vermont. In his book *The First Vermonters*, former University of Vermont anthropologist William Haviland remembered that the Abenaki Indians recounted stories of a forest wanderer, a giant humanoid creature that occasionally left footprints behind. The accounts parallel Algonquin tales of the windigo said to be a hair-covered cannibal giant. The windigo legend of hulking, hairy man-beasts can be found throughout the New England States among all Algonquian-speaking people. According to one early-day Native American description of the windigo, it is a giant thing, swift ... and covered with hair; it has eyes like "two pools of wild fury." They say his smell is like rotting meat.

This description is similar to reports today, except that not all Bigfoot carry an odor.

Slapping His Sides, a Sasquatch Chases a Coyote

A description was sent to me recounting a coyote being chased out from an elm tree woodland area. He never spoke to anyone about his 1980s incident until 1996. While counting trees killed by Dutch elm disease, the former inspector for the Ag Department reportedly observed "a Bigfoot slapping his sides as he galloped after a coyote." The inspector said the hair on his head was wild-looking, dark brown, and curly, and that there was an unmistakable stench in the air that caused his nose to run. "If it was not a Bigfoot, if my eyes deceive me, then it was a tall wild man loose in the woods of a USA National Forest Reserve wearing a bear's skin coat on a day when the temperature outside was 96 degrees. Of the coyote, I am sure; it was not a fox, a wolf or a domestic canine."*

---

* Charles A.R. (2002).

Chasing Two Rottweilers

One more version like that account was of a light-brown 8 to 10-foot tall Sasquatch chasing a family's two yelping Rottweilers across the Quinault River in Washington State, in 1993. The event, casually told to me in 1998 by the late ISC Secretariat J. Richard Greenwell, named the three observers Rich interviewed who argued over the height estimate, which ranged from 8-feet to 10-feet tall. He said the men were so ensconced in arguing over the height of the Sasquatch that only one of the three noticed other details, such as its color or whether it was male or female. Rich grumbled in character, "…the damn thing could have been deep purple or green with stripes and they didn't notice!"[*]

Chasing a Rabbit

A West Virginia fish hatchery management worker described watching a bellowing Bigfoot "hauling butt" after something running in deep grass that he couldn't make out but thought it might have been a rabbit. Apparently, the Bigfoot was chasing whatever it was with flying leaps out into the field, each time falling down but regaining itself to continue the pursuit, which lasted maybe 2 minutes before the worker went back into the building. The Bigfoot was black haired, built well but thin-looking, and about 6-feet tall.[†]

The Meddybemps Howler

---

[*] Richard Greenwell.
[†] Posted to the Sasquatch One discussion list (1996).

Jackson and Tulane Porter knew of several sightings, this one also involving a rabbit. A fellow told them a family of hairy giants was seen crossing Stud Mill Road, north of Lower Sabao Lake in northern Maine. What made that behavior memorable was that the hairy giant was carrying a snowshoe hare by the ears that was alive, kicking, and squealing.[109]

Eating Rabbit

East Coast Bigfoot author Bill Brann posted an interesting article published in the Capital Journal in Salem, Oregon, which said in part that Utah Wildlife Division Officials were investigating a sighting by multiple witnesses. Eight North Ogden residents reported seeing a 10-foot-tall creature covered with a mantle of white hair while hiking a ridge at the head of the Weber Drainage between Pass Lake and Cuberant Basin. Witness Jay Barker told the Utah Conservation the group looked down and observed the creature standing at the edge of a small alpine lake. It walked off after a youngster in the group knocked a bunch of rocks loose. The hikers found a dead rabbit near where the creature was seen; it appeared to be skinned and partially eaten.[110]

For all the confusion, disbelief, and opinions floating around, there are still great reports of encounters with the Sasquatch that echo the same description on the west coast through mid-America to the eastern seaboard...it appears there are no differences in descriptions; no subspecies. If we accept that the Sasquatch is a fully modern human with a few genetic differences that cause the physical distinctions, then I think a sub-species can be eliminated.

Hudson Falls, New York archaeologist Dr. William "Bill" Brann, founder and director of Northern Sasquatch Research Society109 is an investigator, researcher, and co-author of the 1992 book *Monsters of the Northwoods* along with Paul Bartholomew, Robert Bartholomew, and Bruce Hallenbeck. The book is one of two that speak solely to the issue of Bigfoot in the eastern USA. Brann filed a report with Bigfootencounters on March 17, 2000, regarding the creature allegedly crossing a road in front of a fire engine in Chemung County, New York. This eastern Sasquatch was described much like the western archetype, except the one in Brann's report was much thinner. A portion of Dr. Brann's report read this way:

The man who put it out over the web was also the driver of the car that almost hit the creature. He is 29-year-old Joe Sabin. He and his brother encountered what they described as being a 7-foot 350 lb Bigfoot. It was 9:00 p.m., the creature moved from the left of the road directly in front of a fire truck. It was stooped at the shoulders, with arms swinging at its side, dark in color. The entire sighting took exactly 3 or 4 seconds. The approximate speed of the fire truck was 60 mph so they nearly collided with the Sasquatch. At this point, he states, "I felt that I'd seen something I shouldn't have." He and his brother said almost simultaneously, "It's a Bigfoot! It didn't look anything like the one in the Patterson film. It was much leaner, resembling a basketball player in a fur suit. I first thought it came out of the corn field by the side of the road," he said. The next day he went back and found broken branches where it came up out of the swamp, which also borders this particular stretch of highway. "I feel" he continued, "that the siren on the fire truck probably spooked it."[111]

Beast Seen in Utah

For Easterners hungry for listings on the right coast and the contiguous states, the book with the greatest number of listings would be Rick Berry's 1993 five-star rated, *Bigfoot on the East Coast*. There is a staggering amount of information in these two books with descriptions galore. I waited ten years to obtain my copy of Rick Berry's book and, with the help of Roger Knights, located a single copy. I cannot believe what I paid for that book; I dare say neither could Knights! Bigfoot enthusiasts new to research make a common mistake: they rely on Internet website reading when the best information is hidden deep in some of the books written BEFORE the Internet ever came to fruition. That's truly where the good stories are listed.

Chasing Salmon Up the Nisqually River

Also from Washington State in 2001, a Nisqually gentleman, Charlie "One-Eye" (nicknamed that way after he lost his right eye in a dart game with drunks) described a tribe of Sasquatch chasing salmon up the Nisqually River;

> ...they fish with their hands and take only what they can eat in a day. You see them if you don't look away, they are quick! It is not a good sign to see one Steta'l by himself; it is a good sign to see a family of the Steta'l; they are the hidden ones who guard the river salmon.[*]

Hair Covering Bigfoot's Face

The example below describes a Sasquatch with hair covering its face, which is a common feature in reports. Similar descriptions of hair draped over the forehead or hanging in the face have been reported in Texas, Missouri, Tennessee, and the Pacific Northwest. Here is another example from Chenango County, south of Bainbridge, New York:

---

[*] Suttles, Dr. Wayne (1918–2005), noted anthropologist and friend to the Bigfoot community. Personal correspondence and help with Salish languages and the meanings of terminology meant to reference Sasquatch-type creatures color much of the name inventory.

My Bigfoot sighting occurred on our dairy farm in Chenango County, South of Bainbridge, New York in May 1961. I was 14 years old. The sighting was around 1 p.m. in the afternoon in our farm hillside woodlot which was made up of primarily Oak, Maple, Cherry, and Beech trees. At the time, I was active in boy scouts, and having my own camp site was a priority. I located my campsite next to a smsall spring. Now, to a 14 year old boy, this meant all the comforts of home in a camp site; plenty of wood for campfires, water and protection against the elements in this section of woods. I was making my way to the campsite, when I heard a rustling noise at the spring. I thought it might be a deer coming in for a drink, so I moved as quietly as I could in the underbrush. Instead of a deer, about fifty to hundred feet from me, up rose this coal black form, looking directly at me. At first I couldn't figure out what I was looking at. My brain just couldn't sort it out. It wasn't a bear. In the shade of the trees, its eye reflected a brilliant yellow, and its coat was shiny black. Very broad shoulders, no neck to speak of and its head was rounded like a human's. What bothered me was I could not discern a face. It seemed covered in hair. The eyes seemed to be peeking out through hair that fell over its face. Its arms were at its side, and I could not see below its torso, as brush covered its lower half, so I could not see its hands or feet. It had a very broad trunk; its estimated height was around 6 feet. It just stood there swaying side to side looking at me, as if to say, "what are you looking at?" It never made any sound.[112]

Chenango County

Sasquatch Runs Alongside Vehicle

Oregon City veteran Sasquatch investigator Cliff Olson was able to recall for this effort a story about a Sasquatch giving chase. He wrote:

…it might have been from Ray Crowe's *Track Record*, but the story goes that this older gal was driving south of La Pine, Oregon on Highway 97 headed for Chiloquin when this Sasquatch ran up alongside her vehicle on the shoulder side of the road and was able to somewhat bend over while running and look through the window, scaring the bejeezus out of her. She sped the car up and the Sasquatch veered off. Seems that there were other cars on the road at the time too.[*]

The Track Record was a monthly newsletter Ray Crowe published in Hillsboro, Oregon, often referring to the newsletter as the TR. *Track Record* Issue #1 was published in July 1991, and the final issue #144 was published in December 2004. Joe Beelart told me *The Track Record* was sold April 30, 2008. Crowe always reminded people to put on their "skepticals" when they read his newsletter. I took his warning to heart and put aside many cases simply because I didn't believe them at the time. When I asked Ray about some of the questionable reports he published, Ray told me, "...great entertainment, Bobbie." I knew at that moment that Ray had never seen a Sasquatch – "entertainment," for me, was the last adjective I would have used to describe a Bigfoot sighting.

To Ray's credit, he worked tirelessly with his wife Theata (famous for her yeti spaghetti) until her passing to keep Bigfoot research solvent in years when interest was low. Ray was the muscle behind many of the summertime West Coast conferences, every year beginning with Bigfoot Daze, an outdoor gathering for Bigfooters generally held in Carson, Washington, for five consecutive years, then in Hillsboro, Oregon, for another 3 years (*IBS), and finally four years' worth of conference meetings in Sweet Home, Oregon, where Vice President Patty Reinhold took over reserving the park. All of Ray's events were successful, including once-a-month dinner meetings that included speakers and lively discussions at "Dad's" in Portland and then "Home Plate."

Regulars included Trapper Steve, Woody Woodruff, Dr.'s Ruth McFarland and Lloyd Sipes, Joe Beelart, Henry Franzoni, Dr. W. Henner Fahrenbach, Rainy Knight, Cliff Olson, Peter Byrne, John Cordell, Todd Neiss, Sally Newberry, Patty and Bob Reinhold, Dar Addington, Datus Perry, Fred Bradshaw, Bill Harper, Rob Butler, Dave Mann plus

------

[*] Cliff Olson, Oregon City, Oregon.

others whose names I've probably forgotten; so many are gone now. The first meeting was held in July 1991, and the guest speaker was Datus Perry. The first outdoor conference in Carson, Washington, was on September 19, 1992. Rip Lytle talked about Gilgamesh and Beowulf. The meeting included a trip over to the Ape Cave site; Mt. St. Helens, Washington, in August 1991.

The overwhelming opinion in the decades of the 1980s and 1990s was that the Sasquatch was just an ape and shooting them was permissible. Canadian newspaperman John Green in Harrison Hot Springs, British Columbia, was the cause of that heavy influence – but he was wrong. Those who were in Green's camp were also wrong. Why? Because the Sasquatch could not be an ape and still be able to produce viable offspring with Native American women. Humans can only reproduce a viable offspring with other humans. There is no hybrid human/ape cross. The Sasquatch must be human to a major extent for the early stories of live births between the Sasquatch and Indian maidens to be true. I puzzled over most of the PhDs interacting with this research and others who swore Bigfoot was real and that they were apes that evolved to walk upright. No ape has evolved to walk upright. No ape/human cross exists. The genetic makeup of each would need dramatic changes for that to occur. So I puzzled over the insistence of anthropologists and anatomy professors who (conference after conference) postulated that hypothesis.

Humans cannot reproduce anything with an animal, apes in particular. Green, of course, went about demeaning government teacher John W. Burns and his work for suggesting there was any truth to the Chehalis stories of captive Indian women giving birth. Again, Green was wrong. According to the work of Dr. Ed Fusch, Ph.D., (beyond the work of J.W. Burns), there are still living descendants of Sasquatch and Indian couplings alive on the Colville Indian Reservation today. It wouldn't surprise me to find Sasquatch DNA on other reservations, particularly the Chehalis Reserves.

But I digress. Back to the Oregon Sasquatch types, I was recently reminded that "Cape Apes" is a 200-year-old Oregon coastline idiom for a Sasquatch-like life form which, it was said, frequented the beaches of Coos Bay, Oregon, at low tide to harvest rich beds of oysters, clams, mussels, and other shellfish during certain times of the year, both at dawn and sunset. The term Cape Apes was early white man slang.

The Mishikhwutmetunne/Coquille, Umpqua, and Siuslaw Indians watched from the dunes and learned from the haired ones where the largest clam fields were located. Other tribes often joined in the seasonal dig. The hair-covered giants were seen digging without a care and then observed crushing shellfish between the palms of their hands, picking out the shells, and then eating the meat. Some Cape Apes would break open the shells with their teeth, but most opened shellfish with a quick slice from their thumbnail.*

I have these brief chase listings: A white Sasquatch ran after a departing Volkswagen Bug following it up a dirt road in Texas at roughly 30mph; that was Arizona Bigfoot enthusiast Randall Chapman's father, a story he told on discussion lists back in late 1996. Ken Joholske cited an incident where an off-white Sasquatch chased a group of kids off a bike path not far from Jamestown, New York. Joholske reported that during his own frightening encounter, "...there was no smell associated with his sighting and no vocalization, only heavy breathing, a low guttural growl and some form of what sounded to me to be lip smacking."[113] As time goes on, I've come to realize that low tones that sound like growling as well as heavy breathing and this lip-smacking behavior is apparently a common notation by witnesses. Bears also smack their lips and make mouth-popping, tooth-clacking noises. In apparent contrast to the Sasquatch, however, bears will eventually wander into camp or make themselves known. Sasquatches prefer to stay covert. I don't know which I'd rather meet up with –

---

* Personal correspondence, Dr. Wayne Suttles.

maybe take a chance on the Sasquatch since bears are so unpredictably vicious, especially sows with cubs.

Aggressive Behavior? Or Is It Just a Game to Them?

Attacking Cars

In an article published in The Minneapolis Star-Tribune in 2002, long-time researcher Mike Quast, a resident of Moorhead, Minnesota, is quoted as saying,

> I think one of the main reasons why science doesn't take this animal seriously is because we have labeled it a monster, and nobody is supposed to believe in monsters," he said. "If it had just been thought of as a new species of wildlife, there would have been scientists out there looking for it.

Mike told a great story, one of the first he would chronicle, about a car being attacked by a Sasquatch. Captivated by the Sasquatch's behavior, I noted the reported conduct in an old computer; then, in 2010, I found the reference again to this unusual behavior.

Ever the investigator, Quast tracked down a mechanic who told his brother-in-law that he, his brother, and his brother's girlfriend were driving around in a wooded area near Vergas, Minnesota. Suddenly, as they went by, a hair-covered creature leapt out at them. When they turned the car around to take another look, it attacked their car. They later found a large dent in the trunk lid. The description was typical; weight approximately 300 pounds, standing 7 or 8 feet tall.[114]

I wondered how anyone would explain a dent that size to their insurance adjustor. "An angry Sasquatch chased my vehicle and with his fist, dented the trunk of my car." Right! What insurance adjustor in their right mind would believe that story?

Bigfoot in Minnesota

Chasing and Attacking

A swarm of devil creatures chase man: The Harry Colp Story, as told by his daughter Virginia, is fairly well known, and being attacked by hairy giants is worrisome. Here is just the pertinent excerpt:

> Looking over the top of this tree from where I stood, I could see out on Frederick Sound, Cape of the Straight Light, the point of Vanderput Spit (Point Vanderput); and turning a little to the left, I could see Sukhoi Island (Kodiak) from the mouth of Wrangell Narrows. Satisfied with that, I turned half round to get a back sight on some mountain peaks, and lying below me on the other side of the ridge from the ledge was the half-moon lake the Indian had told me about. Right there, fellows, I got the scare of my life and I hope to God I never see or go through the likes of it again.
>
> Swarming up the ridge toward me from the lake were the most hideous creatures. I couldn't call them anything but devils, as they were neither

men nor monkeys, yet looked like both. They were entirely sexless, their bodies covered with long coarse hair, except where the scabs and running sores had replaced it. Each one seemed to be reaching out for me and striving to be the first to get me. The air was full of their cries and the stench from their sores and bodies made me faint. I forgot my broken gun and tried to use it on the first ones, and then I threw it at them and turned and ran. God, how I did run! I could feel their hot breath on my back. Their long claw-like fingers scraped my back. The smell from their steaming, stinking bodies was making me sick, while the noises they made, yelling, screaming and breathing, drove me mad. Reason left me. How I reached the canoe or hung on to that piece of quartz is a mystery to me.

When I came to, it was night; and I was lying in the bottom of my canoe, drifting between Thomas Bay and Sukhoi Island, cold, hungry and crazy for a drink of water. But only to satisfy the latter urge, I started for Wrangell and here I am. You no doubt think I am either crazy or lying. All I can say is there is the quartz. Never let me hear the name of Thomas Bay again and for God's sake help me get away tomorrow on that boat! So passed Charlie from our lives. We put his story down as a fantasy caused by loneliness and morbid thought.[115]

The Colp story is more an account of a Sasquatch 'attack' rather than a chase story. For me, the realism of it came when I read his words: "… stench from their sores and bodies made me faint;" which brought it home! It would take a special kind of field man to soldier through an ordeal like Harry Colp endured. Of interest; Thomas Bay, Alaska, gained the name Devil's Country when, in 1900, people claimed to have seen devil creatures in the area. The locals refer to it as the Kush-taka, a shape-shifting creature of Tlingit legend that can take the form of either man or otter.

There have been older reports of lives lost in untamed regions of Alaska. I remember I was sent an old September 1930s issue of Sports Afield Magazine, which ran a blurb about a hairy giant the Nelchina Aboriginals called Gilyuk. In the article, it said the cannibal giant killed one of the Indians, and it left a sapling tree twisted to shreds as a sign of what he had done.

Thirteen years later, John McQuire, known as The Flying Dutchman, was in de Wilde's camp some eighteen miles down the Yukon from Ruby, Alaska, when a Sasquatch attacked him. McQuire fought back but later died of internal injuries. Bob Betts acquired the story first and then sent it to John Green. Many of these are very old stories, but it tells those of us in general research that they continue with no regard for time or calendar.

In 1920, Albert Petka died after fighting with an Alaskan Bushman who openly attacked him on the boat where he was living near Nulato, Yukon-Koyukuk Borough, Alaska. Petka's dogs drove the bushman off, but Petka died later from his injuries.[116]

One of the Tanana elders reported 19-inch tracks crossing Berry Picking Trail in Northwest Nulato, Alaska, in 1996. The stride length was reportedly five-foot in deep snow. Snow melt may account for some discrepancies in track length measurements. Attempts to get a bush pilot to follow the tracks failed, but the informant was sure it was the sign of the dreaded Bushman or one of the Black Giants.

In 1996, George Yellowhand was fishing the Yukon with his brother when two male Bushmen began throwing rocks from the banks. Startled, if not completely astonished, the two brothers watched the two black, hair-covered giants wade into the river up to their waists, gathering rocks as they approached the brothers sitting in their john boat. The rocks gained accuracy, and the men finally realized their situation and left the area. Yellowhand wrote that before they noticed the two Bushmen, they heard loud whistling but didn't know what it was, probably some strange birds, but when the whistling stopped, the rocks began flying. They have not been back since and Yellowhand had no wish to talk about it any further, so upsetting was the subject.

It seems most of the brutal attacks occurred in years past. We don't hear much about deliberate attacks anymore. Are these attacks happening and just being covered up? Perhaps written off or blamed on bears?

The Fred Beck attack story in 1924, I believe, was in retaliation for the shooting of a Sasquatch family member earlier in the day. Be mindful of what you might be in for if you shoot one. The Anchorage Daily News reported that a teacher and his wife at English Bay stated that a hunter from Portlock had failed to return home. In 1949, 63 years ago, giant manlike tracks 18 inches long were found closing in on a moose kill; tracks were found indicating signs of a struggle. The 18-inch manlike tracks headed up into the higher mountains. Residents were afraid to talk about the incident there in English Bay and, eventually, the village was abandoned; so great was their fear.[117]

The journalist for Sports Afield Magazine reported Gilyuk, the cannibal giant, killed one of the Indians in Nelchina Plateau, Alaska, in 1930. According to Rene Dahinden, the article said the sign Gilyuk left behind was sapling trees twisted to shreds; one end twisted left, the other twisted right. One could postulate that the thick trees twisted into shreds may simply be a show of strength; or it could be a warning to come meaning "notice what I can do to this tree limb, I am able to do to you too." A horrifying thought!

Notice also that the mention of tree twists is not a product of this new internet generation; apparently, it goes back to the 1930s and maybe further. Little is understood about the branch-twisting or the snapping off of the tops of trees. Some of them might be way markers, a release of frustrations, or perhaps a message meaning, "see what I can do?" Blaming the broken top of a tree on weather conditions doesn't always work, especially when only one or two trees among many were tipped, the others remaining untouched. Some of the First Nations people call the broken top trees "a sign of the black giants."

To the Dena'ina people of the Chickaloon region, Gilyuk was not a legendary creature. Their father's grandfathers told them he was a reality, and they spoke of the Gilyuk people, who had all the same realities as the bear and wolf. Gilyuk, they said, was a shaggy-haired giant who wore a little hat and ate men, women, and children – so goes their folklore. And according to the Athabascans, "Gilyuk doesn't molest white men…"[118]

The journalist for the Sports Afield article was Russell Annabel. He stated it this way:

> The Gilyuks are a remote tribe of native people of Siberian ancestry who claim there are animals inhabiting the frozen forests of Siberia that have human feelings and travel in family units.[119]

However, in 2005, Ken Howell of Quemado, New Mexico, wrote,

> Russell Annabel, a neighbor when I lived in Alaska, was a facile, skillful writer of pure fiction. His adventures were creations of a fertile imagination fed by others' experiences.

I like to think of one's imagination as his intelligence, having a bit of fun. At any rate, perhaps Mr. Howell was a skeptic when it comes to stories of the haired primitives – because I find it hard to understand how Russell Annabel could fabricate a truth as regards tree twists in the 1930s. Eighty years later, we are still finding twisted tree limbs and tree trunks! Was Annabel a liar? I think not.

The Strangest Story Ever Told | Black Giants | 18 Older
Alaska Reports

The Alaskan Dena'ina, also the Tanaina, are people whose traditions are not unique to them alone; many First Nation and Native Americans have similar stories of kidnappings, killings, and wars that broke out between them and the haired ancients. They are not difficult to believe – so I am hard-pressed to think the Gilyuk stories are untrue. The Right Honorable Sir Winston Churchill, Great Britain's Prime Minister in the early 1940s said of Arthurian legends, "They are all true, and if they are not, they ought to be." From time to time, I think that is applicable to what we hear about the Sasquatch.

Sasquatch and Bears

Rene also reminded me that Roger Patterson had an interesting story about a group of Indians that came upon a small box canyon in British Columbia. The Indians were horrified to see a huge hairy giant going at it full battle with a great brown bear in what Roger later wrote was an ear-shattering battle. On page 118 of Patterson's 1966 book, *Abominable Snowman*, he is quoted as saying, "it was a long hard fight, but the giant finally strangled the bear to death." For someone who hadn't seen a Bigfoot in 1966; Patterson was able to sketch a fair likeness of both.[120]

It was hard for me to imagine how the Bigfoot escaped the lethal swipe of the great brown bear's four-inch long talons, and the fact that the skirmish lasted as long as it did is amazing considering the strength of each participant. Of interest, author of *Bear Tales for the Ages*, Larry Kaniut cited a story where a brown bear and bull-moose fought to the death. The battle lasted 8 hours, and the moose won.[*,121]

I recall the chase behavior being reported back in the day by Dahinden that occurred south of Golden in British Columbia in 1967; Rene

---

* Kaniut is the author of seven books on bears: *Alaska Bear Tales, More Alaska Bear Tales, Cheating Death, Some Bears Kill, Danger Stalks the Land, Bear Tales for the Ages,* and *Alaska's Fun Bears.*

exclaimed, "…they said the damn thing chased some loggers out of the bush and sent them running for their lives."

There is little doubt that the Sasquatch can catch that which it chases. Why they chase at all makes me think it's a bit of fun for them; some kind of perverse thrill they get watching us flee in terror. How entertaining can we be? Others have suggested that the high numbers of chase incidents reported might indicate that chasing humans in cars, in the field, or on bikes is a "rite of passage" of some sort since the chaser is usually a male. Whatever reason is behind an all-out chase, it has the same terrifying effect on the person being chased.

Alaska Pilot Watches as Sasquatch Carries off His Bride

Heavy Breathing

Hearing heavy breathing is a common thread among witnesses before a sighting occurs. Andy Robson also heard heavy breathing and footfalls before he sighted the Sasquatch in October of 2010 in Linn County, Sweet Home, Oregon. Andy later found footprints. His grandfather also sighted a Sasquatch in Bella Coola while camping with a friend. Both sightings were brief.

The Duke and Whitmore families were awakened by heavy breathing and footfalls outside their tent while camping in the White Mountains of New Hampshire, in the Wildwood Campground/picnic area, approximately nine miles from the town of Woodstock. They went back to sleep, thinking it was just another camper walking by. The next morning, Mr. Whitmore's son, Teddy, discovered 18-inch bare footprints circling their tent. This behavior is often reported and tends to be a non-threatening/curious kind of Sasquatch behavior.

Sasquatch Coughing, Pounding on the Trunk of a Car

Wildlife educator Larry Battson related a story in 2007 that he acquired while working in Parke County, Fallen Rock, Indiana. Battson's informants described a Sasquatch with a raspy cough. Fleeing for the safety of their vehicle, they observed an 8-foot tall, brownish-black creature standing upright. The nervous young man behind the wheel flooded the car by constantly pushing on the accelerator, causing it not to start. By this time, the creature was behind the vehicle as the car finally turned over, backfiring at the same time. Startled, the Sasquatch pounded the trunk with one huge blow using both fists. The car sped away, fishtailing and spraying gravel on the Sasquatch. They drove straight to the Sheriff's Office, where law enforcement did not believe their story and accused them of beating the trunk of the car with a sledgehammer.[122]

Now, there is a behavior we don't hear about very often.

Park County, Fallen Rock, Indiana

Rock Throwing with Aggression

In 2007, Mr. C. Hamilton recorded this stone-rock throwing-chase report near Cable Air Field, Upland, San Bernardino County, in Southern California.

I was leaving Cable Air Field late on a Monday night when my Ranch Wagon crapped out down around Foothill, in Upland. I was supposed to be joining a group from my Law Office over at the Sage Hen Cafe, so I started hoofing it and finally stopped in at the Upper Crust to use the telephone and leave a message for my friends. Leaving the Upper Crust and walking west on the north side of Foothill, I entered some scrub to take a leak - and that's when I saw him. He had to be about 9-feet tall and 3-feet across the shoulders - and it was definitely a male. I think I startled him from what appeared to be the construction of a crude lean-to, or ply-board shack or something when he saw me. He let go with a horrible scream. I froze at first, and then I turned tail and started trying to get back down to Foothill. The creature threw a huge stone – big as a bowling ball – and started coming after me. I made it out to Foothill about 15 yards ahead of him and tore back towards the Upper Crust, never once looking back. I was so damn scared I tripped over a curb in the parking lot of the Upper Crust and hit my head pretty bad. I think I was out for a while, and lucky that thing did not keep chasing after me. When old man Miller left the restaurant for the night he found me conked out. I talked with a fella from the Daily Report the next day down at Alphie's Coffee Shop, but he never did anything with the information.[123]

Bigfoot in the Inland Empire and Fontana Especially

Singing, Screaming, Wailing

There must be several hundred reports of deep guttural screams and soulful wailing, almost too many to begin to list them all. Few reports mention seeing the individual in the process of actually screaming, yet the screaming and the wailing described are usually nothing like they have heard before. Some describe the screaming as the "deep chest rattling type" or the kind that will "easily put the fear of God in a grown man."

Screams are generally described as deeply guttural, reverberating, and trailing off into a prolonged wail or howl. Many witnesses to the screaming of a Sasquatch say that if it occurs nearby, it is beyond deafening, and is so earsplitting that it causes an unbelievable surge of adrenaline and complete terror.

I picked this one - a gentleman's report named "Bob" from Monroe-Shelton Line, Connecticut, because he described the intensity of the 2002 screaming quite well.

> I would walk outside late at night to enjoy the peace and quiet. Many nights I would hear a strange screaming sound far off in the distance. It was so far away I could just barely hear it. One night just after dark I walked out the front door and suddenly there was that same scream but this time it was very close and very loud. I backed up through the door and locked it! I was left with the impression that it wanted to be left alone so I did; I never really saw anything because it was too dark. To this day I regret not getting at least a look, I also don't think a locked door would have been a problem at all, from the way the scream sounded, and the last thing I would have wanted is to have it upset with me. It sounded huge and bad tempered! But the sound I will never forget, I have not heard it since.[124]

Cody Richard's definition of a deep guttural, long-lasting scream he and his brother heard in the Kings Canyon, Jackson County, Colorado, in the summer of 2002 was so chest rattling he was sure it would "level the entire mountain."

> The electrical shock that went through my body was paralyzing, it was THAT close and THAT loud. I grabbed my jewels, Dude, and hung on frozen! Now, in the telling of it, I can only imagine the size that thing must have been. No bear, no cougar screams last that long, that deep or that loud. My brother and I haven't been camping since.

But Elizabeth Wazniak-Clarke remains traumatized to this day some 6-years after an unseen force screamed at her. The screaming session she described happened while she was walking home, taking the usual shortcut through the woods after the school bus let her off at the main cattle gates to their Wisconsin farm.

> It was ghastly, deep and it hurt my chest. It lasted nearly as long as it took me to run home and I am still unable to get near the woods to my parent's place without my husband. The nightmares from the experi-ence have been brutal, my parents have seen the Bigfoot before but I never want to see it, ever! My parents have also heard them singing but the singing was soft and in the distance, coming from higher up in the mountains. There are no campgrounds up there either.

Anthropologist Dr. Connie Cameron also mentioned reading reports about Sasquatch's singing. I smile when I think of Connie; she published the Bigfoot Co-Op Newsletter and contributed to this research for twenty-five years with outstanding reports that included a wide range of reported behaviors. Everyone looked forward to reading Connie's newsletters; she published them in 1980 and continued without interruption until 2005, when she retired. Connie, as we called her, was one of the most knowledgeable women in research and one of the sweetest, most unpretentious people I've had the pleasure of corre-sponding with during her time with the Bigfoot CO-OP newsletter. She is still in semi-retirement from the Bigfoot world and deserves the title of "First Lady of Sasquatchery," a title that would probably make her laugh. But I'll say from experience – producing a newsletter for 25 years is no easy task.

The idea for The Bigfoot Co-Op Newsletter was originally the joint brainchild of Connie and longtime field researcher and friend Peter Guttilla. It was a hand-typed newsletter, much of it before computers, devoted wholly to what's new in the world of Bigfoot, yeti, and the Almasty. Contributors were many of the notables of the day, including Dmitri Bayanov, Roger Knights, the late Lou Farish, Ray Crowe, Vance Orchard, Randy Stradley, Bill Dranginis, and Jon Erik Beckjord. The Bigfoot Co-Op Newsletter was well received, and I don't know anyone who didn't look forward to receiving it.

Bigfoot in Connecticut

The quarterly Bigfoot Co-Op newsletter was pulled together with the help of Connie's organizer-friends, Peter "Sly Fox" Guttilla, Tom "Green Beret" Muzila, Rich "Lock-n-Load" Grumley, Dennis "Hot Wheels" Ruminer, and later George "Old Spice" Turner who, according to Guttilla, carried the torch for Connie for years. The group met for regular meetings at Connie's house in Whittier, California, where occasional attendees included Bay area researcher Warren Thompson, Pat Macey and Doug Trapp, and various other Bigfoot devotees whose names have faded from memory. Tip 'o the hat to Dr. Connie Cameron; well done. I value the things I learned from her.*

––––––––––––––––––––

* Dr. Cameron received her M.A. degree in Anthropology from California State University at Fullerton where she was Curator of the Museum of Anthropology and

New Hampshire Screamer

Nicholas Flood saw a brief glimpse of a Bigfoot and heard noises off and on coming from a window that was occasionally pounded on; the window was six feet off the ground. The area is in Moultonboro, New Hampshire, not far from Lake Winnipesaukee. Additionally, his family heard ongoing screaming and commented that the screams sounded like a woman being mutilated. Together, they reasoned it was a Fischer cat, a weasel-like creature known to scream like a woman in distress. Mountain lions also scream when in heat and even those screams can be a bit disconcerting. Flood described the screams as "terrible" and occurred 40-50 times from the direction of a nearby swampy field on the edge of miles of wilderness. There was nothing in the area but an abandoned farmhouse. Family members heard the screams and, at the time, Flood did not know screams and screaming were associated with Sasquatch behavior, but he said nobody should have been in those fields in the pitch dark in the middle of the night except a Sasquatch.[125]

Screaming Like a Woman Being Mutilated

Editor of the Occasional Papers. She has been involved with Southern California Archaeology since 1972 with long-term projects at Zzyx (the Desert Studies Center) and at Los Piños in the Cleveland National Forest as well as the Channel Islands to include 1983 and 1984 field seasons on San Clemente Island. Connie presented a number of papers and is published in the PCAS Quarterly, The Masterkey, and Proceedings of the Society for California Archaeology and the Archives of California Prehistory.

More Screaming

T.J. Camp honestly stated his complete fear at hearing the roaring scream from what could only be regarded as something huge. His abbreviated account went like this:

While on a bicycling touring trip from Portland, Oregon, south to Santa Barbara, California, during the summer of 1980, I heard a Sasquatch. We arrived at Fort Ross Historical Park just north of Jenner in Sonoma County mid July. It was marked as a campsite on our map but had no pitches. We camped under some Monterey pines next to a picnic bench, ate dinner and went to bed at around 9:00 p.m. Around 1:00 a.m., came a scream no farther away than 20-feet to the left of the tent. It was a blood curdling scream with various sounds in succession that lasted at least 9 full seconds. It frightened me to my bone marrow. I froze in fear knowing that whatever made the sound was huge. It was so close I could hear the tremor in its throat. Since I'm a musician I realize how much force it takes to make a sound that loud. I've also been camping all my life and have heard various animals but this was different. I started to reach for a flashlight and my girlfriend's hand grabbed my wrist with a vice-like pressure so I didn't move. We remained frozen, listening to every little noise for an hour. I remained on guard with my hands hovering around the tent pole to use as a weapon, thinking that at any moment it would stick its fanged head into our tent. At around 2:30 a.m. I heard another scream down by the fort in the lower parking area.[126]

Sonoma County

Chilling Scream, Woman-Like

And there was this account of a terrorizing scream reported by a police officer in Sumter County, South Carolina:

About 20 years ago, I was deer hunting in Lee Swamp, near the Sumter County Airport with my cousin Steve. This whole county is rich in lore of giant manlike creatures that roam the swamp and forests at night. The forest here connects with the same swamp my father had his Bigfoot encounter years earlier. Steve and I were hunting from ground blinds near a small irrigation pond when we began to hear an inhuman wailing coming from the deeper swamps, across the pond from us. I have hunted swamps all my life and heard wildcats and other big predator cats scream both night and day, but I have never before or since heard a sound like this one. It was a chilling scream, almost woman-like, but not the same as a big cat makes. It was a much higher pitch; it was broad daylight. I was armed with a Winchester 30.06 bolt action and Steve had a 12 gauge with slugs. We took up our positions across a trail from each other, with him watching one side of the pond, and I the other; we could see each other. The sounds gradually got closer and closer. Not a word was exchanged. I looked at Steve, he looked at me, and we both forgot about hunting that day. In fact, I have not hunted that particular swamp since. Whatever we heard, it was not human, nor was it any type of animal that I am familiar with. In retrospect, after having watched numerous nature shows throughout my life, I would say that I recall the sound as being similar to that made by Howler monkeys. There have been no recent stories circulating here and I haven't hunted these areas now in years. [*]

Outraged Screamer

I began corresponding Bigfoot stuff with Keith Foster back in mid-

---

[*] J M renegade80flh@xxxxxxx.com who asked not to be identified. He is local law enforcement.

1990. For a brief time, Keith was associated with the BFRO and the only person at the time in research covering Kansas, Colorado, and neighboring states. An avid bow hunter, Keith chronicled many stories. Among them was this one:

> Veteran bow hunter Terry Coon of Nampa, Idaho, wrote an article titled *It Had to Be Big*, which details an experience he had while bow-hunting elk in Oregon in 1991. Coon described how he began bugling on his elk bugle in hopes of luring a bull elk, but the answering call was not an elk but rather "the loudest and longest scream that I have ever heard." The screaming thing kept screaming then began to loudly approach Mr. Coon and his wife with a steady walking sound. Coon wrote, "the scream that erupted would make the hair on your entire body stand straight out. Whatever it was, it was clearly outraged by my bugle." He also wrote, "…in all my years in the mountains, I have never heard such a sound." The couple hastily departed the area in fear after the outraged screamer loudly circled around them just off trail in the underbrush to within 50 or 60 yards.[127]

Foster was deeply interested in the search for Bigfoot during the early days of the Internet. One of the most interesting men in research, he also filed this account with the discussion lists in the 1990s:

> Chris Mortenson of Avon, Utah, had an experience while hunting elk near the Utah-Idaho border. Mortenson describes a long series of incredibly loud animal sounds. He heard, "…a very loud, low-pitched sound that I had never heard before – like a cross between a shout and a growl" with each blast of noise "lasting maybe one or two seconds." He could hear the animal as it approached him, screaming and popping brush and limbs. Mortenson wrote in an article titled, *Keeping an Open Mind* "the most eerie thing about the noise was the sheer volume! What I heard that October day was not an elk, moose, cougar, bear, wolf, coyote or anything else I have ever heard in the wild."[128]

The term Boji originated in South Central Colorado, Saguache County, near Crestone: 1900-1920s. At the turn of the century, miners at the newly opened Independence Mine, seven miles south of Crestone, reported finding giant man-like tracks near the mine entrance. A life-long resident of the Crestone area, a local hunter and tracker who still lives there said that his grandfather told him of personally seeing a giant hairy man-beast in the late 1920s. Many locals saw the creature during that time period, and they had given the elusive creature the name "Boji".

Bugle Enrages Sasquatch

The Winema Screamer

My partner and I were fly-fishing trout at Crooked Creek in the Wood River Range, Oregon. It's all wetlands, reeds and willows. The BLM (Bureau of Land Management) seemed to be everywhere; we didn't know why. One fellow stopped by, we guessed to see what we were catching and to chat, then they moved on. We ate lunch there and stretched out near the Jeep to snooze but were awakened by a noise. It was still, no bird noises, nothing. Neither of us saw anything, but I personally didn't look. After sorting through some flies, we set out fishing. All of a sudden, this horrific scream interrupted the quiet. My partner thought it a big bobcat. Not really concerned at that point, I waded out into the creek and made a couple of casts. I noticed a black patch we took for lava rocks on the opposite bank upstream, noticeable because black flies swarmed thick over it. We continued to fish. As we were packing up to leave around 5:30-6:00 p.m., the scream came again from the area of the black lava rocks. Looking that way I said to John, "the black rocks are gone." Further away, we saw it, a dark figure walking toward the willows. There was no doubt the screamer was a Bigfoot, no bobcat because of the insane lung power behind the scream. It was deafening! We figured he had been watching us fish, lying down in the reeds, maybe all day, it is hard to know. We cannot help with a description other than it was dark; it was only a flash sighting. We saw it only from its backside then it was gone. Now we wonder why the early morning BLM were in that area; if so, the fellow who stopped to talk never said a word. We got in the Jeep and left. [*]

We do not know the reason for the screaming behavior or why some scream a deafening scream while others simply whistle, but I think it's a multi-purposed ploy they use for many reasons. We don't even know if the screamer is male or female. However, the behavior is often reported, so it must have some significance for the Sasquatch. It could be fear on their part or an intimidation tactic. Jami Morgan suggested that primitive hairy men have simply learned that screaming scares the bejeezus out of most civilized men. That may be true. I haven't heard that kind of vocalization first hand, but I'm sure it would get my undivided attention.

Perhaps the screaming is done to rid an area where campers are intruding. I don't know why, but the behavior is widely reported and often associated with rock and stone-throwing. Statistically, screams, yells, and howling rank right up there with road-sighting reports in high numbers. I have no record of anyone actually seeing Bigfoot in the process of screaming, but not all database sites are searchable; so, one in a thousand may exist. Next to road crossings, screams rank right up there in the high number count, along with steps heard and things being thrown.

---

[*] Bryce and John, Oregon.

Scream Unhinges Hardened Hunters

In August 1981 on the West side of Sleepy Cat Peak in northwestern Colorado, three experienced bow hunters experienced a situation that none of them could explain. After this encounter, none of them have ever returned to the area again. Two of the hunters were police officers. One fellow was a lieutenant and the other a sergeant. The third man was an associate that had been in the Army National Guard for many years. His last unit assignment was Military Combat Police. All three were experienced in the use of fire arms and self-defense.

One evening two of the hunters decided to go down into a low valley from their base camp. One hunter remained in camp. The two hunters split up with one going even lower and the other leveling out around a small valley. Nothing was moving, elk, deer, birds or squirrels; it was dead quiet. As darkness fell, the lowest man became uneasy, much like when an imminent ambush is suspected. It was enough that as the evening fell, he decided to hurriedly head back toward camp. Uphill and at over 9000 feet altitude he walked briskly, not knowing the whereabouts of the other hunter. As he climbed up the side of the slope, he could faintly see a campfire glow in the distance through the thick timber. Stopping for a moment, he turned to look downhill for his hunting companion. He could not see anyone in the dark, overshadowed canopy. He was still very concerned for his safety. He continued to climb until he reached camp.

Back at camp, there was a sense of urgency and concern for the other hunter.

Shaken and out of breath, no words were exchanged between the two men for several minutes. No reason was ever given for this silence that both of them observed. Finally, he asked the third hunter in camp if he had seen the other man; he had not....seconds passed. Turning and facing back down the slope, they finally saw the third hunter coming up the hill at a double time pace. "Did you come from down there," he asked the other hunter? "Yes, I just got here," the third hunter replied,

"I did not like it down there...something is not right with that area." The three veteran hunters stood looking down the slope in what by now was almost complete darkness. Again, they both concluded that there was something wrong down there but neither man arrived at a conclusion. They remained standing, looking, listening, but there was nothing making any noise; it was eerily quiet.

Both experienced men retired for the night. No alcohol was consumed. The early retirement was in order as storm clouds lit up in the west. The fire remained stoked and the night fell silent. The sergeant was in his own tent and the other two were in another tent perched on top of a small hill overlooking a large sloping side of Sleepy Cat Mountain. The area was covered with large formations of rock and patches of thick, black, tall timber. The hour was 9:00 p.m.

As law enforcement professionals and a former military police officer, side arms were kept close by. The night passed quietly until around 1:30 a.m. when they were rattled down to the very core with the most terrifying scream and growl with a long chest-rattling snarl ending; the pitch was a low whooo. The hammers rolled back on their side arms, heart rates accelerated, and there was a profound sense of fear among them. Whispering in low tones..."What was that?" But none of them knew and they agreed that none of them had ever heard anything like it ever before in all of their collective years in the field. They remained on alert, prepared to defend their lives in the event the screamer showed itself. The woods went silent again. There was nothing more and no sounds near or far.

Whatever it was upset two of them to the point of insomnia. Sleep did not come as the persistent need was to remain on guard. After several hours the two men in the double tent decided to sleep in the cab of their truck for the remainder of the night. It was a good choice because a storm with lightning, thunder, and rain erupted, and it persisted until daybreak. Camp was broken down and the truck was loaded. They made for their way out of the area and never returned. Whatever it was that made this uneasy feeling and exploded in such a loud and violent outburst, they figured was not anything known from the forests of this earth. For the former military police guardsman, this was to be the second encounter that would go unexplained. His second was much more complex and absolutely no explanation was offered, even though six other people witnessed the same thing. The one thing that none of them could figure was the terrifying sound of the vocalization. Whatever it was, it had incredible strength and agility in total darkness. It was loud and came from only a few feet of their tents. What beast could do such a thing in the dark? After that terror-filled night, none of these men continued to hunt. "It was the most profound sense of terror I have ever experienced," the informant wrote.

The letter was colorfully written by Missy Jessie Rice and dated December 2011, kinfolk to the sergeant in the story. Missy Rice said one thing about the event – their freezer has gone without venison for two hunting seasons.

Frightening Sound; Trailer Rocking

An encounter's full effect, including a nasty bout of screaming, can profoundly disturb even the hardiest of woodsmen. In 2009, I received the following account through the website by an Adams County, Idaho, man who endured the rocking of his 26-foot Nomad travel trailer, parked with all the stabilizer jacks down and in place. These are his words:

2009 was the third year that I have been able to spend the whole hunting season in the mountains. I retired in October 2007. I pulled my camp trailer up the end of September and set it up for 36 days of camping, hunting, and sitting around the campfire enjoying the outdoors. I spend a lot of time camping and hunting by myself (everyone else is still working) and riding my ATV on the few old logging roads that are still open to 4 wheelers. At 12:24 a.m. on the seventh night, something roused me so I sat up in bed. A minute or so later the rear end of my camp trailer started rocking back and forth. All the stabilizer jacks were down and the trailer was solid, so whatever was pushing on the trailer was very strong. The fully loaded trailer weighed in at more than 5,500 pounds and whatever was moving it was not making any noise while rocking it. My first thought was a bear, a really big bear. I grabbed my shotgun and put a shell in and sat and waited for a few seconds. The trailer continued to rock back and forth so I grabbed the air horn that was sitting on the table and gave it several blasts. That did not stop it so I got the keys to my truck and pushed the panic button, setting the horn blaring. This stopped whatever it was and all was quiet for five minutes. I sat there with the shotgun in my hands listening for any sound. There was no sound, just total quiet.

I had convinced myself that it was just a bear when this awful sound came from the ridge behind the trailer. It started off like a whistle turning into a horse whinny and then going into a very loud howl and finishing off with a growl. All of these sounds were run together with no pause in between them. It lasted maybe 10-15 seconds and then all went quiet. Damnedest sound I ever heard, scared the hell out of me. I got dressed and sat there in the dark the rest of the night, shotgun in hand. I have never had anything affect me like that before. After it was completely daylight I went out to look at the back side of the trailer and to see if there were any tracks on the ground. There were not any dents in the trailer or any tracks on the ground. There should have been tracks because the ground was kind of soft, and out of habit I had raked all the pine needles and forest duff away from the trailer leaving just dirt and grass. This happened on October 5th, 2009, at 12:24 a.m. I need to mention here that a 240 lb friend drove into my camp while I was still outside checking for tracks and looking for any damage to my trailer. He wanted to know what I was doing so I told him the events of the previous 8 hours. I also went back inside and had him push on the trailer to see if he could rock it back and forth. The best he could do was give it a jolt by throwing a shoulder into it. He could not make it rock in the smooth motion that had occurred the night before. This particular event is what finally gave me the incentive to file a report.[129]

The often reported screams in the night, especially late at night, could be an expression of the Sasquatch's own fear or a warning to other primitives traveling nearby. Whatever provokes the big ones to bellow like they do; the behavior profoundly affects anyone within earshot.

Adams County, Idaho

Whale Pass, Alaska, Horrifying Screaming

A trophy hunter working a favorite ridge for Sitka black-tail deer several miles from the Whale Pass area in Alaska had camped for the night. He was asleep in his tent in a small clearing when blood-curdling screaming erupted nearby. The hunter assured me that whatever it was that produced the bloody scream he heard that night made him tremble uncontrollably for hours: "...it was a terrifying ordeal during a night that was darker than an asphalt highway." He had nowhere to go in the dark and was miles away from his old Land Rover so the option to run to the safety of his vehicle simply wasn't there. He had to stick it out. He told me the hours between 2:00 a.m. and daybreak was an eternity; "...my watch never moved more slowly!" Towards the end of the Sasquatch's screaming encounter, the hunter could hardly hold himself together.

Bobbie, I tell you the screaming was like someone was knifing a woman – military might understand – it was like hearing your best buddy being disemboweled by the enemy troops; indescribable shrieking and close by! I never did see the perpetrator and I didn't look for any sign; I was worn down to nothing by the time first light came and just wanted it to end. That was 20-years ago and it still seems like yesterday. I'm retired now and living in River Oaks in the Houston area. There is no reason to know who I am, no name please.

Sasquatch Runs off Anglers by Screaming

Joel White had an interesting experience in El Dorado County, California, in 1984 that would rather rattle the heartiest of men. He wrote:

My brother, a friend and I were fishing at Doris Lake near dusk. Doris Lake is roughly a mile and a half hike from the resort area of Mono Hot Springs. Nothing unusual was happening and then out of nowhere, we heard a scream come from across the lake and up in the mountains. There were no people or animals that we could see anywhere except the three of us. We were in the proverbial wilderness. My brother and I looked at each other and, unable to readily discern what we were hearing, we continued to do some fishing. I did say to him, "if I hear that again I am out of here." Well, a minute later, the same horrendous scream interrupted the quiet. The three of us immediately reeled in and began the incline up the canyon wall and back to the resort...without stopping. I was breathing like a freight train.

I have listened to various internet recordings of alleged Bigfoot, and I am struck by how similar these recordings are to the scream that we heard. I did not see anything, so I can't be sure, but I am fairly certain what I heard was not a human, bear or mountain lion; the screams were elongated (sustained). So...what could it be? Note: my brother and sister worked for several years at Mono Hot Springs. My sister's best friend worked there as well and had a horse. While riding in the backcountry, she claims to have seen Bigfoot walking through a meadow below a bluff she was riding atop. The area was a mountain lake surrounded by deep forest and mountains.[130]

Mono Hot Springs Resort

Crows Circle Heralding the Sasquatch's Approach

Describing a scene where two stands of trees converged is called a "bottle-neck," according to bow-hunter Daniel George. He wrote,

I was convinced it was a deer making its way up the creek. I had plenty of time to spin around, drop to one knee, hook my release, and then get ready to draw my bow. Whatever it was stopped at the top of the "bottle neck," …then quiet. I'm fixed and ready to draw my bow when suddenly a flock of crows burst overhead; evidently seeing below them what I couldn't! All I knew was whatever I heard walking, they could see and the crows made a terrible racket. They swirled around for about a minute squawking and then whatever it was suddenly took off running back down the bottle neck. This is when I became alarmed because it was not a graceful sound like a deer or any other kind of foot-falls; it sounded like a Mac truck crashing through the woods snapping very large limbs in its path.

Continuing on with Daniel's frightening story,

I knew instantly that this was something I hadn't dealt with before. The whole time the flock of crows followed it overhead all the way to the bottom of the bottle neck where the three hills came together, then it stopped again. The crows stopped circling. About another minute went by and the thing never moved. The crows stayed calm and weren't being very loud when all of the sudden they exploded, fluttering up squawking bloody murder at the exact same time this Sasquatch cried out in a soul-shattering scream that reverberated off the three hills! My heart fell into my stomach and then it yelled loudly a second time confirming what I had just heard was indeed real. Ha, like I didn't already know! The thing was less than 30-yards from me and its yell was so loud, the booming reverberation shook my clothes. Then, after this thing yelled the second time, I heard over my left shoulder to the southwest another one answer the first one's scream/call but a good distance away and then over my right shoulder a third Bigfoot yelled towards the southeast. The morning sounded like Jurassic Park! That was it, man I got out of there so freakin' fast I have no idea which direction I took. Finally feeling some degree of safety, I realized I had pissed down my leg.[131]

To me, the amazing part of the Dan George story was the powerful echo-locating type of screaming to other Sasquatch in the vicinity that tends to be reported the most. This echo-locating-scream behavior has been described in other references but not to the same degree. It may be a warning statement.

Bow Hunting Incident

George's remarks about crows circling overhead reminded me of a story I heard where the informant described a flock of gnats swarming around the buttocks of a Sasquatch that stood watching small children playing. Apparently, watching and screaming is a Sasquatch pastime. There are other reports of gnats swarming. One surprised couple reported seeing "a thick black swarm of gnats or something" over the head of a Sasquatch, striding off the side of the Alaskan Highway where biting flies are the soup of the day in some parts.

Ripping Bark, Eating Grubs, Watching Children Play

Inspired by Merle Haggard and Johnny Cash, New Braunfels, Texas-born country singer Kris Allen is also actively interested in Sasquatch behavior; he has had at least 8 different sightings, which is extraordinary on the face of it.

His first Bigfoot sighting was in West Virginia; he described the color as champagne with Caucasian skin. The Bigfoot stationed itself in a huge sycamore tree, just minding its own business, evidently watching children playing in the backyard home of Allen's grandmother. According to Allen, there was a whole bunch of people in the yard watching the creature for an hour at dusk until it got too dark to see it anymore. The next day, it was gone. The family St. Bernard wouldn't go out in the yard; but other things happened, like rocks being thrown, etc. Intimidation tactics appear to be an art form with the Sasquatch.

Allen's next encounter was of a "dead-leaf color brown, its skin was dark, quite the opposite of the first sighting." Constantly referring to the Sasquatch people as "apes," he described a clear moonlit night collecting lightning bugs with his wife and son when he heard what sounded like a deer racking its antlers against a tree. The sound came from across a meadow. From behind a rock, they watched the area where the sound came from, and to their amazement, out comes "a ten-foot-tall ape" along with "a shorter one that was 8-foot-tall, give or take a foot or two."

The interesting part of Allen's appraisal was that he was able to observe the Bigfoot in the process of ripping bark off the trees and eating whatever was underneath, probably grubs, termites, and other insects. I've seen photos of trees with freshly ripped bark torn away but didn't relate it to Sasquatch behavior until I heard Allen describe the activity in detail.

Singer Kris Allen described a third Sasquatch stepping out from the woods, and the first two he observed stepped back into the darkness and out of sight. The third was even taller, described as 12 feet tall with greater arm reach, and began to remove bark from further up the trees than the first two individuals were capable of reaching. Finally realizing the potential for danger in a situation where his wife and child were present, Allen escorted his family back to the camper, but the Sasquatch didn't bother them. All told, it was quite the story![132]

In the past, Canadian Randy Brisson and Joe Beelart in West Linn, Oregon, have sent me photos of such trees in a debarked state; so, I knew there was a potential for such behavior, although I have not seen anything like it locally. It is easily misidentified with the work of porcupines and the rack damage done by deer. Porcupine damage will show teeth imprints, and its bark damage is usually generalized in one area much higher up in a tree than racked animals or where a Sasquatch could reach. Conversely, the Sasquatch strips or tears the bark downward from a high reachable point toward the ground, sometimes severely damaging the trees.

Kris Allen Country Music Star, And Bigfoot Hunter

Glaring, Staring, Swaying

Author of the book, *Ghost Grizzlies*, David Petersen was a regular contributor to many outdoor magazines and has authored other books on outdoor topics such as hunting. One article interestingly titled *Bigbutt* ran in Bugle Magazine, November/December 2002 (Volume 19 Issue 6).

Petersen detailed how he met up with a Sasquatch on an old road cut at dusk while bow-hunting in a forest in southern Colorado. Walking quietly around a bend in the road cut, Petersen was startled to see an odd upright creature coming down the road toward him at a range of only 20 yards. Petersen described the creature as being over 5 feet tall, perhaps 200 pounds, with short legs compared to a man, longer arms than a man, thick through the torso, with an upright posture, and walking on two legs. Petersen was struck by the creature's apparent large buttocks as it eventually turned and stepped off the trail. It was too dark to see facial details beyond his observation that the creature had a flat face. The two strangers stopped on the road cut and stared at one another for a while before the creature eventually stepped toward the edge of the road, where it swayed back and forth for a time as if trying to get a better sense of the bow hunter's intent. Eventually, the creature walked off into the darkened forest, and Petersen went on his way.[133]

Bugle Magazine Article

Pre-Teens See Tree With a Santa Claus Face

Clark County, Nevada – Two pre-teens, Tommy and Raff S., ages 9 and 11, spent a weekend with their parents at the Mount Charleston Lodge, Las Vegas Nevada wilderness area. They were fooling around in the woods between Old Park Road and Aspen Circle on Saturday afternoon. According to the boys, it's dense and dark in a few places. They had been warned about cougars in the area, which "freaked" them out. Hungry and worn out, they headed back to the lodge and, as they did, they saw what they thought was a huge tree shaped like a giant man. The older boy said, "The tree moved" and they became "weirded out." Still thinking it was a strange tree, they got closer, and the tree moved its limbs. At the same time, they saw the tree had hair growing on it. Young Tommy looked up and saw the tree had a face that looked like Santa Claus looking down at him. Tommy said he screamed, and the tree backed up and moved away, walking like a man. They ran all the way back to their parents, but the email, which was generated from a school district computer in 2008, said their story wasn't taken seriously, and there was never any reply to my questions for a better description.

The Nevada incident highlights the Sasquatch's apparent ability to blend seamlessly into its surroundings—or perhaps the witnesses simply needed better eyeglasses. The Sasquatch are seemingly quite capable of standing in one position for hours without moving, looking like part of the landscape.

It doesn't mean big ones are hiding behind every tree or boulder. If we think hard enough about that scenario, we can work ourselves into the creepy belief that we're being watched, which seems to psyche most people out. One's own imagination generates terror in the overactive mind and only the strong manage to keep a tight rein on runaway thoughts. I've seen hardened men cut and run from thinking too hard about things totally manufactured in their imagination.

A Different Opinion, Swaying

Midnight Owl, a tribal member of the Cherokee Nation of Oklahoma, also known as Mr Stewart Taylor, contacted me through the Bigfootencounters dot com website on May 22, 2011. Taylor declared he sought nothing but to show folks, "…these subjects are not the wild creature some would have you believe they are. Sure, there may be a rogue or two around just like in our society."

Attached to Taylor's email was a lengthy MSWord processed declaration of an event he had with Cherokee woman Arla Williams on April 16, 2011. Taylor identified her as a woman who had a close, trusting relationship with a whole clan of Bigfoot near Lake Eufaula, Oklahoma. Mr Taylor's complete letter and the sound track is uploaded on the Bigfootencounters website in toto. For this purpose, I've cited only his description of the Sasquatch behavior.

> Just then about 30 feet away from me to the east, a huge 8-9 foot hairy figure stepped between two large trees into a cleared area fully illuminated by the moonlight. It then began to sway, staring at me. It was the typical shape and build of the common Bigfoot sketches and drawings. "I can see it; it is swaying from side to side!" I exclaimed to my guide. "Sway with it" Arla replied, which I immediately did. At that point I began to sway and another smaller Bigfoot figure rose up from the brush about 15 feet directly in front of me, then another one off to its right about the same size with a smaller figure sitting at its feet I assumed was a toddler. They both intently stared at me; occasionally looking back at what I assume was their parent standing between the trees.

Taylor described the sighting with Arla, "at night, after dark." He indicated he was not allowed to take a camera but had a pocket recorder detailing the conversations between Taylor and Arla. Of interest to me was the fact that the witness never described glowing red eyes or any feeling of impending danger. He was not frightened, weakened, or experiencing any other symptoms previously mentioned by sightings that occur at night. He was not screamed at, or attacked, nor did he feel threatened, in danger, or any of the other indicators generally associated with a Bigfoot encounter. Apparently, the whole tribe of hairy men welcomed his presence. The only behavior he listed was swaying back and forth, which is often reported.

Slavomir Rawicz mentioned in his 1942 book, *The Long Walk*, how he and five other men observed the creatures blocking their passageway on the trail. He wrote that they stamped and swayed when moving about; a description which evokes the locomotion patterns of both man and animals. Stomping and swaying are characteristics of hostile feral persons and occasionally reticent behavior of learning-disabled people who are scared. Horses stomp and sway. In other animals, stamping the foot can be an alarm signal that something is regarded as dangerous. Prairie dogs do this, and deer stomp an alarm, then bolt and run. All manner of swaying side to side and stomping have been reported.

Swaying with Aggressive Intent

Debra Fantalh described her 2002 chance encounter in Taney County, Missouri, with a smallish Sasquatch swaying back and forth this way:

> ...it was less than thrilling; the youngster was about 5-feet tall, stocky in build, barely had hair on his extremities and just stood in one place looking at me swaying back and forth on one foot then the other. The hair on his head was pulled back and braided, the length of it falling down his back. We stared at each other in a non-threatening way for several long minutes during that time he swayed. His eyes darted nervously observing every move I made. There must have been others around I didn't notice. I spoke softly to him but he said not a word. It was at that point he picked up a LARGE sized stone and threw it with such great force that when it hit my shoulder, I fell backwards hitting my head on something hard. I'm not sure what happened next, but when I came to my senses, he was gone. I had blood on my shirt and I

was bleeding from my head. Les took me to the emergency clinic for three stitches. I told them I fell but said nothing about the incident. They would not have believed it anyway.[*]

Bigfoot Grabbed Me

Whatever you think about the behaviors variously ascribed to the Sasquatch being totally charitable and non-violent, on April 19, 2001, the following account occurred in rural southeastern Oklahoma, signed only "Wes" at the bottom, but the header read "Westin."

We were watching the season premiere of *24*, about a Federal Marshal named Jack Bauer. It came on late at night, I forget now, but after midnight. It was a series that you could not get up and run to the kitchen unless it was commercial time. But all through that program we could hear the raccoons working the lids off our metal trashcans outside; it happened a lot. I determined that I would get my pistol, go out and nail a few coons after the program.

Woody, our dog, was sitting on alert facing the wall. Once or twice he would get up and sniff the wall and then back up and stare at the wall some more. The clinking of the trash cans continued and was loud enough to be heard above the TV. At my wife's urging, I finally got up, loaded my pistol and snuck out the back door. It was quite dark outside.

It took a few minutes for my eyes to adjust. There was a creepy eerie feel to the night air that put me on high alert, and that's when I saw a figure bending head and shoulders into one of the bigger trash cans; the lids were off all of four cans, and it wasn't raccoons. Then fight or flight kicked in. I think I said, who would be digging in my trashcans so late at night? Thoughts went through my head as I watched. My eyes continued to adjust to the dim light and now I could hear the dog barking inside the house and clawing at the backdoor to get out. I

---

[*] D.F. Taney County, Missouri.

decided to raise my arm and fire a warning shot to scare off the man going through my trash cans.

So, I did, and this is where it gets weird. As I fired off the shot, someone powerful grabbed my hand and arm from behind and held it so tight that I could not move, and I swear to you the strength it took to hold my arm and hand was unimaginable; I was literally hanging by my upper arm. At first, I went weak from fright, but then I began to fight. I fought like hell.

I forgot about the figure in the trash can and, angling around, I looked upwards at the thing holding my arm up in the air. IT WAS A BIGFOOT PLAIN AS THE NOSE ON MY FACE. It had bright yellowish orange eyes looking down at me! I know I screamed weakly, in hindsight probably a high pitched girlie scream, but I don't mind saying it was terrifying being that close held by such a freak of nature. The pistol dropped to the ground, my ego was bruised but I wasn't hurt, just scared. I crumpled to the ground to regain my composure then went inside to tell my wife and calm the dog. Woody wouldn't come near me, in fact Woody growled at me. My wife believed me because of the stink on me. True story!*

In the continuing correspondence with the informant Westin, he told me that a neighborhood watch was eventually formed where everybody in a ten-mile radius had their neighbor's phone numbers. Other neighbors in his rural community took up arms when one of our neighbors showed them her back door. The door was locked with a push-in type lock on the knob from the inside of the house. The outside knob was completely sheared off and tossed several hundred feet from the porch. The door was ajar, and the screen door was ripped or torn out from its framework. Nothing in the house was missing apart from the woman's little terrier, which was never found. Her cat was found drowned in the toilet. The toilet seat was in the hallway.

---

* Westin, April 19, 2001.

This report came in hours after the death of Rene Dahinden and, of course, it didn't get my undivided attention. In the process of a heavy email load that month, the report was misplaced, and now, eleven years later, I can no longer reach the informant. In honesty, I struggled with the veracity of Westin's report, but perhaps he will make contact once again, and I can learn more. I don't doubt the Sasquatch is capable of that kind of aggression; but grabbing a shooter's arm from behind is hard to visualize. The informant said it happened in Le Flore County, Oklahoma.

When a person sees something that isn't supposed to exist, it's hard to know what to think, and this is what Westin's story is about. Trying to imagine what Bigfoot behavior is typical and what isn't is near to impossible. The ridicule, the discrediting we all go through because we told our story and gave an opinion is part of the ugly side of this research. Sometimes, saying what we know isn't worth the risk of the discrediting, disrespect, and ridicule that comes with it. We've lost many great contributors because of the senseless attacks by those who think their opinion is more appealing than the next guy's.

Unprovoked Physical Assault

My wife and I lived in McIntosh County, Oklahoma. For nearly 33 years we walked an old dirt path every morning through a densely wooded area. Sometimes, even an evening walk, and we've seen all manner of wildlife – but did not know hairy men were in these parts. The idea of Bigfoot was something my wife knows as she is Creek/Checotah.

A morning came when the wife wasn't up to par and didn't want to go out and walk. So I put on my jacket and went off without her. Finally, I felt I had enough, was feeling fatigued and turned around to head back to the house. There, in the morning mist and clearly blocking the narrow path, stood a hair covered man-shaped figure...okay, now I believe in Bigfoot.

I'm a retired Marine but never felt terror like I did at that moment. With no weapon, nowhere to turn, and no options, I froze and stared. No exaggeration, this thing was 8-feet tall, maybe 4-feet wide across the shoulders, and it commenced walking towards me. Thinking back, it was more like marching towards me because it hiked its knees upwards with each step and stamped down its feet. I became irrational, I couldn't think of a way out or around the thing. Then his huge-ness picked up momentum, comin' straight at me. Honestly, at that moment I talked to God. Seriously, it was a "come to Jesus moment." I felt a kind of warmth on my cold right thigh, and I'm not ashamed to admit I involuntarily pissed my pants at seeing it coming at me, Bobbie, and then I stumbled backwards a step or two and nearly fell but needed to see where to run; not that I thought I could out-run it. By then he was almost on top of me, dust behind him was flyin' and I thought, "fuck, I'm a dead man." I don't know why I did this but in that split-second I dropped to the ground and curled up in a tight fetal position like you would if a bear was on top of you. Each step the Bigfoot took made the ground move; he kept coming and stepped over me with a huge amount of force into the ground, narrowly missing my face; it was THAT close@!#@! At the same time he must have grabbed hold of the back of my windbreaker because he jerked me off the ground and now I'm flying through the air! No exaggeration here, I flew a good twenty feet, landed at the base of a tree in forest litter. I curled up again, afraid to move, and this creature let out a "primal scream" that was so horrifying that it made my whole body quiver.

What the hell did I do to cause the wrath of this wild thing? I don't know but this attack was not provoked and if they ever watched us as you suggest, then the wife and I must have been familiar to him. This was, however, the first time I went alone for a walk. No 52-year old man ran home faster than I did that day.

Now look, I don't want to argue the point, but this was no bluff charge, this dude was seriously taking care of business! Reliving that day for you made me sweat profusely; my pits are wet! His color was reddish brown. I do not wish to be known or talk about it again, and I don't want organizations or the media coming here like I read about.[134]

Physical Attack by Sasquatch

One of Bigfoot research's best collectors of old Bigfoot-related articles is Scott McClean of Pacific Palisades, California.[135] Scott has been exceedingly generous with members of this field with the articles in his extensive collection. I mention this particular old account because the history of Bigfoot attacking civilized man – though unprovoked – has always been there.

In this newspaper article, a Sasquatch attacks a man and his daughter - literally in a physical way. We sometimes forget that the Sasquatch is, after all, a wild living being with no specific rules for living that we know about. Using caution around them is smart! Published in The Hillsdale Standard, Hillsdale, Michigan, on Tuesday, January 26, 1869, it reads:

> The City of Gallipolis, Ohio is excited over a wild man who is reported to haunt the woods near that city. He goes naked, is covered with hair; is gigantic in height and "his eyes stare from the sockets." He attacked a horse carriage containing a man and daughter a few days ago. He is said to have bounded at the father, catching him in a vice grip and hurling him upon the earth; falling upon him and endeavoring to bite and scratch him like a wild animal. The struggle was long and fearful, rolling and wallowing in the deep mud, half suffocated, sometimes beneath his adversary, whose burning and maniac eyes glared into his own with murderous and savage intensity. Just as he was about to become exhausted from exertions, the daughter, taking courage at the imminent danger of her father, snatched up a rock and hurling it at the head of her Father's would-be-murderer, was fortunate enough to put an end to the struggle by striking him somewhere about the ear. The creature was not stunned, but feeling unequal to further exertions,

slowly got up and retired into a neighboring group of trees that skirted the road.

Some may rationalize this article is 144 years old, but the prior report from McIntosh County, Oklahoma, was very recent in 2011. Apparently, we just never know what the attitude and demeanor of a Sasquatch will be. For this reason, I am often hard-pressed to believe stories from habituators and other long-term inter-actors. In light of the many statements from witnesses that include aggression or perceived aggression in the data; it is hard to accept that the Sasquatch is totally a benevolent being.

Scott McClean's Website

Washing Food

At first, I thought washing food had to be unusual, but rethinking the idea, I've concluded that we simply have a shortage of reports for this little-known behavior, and that the following is only one of two I was able to find listed in my records, though there may be others. This first account is quite old and was penned originally by Ivan Sanderson, but it's worth mentioning for recording the behavior.

Mike King, a well-known timber-cruiser, was working in an isolated region near the Campbell River, Vancouver Island. He was left to work alone because his First Nation employee refused to accompany him in fear of the horrific monkey men they knew inhabited the woods. It was late afternoon when King spotted the reddish-brown creature bending over a water hole. The interesting behavior noted in this account most certainly had to be that the Sasquatch was observed washing some roots and vegetables before placing them in two orderly piles on the creek bank. The creature then left, loping off like a human being. King said: "His arms were peculiarly long and used freely in climbing and bush-running." The footprints observed by King were distinctly human, except for the "phenomenally long and spreading toes."[136]

Too Bizarre for Science

Sasquatch Ran Like a Deer

Canadian Alex Solunac reported a sighting occurring in 1904. The Victoria Daily Colonist reported that four men from Qualicum were hunting near Horn Lake when they came across a creature they described as a wild man covered with long, matted hair all over its body. "The creature ran like a deer through the seemingly impenetrable tangle of undergrowth, and pursuit was utterly impossible."[137]

Too Bizarre for Science

Strategic Stone Placement

Much of what you will read in *The de facto Sasquatch* about rock throwing and like behaviors came from the assisted research of Roger Knights in Seattle, Washington, and I gratefully acknowledge his generosity and willingness to share a shipload of information.

It is fascinating to think that the primitive Sasquatch found rock-throwing the means by which they could, in some small way, communicate with the civilized world. We puzzle over the reasons why they lob things at us when we know they're quite capable of knocking us absolutely into next year if they wanted to; yet they don't.

Reports of Sasquatches and rocks are many. This next story includes flat stones, but they are not used in an aggressive state of mind. Instead, it is a Squatch having a bit of fun with flagstones, perhaps a bit of juvenile graffiti.

A Native American Pala man named Gibbs, a forklift operator at a rock and stone masonry yard in Southern California, reported something odd he blamed on the local Bigfoot. He locked up and left the high-fenced yard at 6:00 p.m. on a Tuesday, and arriving at work the next morning, found something strange. Large flagstone stepping stones had been displaced from their 4-foot high stack and placed down the middle of the main aisle of the yard. It led up to the section of various stones marked "walkway projects."

"Now, I admit I thought this was probably unrelated to Bigfoot and most likely the work of high-school pranksters until I tried to lift one of the 3x5 foot flag stones. Surprisingly, they were thick and quite heavy. The art of collecting and strategically placing 34 flat stepping stones took some doing."

The story Gibbs told me really came home to roost when he said the stepping stones were placed fifty-inches apart...exactly. The Pala band of Mission Indians, from which Gibbs is a descendent, is known in southern California for its certified organic citrus and avocado orchards; its production is one of the largest of its kind. Gibbs believed the Bigfoot came down from the mountain attracted to the citrus and avocado orchards. Maybe they were just having some fun for themselves in the block and brick masonry yard, and hopscotch on flagstones was suggested. It is also interesting to note that there are reports from nearby growers of trees stripped of their fruit, so the pattern of behavior is there.

In some instances, rocks don't seem to be deliberately thrown at passers-by but lobbed precisely to land in and around hikers. It's hard to say if it's to get attention or a low-dose level of aggression used to rid people from an area where they are not wanted. Certainly, there are written bow-hunter testimonials where Sasquatches have been seen taking down deer with rocks aimed precisely to kill. Apparently, they're quite accurate.

There is another account where a Sasquatch in eastern Ontario side-armed a projectile believed to be a rock at a fleeing snowshoe rabbit and nailed it on its third leap, and a story I was told recently where "something" lobbed or pushed a 400 lb boulder down the mountainside at a terrified trail walker who didn't take kindly to the message. Small avalanches and rock slides have been attributed to Sasquatch shenanigans, and road closures are the result. Speaking of road closures, some of us are quite mystified by a few of the closures that lead into Bluff Creek at certain times of the year.

There is no doubt in my mind that the proficiency they have in rock placement is a learned skill, a behavior perhaps taught to male Sasquatches, undoubtedly becoming a means by which they take down hoofed animals, game birds in flight, and one very brave ole gold prospector in Thompson's Flat, Oregon.

The Kentucky Donks

In stark contrast to some of the revenge displays made by a Sasquatch, this next story showed a compassionate side, or at least this one did. A backwoods Kentucky widow woman's grown children wrote to tell me about this next encounter.

Apparently, they had always had "Donks" come around. They were familiar individuals that frequently hung around; one they named Big Donk, another Mama Donk, and over the years there were several smaller Donks. There was never any problem with them, but they never fed them, gave them treats, or interacted with them other than to acknowledge their presence.

This day, the daughter left her infant baby with her widowed mother to babysit while mom went to the store for diapers. The infant was in a four-wheel baby carriage set near the clothesline while grandma hung the baby's washing out to dry. The phone rang, and grandma ducked inside the house to answer it. While on the phone, a neighborhood dog entered the backyard and jumped onto the baby carriage, tipping it over and spilling the tiny infant out onto the grass. It began to cry loudly, flail, and kick, causing the wild dog to lunge at it. Finished on the phone, the grandma came back out onto the scene and saw the female Sasquatch they called Mama Donk righting the carriage and placing the infant out of the snarling dog's teeth, back into the baby's carriage. The male Donk chased off the dog and, taking Mama Donk's hand, retreated into the woods. Grandma told the returning daughter that the Donks had saved the infant from being eaten by the vicious neighbor-hood dog.[*]

There were other behaviors in the Dodson letters. One was the interest shown in the laundry on the clothesline by Mama Ba-donka-donk. The other was the Donk children's delight in running through the lawn sprinklers, just like any child would. Curious about the use of the term "Donk," I was told it was a slur expression for a woman with a large derrière; large buttocks. Google lists it this way: A "Ba-donka-donk is an Ebonics expression for an extremely curvaceous female behind." I learn something every day.

––––––––––––––––––––

[*] The Bessie Dodson Story, 1988.

According to Betty Sanders-Garner's research, the early Chehalis Indians of the Harrison Lake, B.C., area believed the creatures called "Sasquatch" in their language were descendants of two bands of giants who were almost exterminated in a raging battle many years ago. Those who survived the battle are said to inhabit the remote mountain caves at the top of Morris Mountain. Witnesses relate stories of Sasquatch kidnapping Indian maidens, stealing fish from housewives larders, hurling rocks at prospectors, and killing deer with clubs.[*]

Taking Things and Stealing

The salt shaker caper…

We didn't make reservations but thought if we pulled our rig in early, someone would be pulling out. We were wrong. The River Bend Resort Campground was full that week in August 2007. We backed out and went up River Road to what looked like a dirt pull-out for 18-wheelers and stopped for the night. It was hot, so we set up outside underneath the RV awning, cooked dinner in a Weber kettle and sat around mapping the next part of the trip. The night was clear; the moon was out, a real nice evening. Jan was laid out in her chaise nearly asleep, I got up and went inside and flaked out on the divan facing the screen door. At one-thirty I heard my wife calling out for me. I sat up expecting her to come through the door but she didn't. Finally, I got up, went over and stood at the screen, when Jan gestured toward the trees. Our awning was facing the trees approximately 40-feet away and there stood a dark figure with moonlight shining up his back. He made no movement, just stood still for the longest time. I quietly told my wife to come inside, and she did. We turned off the door light, me watching through the screen door and my wife looking out the sink window. The creature stood there motionless for the longest time; then just when I was ready to close up the outer door, he moves towards the Weber kettle. I left a small piece of kielbasa on the

---

[*] Betty Sanders-Garner.

grill; it was char-burnt. He seemed to be sizing up the sausage. I looked up at Jan and she says, "he wants the sausage." Our watch continued for most of three minutes. He was very cautious, taking a step and standing motionless for periods at a time. He touched the chair I had been sitting in...always going back around the kettle. The creature was big but not as hulking as I had imagined from other reports. He timidly touched the fork that dangled from the side of the kettle then picked up the salt shaker from the side table and went into the darkness of the trees. Less than a minute later he returned again with a stick and used it to flip the burnt sausage off the grill onto the ground. He picked up the sausage and went back into the woods. We waited a while to see if he would return the salt shaker but he didn't ever show himself again. We stayed up 'til three that morning amazed at the whole thing.[*]

Leo Selzer Reported Stealing Behavior

This happened to me when I was hunting alone, if my memory serves me right. I think it would have been around 1979 or 1980. I was hunting and I drove up to a clearing that was probably 20 acres in size. As I ate a sandwich I had a feeling that something was around; like I was being watched. I was starting on the second half of my sandwich when I saw some movement in the bush on the other side of the clearing. Thinking it might be a moose, I put my sandwich on the rim of the pickup box, took my rifle and headed off to circle the clearing. I was gone close to an hour. When I returned I noticed that my sandwich was gone and where it had been there was a huge cone from a fir tree. Somebody or something had stepped out of the bush some 50 yards from my truck, walked past my truck and back into the bush.[138]

As many researchers suggest, there are lots of stories about stealing.

---

[*] B.J.T. February 2, 2008.

Another interesting email from Pacific County, Washington State, speaks again to brazen behavior.

> We have a secondhand story for you. My family and I spend two weeks a year out in a little place called Raymond where we salmon fish with my mother. She's a widow in her sixties, an avid fisherwoman who's been fishing the Willapa River since her parents taught her and their parents taught them. My 6-year-old daughter had a small plastic statue of an ape she got out of a gumball machine up river, and she showed it to my mother.
>
> Somehow the little statue reminded mother of Bigfoot and of a story she was involved with when very young, maybe 8 or 9. It went like this...she was fishing with my grandfather somewhere on the Willapa River during the salmon run. They each had a large fish, enough for the family's dinner, and started back up the path toward home. My mother was skipping along when she saw a large black man step out onto the path between her and my grandfather. She stopped and called out for her paw. He turned to see what she wanted and what he saw astounded him. There was a large black Bigfoot standing there with a half-carcass of a deer under his arm (still bleeding she said) and with him was a kid, you know, a younger model of the bigger Bigfoot. My grandfather spoke softly to my mother telling her to give the little one her salmon. Mother refused, she'd worked hard for that salmon. The smaller one then approached my mother closer and she started backing away from the safety of grandpa. Seeing the persistence, grandfather untied his catch and tossed one to the little Bigfoot. Amazingly, he caught the thing and then the two Bigfeet [sic] scaled a vertical wall with the deer and salmon, and at the top looked back and went out of sight. My grandfather took my mother's hand and all he said was "there will be one less salmon steak for dinner tonight." She remembers asking what they wanted it for, the reply was as best she remembered, "they were hungry and we had more than enough." Mother never saw another one, but the encounter stayed with her for more than

> 50 years. I fish with mother a little differently now, but her story is a
> family treasure.[*]

I think the Fornier story speaks not only to the art of pillaging but also to the brazen defiance of the two Sasquatch. I've mentioned before, what's theirs is theirs, and what is ours is also theirs – or so it seems. The behavior of the Sasquatch is rather unsettling. What might have happened if he hadn't tossed the salmon to them? Alarmed by the presence of the hairy man, not every fisherman would think to do that.

There are other reminders of deer being torn in half. While that wasn't detailed in the Fornier story, they did say the adult carried a bleeding half of a deer under its arm. Clearly, the pair were hunting, and seeing an opportunity presenting itself with fresh salmon, they seized the moment. The hairy beggars were totally on point for this caper... evidently, their culture has no laws or boundaries for a little daytime trail robbery. If I collected my groceries in the same way, I'd have a police record a mile long.

Stealing Grain and Fruit

Bonnie Woodburn of Collowhee, North Carolina, reported a theft of sorts by a family of Bigfoot. The sighting occurred in the Ouachita Mountains in Arkansas on September 27, 2011. Woodburn and her husband had a farm by a stream bordering the ascent to the Ouachita Mountains. Early one evening, her friend went outside to look at her horses. As she neared the stream, she came face to face with a male Bigfoot. Entranced rather than frightened, they gazed intently at one another. The woman said the Bigfoot's eyes seemed startled but not menacing. The Bigfoot turned away, crossed the stream, and disappeared into the woods.

A week later, at approximately the same time of day, she went to check on her horses' grain, which had been diminishing faster than normal.

---

[*] Stephen Fornier, 2003.

When she looked toward the stream, she saw a Bigfoot family – a male, female, and a youngster – carrying off some of the grain as well as fruit from her trees. She noted that her horses weren't at all spooked by Bigfoot moving through the pasture. I thought the behavior of the horses in the presence of the creatures was highly unusual but possible if they were used to having them around. When the Bigfoot family saw Mrs. Woodburn approaching them, they picked up gravel and threw it strategically around her rather than at her. There had been sightings of Bigfoot families taking refuge in abandoned barns and cabins in the wooded areas near water. Wild boar remains were reported inside one of the huts. Mrs. Woodburn said she firmly believes that these non-threatening creatures exist, and deserve privacy and our respect.[139]

Skyships Over Cashiers Website

Rock Thrown, Lineman Quits Job

David Benear had an interesting conversation with a neighbor friend while the fellow was cleaning fish near his front porch. Benear's friend told him that a guy he worked with quit his job the day before because of something that happened at work. With a few edits to shorten up the incident, here is Benear's story, including the hairy man's behavior:

> This guy works for the electric company here in Little Rock and has for twelve years. He was on a call Tuesday night about some power lines that were "on the fritz" west of town, just before you get to the Saline County line, near Paron, Arkansas. He arrived around 9:00 p.m.

and was in the process of loading up a bucket when a large rock landed near his truck that was parked off the side of the road. Within a minute or so, another rock (larger than the first) hit and rolled almost to his feet. He didn't know what to think, but as he was headed toward his truck, out of the tree line stepped a Sasquatch, just staring at him from about 150 feet. He shined his light in the area from where he thought the rocks came from and heard rustling in the trees just before the creature stepped out. He immediately hurried to his truck and took off. This was about all the info he gave other than that he was terrified, and in his fright told his supervisor that he quit because he could not handle going out on night calls anymore. This guy also said to Sam, "you'd be surprised how many of these Bigfoots are seen around here that you never hear about."[*]

Sasquatch Brandishing a Club

Kip Derringer was scanning old Dayton newspaper articles in The Columbia Chronicle, for February 1, 1902, and ran across a Bigfoot story while looking for something else. Here it is:

Eight Feet High, Carries a Club and Yells Like a Comanche

Salt Lake, Utah, January 27, 1902 – According to a Pocatello, Idaho, correspondent at the Deseret News, the residents of the little town of Chesterfield, located in an isolated portion of Bannock County, Idaho, are greatly excited over the appearance in that vicinity of an eight-foot, hair-covered human monster.

He was first seen on January 14 when he appeared among a party of young people skating on the Pointneuf River, near John Gooch's Ranch. The creature showed fight, flourishing a large club and uttering a series of yells, before starting to attack the skaters who managed to reach their wagons and get away safely.

---

[*] D. Benear, 2005.

Measurements of the tracks showed the creature's feet to be 22 inches long and seven inches broad, with the imprint of only four toes. Stockmen report having seen similar tracks along the range west of the river. The people in the neighborhood, feeling unsafe while the creature is at large, have sent 20 men on its trail to effect its capture. [*]

Big hairy things brandishing clubs is a behavior recorded as far back as the 1860s Civil War era when the New York Tribune published a story about "a hairy thing" carrying not only a club but a rabbit. Bloodhounds refused to track the hairy thing.[140] The old stories of Sasquatches with clubs seem lost to research now; we don't hear but a few reports of that kind anymore.

A 1900 sighting occurred at Huntsville, a small town halfway between Waitsburg and Dayton, Washington State. A lone fir tree still stands alongside the highway where the house of the family stood for many years. In that report, a girl went out the back door to tend the family garden when she saw the Bigfoot at the garden gate (brandishing a club) not more than 100 feet away. She turned and bolted back indoors, and the Bigfoot likewise scampered off into the nearby foothills of the Blue Mountains.[141]

Idaho Has a Boogie Man

Barn Door Torn off Its Hinges, Grain Barrels Tossed

Tina Barone was only 13 in 1981 when she and her sister Roxanne entered the dark barn to carry out their evening chores. The two girls were scared to go into the barn because they had heard strange noises many times before coming from inside, but Tina said she would go in first. "As I reached for the light switch, I felt fur, which I thought was one of the goats or something, so I touched it again. It was tall and black and furry and it stood upright like a man. It had a deep growl. I just can't put what it looked like into any kind of form." Tina told the younger Roxanne to run back to the house, then turned and began walking slowly from the barn, but "it started walking out behind me so I started running."

The girl's older cousin, David Barone, grabbed his 16-gauge shotgun to scare the creature away. "It stood there and looked at me; it didn't know what to do either," said Barone. "It was unbelievably B-I-G! It was about 6 or 7 foot tall. I didn't shoot to kill; I shot in the air to scare it away and then it ran into the woods making funny noises. It stood up on two feet, had real long arms between a bear and an ape - that's what I think. I've never seen a Bigfoot, so I have no idea if it was one of those."

A Bigfoot in Thumb

Mrs. Barone stated their first encounter with the creature came earlier that year when her neighbor's barn door was ripped off at the hinges. "I've had fences torn down and grain barrels dumped over and eaten before," Mrs. Barone said. The family dog often barked at unseen intruders in the trees, and their farm animals are occasionally spooked by unknown predators. There is nothing spookier than a dog on point staring into the darkness, not barking, not moving – only watching intently, ears pricked forward, ever alert to a scent they cannot quite identify. The report was filed with the St. Clair County, Michigan, Sheriff's Department on November 22, 1981, carried by the Detroit News Sunday Edition, and cataloged by investigator Ron Schaffner in Creature Chronicles.[142]

Sasquatch Flags Down Logging Truck

Logging roads are a significant feature in the forest landscapes of British Columbia and Alberta, Canada. I was told by Jim Cheng that there were well over 80,000 kilometers of such roads in British Columbia alone that provide access to forests for timber harvesting.

In conversations with Cheng, formerly a resident of Blaine, Washington, and now living in San Diego, he told me a story about a B.C. log hauler. The fellow told Cheng that a Sasquatch blocked the narrow road when he was negotiating a hair-pin turn-around with a full load on board. In fact, Cheng (a truck driver himself) said the man was behind the wheel of a 2007 Kenworth T800 - 500hp Caterpiller engine and had to bring his load to a full stop in order not to hit the giant standing directly in front of his radiator. What was so unusual was the height the driver described. He said it was taller than the cab of the truck, so this particular Sasquatch (a male) was not only more than nine or ten feet tall, but he waved his arms like he was trying to fly. The driver sat stunned, waiting for whatever was to come next. He told Cheng that two very small copies of the big guy (twins) came out from the forest and walked to the big fellow. He picked up both of them (the little ones) and went off into the forest on the other side of the road.

Cheng wasn't sure he believed the fellow until the man next to him set down his beer and declared he was the driver in the truck behind him and the story was true.[*]

The Cheng log-hauler story reminds me of another that occurred in the early 1960s where Canadian John Bringsli spoke with two men from the Doukhobor settlement who were logging up Kokanee Glacier Road near Nelson, B.C. Both of these men witnessed a Sasquatch dumping logs off a logging truck. Neither man would give their name.[143]

Logging Camp Thief

I vividly remember being told a story back in the late nineties by Dr. Henner Fahrenbach that took place in Marion County, Oregon. At the time, I believe the story was already twenty years old, by which point the young girl telling it was an adult. The account itself isn't terribly remarkable, but the behavior of the Sasquatch stayed with me all these years. It was about a young girl who had been taken by her father to his workplace, which was a logging camp near Detroit Lake. During the night, she was awakened by a noise and opened the door to the cabin to find this female creature standing in front of an open cooler with a 20-pound piece of meat tucked neatly under her arm. After exchanging lengthy glances, the young girl screamed, arousing the men, at which point the slick, opportunistic Sasquatch left with the meat. The witness described the Sasquatch as six and a half feet tall, and it left 14" tracks. Regarding the behavior, Dr. Fahrenbach wrote:

> Although the cooler contained a variety of vegetables and fruits, the Sasquatch selected and kept the meat only. The door to the cooler had been opened in normal fashion by the handle rather than torn off bear-fashion. The relaxed response of the Sasquatch to the girl brings up the question of whether a Sasquatch recognizes a human female as such and responds in a different fashion to her, perhaps as a function of the sex alone or different body language conveyed by women or children, for that matter. I explored this possibility by way of John Green's

---

[*] James R. Cheng, 2007.

records. We segregated the sightings into male and female human observers, singles, couples, and groups and indexed them against the length of their encounters. The time difference between male and female encounters with a Sasquatch did not differ. On the other hand, it may not mean very much, because Green mentioned that his database did not record who first broke off the encounter, the Sasquatch or the witness. Hence, if there is a systematic difference in the readiness with which human observers, male or female, break off the meeting, then it would tell us nothing about Sasquatch behavior, only about that of the observers.[*]

There are any number of 'stealing stuff' stories told by surprised witnesses of hen house break-ins, eggs and chickens being stolen. Often, the Sasquatch will snap the neck of the chicken to keep them from squawking. Derek Jacobsen remembered his father talking about seeing a large, dark Sasquatch in the barn that lobbed a pitchfork at one of the barn owls nesting in the loft.

Debbie Grayson wrote in 1995 to say they often saw Bigfoot people carrying off an armload of apples from the orchard next to theirs. Mike Dardanos recorded a produce grower in the San Joaquin Valley of California saying several rows of onions were uprooted and missing from his acreage.

Over time, there have been reports of calves missing, and one report from Georgia told of a Sasquatch burglar who routinely ran off with pigs. Stranger stories filter in; stealing behaviors are common, so common that I wonder about the many that go unreported.

Use of Bow and Arrow; No Language

Writer Ioganes Johnson wrote an interesting piece in which he cites an old man with recollections of the early days (1800s) when "Indians were seen over 8-feet tall." Yes, he said, "Indians." In fact, the teller

---

[*] W. Henner Fahrenbach, 1997.

said he traded with one of the giants. Notice two things in this account: the giant shot a deer with an arrow, lending interest to the behavioral use of weapons other than what the Sasquatch can throw, and the fact that the giant Indian never spoke.

If what I suspect is true, perhaps the inability to speak is inherited. It could be a physical disability, refusal, perhaps mute, or living so remote that they never learned to do anything but wail, howl, and scream. Certainly, there are accounts of both in the data, with regional reports so widely varied that it's hard to say what the reasons are for some reports of language that indicate some Sasquatch are mute, for lack of a better word. My statistics reveal that more accounts say the Sasquatch made no sound or "didn't speak," than with language being identified and understood.

Bartering

In 1946, I was sitting on the porch of my hotel after supper, leafing through some old magazines when in walked a character who looked much like some pictures of Buffalo Bill I've seen, only much older. He seemed around a hundred years old; his shoulder-length hair was snow-white. He wore an Indian-made fringed buckskin jacket. Having nothing better to do, I listened in on the conversation, which soon brought out that the oldster had been the first white settler in the area and still lived in a cabin some distance from the village. The talk soon got around to the Sasquatch giants, and I became interested when the old boy blandly asserted that the stories were true and that he had seen many Indians over eight feet tall when he first moved up the lake some sixty years ago - roughly 1886.

"They were peaceful then," he said. "There was one big fellow, in particular, who used to come and trade with me. He never said anything, just gave me the creeps the way he would suddenly appear out of the bush with a deer on his shoulder. The deer were always killed with an arrow. He would put the deer down on the grass before my cabin and would just stand there looking at me. I would go to my cabin and come out with a bag of salt, which is what he wanted. Once I offered him a smoked salmon and trout but he only shook his head, grunted and slapped his belly to show he had all the fish he wanted. I saw this big guy kill a cougar with a club he broke off a tree..."

"How did that happen?" I asked.

The oldster continued, "I was out in my canoe fishing just in front of my cabin when a cougar (this area was full of them then) attacked my dogs, and they ran yelping to a little wharf I had built with the cougar hot after them. The dogs kept right on going and hit the water, which was the best thing they could have done. The cougar was perched on the wharf, spitting and snarling at the dogs, when this big Sasquatch came out of the bush with a club and killed the cougar like it was a pussycat. It almost wrecked my wharf, too, because his first swipe missed and broke some of the planks. The second time he didn't miss."

"What had become of these big Indians?" I asked.

"Why, they just went up north when the loggers came in," the old fellow explained.

"How far north?"

"If I know them, they went far enough so they won't be bothered too much," the old boy said.[144]

Is the Missing Link Living in Canada?

Rock Hurling

We have in our history the story of Alexander Caulfield Anderson, a well-known explorer and an executive of the Hudson's Bay Company, who was doing a 'survey' of the newly opened territory and sought a feasible trade route for his company. It is an old story to those of you who have been around in research for a while. Anderson reported hairy humanoids hurling rocks down upon him and his surveying party from more than one slope in 1864. So this rock-throwing business is nothing new if we take time to consider this 146-year-old entry.

There was reportedly a Sixes Wildman in and around Coos County, Oregon, who, from the early 1800s into 1900, was written up as a hairy, mean, rock-throwing monster that harassed miners and gold prospectors near Myrtle Point and Thompson Flat. The creature was also termed the "Thompson Flat Monster." Many accounts are filed in the historical society and published in the Lane County Leader in Cottage Grove, Oregon. One dated April 7, 1904, called the creature "the Sixes Wildman."

Out Run, Out Jump

In Cottage Grove, Oregon, the Lane County Leader News described the creature as "a reality, something after the fashion of a gorilla and unlike anything else either in appearance or action. It can outrun and outjump anything else that has ever been known, and not only that, but the seven-foot-tall creature could throw rocks with wonderful force and great accuracy. It had broad hands and feet and copious amounts of hair covered his body. In short, he looks like the very devil." Over time, it appears the State of Oregon, in particular, has not been without its stories of Sasquatch aggression. A close second is the State of Alaska, or so it seems.

What we can take from these older reports is that this rock-throwing phenomenon is nothing new to this field of research; it's old hat and a ritual Sasquatches evidently find as a useful means to create havoc and induce fear in surveyors, loggers, miners, hikers and backpackers, and why not? The strategy works well for the Sasquatch and, frankly, it wouldn't surprise me if they didn't sadistically enjoy the reactions they get from us. I think we are to them – great entertainment.

Boulder Throwing

Most rock-throwing sightings are relatively uneventful, but one angler had a notable experience while fishing the spring run-off in a low area of the Klamath River, close to a forest service road. Lester Wheatcroft, who was 73 years old at the time, was fly-fishing and busy casting when a large stone came "flying out of nowhere," landing eight to ten feet in front of him, close enough that he heard the incoming sound. He said it displaced an enormous amount of water. Disturbed, Wheatcroft eased down the river to the spot and could see that the stone's size was more a borderline-sized boulder, and he could hardly lift the thing. He thought it might be teenagers and looked all around and saw nothing, though he did notice a putrid smell in the air. Wheatcroft said after some thought as to what could lob something that large into the river, he decided to leave the area. If the intent was to scare off the fisherman, the behavior of the Sasquatch wins again. [*]

In August 2001, yet another fishing tale came to me from Bill Meszaros, who shared this account of rock throwing along the Salmon River in Idaho:

We were bringing out...um...illegal plants from the rough and mountainous terrain along the Salmon River in Idaho. It was about two in the morning and we were paddling out by moonlight. Suddenly, there were splashes ahead of us and to the left. We looked towards shore for the source of these splashes and saw a large manlike figure shadowing

---

[*] Ernestine W, 1987.

our canoe on the bank, hurling what we thought were large boulders. We paddled on.*

A Wandering Behavior

While vacationing at The Broadmoor in Colorado Springs in 2003, a golfer of some minor fame and his wife told me two winters before, there were 16-inch footprints found in the snow on the front nine of the east course. The snow tracks ran in circles around the first tee several times and then wandered off down the fairway and out of sight. The golfer remarked that it looked like a flat-footed man was having some fun in the snow. "…a man with feet that big in what must have been freezing weather?" I asked. The golfer looked puzzled and replied only, "I guess."

Hurling Rocks

Other behaviors by Sasquatches have been observed, in addition to rock throwing and stealing. Keith Foster wrote in The Musings of a Bow Hunter, available on the Bow website since 2003:

> Two motorcycle riders reported seeing a Sasquatch above a timberline while riding east of Silverton, Colorado. They were speeding along and evidently got between it and the cover of the forest below. They reported it evidently felt threatened because it started screaming at them and hurling large rocks down on them. One of them reported he was almost hit with the first throw. They left, of course.

Again, the Sasquatch wins the day with the ole rock throwing tactic. It would seem they've got us figured out, haven't they?

Quite a few other bow and black powder hunters have heard those loud, odd screams that are unmistakably out of place and abnormal for

---

* WM. Meszaros, 2001.

Colorado, but we just can't say for sure it is a Sasquatch making the noises. Foster went on to pen this:

> There are only a few cases where something killed a hunter and left tracks at the scene that might have belonged to a Sasquatch. I have not investigated a report that included a Sasquatch attack; the merit of such aggression is up for grabs. Most encounters where a Sasquatch has been aggressive were misidentified false charges similar to the way a gorilla bluff charges. It amounts to an overt charge forward towards the informant, a sudden stop and that's it.
>
> A Sasquatch could easily catch a man, but apparently they don't want to come into physical contact with us for the most part. Bluff charging is a scare tactic that generally works well to scare off the human intruder; rock throwing is very common. If large rocks start plopping down around you in the wilds, you might want to investigate the source or do the wise thing and leave. If something starts throwing huge rocks at me from some hidden location, I will not run away from it but rather take off running toward it to see just what the hell it is. If it kills me, I hope a crime scene investigation is done thoroughly. For now, though, I have quit collecting Sasquatch evidence and just wait for it to come to me while I am out there fishing a timberline lake, or bow hunting some herd bull or timberline buck.[145]

Female Feeding a Youngster

In the age of internet and e-mail, I was surprised to receive this report by forwarded ground mail postmarked July 2005 from Wrangell, AK 99929. The letter has been spell-corrected, but the wording and sentence structure remain as original as possible. It was written by hand, and readability was difficult, perhaps done by a senior citizen who couldn't see well. Still, the letter contains interesting observations.

From E. Petermann's 1947 narrative, *On his Grandfather's Knee.*

In 1918, a German gold prospector of a stature half-starved made his way (a day's walk) back to Wrangell from a northern most mining camp. He was looking for food and provisions.

Lacking in strength from dietary neglect and penniless except for a pinch of garnered gold, in route to the settlement he sat down to pick new sprouts of fireweed plant to eat, which was mixed in a scraggly field of berries. He ate what his stomach could tolerate and fell asleep curled up in a bed of grass in the warm afternoon sun.

The story goes on...

The prospector claimed persons talking nearby awakened him. Glee-filled to have company and needing direction to the settlement, he worked his way twixt high berry brambles of thorn to see who was there and meet his company. His eyes beheld a bushwoman! The hairy woman was sitting on the ground feeding a small one berries hand to mouth. The little one was sitting inside the circle of her huge legs. "... the bulk of my being was in great astonishment and fright for my safety in the presence of the giantess." Later he exclaimed, "...now in control of my faculties, I take leave of my civil upbringing to declare she is the ugliest woman ever a lonely man set eyes upon."

His journal indicated the bush woman talked to the smaller one in words sounding of the same kind to the Tongass Tlingit Indian, which he knew was the Native tongue. She was of brown colored hair about her face and body, unclothed bosom in nakedness of great size, a length of darker hair on the back of her head and neck and fed the infant berries left-handed.

The note is blurred, ending with, "...heard the bushman on the Stikine River... (a blurred or stained space) ...capsized his dugout last spring."

No one knows what became of the bushwoman, but his youngest son found the prospector's bones in his camp four years hence. There was no disturbance or clamor in camp and no tins of food. It was deter-mined father died of delirium from starvation and cold; a length of cord was found tied such to hold up his trousers around his wasting figure. Tools and bedding in his tent were untouched.*

Skipping Behavior

A donut baker named Sweeney, leaving for work at 3:00 a.m., reported a large Bigfoot traversing a meadow below his property in Michigan. The behavior he listed was interesting. The Bigfoot was with a youngster trailing behind him, "skipping along like any kid might."

An Apache truck driver running his bottling route in Las Animas County, Colorado, in the early morning hours reported a Bigfoot-looking figure with dense red hair on its body cross over Highway 12 about 3 miles short of the Trinidad I-25 junction. "I swear to you the thing was auburn colored and it was skipping!"

Joshuah Bearman interviewed Diane Vaughan in 2002 and recorded a sighting close to Los Angeles County, California. Vaughan began a 1989 hiking trek at the top of Lake Avenue in Altadena, California. She apparently encountered a "hairy one," whom she observed skipping down the mountain. Vaughan said Bigfoot was last seen prancing around within Vaughan's eyeshot. Using Vaughan's detailed description, Bearman followed her exact route through some very rough terrain all the way through a clearing with the stream, a wash, an overhanging tree, and the ridge with the brambles.

Eventually, they made it to the exact spot where Diane Vaughan saw her specimen.[146]

The recorded behavior in the Vaughan account was "skipping and prancing." Evidently, a skipping Sasquatch is not an unusual visual. Dwight G. and his two daughters were out for a short hike near their parked camper truck in Warner Valley, St. George, Utah, when they encountered large tracks in the road. The road was mostly dry powdery red-rock silt, making the tracks "plain to see." The informant stated

---

* A. Petermann, Wrangell, AK.

that either the maker of the track was somehow crippled, leaving scuff marks ever so often, or it was "skipping in an intermittent manner."

Legends Looking for Los Angeles Bigfoot

Dreadlocks, Skipping, Mummers' Dance

A van load of spring break college girls reported a "very strange looking something" described as "seriously tall with body hair and dreadlocks" going down Park Road "literally skipping" in Tishomingo State Park in Mississippi. Carol G. reported in 2010, it "freaked them out – it was no costume." Jennifer C. described the 'skipping' as more like a New Orleans Mummer's dance. When described that way, the other girls agreed and laughed.

I've also heard of skipping behavior in St. Charles County, Missouri, in the 1970s, evidently during a flurry of media reports articles about the "Missouri Momo." The news item stated the "creature skipped merrily down the road."

Trash Cans Thrown Around

In July of 1997, in the Trinity Alps north of Weaverville, California, a group of campers from Nevada filed a report indicating they both heard and observed two Bigfoot rummaging around the campground trash can in the middle of the night. The next morning, trash receptacles were thrown about, and garbage was strewn all over the place, much the same as a bear might do. The difference evidently was 16 x 6-inch and 10 x 5-inch footprints that bears did not make; no claw markings. The larger track example displayed five distinctly splayed, human-like toes. Both tracks were found in the mud trailing off into the timber behind Ripstein Campground, a forest service/BLM maintained camp-site area. The story was related by retired law enforcement Captain Tom Akren, Los Angeles County Sheriff's Department, who said after interviewing the two couples that they refused to report it to BLM or Forestry agents because they feared for the welfare of the Bigfoot. Instead, the witnesses cleaned up the mess and left behind the food they had left over.[147]

Weed Whacker up a Tree

Captain Akren was unashamedly keen on gathering information on the Bigfoot from everyone he met. His enthusiasm was contagious. He made it his business to chase down reports and stories, and he did it with great interest, often with his wife Marie at his side.

In his time, Akren met up with a couple who owned recreational prop-erty in Plumas County, California. As I write this, I am no longer sure of the year, but 1996 sounds about right. During the course of that friendship, they told him of their problem with black bears that often came around the place. In the process of looking for food, the bears destroyed metal trash cans set out for pickup. One week, however, Akren's source told him he found his two trash cans set on top of the hood of his Camaro, no scratches; just neatly placed there. That was an odd occurrence, but the following summer, the same source found deck chairs placed more than 100 feet from the main house and the umbrella table two blocks away. The informant put notices for a block meeting in all his neighborhood mailboxes in an effort to take the problem to his neighbors. Sure enough, other odd-ball things were happening. For instance, a weed-whacker was found 16 feet up a pine tree with the electric cord trailing down swinging in the breeze. Akren saw photos of the incident and said he was "blown away." Of course, the weed-whacker could have been thrown up the tree, but the few cabins there all housed adults, no wayward teenagers or younger juveniles. Who or what does that? Another neighbor hesitated but finally conceded that she thought she actually saw the creature but was afraid to say. Akren interviewed the woman, who was unable to describe anything more than a large dark man, taller than usual, walking through her backyard in the middle of the night. During my conversation with the woman, Joan, she told me she looked down on the figure from a second-story window and guessed that his height was level with her second-story balcony.*

Beer Bottle Thrown

In another instance, a couple necking in their parked car by a secluded pond were surprised when something or someone hurled a beer bottle out from the darkness at their vehicle. They were ten miles off the beaten path when this occurred in the pitch black of night and had pulled off on an old frontage road that led to a logging area. The informant told one of Akren's officer's, "...bears don't throw beer bottles, do they?" Many were the stories Captain Akren collected; his doting wife Marie died in February 2010 and Captain Akren followed her two months later. I miss having his stories and enthusiasm. Akren's final days were in Post Falls, Idaho. It was there he gave me one last story. This time, it was just a scream, but beyond that, it demonstrates how the Sasquatch is reported to crash and make crunching noises as they parallel people walking logging roads and hiking trails. Here is that last report.

Bonners Ferry nestled along the banks of the beautifully scenic Kootenai River in North Idaho, fall duck hunting season, 1987. Credible businessman recollects an incident en route to his favorite duck-hunting pond with a cousin and two others.

---

* Capt. Tom Akren, Ret.

That morning my cousin Steve and I were heading south towards the duck blind at our usual duck hunting pond-site near Bonner's Ferry, Idaho. Bonner's Ferry is located in the panhandle of Idaho near the Canadian Border. There were four of us, two already waiting at the pond. My cousin and I left the parked car alongside the logging road and began walking towards the pond. It was approximately 6:15 a.m. In the stillness of the morning, as we walked along the logging road towards the duck blind, we heard trees snapping about 50 yards away, and some kind of movement in the timber. Being anxious to get to the duck blind, I didn't think much about it at the time, and just assumed it was elk or deer. Thinking back, that didn't make sense. As the morning progressed, I began running short of shells and decided to walk back to the truck to get another box of shells, which were left there. I was younger, and a poor shot back then.

I left the group and backtracked from the pond to the logging road where the truck was parked. It was 9:30 a.m. Walking back along the road, my shotgun dangling through my arm, I heard that same breaking of branches moving to the side of me going in the same direction, along with obvious movement in the thick timber and under-growth. I stopped, it stopped. This time I thought it might be a bear or most likely elk. But what was happening didn't fit the known behavior of either animal, I thought.

Nearing the car, I stopped again, looked in the direction of the noise and, hearing branches breaking again, I raised my shotgun. Hell, I didn't know what I was going to do and I was out of shells. As suddenly as I raised my shotgun I heard this terrible scream! It sounded like a woman screaming, but deep throated, guttural pitched sound about 50 yards away. It's difficult to describe something you've never heard before and I've never heard anything like it! It was a loud, long screaming tone that echoed through the trees. I cannot describe the terror I felt. I ran to the truck and locked myself inside, completely shaken. It was some time before I recovered. I know elk, deer and bear sounds very well. It didn't fit. Back at the pond, they heard it too. I wish someone would send me a recording of

Bigfoot, so that I might do a comparison. While the years have passed, it is a sound I will never forget. My home is in Hayden Lake, Idaho. I prefer my name be withheld except to researchers or someone with sound recordings of Bigfoot. Being computer illiterate, I am not online. The sounds can be mailed to my Grandfather in Post Falls.[148]

The Idaho Daily Bee reported a set of Sasquatch-like tracks found by Bonnie Thompson on June 21, 2012, in Bonner County, Idaho. The finder of the tracks was fishing with friends in the Trestle Creek Drainage when she located the large footprint. It was photographed, cast in plaster, and measured 15 ½ inches long by 8 inches at the toes and 4 ½ inches wide at the heel. Interestingly, one of the casts had three prominent bulbous protrusions resembling toes and another protrusion toward the heel of the foot. Miss Thompson said the tracks resembled those cast by the late Grover S. Krantz formerly with the University of Washington at Pullman. She said the professor at Idaho State University, Jeff Meldrum, dismissed her track as an over-lapping elk. But do elk leave a bipedal tightrope trail of 15 ½ inch tracks?[149]

Bonners Ferry, Idaho | Tracks Leave Bigfoot Imprint

Calf Thrown

In Giles County, Tennessee, a shocked farmer watched as a Bigfoot killed one of his calves by swinging it by its hind legs and then throwing it to the ground.[150]

Throwing Dogs

I remember reading a lengthy report from the unincorporated town of Calverton, Maryland. A NASA engineer told the Prince George County Police Department that while driving to work early one morning at the Goddard Space Flight Center, he saw a huge brown hair-covered Bigfoot lumbering along I-95 in the early morning fog. His observation was unusual because a domestic dog was chasing it from behind. Apparently annoyed, the Bigfoot reached down, picked up the dog, threw it from the road, and then disappeared into the woodland trees. This happened near the Powder Road Mill Overpass and I-95 in March of 1977.[151]

Tractor Up-Ended

This was an interesting report to contemplate. The wife of a corn farmer in Iowa wrote Bigfootencounters to say that something very strange occurred on their farm property. She described a day when her husband finished dragging a 17-acre field section with his 1989 - 45hp John Deere 2155, busting up dirt clods. That evening, he pulled the tractor up to the barn with the intent of servicing it the next day. Early the next morning, the farmer came excitedly back into the house and told his wife something had up-ended the tractor; literally turned the heavy machinery over, laying it on its side. There were 17-inch humanoid footprints all around the tractor, leading through one of the freshly plowed fields and into the woods behind the south section. The tracks appeared to wander aimlessly in circles around the field. They wrote asking if a Bigfoot could have possibly done this? What would you tell them?[152]

Hideous Creatures Pelt Couple with Gravel

In the year 1950, a couple from Forks, Washington, went for a sunset stroll early one evening after a large dinner and returned to tell the family they were pelted with gravel from a dirt road area in the

Olympics. They described their terror as "two huge, hideous creatures walked out onto the road way in front of them and began heaving hands full of small pebble-like gravel in their direction." Stunned, neither remembers how they got back to their vehicle, a 1948 Plymouth woody station wagon parked about 75 yards up the road. They related the terror they felt being chased by these strange beings. The word "hideous" was used often in the retelling of this story. Mike and I interviewed them both separately, and independent of each other. They said they didn't believe in Bigfoot prior to this event.[*]

Sasquatch Chews up Styrofoam Toolbox

Pictured is Washington State resident Karl A. Breheim, who was prospecting for gold in the Rogue River area just north of Grants Pass, Oregon, in the Siskiyou National Forest when he encountered a Sasquatch.

---

[*] Mike Dardanos, 1996.

Breheim told the Spokesman-Review that the creature "took a chomp out of his plastic-foam toolbox." Believing the chewed pieces of his Styrofoam toolbox would yield genetic proof needed to declare Bigfoot an endangered species, Breheim sent the evidence to QuestGen Forensic Geneticist Dr. Joy Halverson DVM, MPVM, President and Senior Scientist at the University of California at Davis, School of Veterinary Medicine. Halvorson detected a possible divergent line of DNA heavily obscured by mineralization.

Breheim and Nancy Dean Paulson worked the site during the daylight hours but drove into Grants Pass during night hours. When they returned the next morning, they found close to 50 small trees snapped like kitchen matches. "It seemed to me like a mini tornado had touched down on the trees. Every single one had been snapped off," Paulson said. "That's what I noticed, then we saw the bites out of the toolbox and we got out of there." Breheim said the bites looked like a giant man had munched a white-bread sandwich. Pieces of the chewed-up box were spat out 20-feet across the forest ground. They stayed on the ground for months beneath the piling up of mulch until Breheim retrieved them the next spring. There were other signs. Apparently, Breheim found sticks broken into similar lengths and piled 9-feet high, which he photographed. He found long, steaming dung samples as big around as a ship's rope - approximately 2 and 3/8 to 3-inches in diameter. And he found marmots, carefully plucked clean of their fur, placed at the doorstep of his camper. Breheim found suspicious shapes in the woods, which he filmed with an infrared camera.

"...Bureau of Land Management employees might have made the stick mounds," said Abbie Jossie hypothetically. She was field manager for BLM's Grants Pass Resource Area. The BLM has been piling up sticks in the Pickett Snake area of the Rogue River drainage to reduce fire danger. But piling up sticks to reduce fire makes no sense because a 9-foot pile of sticks most assuredly equals a bonfire! It was interesting to note that the area had been contracted for logging, and any notice that Bigfoot was in the area might be the reason the BLM totally disregarded any references to a Bigfoot in the area. That region, however, has a long history of Sasquatch sightings.[153]

Joy Halverson, DVM, MPVM, President and Senior Scientist
| Karl's Journal | Man Says Bigfoot Took Bite From Toolbox

New Sasquatch Family Arrives in Bluff Creek

In October 1958, California road building contractor Ray Wallace found human-like droppings the size of those a 1200-pound horse might leave. Interestingly, a similar pile of droppings were found and filmed by Rene Dahinden on Blue Creek Mountain Road and on the sandbar at Bluff Creek in 1967. Wilbur "Shorty" Wallace, Ray's brother, found an unopened, full 55-gallon oil drum carried to the edge of the road and thrown down the hill. He also found a 20-foot length of 18" metal culvert carried some distance away and a 700-pound tire and wheel for a carry-all, which had been rolled for a quarter mile and hurled into a ravine.[154] Seems like the Bluff Creek seven were very angry about the new road, Highway 96, being cut through their territory? No doubt.

In July 1963, Dave Blake found big footprints all around where a barrel of diesel fuel was thrown off the side of the road in the construction region of Bluff Creek, California. In August of that same year, Bigfoot tracks approximately 15-inches long were found at Bluff Creek logging operations, with boxes of spikes thrown around and sticks of dynamite bitten into.[155] The anger, frustration, and displeasure of the Sasquatches in that region did not go unnoticed. What was a pristine, tranquil region had been up-ended by the noise and diesel smoke generated by large machinery required for cutting roads in that region – the Sasquatch undoubtedly were alarmed by the intrusion.

Nearly twenty years of this kind of behavior was recorded in and around Bluff Creek from the late 1940s to 1967. Then suddenly, after 1967, it all stopped and for nearly 45 years there was no more mention of Bigfoot activity in the region of Bluff Creek drainage. No sign of the former familiar tracks ever surfaced again. What happened to the makers of those seven tracks? After putting up with all that goes with cutting a new road through their territory, would the resident Sasquatch just up and leave? I don't think so, because their tracks never showed up elsewhere. What happened to the famous seven Sasquatches of Bluff Creek fame? Whatever the cause, life does rejuvenate itself. Recently, brand new tracks were found in the drainage of Bluff Creek between the Notice Creek Bridge and the Bluff Creek Bridge. Not all the tracks were measured because there were "hundreds all over the place." It was like a new tribe of Sasquatch had moved in and had themselves a Pow Wow. The substrate was hard packed, making exact measurements difficult. On June 10, 2012, Ken Iddins and M.K. Davis located a clear track set quite deep in the sandy loam of Bluff Creek that measured 14 x 6. The tracks were found one quarter mile upstream from the Patterson site, one of dozens of different-sized, newly discovered Sasquatch tracks under fourteen inches in size.

On that June trip was Don Monroe, seen in the first photograph waiting for the plaster to harden in one of the tracks they poured that week. It was a baby track measuring 6 inches long. It is an encouraging testimony that new life continues, with new tracks and a new resident family of Sasquatches living in the Bluff Creek drainage. It was thrilling to learn about this turn-of-events and new life being reborn in northern California.

Then, as Davis and Iddins hiked further up the road, it became apparent that they were being followed by juvenile Sasquatches racing alongside Bluff Creek Road, just out of sight. Coming around a turn in the road, Davis figured they surprised the juveniles, who then ducked under this yearling Douglas fir tree. Davis snapped the photo below showing the partial hand sticking out from the tree's skirt.

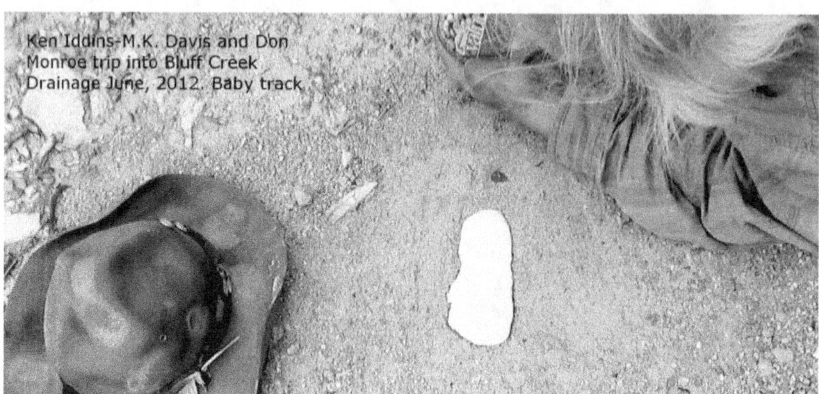

Photos © film analyst M.K. Davis 2012.

It was also determined on that same trip that not only had the gates to Bluff Creek been closed and locked by the U.S. Forestry in the fall of 2011 but that the Forestry was showing a new determination to keep cars and bikers out of the region. There isn't much they can do to keep hikers out, but it's one whale of a hike from there into Bluff Creek!

The Forestry built four-foot-tall berms across Bluff Creek Road and brought heavy machinery to chisel plow massive ditches across the road to prevent motor scooter access. The reason given by Forestry is, of course, the false notion that vehicles spread Port Orford Cedar Root Rot Disease, but so do bears. The Cedar fungus has been around for thousands of years, so why close and lock gates, dig ditches, and build berms at this late stage – isn't the horse already out of the barn?

One forestry official told Davis that "...you could all be killed," after a woman's remains had been uncovered in the area. It sounds like something else is going on, and only the U.S. Forestry knows what that is. I could find no press coverage of a woman being killed in Bluff Creek even by bears. The following photos were generously provided by M.K. Davis, showing a four-foot berm blocking vehicle access up

Bluff Creek Road. Further on up the road where the trio hiked, they found a machine-carved channel cutting across the road, essentially blocking motorbike access into the Bluff Creek drainage.

Trees were felled and ditches were chisel-plowed straight across Bluff Creek Road in 2012.

I doubt that the prevention methods employed by the Forestry will keep out visitors to the famous Bluff Creek region, but only the hardiest souls will make the entire trip; it's a long way in on foot.

California Sightings

It was heart-warming to learn that new tracks were being cast, including a newborn generation of Sasquatches in the area. It was a long time coming.

Sasquatch Unhitches Chained Dog

Marian H.'s red husky was routinely chained at night to keep her from running off and to protect the front door. In 2009, the widow woman wrote to ask if I thought a Bigfoot could work a chain attached to the dog's collar with a slide snap hook. The short of that exchange was that something was coming in the night and unhooking the snap hook that held the husky confined to the porch area and yard. Several mornings a week, she found the dog running loose, and she knew it couldn't get that way without human help. Two months went by, and the woman wrote again, telling me that the ground anchor for the dog's chain was cemented in the ground; it had been pulled up and taken down to the lake some 50 yards from her cabin. The dog was found loose and asleep on the porch. I sent Jim Fischer over to see what he might find out, and he wrote to say there was a sign all over the place and one clear track down by the creek that measured 15½ inches in length, which he later cast.

Fischer said the woman was unarmed and frightened, and invited him to stay the weekend. Fischer camped out in his tent but said the sudden appearance of his truck may have put off the Bigfoot because it never showed while he was there. Odd things continued to occur. For instance, Mrs. H. described finding a pile of Barred owl feathers near the lake as if it was killed and plucked on the spot. Finally, the problem was solved when Mrs. H. brought in a retired police dog; its warning bark kept the hairy visitor at bay.[*]

---

[*] North Hamlin Lake region, Michigan, 2009.

Rocking Vans and Campers, Kicking Tires

There remains an old story out of Trinity County, California. Mike Gordon, while sleeping in his Dodge van at Gray Falls Campground, woke up at around midnight because a Bigfoot was kicking his tires and rocking his van. Mike could see the Bigfoot's hairy, bearded chin, chest, and hand through the van's windows. The Bigfoot, approximately 8-feet tall, continued to harass the van off and on until finally, Mike blew the car's horn, and then it stopped. The source of that story, the late Fred Bradshaw, also told another story about the behavior of "trailer rocking" in Pierce County, Washington State, near Fort Lewis Army Base. Bradshaw was in the travel trailer when his hunting trailer was rocked violently. He said, "...it wasn't funny."

Bigfoot Showers Camper with Pebbles

In 2010, Bigfoot enthusiast and family friend Peter Williams complained constantly that I had neglected to upload his encounter. He was so irritated with me that he finally wagered me $100 that I wouldn't publish his story. He often took his teenage son camping at Patrick Creek Campground, which is 8 miles east of Gasquet, California, on old U.S. 199. It's in the Smith River National Recreation area and the attraction for them was the barrier-free hiking trail he thought was best for teaching his young son the art of hiking.

For years, I listened to him grumble about nothing ever happening to them while on their hiking campouts; not a stone was thrown and not a scream was heard. Finally, one year, very late in the season, he took his wife along; she's a beauty contest winner from the Midwest; the young son was not with them.

The first afternoon and night, just the two of them were sitting around the campfire talking. The second night, he tinkered inside with the radio, and she busied herself around the campsite, cooking, washing up, stowing away the garbage, and a little after 11:00 p.m., they retired inside their cab-over camper. Within 30 minutes, rocks started raining down on them. Pete switched on the porch door light and stepped outside but he could see and hear nothing, and no rocks fell on him.

Giving up, he retired again and went inside. No sooner than he closed the door and turned out the light than the rocks came flying in again, and whatever it was pushed on the camper but did not rock it. This persisted until, finally irritated, he went outside and fired a round from a handgun. All went quiet, and it stayed that way. Pete believes the Sasquatch was interested in his wife, and the pebbles were in hope she'd come outside, though she never did.

So Pete, there's your story. You owe me $100 bucks, Buddy.

More Camper Rocking

Sandy Glencross and other women were camping near Benton, New Hampshire, in a Ford truck with a camper shell on the bed. The behavior of the Sasquatch she cited appears to be common among Sasquatch narratives; it's the rocking or pushing of cars, campers, RVs and camper shells. She wrote in part:

> ...in less than probably 5 minutes that camper started rocking back and forth as if whatever was doing it wanted it to tip over; it rocked and rocked. I had my rifle in my hands but was too scared to get out of bed; we were frozen in fear. We thought, "bear?" I said "not." Whatever was rocking the camper was pushing from the top; a bear would have taken their camp food. But this was no bear, no moose - nothing other than a Bigfoot with the height and strength to rock my camper truck the way it did. We could hear it walking outside through the screen window near the top of the camper. Then it stopped and everything went silent. There were no scratch marks on the camper the next day. The only things touched were our nerves, we were terrified.[156]

Sasquatch Rocks Truck Violently

Ted Brock wrote:

> After driving all day and into the night, trying to get home for Thanksgiving one year, I pulled over to doze for a while somewhere off Interstate 10 in New Mexico. It was a rest stop area and when I drove in there was only one other car present and I think they drove off as I fell asleep.
>
> I slept in the cab compartment of my 2-door Chevy Colorado. Let me explain, Bobbie, it's a 2-dr truck with stainless steel nerf bars, which are like narrow running boards underneath each door and a 3.5 suspension lift kit, okay? So, when a 700 pound 8-foot Bigfoot jumped up on the truck, you get the picture of how the truck leaned. So, it's pitch dark, dash clock says it is 2:30 a.m., and I'm awakened by this bruiser rockin' the boat. Now you see it was an intense way to be awakened. There isn't much left to tell; the Bigfoot jumped on the rail-board and rocked the truck back and forth with his weight alone. It felt violent and it got my chicken skin working, you know out of a sound sleep you wake up fighting? Looking out the driver's side window, all I saw was his midsection, which was not very hairy, not like his arms and legs. Then as fast as he started, he quit. That was it. I don't know where he went or why it happened but I started up the truck and got out of there. There were no other cars parked anywhere around, so it wasn't another person.[157]

Trash Bin and Dumpster Divers, Oh My

Cindy Herold, a nurse and friend of mine who lives in Butte County, California, told an interesting story in 2010. Her story concerned a fellow who worked at the Mule Creek State Prison at Elk Creek. His name is Steve McCall, and he lived with his wife in the nearby City of Paradise in the northwest foothills of California's Central Valley in the Sierra Range.

The McCalls were deeply religious and lived a simple life in a remote area of the town. When Cindy met Steve, he told her he was deeply troubled and felt the Devil was trying to get him - the subject became centered on Bigfoot. Steve said, "...there is something outside at night where I live that knocks on my mobile home walls." Thus, began Cindy's ongoing interest in Steve's observations.

One incident Cindy learned about occurred when Steve and his wife left the windows open on hot summer nights, making it easy for them to hear the foot traffic running around outside. It started around midnight and continued until sun-up. Steve told Cindy, "...I could hear deer followed by something heavy on two legs running in one direction, then another came from another direction. It's wild out there at night. I've heard stray dogs sound like they were getting killed in the brush, it is a horrible sound."

After months of listening to the night sounds, a night came when one of the big fellows came up on Steve's porch. Finally, Steve braved it and, getting up the courage, yanked open the curtains. What he saw had a very large set of black-colored hands as it pushed off the window pane. At first, he said he thought it was a black man; in a momentary flash, he considered calling the police, but then, coming out of his shock, he realized the hands were far too big to be anything but a Bigfoot.

Time passed, and Steve finally contacted Cindy and told her about another incident with the Bigfoot. His second encounter came one night when he locked up his chickens in the coup. Walking back to the house, he heard something crashing through the brush and, instinctively, he swirled around, aiming his thousand-candle-power flashlight toward the racket just in time to see a reddish-brown Bigfoot standing in the brush. He could see the top half and part of a thigh; then just as quickly, the creature was gone. Steve also told Cindy that there was a large neighborhood trash bin receptacle where people were sometimes surprised by the Bigfoot. A peanut butter jar had been unscrewed and licked clean, and the trash always looked like it had been gone through.

Incidents like this often happened to the McCall couple in the woods surrounding their trailer. One year, the visits stopped, and the night sounds were no longer heard. It wasn't long before he heard a rumor that one of his distant neighbors shot a large bear trying to break into his mother's house. The mother said, "it was no bear."

Steve believed the bear his neighbor shot to death was really the itinerant Bigfoot that frequented his trailer and the rest of the neighborhood at night. According to the neighbor, the body was never found.[*]

To the avid researcher, it seemed a familiar story. Many narratives define a given Sasquatch as a slick opportunist. It isn't hard to believe they find trash bins and rural garbage dumps an easy food source. They likely got a clue from watching bears pillaging trash cans. I heard from Cindy again in May of 2011, and she had lost track of Steve and his wife. But stories from Butte County, California, are many.

The Bag Man Story

One distinctly different case proved amusing. The informants wrote to report an encounter with a Sasquatch that occurred (as the crow flies) a short distance from the Concow Reservoir in Butte County, California. The very tall reddish-brown-colored Sasquatch crossed over Concow Road in the early morning hours in the summer of 2003. Nothing unusual about that report except for one thing; I spoke twice with the couple, and both said independently of one another, "…the Sasquatch had a plastic bag on its head, the handles draping down over each shoulder." After a good laugh, I put that one in my *Who's Going to Believe This* file; I mean, really! How would I ever be able to verify a report like that one? Some reports you just have to take at face value and enjoy.

---

[*] The Cindy Herold Story, 2010.

Bigfoot Wearing Yellow Hard Hat

There are numerous reports of Bigfoot wearing various hats and now plastic bags. One report I took from a retired logger by the name of Swain. This fellow also lived in Butte County, California. What he reported was surely a novelty.

Swain wrote that he was startled to see a dark-colored Sasquatch crossing the road wearing one of the yellow hard hats commonly used by Cal-Trans highway workmen. Talk about funny, the mental image that conveys is hilarious; hairy, naked as a jay-bird with a yellow hard hat on its head.

The same Sasquatch reportedly crossed the dirt road in two steps and appeared shorter in height than most reports out of northern California, but had incredible bulk for such a short Sasquatch. Swain remarked it was probably a juvenile, but he was built "unbelievably well." The informant went on to say the Sasquatch evidently was not concerned with the heavy machinery working the roads that day, which caused me to laugh even harder at the prospects of this Sasquatch feeling protected by the hard hat. Is the story true? I don't know, but it lightens the load, makes me smile, and I suppose a Sasquatch can be eccentric and playful, too.

Bigfoot Wearing Clothes

The late Jon Erik Beckjord, Sasquatchery's bad boy, often had great insight; he rarely gave up on the weird, the supernatural, and the unusual aspects of Bigfoot research. A 2008 story in the Yakima Herald-Republic quoted a gentleman with the SRP (Sasquatch Research Project), Eric Beckjord, who said that a recent computer enhancement of the famous 1967 Bigfoot film footage revealed a metal cylinder on the creature's right arm. Beckjord quickly concluded that Bigfoot was a product from outer space. "An ape doesn't have a cylinder on his arm unless it's an experimental creature," Beckjord said. You would need to know Beckjord to understand how absurd some of his conclusions were. Often delusional, Erik imagined babies clinging to the creature's chest in the film clip attributed to Roger Patterson. My great annoyance with him was not so much his fringe ideas, but in his frightfully over-bearing way. He shoved his ideas on others with great insistence. My clashes with him were far scarier than any chance meeting with a Bigfoot, in fact, I was unashamedly afraid of Erik, often for good reason.

Erik Beckjord often quoted Dr. Vaughn M. Bryant of Texas A & M University; his specialty is paleo nutrition, the study of coprolites and fossilized fecal matter.

According to Erik, Dr. Bryant reported an event concerning a woman who said she saw a Bigfoot wearing dirty jeans; seriously. As big as the Sasquatch can get, that must have presented a very funny image.

Another account was investigated by Marine biologist, Dr. Peter Rubec in Florida, who interviewed a family that claimed a hair-covered youngster played with their children. If I remember the story correctly, they clothed the hairy male child in a pair of overalls mainly for coverage because it played with the small daughters of that family.

Mike Dardanos tells a story about a Native couple in Washington State who occasionally would see a Bigfoot watching children at recess playing near a tree line. Mike suggested the big male was 'henpecked' because the primitive wore a frilly apron in the style of a loincloth. The makeshift apron was not tied in the back but twisted and was probably a stolen tablecloth from a clothesline somewhere. Nothing made Mike laugh harder than to tell his henpecked Bigfoot story. Mike swore the sight was too funny and did not have any truth to it. Could it be the primitive understood his nakedness was objectionable around play-ground-age children?

Big Scott Mullis repeated a story to Dardanos in Maine on the Meduxnekeag River, probably sometime in the 1960s. The strange behavior occurred when a Maliseet woman was hanging washing on a line strung between two trees and left to dry overnight. When she went to fetch her dry clothing off the line the next morning, she found they'd been removed and draped on two adjoining conifers. How was she sure it was the hairy man? The clothes were draped on the tree way above her reach. Gugwes is a northern Maine Algonquin Indian term for Sasquatch; also, koakwe and kookwe.

Sasquatch in a Skirt

Rhonda Whetstone wrote that the Marshfield Terror lived in the forests surrounding Auburndale, Wisconsin, in October of 2010. She reported that the creature occasionally appeared out in the open and, strangely, it was wearing only a shirt that was "more abbreviated than a Scottish kilt" and he was neither a hoax nor a hallucination. That must have been a sight.

Calling him "wild as a hawk," Whetstone said he hung out in the woods near George Zollinger's place and described him as "unkempt looking." Those who observed him said he had the speed of a deer and was seen putting one hand on a fence post, vaulting a five-wire fence as easily as a college athlete. His speed defied pursuit, according to one story Whetstone wrote. The local berry pickers gave his area of the thicket a wide berth and thought him a throwback to early primeval wild men.[158]

Wood County Wild Man Root of Bigfoot Legend

The Watcher, the Opportunist

In the summer of 1992, I received a report from a woman named Cassie. We met while browsing the Port Book & News Store in Port Angeles, Washington. In the aisle for Bigfoot books, she engaged me in conversation, telling me of her surprise at seeing the haired ones for herself. We stood in the aisle and talked about primitive wild men as excitedly as any two women might for over an hour. She told me she was in the backyard one fall morning when a Bigfoot shot out from around the far side of her home out of nowhere and grabbed a blanket airing on a clothesline. As it ran off, it wrapped the blanket around its shoulders. "You wouldn't believe how fast he ran!" She believed it was the same Sasquatch who watched with curiosity her two boys jumping on the backyard trampoline from his vantage point 25-yards away in the trees. Her children were small, so she and her husband had the yard fenced to be safe, and she never saw the Sasquatch or the blanket again. "In my heart I knew the fence wouldn't keep this thing out of the yard but at least my boys would be unable to follow him into the woods. The thought that the Sasquatch might carry my boys off thankfully had not occurred to me, not at that time. We had a "stay safe" conversation with the two boys but you never know how much they assimilate at such a young age. I frequently wonder what that Sasquatch did with Kevin's blue blankie."[*]

Sasquatch with Footwear

In 1996, I took a report from a Native American woman at her home in Shields Valley, Montana, where she had a brief visual (at a distance) of what looked like a Sasquatch with deer hide wrapped around each of its feet. I thought that very unusual. That was her only sighting, and she was quite sure of what she saw. In Montana, there is no shortage of stories in almost every Native American family history; most are trail-side or roadside sightings. The woman had a distant relative who told

---

[*] Cass D. July, 1992.

her about another incident. The relatives claimed they saw a creature watching them put out salmon in the smoke-house. It seems, in some cases, the hair people don't miss much. They are very observant and many are the reports about Sasquatches seen studying our outdoor activity; usually from a distant vantage point. Whoever this woman was in the smoke-house tale included a relative who saw a nine or ten-foot Sasquatch while wild boar hunting in Saskatchewan, Canada. I recall reading the boar hunt report to Rene Dahinden at some point; of course, he didn't believe the story. Whatever year that was, Rene had just finished an interview with Rick Noll. It's hard to know how to assimilate all that comes with informant perceptions during an encounter. Visuals can startle people to the degree that the facts are twisted and often misinterpreted. Canadians tend to report taller Sasquatch.

Wrapped in Hides

I failed to check back with an informant who wrote in the early 1990s from Teton County, Idaho. The informant, a retired policeman signing himself with the screen name 'Tinish,' related seeing a Bigfoot carrying a bundled young one cradled in its arms. He believed it might have been an infant wrapped in some kind of hide. This was another report that somehow got past me – so many did. I do remember posting it in one of the underground mIRC hunter-type chat rooms one night, but nobody was willing to give it much credence. Who knows? If Bigfoot is human, then humans do what humans do!

Speaking of odd apparel, the late Datus Perry, eccentric though he was, is recorded as saying in 1979 that he saw a Sasquatch in the Central Sierra Nevada Range on the California side near Grant Lake. From a distance Perry said it looked like it was wearing something like a musk ox hide on its back.[159]

In 1985, old Datus Perry had a face-to-face run-in with a female Sasquatch. In Perry's own words, "She followed me over half a mile to my shelter and stayed behind a tree while I repaired my shelter. Then she came down closer to my shelter and seemed to be indicating she was...uh, ...available. She was back a couple more times leaving tracks and droppings." It's hard to imagine what lewd and lascivious gesturing the female Sasquatch might have done to give Perry that impression, but those were his very words. I was amused when I read that report – and laughingly said, I thought Perry's Sasquatch didn't know a civilized man had soliciting laws. When I first read about Datus, I didn't believe all of the stories attributed to him; this one was by far the most amusing. And isn't it interesting that in the case of Albert Ostman's kidnapping, he also felt he was captured to be a mate for his captor's daughter. More interspecies soliciting between primitives and civilized man. I used to think female sightings were rare, so I blew off the stories like these two.

Datus Perry was a peculiar character who told many stories, some true, some would make you wonder...nobody knew if he was telling the truth or telling a big whopper.

Datus Perry

Three 2 by 4s Short of a Load

I call myself a serious researcher, but more often than not, I amuse myself by finding the humor in it all. Reports have not been without a funny side, and maybe that's what keeps me sane.

The yellow hard hat story reminded me of a second-hand story with no name attached other than it was from "honkytonkgirl9" on the Alt-

Bigfoot site. A restaurant waitress revealed her neighbor had an encounter with a Sasquatch on Highway 299 westbound toward Willow Creek, California, one night quite late. What was odd about that? The Sasquatch was carrying three standard-length two-by-fours under its right arm, seemingly with little effort. She said he was as typically described. A building contractor would have difficulty believing a Sasquatch carried off construction lumber. Most likely some poor carpenter in need of keeping his job probably got blamed for that heist.

And speaking of heists; Mrs. R.F. wrote that she believed one of the Bigfoot that hung around her property made off with an Easter basket she and her husband left on the front porch for their 4-year-old son to find Easter Sunday morning in 2004. The woman wrote that it was a 24-inch basket wrapped in blue cellophane with assorted chocolates and a white fuzzy bunny inside of it. The mother said angrily, "...that basket didn't just get up and walk away, it was taken by someone during the night." Apparently, the rural mountain property in Kootenai County, Idaho, had a history of Bigfoot sightings.

Sasquatch and Rabbits

I uncovered three similar reports of male hair-covered bipeds carrying rabbits. The first account was told to me by the late Rene Dahinden about a dead rabbit described as dangling by the hind legs as the Bigfoot walked through a small clearing near Jeune Landing, Port Alice, Vancouver Island, BC.[160]

In the other report, the rabbit was apparently still alive, kicking and squealing in the hands of a Bigfoot who was carrying it by the scruff of the neck. The incident evidently occurred near Fort Totten, Benson County, North Dakota. Interestingly enough Fort Totten is very close to a place known as Devils Lake.[161]

The last rabbit case file was from a New Mexico resident. Traveling down Bitter Creek Road, near the little town of Red River, a woman wrote in great fear of being ridiculed that she observed a Sasquatch with shaggy gray hair crossing the road in front of her place. She previously wrote to me through the website about finding 16-inch tracks around her hacienda's garden several months earlier. The dead rabbit was strategically placed in the walkway up to her front porch, its neck snapped and nearly twisted off. The woman wanted to know if I thought the maker of the 16-inch flat-footed tracks might have left the dead rabbit; what did it mean? What would you have told the woman?

Grey-White Sasquatch Throws Pine Boughs

Summarizing the following account related to me by two men fishing the Powell River in British Columbia: Two anglers were sitting on a rock-strewn area of the Powell River, busily sorting through a tackle box. The sun was out; the morning was peaceful except for the chatter of birds. His brother finally got up, waded out into the shallows, and began fly casting. Macintosh tied the chosen fly onto his line and got up. Just then, he said he heard a very loud crackling sound echoing through the woods behind him. "I turned to look in that direction, but inside the trees was very dark, pitch black in places, and I didn't see anything but the sound was unmistakably out of place that I'm thinking – grizzly, maybe." Checking to see where his brother was, he began casting. "Crack!...it happened again, only this time the cracking was like the report of a bull whip causing me to whirl around and look once more in that direction. It wasn't a continual noise, just a loud crack like a large breaking branch, then the echo and silence again." The informant's half-brother made his way back toward Macintosh exclaiming, "did you hear that? A griz...do you think? But we have the .44."

The two men prepared to open the tackle box again and sift through the firearm's drawers. They quickly loaded the .44 and set it atop the tackle box while keeping watch. According to their story, the silence continued for about ten more minutes then, two quick snaps, very loud snapping sounds were heard, and the thoughts of a tranquil day fishing the river ebbed away. Both men assured me there was no doubt a dangerous grizzly was about the place they wanted to fish.

By that time, the two men were spooked; they moved back toward the firearm, they stopped, and suddenly, at the edge of the tree line, the two men saw what they described as a "ghostly hair-covered apparition" moving out from the darkness of the trees and onto the beach of the Powell River.

Listening to their story on the phone, Lou's voice became shaky as he retold the event. He described a very tall Sasquatch-looking giant emerging out the tree line with a load of tree branches and pine boughs in his arms. They knew in an instant what the apparition-like figure was. The Bigfoot was enormous in height, definitely male, with "gonads the size of grapefruits."

The creature was thick of legs with a powerful chest, and the size of the giant alone caused them alarm. "Bobbie, he projected a powerful image standing there! I've never seen any man that big or ever dreamed of a man that big, he was very intimidating; it was the same feeling you might have if a giant Mac-truck was barreling down on you, with no chance of escape. I never want to see anything like that again."

The creature took a few more steps toward the anglers and began throwing the pine branches (boughs) at the two with great accuracy. Next came a few sticks and twigs. Lou exclaimed that the creature was a head and chest taller than he was, much taller than they had ever heard of the Sasquatch being before. Clarence grabbed his firearm and, releasing the safety, discharged his weapon in the direction of the advancing Sasquatch, but he was admittedly "so frightened for his life" that he was sure the shot was off to the right because he heard it strike a tree trunk. Stunned by the noise, the Sasquatch looked startled and dropped the remaining pine boughs before turning and walking back into the darkness of the woods. The two brothers were so disturbed by the event that they left behind two folding chairs in their haste to get away and back to their main camp, where their guide and other men were bivouacked.[*]

I think these few examples give us an insight into the Sasquatch's ability to throw things with savage determination and do it seemingly with some semblance of aggression and precision. There was some measure of conversation afterward about what would have happened if the first shot had hit the monster and, also, the size of the tree branches thrown were more like whole limbs ripped off pine trees. There are other behaviors to consider, for example...

Bluff Charging

In the mid 1990s, when I was interacting with former Los Angeles Deputy Sheriff Captain Tom Akren and his wife, Marie; he had an interesting story. The narrative was about a silver miner who made camp in Glengowan in the Matzatzal Mountains, Maricopa, and Gila County, Arizona. His story is lengthy and dates back seventy-eighty years or more when mining silver was a successful venture in and around the Tonto National Forest. The behavior I noted for this purpose stemmed from an incident on the trail going up and out of a steep canyon ravine en route to the Globe Stage Coach Line to Phoenix, which came through only once a month. The miner packed up his team of nine mules with ore and was single-filing his mule team up and out of this steep canyon on a very narrow trail. Suddenly a Sasquatch jumped in front of his mule team, facing the startled miner. The Sasquatch, Akren reported, stood his ground on the trail waving his arms and wouldn't move. In the first story I heard him tell, the male Sasquatch waved his arms violently in what appeared to be a bluff charge, stamping his foot forward several times on the ground, and wouldn't let the mules go any further.[†]

There must have been a reason for this peculiar behavior, but whatever it was escaped me unless it was for the amusement of the Sasquatch or

------

[*] C. & L. M., 2001.
[†] Tom Akren.

the protection of others, perhaps young Sasquatches ahead on the trail unseen by the miner. To see a Sasquatch child is rare; we see their tracks in the snow, but according to the data, we never see the little ones themselves. This bluff charging is echoed in other stories told by hikers who talk about Bigfoot-like beings jumping out on a trail and blocking their only route.

Senior Bigfooter, author Will Jevning and I were reminiscing about some of the antics by the late Rene Dahinden one night; I've never laughed so hard in my life! Will goes way back and knew Rene long before some of the current claims. Some of the older crowd in research will remember Will's Bigfoot newsletters *Notes from the field*.

Anyway, during that exchange, Jevning related a story that involved a bit of bluff-charging behavior by a Sasquatch. I asked him for permission to tell it again and he graciously agreed. Here it is, in Will's own words:

Hugh Brown's encounter was, I think, one of the more interesting ones I have investigated. The man I met on the logging road, one Kevin Gerde, had known Hugh for a number of years and said he was a very honest man. Kevin told Hugh that he should go to a location in northern Oregon not far from the Bridge of the Gods at Wyeth. This is just across the Columbia River from Stevenson, Washington. Kevin told Hugh he had seen "steam vents" and that Hugh should go check them out. What Kevin had mistaken for volcanic steam vents were just rotting debris from a covered up logging landing. When it got cold and wet the heat vaporized the water that seeped into the debris pile underground, emitting steam from surface openings. One day Hugh and a friend of his, Jeff Strough, went there. They walked after driving as far as they could to the spot and saw where a small amount of steam came out from a small opening in the ground. They stood there for a few moments, and were about to leave when they heard a "roar" down slope from the edge of the ridge where they stood. They kept hearing this "roar" periodically and it sounded as if whatever was making it was coming up the hill in their direction. It kept getting closer and louder. When it sounded like it was just below them, they caught a glimpse of it and at first thought it was a bear; it then went into the brush. Jeff took off for the car, not wanting to be there if a bear decided to come after them. Hugh stayed a few moments longer hoping to catch a glimpse of the animal again, saying he didn't think it looked quite like a bear.

A few seconds later, a deer burst out from the brush and ran right at Hugh, stopping close enough he could have touched it. He said it acted very scared. The deer suddenly took off running out of sight, and then this huge creature came out near where the deer appeared and when it saw Hugh it ran right at him! Hugh said he must have been in shock, because he froze there. The creature ran toward Hugh, being down slope from him, stopping just 15 or 20 feet in front of and slightly below Hugh. It stood there staring at Hugh and Hugh back at it. Then after what Hugh estimated later to be around 20-seconds or so, it turned to its right and casually walked off into the forest and out of sight.

Hugh then ran for the car and told Jeff what had happened as they got out the area. Hugh said he thought he was a dead man because he knew it was coming to get him; thinking perhaps it was competing with him over the deer. Who knows? Maybe it was, but the mock charge was very interesting behavior to me. Sasquatch behavior is one of my favorite parts of all this. *

Trail Blocking or Is This Herding?

I hesitate to call this next story bluff-charging – to me, it is more like herding or, for lack of a better word, trail-blocking behavior; but I'll relate the story, and you'll judge it. It's a great story and true, as told to Oregon's senior investigator Cliff Olson by the Estacada Police Chief's son Robin as he sat in the dining room with his homework. Young Les told his dad and Bob what had happened to him and his friends up the

____

* Will Jevning, 2012.

Clackamas River. This all came down some years before the 1967 Patterson film clip was made public. It was a time when the Mount Hood National Forest was logging big time, causing a great deal of Bigfoot activity due to the disturbance from machinery noise.

Les K. was Public Work's foreman for Estacada, Oregon. This particular Saturday, he planned to take his kid fishing on the North Fork of the Clackamas River above Estacada; they loaded up and headed out. He didn't want to hike upstream to his favorite fishing area, so he drove up Ladee Road, hiked a trail to the canyon breaks and then downslope to the North Fork where he spent the day fishing.

They drove to where they could take a trail to the breaks and headed toward the canyon. They parked about a third of a mile from the lip of the canyon and then downslope another half mile or so to the stream. They hiked through the heavy timber almost to the breaks, where they saw the timber thinning. They knew they were almost there.

Suddenly, a very large male Sasquatch stepped out onto the trail just in front and stood there glaring at them. The appearance of the creature and its huge size sent the kids into hysterics; they had been in the lead on the trail, and just that quickly, they were behind their Dad, screaming and hollering and tugging on his clothes, scared to death. The creature just stood there as Les struggled with himself and his kids to gain some composure and head them back up the trail.

As they were about to head back up to the car, the creature started walking toward them, adding to their need to vacate the area. The children wouldn't head out by themselves; instead, they just clustered near their Dad, slowing their progress on the trail. The Sasquatch advanced on them to the point that Les, in his fright and concern, used the only tool he had - a 7 ft. fly pole - shaking the tip of the rod at the creature's chest as he walked backward up the trail. He persisted with this until the creature stopped just a few feet from their pickup truck where it stood while they clambered inside and left.

Les drove straight home, dropped off his kids, and then drove to the Police Chief's home to tell him what he had just experienced. Bob W. could tell Les was really rattled and had him sit down. Les was not a drinking man; a complete tea totaler, but when Bob W. offered Les a drink to settle his nerves, he took a big one.[*]

Incredibly, this is a true story, and in the process of relating it to me, Cliff figured the big hairy guy was probably a guard for his family or others on the canyon slope picking berries, gathering roots or perhaps fishing. He did not want them in his area and meant them no harm if they left...that was obvious. I'd call his behavior in ushering them back to the vehicle unusual. Thanks, Cliff, for relating this great story. This was a behavior I had not heard before.

Peeping Toms

Many notations in the database described a Sasquatch looking through windows not only of remote cabins but in rural residential areas. One such incident was described by a woman living on a reservation; large footprints were found all around the soft soil under a bedroom window, indicating something shoeless and very large had watched the family inside at some point the previous night. The reservation police and forestry tracked the creature into the nearby woods, but the Sasquatch was never found. One of the elders asked that I not identify them or the individual.

A Montana resident wrote in 1997 to report that he observed a Sasquatch watching the family through a living room window. He phoned his neighbor, who ran out the door and fired twice into the air to scare it off. The next night, however, the persistent Sasquatch was back peeping through windows.[†]

---

[*]   Cliff Olson, Oregon.
[†]   J. Melon.

Orange Haired Peeping Tom in the Catskills

Brian from Delaware County, New York, had an unusual sighting:

One night after nine o'clock, my sister and I sat at the kitchen table eating sandwiches for dinner while my parents had cocktails in the front living room. The kitchen was at the rear of the house and the windows faced a drop-off in the property elevation, which ran down to a clear running stream. As I was eating my dinner, I was gazing out the window. It was a dark, overcast and moonless October night and there, illuminated from the light spilling out the kitchen, was a huge, ape-like face staring back at me. It had a broad, wide face, with no discernible neck and shoulders that spread out beyond the four foot wide window. HUGE. The brow of the creature was heavy and I do not recall any expression on its face. It was clearly a Bigfoot, but what was different from any description that I heard before about a Bigfoot was that the hair of this creature was more orange-like, not brown or black.

My father and I took flashlights and went outside to look for it, but the ground was hard due to a cold autumn that year. What we did realize was that the creature would have to be over nine feet tall for its face to be visible through the window at the kitchen, since the basement level was exposed at that part of the house, as the farmhouse was built into a hill. Two weeks later we read a local newspaper article in which a farmer said he spotted a big hairy creature breaking into his henhouse stealing chickens. The color of the creature's hair? Orange![162]

Bigfoot in the Catskills

The Humpah Man

Children playing on a wooden porch near rural Estes Park, Colorado, told their mother the "Humpah man" came to play again. Thinking it was an imaginary friend, the mother paid little attention and enjoyed hearing the children squeal every time the electric model train blew its whistle and puffed smoke from its stack. Apparently, this was an attraction a visiting Sasquatch enjoyed as well. Running into the house, the 6-year-old told his mother that the "Humpah man" was laughing and excitedly said, "Humpah-Humpah" every time the train whistled; then, he would laugh. Paying better attention and upon hearing a man's deep laughter, the mother stepped out onto the porch and saw a reddish-brown Sasquatch astride the corner of the porch, casually watching her children play with the electric train. He wasn't very tall, but he was big, and her screams sent the Sasquatch running towards the woods. The men in the family gathered up their rifles and set off into the woods to confront the stranger. But he was nowhere to be found. The following spring, the children reported seeing the Humpah man again peeking through their bedroom window. Now an adult, the report was written by the young lad in the story along with his 55-year-old mother. Now, living in New Mexico, the story is still talked about by his family all these years later. [*]

Dr. Connie Cameron recalled reading about laughter and the Sasquatch but couldn't remember the origins of that story. Stephen and Lucius Foley reported hearing laughter in the middle of the night when he and his two cousins camped near a fire-look out in the State of Washington in the summer of 1984. Lenny M. mentioned hearing laughter while hiking the back country in Mount Rainier National Park, Washington State. He stated nobody was around for miles, yet he and his girlfriend heard laughter that continued sporadically from 2:00 to 3:30a.m. They could see no campfires or other people. The next morning, they stopped to talk with a park volunteer about what they heard. The man

---

[*] Private Correspondence anonymous.

had no answers and said nobody was up there in that meadow but them. The informant was adamant that he heard laughter coming from the forest.[*]

Whistling in the Blues

Long-time friend and Bigfoot investigator from Cincinnati, Ron Schaffner, provided me with a Cleveland Plain Dealer newspaper article; in it, there was written an account that mentions whistling where former game warden Bill Laughery met up with the late Wes Sumerlin in the Blue Mountains of Washington not far from Walla Walla. There, they encountered two hair-covered Sasquatches. The bigger of the two hairy ones jumped the trail, 15 feet in one leap ahead of them, the other wandered off down the canyon. Laughery and Sumerlin could clearly hear whistles, grunting, and crashing in the bushes.[163]

Singing/Chanting Up Notice Creek

The reports of singing and that sort of behavior remind me that during one of a dozen treks into the Bluff Creek region of Northern California, an incident was reported up Notice Creek in May of 2009 by Don Monroe, M.K. Davis, and Bryan Davis. The three men stopped deep into the bush country to camp out one night. In the quiet of the night, Davis related that they could hear a singing kind of chanting wafting in the distant air; the tune and words unrecognizable but clearly audible. This occurred 13 miles up Notice Creek, California (above Bluff Creek), which was completely off-trail where nobody could possibly be. In every sense of the word, that region is pristine wilderness. I'd like to think the locals were enjoying some kind of social gathering, but who really knows?[164]

---

[*] Lenny M.

Singing and Banging on a Cabin

In 2011, a woman of Southern Paiute heritage wrote to tell me she lived alone in a cabin located on the Russian River in California and believes she saw a Sasquatch up in a redwood tree on her property. It was a fairly young one, either sleeping in the tree or hiding its face from her. She told me she sang to them and believes they come around to hear her singing. One night, the woman said she had stoked the fire and turned in for the night. At about 2:00a.m., she heard and felt two distinctly, "...loud and hard bangs from a fist just below my window, which is located on the second story of the cabin. I felt the fear run through my body like a shockwave and lay frozen in my bed wondering what could have made this whole cabin shake so hard. Then I wondered about Bigfoot and fell asleep after the fear subsided."

Sonoma County, California does have a history of earthquakes, and it might have been a sudden jolt she felt, but it happened a second time. Continuing on, she wrote:

> My medicine woman said it was the Bigfoot and they liked my singing and I didn't even tell her about the singing, she just knew, so weird. The second 'banging incident' occurred exactly like the first one right down to the fear and finally falling asleep. [*]

Not all earthquakes are rolling types; many are sudden jolts. Perhaps the Sasquatch can move a house with that much force...I wouldn't want to meet up with one who could.

Young Bigfoot With a Dog, Watching

In a separate account, a young northern Minnesota mother wrote that two young Sasquatch children frequently watched her three children from outside the chain-link fencing they put up to keep the coyotes and

---

[*] The female informant asked for anonymity.

wolves away. The interesting part of that 1998 report was that each time the mother observed them the two young Sasquatch children were accompanied by a "mixed breed looking dog" and the canine appeared tame and protective of the little hairy ones; it was always with them. She never saw any adult Sasquatch but reported the two young hairy ones were dark brown and neither was over 4 feet tall. Their hair was "parted in the middle and hung straggly." Their faces were bare of hair, but their bodies had a light covering of dark brown hair that was very short. They walked upright and sometimes clung to the chain-link when peering through. Once or twice, they tried to climb over, but never did that she saw.

Sasquatch Stride Length

An intriguing story was written up in April of 1987 about three itinerant loggers at a picnic area off Highway 89 between Truckee and Sierraville, California. The three men, Claude Dudley, Tom Ruffing, and Lee Janet, reported to Sierra County Sheriff Sgt. Joe Mosley that they were brewing coffee when they began hearing screeching noises around dusk.

Loggers Swear They Found "Large" Bigfoot in Sierra County, California

They described an upright walking animal between 9 and 10 feet tall coming toward them. When the creature saw the three men, it turned away and ran toward Prosser Lake, knocking over a small tree that stood in its path. According to Gary Horn, a California Fish and Game

Department Warden who conducted the initial investigation, the animal moved with a five-foot stride, crossing Highway 89 in only two steps. The Warden said, according to one of the witnesses, "one guy told me...two strides was enough for me, I packed up my grub and got the hell out of there." The loggers drove directly to Sierraville, where they reported the incident.[165]

Sasquatch Hiding

Broken Mirror Campground got its name from an early 1990s incident when a log struck and broke off someone's driver's side rearview mirror. The van was parked in the northernmost part of Arizona's high Mogollon Rim Country, Coconino County. The presumption, of course, is that a Sasquatch tossed the log that broke the mirror because what other rim country creature throws things? Not bears.

I found an old reference to this same camping area that occurred during Easter week of 1996, where three witnesses approaching this remote campground saw a large dark figure move behind a tree; its color did not match that of the tree according to the witnesses. The linemen who told me the story said they were familiar with the elk in the region but never saw one stand upright and hide behind a tree trunk like this dark image was seen doing. The figure stayed behind the tree, which was later measured at a guesstimate of 36 inches in diameter. The witnesses commented that once behind the tree, the figure didn't show on either side except in the region of the shoulders. The informant's girlfriend, Shauna, also observed the figure's head as it went behind the tree and reported seeing no eye shine but thought the figure was a human shape, roughly 7-feet tall, and they felt it was a Sasquatch hiding behind the tree. They watched the tree for more than ten minutes. Then suddenly, the woman coaxed the other two linemen into making a dash for their truck. They didn't look back but returned the next day to measure the tree. They found 15 x 6.5-inch, 5-toe footprints. Evidently, the creature knew how to hide well. I remember trying to contact Lyle Vann in regards to this report as he was the only person I knew at the time who was investigating Arizona sightings, but we never did connect, or if we did, I sure don't remember.[166]

The story of the hiding Sasquatch was followed by another that originated nearby in late 1996 when an employee of the Coconino County Sheriff's Department told a security officer visiting Fort Tuthill County Park in Flagstaff that he saw a light-colored figure leaping hunched back across Arizona's I-17 not far from exit 337. It was dusk when he pulled his truck off the road and watched the figure run in leaping motions into the sun and hide itself behind a set of old growth Ponderosa Pines. He sat off the highway and watched those trees for several minutes, but unable to see much more, the informant drove off convinced that he had witnessed a Sasquatch.

Coconino County, Arizona's Mogollon Rim Country

The Owens – Herriott Story

When I reread the rather famous account that Daryl Owen and Scott Herriott told oh so many years ago about their encounter with a Sasquatch, I imagined the Sasquatch they saw was doing a bit of this same hiding behavior, trying to stay away from the twosome. I couldn't figure out who was more afraid, the Sasquatch trying to hide from the approach by these two guys or Daryl and Scott at seeing it. The story was far funnier to hear Scott tell it; reading it does it an injustice. But it was a fun read in the '90s. Drawing from part of their story is the following...

On October 12, 1992, Bigfoot hunters of the day, Daryl Owen and Scott Herriott, ventured into the woods near the mouth of the Klamath River armed only with their video cameras. Their goal: to capture an image of Bigfoot. The incident occurred in Del Norte, California, near Requa, and it wasn't long before they got lucky. Of course, in hindsight, calling their encounter 'lucky' may be a matter of opinion from their point of view.

Once deep in the bush, and when they actually got close enough to realize what they were looking at, they found the Sasquatch positioned low in the bushes, lying prone on the ground, hiding as the fearless duo blundered into its hiding place. The photos emerging from that day revealed the outline of the body and eyes that so terrified Owen that all he could say was the f-word repeatedly, and many times since!

Forgive me, I don't know why, after all this time, I found this funny, but here is a small part of the tape-recorded dialog that transpired between Daryl and Herriott; Daryl holding the camcorder:

"…all right, I'm recording right now…"

"…you can see that little thing; it looks like maybe…an eye!… fuck! It's a PAIR of eyes; he's looking right at me…"

<their two voices rising in tempo to high octave soprano> "…yeah?" Herriott responds… "Holy Shit!"

"…that's a fucking Sasquatch, man!" <voices are wild>

"I got it on fucking tape!" <Owen's voice screaming in a high-pitched tone> "I can't fucking believe it!" <Voice even higher and trembling with terror> "…he's looking right back at us…" <high squealing voice>

That outlines the scene. You get the picture.

No one ever left a scene faster than Daryl Owen did that day, fleeing in complete terror with camera in hand. I phoned Scott in Los Angeles one night in 1996 to hear the story from him personally. His roommate answered the phone and when I asked for Scott, his reply in serious alarm was, "oh no, not again, I have to hear this story again? Oh no, spare me, not again!" He went on to explain how many times he had to listen to Herriott retell his encounter. Then, with intermittent laughter and frustrated resignation, he handed the phone over to Sasquatchery's handsome, funny man, Scott Herriott. It was a great story for its time! I don't think there's been one like it since; probably never will be. There was nothing funny about their terror and Daryl, of course, never returned to the Bigfoot arena again. Their encounter made television; A & E's *Ancient Mysteries: Bigfoot*, a series that aired in 1994, and the Learning Channel's *The Quest: Bigfoot*.

Disguised as a Tree Stump

We were camping in Northern California, on the coast, spending time in Arcata and Crescent City. We went inland to camp, but weren't sure exactly where we were. I only moved to California from Brooklyn about a year ago, so big trees and salmon-filled rivers are new. The incident occurred the first week of October 2003. In the late afternoon, the three of us ate and were scrambling for some firewood. It was late in the season, and the area had been cleaned. We fanned out, and I started away from the creek, heading into the deep woods. I looked around and saw large trees and a few big stumps. Suddenly, one of the stumps seemed to disappear. I was about 25 yards away and could swear that a large redwood stump moved! I moved closer and saw a man walking away into the deeper woods. I saw him for about 10 seconds. I yelled out, but all I got was a "whistle." I could tell he was big because another stump he walked by was later measured about 6-feet tall and he was at least a foot taller than that stump. It was evening, but the light was not gone completely. I thought he seemed to be wearing bulky, dark clothing. I didn't get a clear view of anything except his silhouette. I whistled and got a reply of a similar whistle, but if it was him, he had already moved a couple of yards further away. Only in the morning did one of my friends mention Bigfoot. We followed what we assumed was his path, but there was no sign of a campsite anywhere near or any human activity. The woods just got deeper. Who knows? It was cool, though, the stump Bigfoot.

Carrying Things

I listened to Arla Williams on one of the Blogtalkradio programs in 2011, where the discussion centered on Sasquatches seen eating acorns. If you're not familiar with acorns, they are quite tough-skinned. I cannot bite into them, I lack the jaw power, but the early Native Americans, using grinding stones, ground the acorns into powder for making flatbread with other wild seeds incorporated into the flour mixture.

The conversation on the radio eventually turned to how the Sasquatch managed to store dropped acorns from beneath oak trees. Arla, a Native American Cherokee woman, told her radio audience that the Sasquatch weaved baskets to carry large loads of food stuffs to be cached for winter use. Asked how she knew about the baskets and how the Sasquatch used them, Arla replied she had seen them for herself. Arla befriended the Sasquatch in Oklahoma and claims to be a long-term witness with an unusual trusting relationship with the Sasquatch people.

Arla's testimony reminded me of a Native American/Hispanic woman in west Texas, Edna S., who told me that while visiting her daughter in Rio Arriba County, New Mexico, she saw a small Sasquatch basket that seemed to be made from fibrous strips of cactus plants. Edna went on to say that, when allowed to dry, the strips of woven fiber formed a vessel quite large and sturdy enough to pack any number of foodstuffs for storage and, supposedly, the cactus prevented mold and kept away insects. But my question was, in summer, when temperatures soar over 100 degrees many months of the year, -where were they storing these food items so they wouldn't spoil or be eaten by squirrels. Her answer: "...underground where cool temperatures are maintained year round."

In many instances, a theme tends to develop that suggests the regions where Sasquatches are often seen are areas with underground cavern-like tunnels; usually of lava rock formed by volcanic pyroclastic flows centuries in the making. Such is the region around volcanic eruptions like Mount. St. Helens in Washington State and California's Mount Shasta and Mount Lassen areas.

Caching and Storing Food for Winter

Along those same lines, I located two reports from hunters independent of one another. The reports were filed by a bow hunter and black power deer hunter who reportedly found foodstuffs cached above timberline buried deep under moss where snows are perpetual. A small cache of dried meat and nuts were found above the north end of a lake, in British Columbia, Canada. The hunter's retriever discovered the cache digging nervously into the ground.

The largest cache was found high in Gunnison County, Colorado, in 1992. Besides elk meat, a rudimentary sort of Bannock bread was observed, which traditionally, I'm told, is a large, round, or rectangular loaf-like substance that requires baking, which would also suggest Sasquatch fire use. Bannock was usually made from crushed acorns, wild berries and seeds, barley, wheat or oats, and other wild ingredients that vary according to region, which is held together by any available lard. In this case, it was believed to be rendered elk lard.

In that same stash of food, hunter Mel Whitlock found an unidentifiable root vegetable on the order of a leek, corn still on the cob with shucks still on, and the cache was cleverly lined with unshelled walnuts. The temperature in the cache was near freezing, and none of the food items were molding; some were shriveled. Whitlock said there was no ventilation into the cache. It measured approximately 5' x 6.5' and was 18" to 24" down underground covered in mosses supported by sticks and whole unshelled walnuts. There was no evidence of bears or raccoons having disturbed the cache. Whitlock mused over the find and was intrigued by the lining of the cache, as big as it was, with walnuts that had been methodically pressed into the ground, lining almost every inch of it neatly and painstakingly. In the process, the food stuffs were held up and away from any drainage that might occur on the ground of the cache. I agreed that it took some mental acuity. Cooking items such as Bannock may be unseemly to those who haven't considered the human element of the Sasquatch. But it's not out of line if the Sasquatch interacted with the Aboriginal Indians. Some records indicate they not only warred against the early Native Americans but traded with them in age-old times that were.

Bannock bread was, and may still be, in some instances, used to store for the winter months. It is baked together (without eggs) with bear or elk lard and often wrapped in the leaves of skunk cabbage during storage. Loaves have been reported to be found alongside cached rabbit, wapiti, and elk parts that had been dried. Bannock is often nasty smelling, nevertheless sustenance when winters are unusually harsh… it's all about survival whether it tastes good or not. The bow hunter reported dried root vegetables were layered among leaves, and underneath those layers on the very bottom was another layer of tiny apples, which were not dried but whole. I wondered how many times hunters had walked over these cached fortresses without knowing it?

Bigfoot Leaves a Gift of a Silk Flower

One of the strangest moments in researcher Paul Graves's life occurred when he was alone in the William O. Douglas Wilderness in the Cascades Mountains of Washington State. After merrily playing his flute one evening, Graves went to sleep in his one-man tent at about 1:00 a.m. When he woke up the next morning and unzipped his tent, "Right there, right outside by my tent, was this big old white-looking flower - one of those silk fake ones." Had the Sasquatch left it as a gift for Paul in gratitude for the evening flute concert? How did it get there so deep in the wilderness?[167]

Hairy Beings and Nothingness

Sasquatch Gift Giving

Fred and Nancy de la Rosa wrote me in 2003 from their ranch home that was carved out deep in the forest near the California-Oregon border. As I understood it, they had been living alone on the property for almost 35 years. They raised their family there and lived alongside a family of wild forest people with no problems and with minimum interaction. During the correspondence that year, one facet of their report stayed with me. It was an incident where they found a neatly placed row of hen's eggs lined up in a row, about 3 feet from the front door on the porch one morning. The de la Rosa's had no chickens or known neighbors nearby. Who left the neatly aligned row of seven eggs? When you consider eggs major sustenance, that was quite a gift they left, and the gesture was huge.

Along those same lines, a beautiful Canadian woman from Mount Currie, British Columbia (and my friend Marie Abraham), made a comment about Sasquatch gift-giving that struck a chord. I sought permission to quote her, and she generously gave it. In September 2011, she was recorded as saying about the Sasquatch people:

> They understand gifts. Some older ladies used to go fishing along Lillooet Lake; they would leave an extra fish on the log near the edge of the forest in the evenings, and in the morning the fish would be gone. My sister saw a Sasquatch along Duffy Lake Road a few years

ago. When we go by there, sometimes, we leave apples, cucumbers, and plums for them. My cousin use to tie bannock in a plastic bag up a tree for the Sasquatches, and it would be gone in the morning...gifts to the sasquatches. This is one way to thank them, though they don't expect to be thanked like everybody else. They don't expect a medal, a flag, handshakes and pictures taken like other heroes get.[*]

Pinecone Seeds in Exchange for Chanterelles

In another bit of correspondence, I found some frequently reported behavior. Following, watching, forgetting themselves, and the taking of gifted mushrooms and return gifting of pine nuts:

My brother and I were sent out to gather chanterelles, mushrooms that grow at the base of oak and Douglas fir trees in an area where we live. We are Yurok and at $29-$30 a pound, it helps the family income. I know the forest, I know where they grow. This day was bloody hot, over 100 degrees, so there wasn't much enthusiasm when my father told me to get to the mushroom picking. I went down to the creek, waded across, and coming up on the other side followed the game trail about a mile up an incline where the north side has a secret growing area for chanterelles. The hills are full of such secrets; I won't tell where.

My little brother, age 9, was making a lot of noise with a small boom box and rap music. Thinking it over, that was probably what brought in the Bigfoot. There were two of them watching us pick chanterelles. Both were small, I think children, and they came right out into the open and watched. They were not very hairy types; one bigger than the other but both under 6-feet, maybe my father's size and he is 5 feet, 8-inches tall. We did not acknowledge them but continued on, and the picking was great. We moved through the area quickly and within an hour had nearly a pound and a half. The Bigfoot followed, sometimes

---

[*]   Marie Abraham.

directly out in the open and other times from behind trees. They made no noise, just watched. We smelled no stink and they did nothing to draw attention to themselves. Since we had more than enough, I left a handful on top of a fallen tree and we left. They followed all the way to the creek crossing then we didn't see them anymore. The next day we returned to finish picking the adjoining area on the incline. The chanterelles were gone and in their place were three pinecones, dried and wide open with nuts almost visible.[*]

For readers who don't know, pinecones require heat and dry warmth to open up enough to make their seeds accessible. Thai cuisine often uses pine nuts, and I know an Italian restaurant that serves spinach salad with pine nuts. They are delicious and nutritious.

The Oklahoma Watcher

The chanterelle mushroom pickers in the previous story were watched but not interrupted. In Texas, North Dallas Urologist Dr. Nathan Graves filed his 1993 sighting with me in late October 2012, also about "watchers." There are many stories about dark watchers observing human activity from great distances.

Murray County, Oklahoma

---

[*] Martin.

I had a sighting in the Arbuckle Mountains near Dougherty, Murray County, Oklahoma. We looked up 400 yards away where there was a 14-foot cedar tree. A large black 9 foot creature (3-4 feet wide) stepped out from behind the tree, stared at us and then stepped back behind the green cedar tree. The creature was dark black. The other person with us said he thought the watcher was big as a truck. Two weeks later I went and looked at the tree and surrounding terrain. Beneath the tree was mainly solid rock. This area of the Arbuckles has a lot of underground caves. I am a surgeon in the Dallas area with 20/15 vision.[168]

Gifting, Language, and Arguing Sasquatches

I've always enjoyed my exchanges with Leo Selzer. He lives a long ten hour, thirty-six minutes north of the USA/Canadian border in an amazingly beautiful untouched wilderness region. The town of Prince George is roughly 489.7 miles north from Vancouver up the Cariboo Highway in British Columbia. During a conversation about unusual Sasquatch behavior, Leo generously shared what some in research refer to as gifting, or swap-outs, between the primitive Sasquatch and trusting humans. Here is the pertinent part of my exchange with Leo:

The incident with the apple being traded for the stick and rock happened about 70-80 miles drive into the bush from down town Prince George City. The trading of a sandwich for the fir cone happened about 30 kilometers (18.6 miles) from town. What strikes me is that in two different locations, that far apart and about a year apart in time, I experienced two incidents of trading rather than the opportunistic taking of things.

I suspect that when circumstances are in certain ways, the Sasquatch are apt to think more along the line of trading what they want, with something that they consider to have value. The rock was very colorful, cleaned, and appeared to be hand rubbed to look nicer. The stick was rubbed nice and clean. The cone from the fir tree had to come from a distance away as there were no fir trees anywhere nearby. If it was a youngster or teenager who took the sandwich, perhaps he/she had been carrying the cone for a while as a possession of interest. I wondered if the intention to trade rather than just take might have been an attempt toward friendship? In September 2007 a Sasquatch left me a huge mushroom in what I believe to be a friendship offering. He/she had likely become used to my vehicle and my being in the area over the years and decided to make a positive move towards communication. I have heard of similar stories that other people supposedly experienced but I have no way of knowing if they are true or not.

I just remembered a story that I was told first hand by the witness while I was investigating an occurrence on his property in August 2007. The gentleman's name is Collin Stone. He lives east of Prince George, about 18-kilometers. There is a lovely pond 250 yards from his house. Toward the pond and 100-yards from the house is his workshop. He was in the workshop and his dogs were with him. One evening shortly after dark, he had what he believed was a group of Sasquatches on his property. On the far side of the pond he heard what sounded like people talking in some kind of Indian language. Then it erupted into yelling, screaming and fighting. The noise was so loud and scary enough that his dogs ran back to the house and hid under the porch. He immediately followed the dogs to the house and got his rifle, shotgun and a handgun. He loaded them and went back to the workshop. The dogs would not go with him. He said the ruckus lasted off and on for a good five minutes or more. The next morning he went to investigate and found a lot of brush and debris had been tossed around. The grass was knee high and sparse, and the ground was very hard. No clear tracks were found. I couldn't arrange coordinating times with him to get out there for over a month. When Mike and I did get there, a tall thin poplar tree the size of my arm was broken off and angled out into the pond. The driveway runs right beside the pond so if it was that way when he came home he would have noticed. All throughout the summer he bought fluorescent green tennis balls for his dogs to play with. If he forgot to pick them up in the evening, they were gone by morning. He kept buying them and they kept disappearing. Then, in early August, the week before Mike and I arrived, Collin's lady friend came to stay for the weekend. He has 40 acres of land. Behind the house is an old logging trail that is grown over to the point of being just a wide game trail that runs way back into the hills; it is used by deer, bears, and sometimes moose. Collin and his lady friend went for an afternoon walk along the trail. About 300 yards from the house, right along the side of the trail, was all the missing tennis balls. There was a dozen or more of them arranged in a perfectly straight line 1-2 inches apart. He decided to leave them there. The Sasquatch was obviously enjoying them and he had just bought a bucket full of tennis balls for his dogs.[169]

Children Playing with Sasquatch Children

In a straight line through the bush, Collin's abode is only about 5 kilometers from a place where a man, his wife and two daughters live in a small house, back off the highway and close to the bush; this is also in Prince George, British Columbia, Canada. I interviewed the lady and her girls one afternoon and they explained how the girls had been playing back in the bush with a naked hair covered youngster. Sometimes the big hair covered mother would stand back and watch them play. The girls were 5 and 6 years old at the time.

The following summer they only saw the hairy youngster a couple of times. When the girls convinced their mother that the youngster was real she told the girls the next time the youngster shows up they should run to the house and tell her. Shortly afterward the girls came to the house to tell their mother and she followed them out into the bush. When she saw the youngster and the huge mother she forbid the girls to go into the bush without her or the dad with them. When I spoke with the girls, they felt it wasn't fair that they weren't allowed to play with their friend anymore. Their friend never said anything, just played and smiled a lot. When I asked the girls what their friend looked like, they said he "just looked like any other kid just all covered with brown hair." They think the youngster was a girl, and she had quite long arms with big hands and dark skin under the hair. They did not feel afraid because the youngster came to them when they went to the end of the trail. The mother never came very close; she just stayed back and watched them attentively, playing and doing what children do.*

Selzer, the investigator in the case, questioned the children extensively regarding verbal interaction with the young Sasquatch. But apparently, the hairy child never spoke; it squealed happily, laughed, and followed instructions with apparent understanding. The children's mother had no idea about the interaction between her children and the hairy child and did not know how long they had been playing together. It could have been going on for months.

Sasquatch Adoptive Parenting? Guttural Sounds

In July of 2001, my friend Ken Kristian, a resident of beautiful Stuart Island, British Columbia, sent along a news article with testimony from a Vancouver dentist named Dr. Arthur Gosten. He told the most amazing story I think I've ever heard or read.

The doctor went camping in the Rockies with his family and was awakened by the frantic cries of his 12-year-old daughter, who told him a "wild boy" was stealing their food. To Dr. Gosten's complete astonishment, he recalled for me the following:

> I looked where she was pointing and saw this half-naked boy slinking off into the trees with an armful of canned goods.

Shouting after the boy, Dr. Gosten gave chase and caught up with him at the edge of a clearing.

---

* Twenty-seven years' worth of story exchanging and interviews with Peter Williams.

> I couldn't believe my eyes! The boy was standing next to an enormous
> hairy man-like creature at least 8-feet tall. The giant took some of the
> boy's load then they ambled off together into the woods, both of them
> walking with the same hunched over gait.

Since the Gosten sighting, at least 33 people have reported seeing the naked wild boy and his hairy companion. Witnesses include clergymen, forest rangers, and even members of the Royal Canadian Mounted Police (RCMP). The report went on to mention the unlikely duo had been heard exchanging guttural sounds as if talking to each other, and they said the youngster had all the earmarks of a feral-human.

A few investigators of the day (in Vancouver) believed the wild boy sightings might be connected to the 1989 crash of a private airplane carrying a family of French tourists visiting the region. According to the report filed with the RCMP, the pilot and passengers were all killed, including a young mother listed on the manifest as Madeleine Dusoire. Her tiny infant son Marcel was missing and his remains were never found. If any part of the story the dentist told is true then it is a remarkable account of an infant being rescued and raised by a Sasquatch family. At this writing, the child would be an adult and undoubtedly given to the Sasquatch way of life.[170]

The ramifications of a human newborn being raised as a wild Sasquatch are interesting. It reminds me of the instances Dr. Ed Fusch wrote about and the possible interbreeding between the captive Colville Indian women and local Sasquatch husbands.

The French adoptee, however, is the reverse. Now, as an adult human male living the only life he knows with the primitive ones, would he take a Sasquatch wife? We would be foolish not to think that highly probable. Would the children of that union be haired? Many questions arise. Apparently, when Dr. Gosten saw the feral boy, he was still under the tutelage and watchful eye of a large male Sasquatch. Stories like this are indeed rare but fascinating to read, and I found this account astonishing! Here is the news article published in Vancouver Sun, regarding the wildchild story:

May 19, 2000 - VANCOUVER, Canada - Excited researchers are combing the wilds of British Columbia in response to recent sightings of Bigfoot accompanied by a blond-haired boy.

More than two-dozen people claim to have seen the human youngster dressed in animal skins and loping along beside the towering man beast. Investigators speculate that the mystery boy may be the missing survivor of a plane crash that occurred in the area 11 years ago, raised from childhood by Bigfoot.

"This is the most tantalizing development in Bigfoot research to take place in decades," said Dr. Rob Worrier, Ph.D., a zoologist involved in the hunt for the elusive forest creature. "It suggests that Bigfoot is not some shambling monster as he is often depicted, but a gentle and intelligent being capable of nurturing behavior and compassion."

Dentist Dr. Arthur Gosten who was camping in the Rockies with his family first spotted the boy, described by eyewitnesses as lean and wiry with long, matted hair, in late March.

The Vancouver man was awakened in the early morning by the frantic cries of his 12-year-old daughter. When he emerged from his tent, he saw her pointing into the woods.

She said that a 'wild boy' was stealing our food, Dr. Gosten recalls. "I looked where she was pointing and saw this half naked boy slinking off into the trees with an armful of canned goods." Shouting after the child, Dr. Gosten gave chase and caught up with him at the edge of a clearing. "I couldn't believe my eyes. The boy was standing next to an enormous, hairy, man-like creature at least 8 feet tall. The thing took some of the boy's load before ambling off together into the woods, both walking with the same hunched over, ape like stride." Since that sighting, at least 33 people have reported seeing the wild boy and his hairy companion. Witnesses have included clergymen, forest rangers and members of the Royal Canadian Mounted Police.

In many cases, the mismatched duo has been heard exchanging guttural sounds as if talking. "This youngster has all the earmarks of a feral child. A child that has had no human contact and has been raised by an animal," said the Seattle based Dr. Worrier. "The fact that his gait is similar to the Bigfoot and that they can communicate is evidence that the creature is his surrogate parent." Researchers believe that the wild boy sightings may be connected to the 1989 crash of a private plane carrying a party of French tourists visiting the region. The crash left the pilot and four passengers dead including young mother Madeleine Dusoire. Madeleine's baby Marcel was missing and the remains of the 1-year-old infant were never found.[171]

Note: This has to be the most remarkable account I've ever read!

Bigfoot Roaming the Wilds with a Child?

Chatter Like a Tape-Recorder Running in Reverse

The behavior listed was "stooping over a salmon-run pond scooping up salmon." The other interesting aspect of the interview was when the informant said the sound the Sasquatch made was like a tape-recorder in reverse. We've heard linguist Scott Nelson talk about how fast the Sasquatch seemingly speak, so it makes sense that what we hear might sound like a reversed tape recording.

January 21, 2006: Ken Kristian mentioned a report by Brad Hay, who became a true believer during a prospecting trip a few summers before. In a rugged area known as Spindle Creek, in the Lower Mainland, he had a close encounter with a large, hairy creature that made sounds "like something played through a tape recorder in reverse."

In an interview, Mr. Hay said he and a friend were hiking along a creek northeast of Vancouver when they saw the animal stooped over a pool, apparently scooping salmon fry out the water. "I thought it was a raggedy old bear at first. But when it stood I thought, holy crap. Then it started making this sound and chills just ran through me. It freaked the hell out of us." Mr. Hay said he and his friend ran one way and the creature, which they believe was a Sasquatch, ran the opposite way. Asked whether he could have seen a bear standing on its hind legs, he insisted, "oh no. This was no bear, it had hands."

He described the animal as being muscular and between 6-7 feet in height. It ran upright on its hind legs in a "quick jaunt," exuding a smell that nearly choked them (a strong, pungent smell is so closely associated with Sasquatch sightings that in some places, specifically Florida, the creatures are called skunk apes). Mr. Hay is certain he saw a Sasquatch. "I really don't care what people think," he added. "I saw what I saw and I can tell you, I'll never go back there without a gun."

Kristian said that while many reports are suspect, Mr. Hay's account has a ring of truth. "This is pretty exciting. He's a guy who knows the bush, and he won't see a black bear and mistake it for a Sasquatch."[172]

The Giant Hairy Beast Is Out There

Watching

Wildlife educator Larry Battson told another story about morel mushroom pickers along Big Walnut Creek in Putnam County, Indiana. The case account Larry told me about involved a husband and wife who noticed a field of morels already picked. Scouting around for a different area of unpicked mushrooms, the husband wandered off. The wife located a mushroom that had not been picked and as she bent over to recover it, she heard heavy, forceful breathing. Looking up from her picking, she found a large brown/black Sasquatch watching her, half of him sticking out from behind a tree. The sight sent her screaming back to their vehicle in horror.[173]

Putnam County, Indiana

More Watching

Oklahoma researcher Matt Knapp had some interesting observations and offered the following behaviors attributed to the Sasquatch:

A lot seems to happen in and around Native American communities. I've heard some pretty strange stuff from Dan Ricke that he has passed along. There was one instance where there was an evening soccer game at the local school or some similar type sporting event, but I think it was soccer. Apparently a Squatch, or a few Squatches, had come up to the tree line about 50 yards away from the where the children were having this game. Their total attention was on the children, watching them, and didn't seem to care they were right there in front of a large group of people. I think there was something close to like 30 witnesses or so to that event. I've also heard accounts of them at Pow-Wows coming right up into the crowd of people or up around the large fires where everyone was at. Of course the Pow-Wows would end abruptly at that point.

Luke Gross down in Texas had a sighting at his mother's house where a Sasquatch came right up to the glass front door and just stood there staring at him.

One of the strangest stories I've ever heard came from this Native American woman in south-central Oklahoma who claimed that when she was a young girl, a Sasquatch followed her right on inside her house. The men in the room jumped up and began yelling at it, trying to get it backed out of the house, and it apparently showed its teeth and let out what they referred to as a laugh, and then it turned and walked out.*

Destroying Trace Evidence

Wildlife educator Larry Battson amassed many reports where the behavior was either an exchange of stares or watching from afar. One other report occurred in a man's backyard in Morton, also Putnam County, Indiana, in August of 2007. In that same report, the informant told Battson that while sassafras was hunting, he found what appeared to be a nest that contained matted hair. He went to get his brother to show him the find, but when they got back to where the nesting area was, it was completely destroyed and the clump of hair was gone. Apparently, Battson's informant was watched the whole time. I don't think field people should readily assume they're being watched, but in a field of potential food, where it's obviously already picked over, the opportunity is there.[174]

---

* Matt Knapp, Oklahoma Bigfoot investigator; private correspondence.

The behavior of destroying their own trace evidence is something I didn't have in my data. I do recall ten years ago there was a rumor floating around that the Sasquatch would sometimes obliterate their telltale footprints. Someone in the course of time mentioned seeing a Sasquatch dragging a branch behind itself to destroy its tracks – but I could not confirm that story. Some Sasquatch may hide trace evidence, but I do not believe that can be said for all of them as a universal trait.

Speaking of stories difficult to verify but kept alive by the perpetuation that is inherent in the internet world, there was this one:

When I entered the Bigfoot search scene in the 1980s, there was a story circulating about a hunter who a Sasquatch rescued. It was one of the first stories I ever heard. I don't know where the story originated, and I cannot remember now who first told it to me, but it is still talked about in Bigfoot circles more than 30 years later, at least that I remember. It was one of those hard-to-believe stories grossly embellished by some accounts I've heard.

Morton, Putnam County, Indiana

As it was told to me, the story centered on a couple of deer hunters deep in the wilderness. One of them fell and fractured his femur, a compound fracture rendering him unable to walk. Unable to carry him out by himself, his hunting companion went for help. The hunter's pain was excruciating, and a Sasquatch allegedly heard his agonizing cries (it was said), heroically scooping the injured hunter up before carrying him to a safe place where he was later found. It was a wild story to hear back in those days, and it continues to make the rounds. Was it true? I mention it here to confirm that nobody I know has ever found any source for the story, with no article and no citation anywhere. There may have been some truth to it but I think not, however, I've been wrong before.

Evidence of Physical Rage and Aggression

In 1997, marine biologist invertebrate expert Dr. Henner Fahrenbach lived at the time in Beaverton, Oregon, and he shared an interesting story told to him by a fellow Bigfoot tracker/enthusiast from the Eugene area who had been tracking a rather large Sasquatch up through an old logging road.

In 2011, with my memory fading of the 14-year-old incident, I asked Dr. Fahrenbach what he remembered of it. Recalling the conversation, Henner said:

> That fellow was sort of a loner from Eugene. He had a tendency to follow and encroach on the Sasquatch in that very unappealing forest down there - no old growth, lots of patchy clear cuts, abandoned lumber roads, probably no traffic all year other than for hunting season. As I remember his story, it sounded to me like the Sasquatch tried to do a 'scare display' to get Bruce to leave the area and acted like a male gorilla in the process, stomping and ripping up the vegetation.*

It was a story hard to forget, and I thought the behavior described was unusual in that the informant's presence in the woods either offended or upset the Sasquatch, who literally laid waste in an area of timber and vegetation nearly 12-foot square. It was hard to imagine the sounds that calamity must have created. The distressed wild man uprooted vines, shrubs, trees by the roots, threw dirt clods, and generally deci-

---

* Conversations with Dr. Henner Fahrenbach from 1996/7 to present time.

mated a huge area by turning a green growth swathe into a moonscape. It's hard to know whether the scene was an act of intimidation by the Bigfoot, anger, frustration, or simply an attempt to get the tracker to leave the area. There are other such reports in my files.

After inspecting the upheaval, the informant Bruce decided it was best to leave. Upon investigating the area at some later point, Dr. Fahrenbach reported:

> I found a good Sasquatch track (with my own eyes) as we were driving along overgrown dirt tracks, with nice toe prints under the overhanging, uphill side of the road cut and then a continuation through dusty ferns. We camped out one night. Bruce had his smallish Bigfoot dog along. It certainly gives one a creepy feeling when the dog suddenly runs a few steps, stops and stares silently into the dark forest, when he usually barked like crazy at all other animals! [*]

Decimated Vegetation

While fishing for salmon, Moesha Carra came upon a similar area, although the destruction described this time wasn't fresh. The vegetation had withered and turned brown, but the area was about the same size as Fahrenbach described in the mountains around Eugene, Oregon. In this instance, the area faced the river where he and others frequently fished during the October sockeye salmon run near Kamloops, British Columbia. The destruction extended on the trees some 4-feet above Dr. Carra's reach, and the remaining trees were stripped of their lower branches and tossed over the tops of towering trees that surrounded the path of destruction. Treetops were broken over and left hanging. Other small saplings had been pulled from the ground and thrown into the surrounding forest – not only thrown through the columns of trees but up and over the tops of trees where many were still hung up and withered. Apparently, the disturbed Sasquatch cut a swathe wide enough to

---

[*] W.H. Fahrenbach.

allow sunlight into an otherwise dark and foreboding bit of the forest. The behavior is intriguing.

Dr. Carra recounted a story shared with him by an elder of the Tk'umlups Indian Band in 1989 in Kamloops, B.C. Two of the First Nation women were cleaning salmon on the banks of the Adams River late one afternoon when the hairy man appeared out from the trees and walked brazenly up to the two frightened women. The younger woman ran off screaming, and the other extended her hands with a cleaned sockeye to the giant. After a lengthy bit of staring at the woman, she again gestured for him to take the fish. Finally, the salivating giant took it from her and continued to stare, standing firm a few feet away. She could hear the fully bearded giant breathing, so close was he to her. The unnamed woman illustrated the length of the wild man's beard with her hands, saying it was twisted into a single braid, the length of it touching him mid-chest, which is an unusual characteristic previously not in my data that conjured up a mental image of Rip van Winkle. At that point in Dr. Carra's narrative, the younger first woman returned with three tribesmen who fired rifles into the air. Only then did the great giant return to the trees with the fish he had been given. The storyteller thought he probably wanted more fish, but of course, she stood firm and resisted. I don't know what the hairy man's intent was, but she was very brave to stand there with him glaring at her. Dr. Carra wasn't so generous; he thought the creature wanted her AND the fish...as many of these stories go. We'll never know.

Dr. Carra must have had some sort of herpetology knowledge. In a subsequent email, he related one other sighting in the same region that involved a young Sasquatch male who was seen in transit crossing the great Thompson River in the vicinity of Kamloops, British Columbia. As it forged the Thompson, it held a fist full of newly hatched snakes above its head. Carra's remarks were interesting in that the Sasquatch seemed oblivious to the bites he was enduring from the wriggling, obviously annoyed hatchlings. The description does paint a rather interesting picture and I was left transfixed by the visual it created. In 1995, all those years ago, I was hard-pressed to believe his stories.

Today, it all seems plausible. Dr. Carra described the individual in the snake tale as "an eight-footer, black-haired male, fully bearded Sasquatch with hair so long and fine that it trailed behind him as it forged against the windy Thompson River."*

In my data, there is frequent mention of bearded male Sasquatches and a few females as well. Strangely, the female in the Patterson film appears to also be bearded. But in 2003, I received this counter response from an out-of-touch John Green:

> The 4000 reports in my computer files contain no indication that male Sasquatch are bearded or that Sasquatch are normally in family groups.†

Digressing for a moment here, I am left to believe that Green is often out of touch or forgetful because I can think of several reports of family units being observed, not the least of which was Todd Neiss's encounter with a male, female, and juvenile Sasquatch observed and reported in the Military Chapter of this book. The second instance would be the bearded face of the subject "Patty," in the short film clip Roger Patterson filmed.

As recent as September 2012, a Bigfoot family was reportedly observed in Ontario, Canada, in an article titled *Wunnumin Lake's Mysterious Bigfoot Family*. Apparently, stories of the Wunnumin Lake Sasquatch family are "as old as the hills," according to counselor Gordon McKoop.[175]

Finally, for as long as I can remember, John Green has been a member, curator, and advisor of the BFRO, yet he doesn't seem to know about the cited reports. Todd Strong filed what they like to label a class A report from multiple witnesses in Bear Lake County, Idaho, who observed a Bigfoot family. The report was unusual in that it included

---

* Various email exchanges from Dr. Moesha Carra; 1995-2001.
† John Green Wednesday, May 21, 2003.

this statement: "They had dome shaped heads and no fur on their faces."[176]

I thought it a most unusual statement inasmuch as the data tends to show male Sasquatches with facial hair, even the females. As with the subject in the film attributed to Roger Patterson, analysis has shown that the female subject had a human-shaped skull/head, not a domed head. What had previously been perceived as a dome-shaped head or cone shape was a stack of piled hair that moves to and fro with every step the Patterson female subject took on the Bluff Creek sandbar in 1967. There are one or two descriptions of "dome or cone-shaped" heads in the data, but I think it isn't the skull but a piled amount of hair. And too, not all primitive Sasquatch are reported to have Ozzy Osborne style hair; that is – parted in the middle, hanging straight, stringy, or straggly. All manner of hairstyles are listed in the data; some have even been reported with hair hanging down over their faces in the manner of a sheepdog. There are even reports of braided and twisted dreadlock-type hair, bangs, and adornments.

Nothing Fishy Going on; Just Winning | Several Years Later
Bowhunter Confirms Sighting of Bigfoot Family East of
Montpelier

Angry Display

The late Vance Orchard accumulated data in Walla Walla County, Washington, for the most part, but he also fielded reports from other areas. His report in April of 1999 came from Marion County, West

Virginia, and involved several 4-wheeling funsters riding their ATVs in the Rivesville Hollow.

Following what they described as a horrible stench, the men saw a dark figure crouched or squatted down behind a tree. Trying to get a better look, the hairy man stood up and left. Checking the area, they found footprints five feet apart. The brother and wife of the original informant also observed what they thought at first was a bear; they turned off their ATVs to watch. The Sasquatch, in turn, stopped to watch them. The glances back and forth continued until the Sasquatch walked on. It was clear from the description that it was not a bear. Tracks were also found, but no measurements were given in Vance's report. The encounters continued in that hollow, basically in the same location. Watching it through binoculars, it was described as "...nothing they had ever seen before."

Two days later, Vance's informants were out picking mushrooms when they heard a brief rapping sound and then screaming that became louder and louder followed by thrashing/crashing around in the woods that apparently persisted, causing some amount of destruction in the surrounding forest. The rather dramatic ear-piercing noise could be heard over the engines of the ATVs. The area was a popular place for mushroom picking, which may have been the reason for the angry upheaval. This report was initially uploaded on Jeff Rense sightings by Vance Orchard, Ron Schaffner for the BFRO, Bigfootencounters dot com and several other websites of that day.

Near Rivesville and Jordan, Marion County, West Virginia,
Bordering Monongalia County, Along the Monongalia River

The discussions of that day centered mostly on the aggressive behavior of the Sasquatch, which was not aimed at the people on the ATVs, but in general, the aggression was taken out on forest vegetation. Whatever the reason for the Sasquatch's behavior that day, it is noteworthy that the display was apparently not aimed at the people on the 4-wheelers.[177]

Raging Sasquatch Rips up Trees and Destroys Vegetation

The behavior of the Sasquatch ripping up vegetation probably has more than one explanation. It may be that there were no rocks available; the alternative behavior would be tearing up jack... as the saying goes. I have only this last account where a witness actually had visual contact with the perpetrator in the process of decimating an area of vegetation.

My friend and longtime subscriber to the Bigfoot Newsletter, Jerry Padilla of the Taos News interviewed Arturo "Homie" Martinez of Costilla, New Mexico, in 2006. Martinez's testimony was similar to those of Doctors Henner Fahrenbach and Moesha Carra. Padilla wrote that as hunting season neared, Martinez was out scouting elk in the highest peaks of the Sangre de Cristo Range in southeastern Colorado. It's beautiful country; the high peaks are pristine, naturally untouched forest, and the aspen trees at the time were a deep yellow. New England has nothing on the fall colors I've seen in the Sangre de Cristo Range. It is breathtaking watching yellow leaves blow away from the aspen trees from the comfort of a camp chair; it is dynamite!

Homie Martinez, scouting the high range with a friend, was driving on a section of a roughly carved-out road when they discovered the tops of many aspen trees broken off. "The aspen," he said, "ranged in size from 4-inches to 8-inches in diameter and were cleanly broken off about 15-feet up the trunks of the trees; there were no tracks of any kind." Continuing on, the informant told Padilla, "there were two big aspens completely uprooted and thrown away from where they had been growing. If bears had broken them, there would be clawed markings." The broken tops of trees were lying in the road as if something or someone wanted to say, "nobody is welcome here," or perhaps "don't come here." Then, rounding a curve, Martinez blew a tire, and things began to get scary. "We could hear elk bugling up in the higher country. We decided to walk back down since it was late afternoon," Martinez said. "We needed to get a spare tire and come back to change it. We were taking our time checking out more broken trees; there was easily over 100 broken trees snapped off in the same way. That is when I heard the scariest noise I have ever heard in my life. It started at first sounding like an elk bugling then it turned into a scary roar so loud it kept echoing through the canyon. The elk up high stopped bugling. It kept making that noise at us, and reminded me of the noise the devil made in *The Exorcist*. Whatever made that sound started breaking trees and throwing them in our direction. Then...I saw a HUGE creature moving through the edge of an aspen grove about 30 yards from me. It walked upright hunched over, maybe was six feet tall bent over but standing straight up was seven or eight feet tall with very dark hair all over. It was not a bear. Bears don't walk like humans. I am convinced I saw what many call a Sasquatch."

Padilla picks up the story again. "The two men fled down the mountain and Martinez said every time the creature roared, the noise continued reverberating through the entire area. "I felt like at any moment something was going to grab me from behind all the way out of there." They arrived on foot in Costilla well after dark and decided that no matter how scared they felt, it was necessary to return to the canyon, change the blown tire and bring Martinez's vehicle back.

"They did return, changed the tire, and decided to spend the night because it was after 2:00 a.m., Martinez continued, "we decided to stay until daylight and try to find out what it really was we had experienced. It was deathly quiet the whole time; nothing moving, no elk bugling, not a sound. At sunrise we checked around and found more aspens broken in the same way. Nothing else happened to us."

One familiar notation I often hear from such informants like Martinez is the wish to be believed and to understand they know the difference between a Sasquatch and a bear. So many times, I've heard witnesses tell me that when they told officials such as the police, sheriff or forestry, they were rebuffed and sometimes even ridiculed and laughed at. Where Martinez and his friend got the stones to return in the pitch black of night, up that darkened road, armed only with flashlights, I'll never know, especially when returning to an area where the Sasquatch was clearly not happy about something! Perhaps it was just their presence that ticked off the rage that caused the physical destruction of that area. It was a great story, and I was glad Padilla published it. Colorado has a long history of sightings, especially in the Sangre de Cristo Mountains, not only of hair men but of Little People.[178]

Aspen Trees Broken, Uprooted and Tossed in Roadway

Horse Killed by Bigfoot

Russ Spence put me onto a story Tom Hernandez told him that happened in Wyoming. We don't hear much from hunters, hikers, and riders up in that part of the country, so I was delighted for his story to come my way in December 2011. The report spoke to the issue of aggressiveness with horses.

Trimming the account down to just the behavior of the Sasquatch, Hernandez wrote:

I was 13 at the time we saw it at my grandfather's place near the Boulderflats area in Fremont County, Wyoming, near Lander. The creature jumped up on the road next to us. I was on a horse that stood 16-hands and I was a little over 6-foot and had to look up at this guy.[*]

He was only about 4 or 5 feet from me and I got a pretty good look at him. He ran the same direction we were running. I'm not sure if it was chasing us but I didn't feel a real sense of the Bigfoot trying to harm us. It scared me of course, but if it wanted to it could have grabbed either one of us right from the start.

Anyway, that night something killed a two-year-old horse we were working with and carried it up to the house. Whatever carried it was so tall that only three of the horse's legs dragged the ground as it walked. It left the horse by the water trough and took off. The dogs tracked it to the mountains, and the police/sheriff's office made plaster casts of the tracks—and that was that. The incident made the papers and the Salt Lake City news; some of my students even found the newspaper story on the internet. I am a believer, but not as sure as I once was.[179]

Is Bigfoot in Fremont County, Riverton, Wyoming?

---

[*] A horse 16 hands high (16hh) is approximately 5 foot 3 inches at the withers. With head raised, the horse is actually taller. A hand is 4 inches. 16hh x 4= 64 inches. A rider seated in a saddle who is over 6 feet tall having to "look up" at the Sasquatch would probably put the Sasquatch in the 8-9-foot or taller range.

Bigfoot Attacks Horse and Rider

Diane Stocking filed a 1974 report of an incident that occurred in Douglasville, Georgia. It involved a young 18-year-old woman who had been riding cross-country endurance training sessions for a local rancher since she was aged 14. On this particular day, the rider was training a 16½ hands-high black Arabian stallion. Stallions, regardless of the breed, are notorious for being strong-willed, high-spirited, easily spooked, and often difficult to handle. The young woman must have been a very accomplished rider to have had the skills and know-how to handle a young stallion on an endurance ride.

On this day, she was twenty miles into the woods on a dirt road when she crossed a bridge that snaked into an 'S' curve road. Instantly, the rider heard something, and then a loud shrill scream. "Something" from the side jumped out, panicking both rider and stallion. Whatever it was, it was massive and human-looking and had hair over its body. It jumped out, grabbing the horse's back-end and rear of the saddle. A flash struggle ensued between the horse and the perceived Bigfoot. The rider testified she threw herself around the stallion's neck for lack of a saddle horn and hung on as the panicked horse took off in a wild run. It was not known if the ranch owner believed her, but the scratched saddle told the story. What a horrifying encounter, and I don't have another similar behavior in the records quite like this one, but the conduct of the Sasquatch was not all that unusual. If it wasn't outright aggression, then perhaps a bit of fun gone wrong?[180]

Terrified Horse and Riders

No stranger to Bigfoot stories, long-time friend Sheryl Jenkins often rides the mountain range near her home on horseback. It's a great way to clear the mind, get your face into the wind, and enjoy the mountain air and all it has to offer. Luckily, Sheryl had daily access to the same Mill Creek Watershed in the Blue Mountains of Washington State we've all read about; Paul Freeman and Wes Sumerlin frequently talked about their experiences in the Blues with Bigfoot. It's no surprise then that Paul Freeman's famous Bigfoot footage, "Oh there he goes..." was filmed in the Blues, as were some of his tracks—both real and faked. There's no shortage of sightings from that region. Master tracker, Joel Hardin (who Rene Dahinden often bragged on, claiming he could "track a mouse across a concrete floor") wrote a twenty-page dissertation on his time in the Blue Mountains of Washington State. It is also worth noting here that Hardin was flown in by the U.S. Forestry Service to track footprints that Paul Freeman had reportedly found. His account is recorded in a lengthy twenty-page chapter in Joel's 2009 book, *Tracker*, available through Joel in Clearwater, Idaho. The late Vance Orchard penned many an article about Bigfoot and horses in his newspaper column for The Times in nearby Walla Walla, Washington, and he wrote two books covering stories of Bigfoot and the Blue Mountains.[181] Brian Smith is another long-time enthusiast who found tracks up in the Blues. The list is long.

Sheryl Jenkins is a seasoned horse woman who has seen Bigfoot often in the Blues, but neither her horses nor mine ever reacted with the same wild terror other horsemen have. Yet all horses I've owned give off well-defined signals or physical signs when they catch the scent of mountain lions, bears, coyotes, wolves, etc. With an olfactory nose the length equines have, they don't miss much, especially seasoned trail-savvy horses. A horse will throw its head around, loudly snort the air with flared nostrils, buck wildly, jerk its head back, and dance around nervously. Some grumble with an audible snort upon detecting something unusual in the air. Some will stand and fight, and others will take off running in a panicked state. Occasionally, they will simply lower their head and buck violently. Once you come to know the horse, his behavior, and what it means, you can pretty well figure out the exact stimuli the horse is experiencing.

There have been interesting conversations with equine veterinarians on scent reactions. One vet related that horses, like wolves and bears, react to the chemical gases in the air emitted from dead animals much more than they react to the scent. A horse must be trained to carry anything dead, so violently opposed they are to the secreted gases from anything dead as each dead and decaying animal carcass has its own unique stench. Packing dead bodies out of the mountains will generally take a special kind of horse. Mountain horses quickly learn scents at a young age by watching their mother and other horses. The equine ear is amazing. I remember a trail ride on the Grand Mesa over on Colorado's western slope when my mount stopped abruptly, pricked her ears forward and stared head high and fixed without moving. The brush was dense manzanita and scrub oak, and not knowing what she sensed, I urged her forward, but she stayed fixed and motionless, her ears pricked forward. The air was quiet, I heard nothing for several moments, and then, maybe 3-4 minutes after she alerted me, I heard the rattle of a western diamondback coiled off to the left of the dirt trail. If I had been paying attention, I would have noticed the signs in the trail dirt heavy with snake sign. The incident was brief and uneventful, but it spoke volumes about the highly specialized senses of all animals with long noses and directional ears.

Given the circumstances the subject "Patty" was under at the time Patterson's horse began bucking, Patty may have been giving off sudden fear pheromones the horses were able to detect, inhale, and react to. Then again, other bodily gases may have caused Patterson and Gimlin's horses to react the way they claim they did, if any of that story is true.

In Sheryl Jenkins's *Bigfoot sightings in the Blues*, the Bigfoot did not run from her. They stayed, watched, and stalked her and the farrier friend riding along. This was the case in Arizona when a male Sasquatch stood his ground and watched a group of single-file horsemen ride the opposite canyon wall; I was among them that year. Horses are great sentries during a forest ride. That day, my horse was bucked by the one in front of me, and more than anything, I feared the horse would panic and take me over the sheer drop-off to my right. It was a harrowing experience, such that I didn't get much of a look at the Sasquatch everyone was yelling about other than it was huge. Here is a condensed version of Sheryl Jenkins's report as she wrote it.

The day we were followed by a Sasquatch, Sept 19, 1987, I was riding Star. My shoer* was on a horse of his own and a friend of his was on my horse, Tiger. We were going along the main Mill Creek Watershed Trail checking for elk hunting possibilities and were riding easily along at a walk pausing here and there to scan for elk in the canyon. I should mention my shoer had more mountain experience than me as he spent several years herding cattle in the mountains. We rode past the electric gate, the only place in the trail that meets the road for a few feet, and then up the hill along a curving trail, out into an open meadow, down the other side going thru brush and trees in many places but on the Watershed Trail. No problems riding out.

When we decided to turn around and come back, my shoer noticed some hair on a low tiny tree or bush. We had just ridden past this point an hour before and there had been no hair then. My shoer friend stopped to inspect it, we both dismounted. Suddenly the three of us heard something move, a loud unmistakable noise below us in the trees/brush. The three of us, along with our horses jumped at the noise; this behavior is unusual for my horses. We decided it best to mount up and ride out of there, this just wasn't normal and the horses were uncharacteristically nervous. I remounted as did my shoer. I was worried about mounting as Star was nervous and starting to act up, moving instead of standing still, wanting to leave. The horses were not happy with whatever was behind us, following as we walked the horses out for roughly a mile. I have to mention that all three of us were nervous turning to scared, the fear increasing as we walked.

We were definitely being followed, zero doubt! We could tell that whatever followed us was getting closer due to the brush noises becoming closer and the horses became increasingly agitated. By now I was on Star who was used to bear/cougar/deer/elk and other forest animals, and she had no problems with them. Whatever was following us that afternoon, this horse had problems with as did the other two horses. By now Star wanted no part of this animal.

---

* In equestrian lingo a shoer is also known as a horse-shoe-er, a blacksmith or a farrier.

All three horses were increasingly stressed wanting to break into a run; in fact, we even felt the need to start running! Star had the best reaction, but we kept all of them under control, forcing them to keep a walking pace despite their jitters. My two were used to walking this trail on a loose rein at a walk with zero problems. That said, we still had a problem keeping them at the walk and they fought us all the way for well over a mile. Ever alert, the horses' ears swiveled backwards towards the rear, listening. They were wild eyed, nostrils flared, just straining to take off in a dead run and this terrified behavior they displayed definitely increased as the Sasquatch gained on us!

Just before we reached the electric gate the horses were at the peak of agitation wanting to bolt into a run but we fought hard holding them to a walk; tensions ran high. At this point we could SMELL whatever was behind us and no doubt the horses caught the scent on wind much sooner than we did; it was obvious by their behavior. We could hear noise in the underbrush ever so often, but the smell by now was an overpowering sickly-sweet stench, intolerable and nauseating. Never before had I seen such a display of wild eyed fear from my horses. The fact Star was so bothered scared me all the more; the all-consuming stench didn't help my nervousness. The creature was definitely gaining on us; we decided to go through the electric gate at this point, and then ride the road around to the cabin. Shoer had trouble getting off his agitated horse and also in remounting her. In our minds, we did not want this creature with the foul stench following us back to the cabin, noting at this point it had been either close by or behind us for nearly a mile. There are no words to adequately express how scared we were.[182]

Sasquatch and Horses, a Personal Story

Sasquatch and the Horse Stable

This appears to be another story where a solitary Sasquatch found food, and when it was withheld from him, it destroyed the place. We have several case reports where people have consistently fed Sasquatch families only to have the homestead torn to shreds when the owners move or die.

In another instance, a Sasquatch family watched television through a big bay window, and when it was shut off at night, they howled continuously. To solve the problem and get some sleep, the cabin owners had to leave the television running all night long. The Sasquatch appear to be short-tempered when the things they grow accustomed to are taken away. Apparently, that happened in this next story.

We maintain a working ranch in western Tennessee. In the stable we have two refrigerators and in one of them my hands keep a 50-pound sack of fresh cut carrots to use as treats for the mares after a training workout. One or two, three at the most cut up into bite sized pieces with an occasional apple in season.

In going over my expenditures one evening, I noted how often these larger bags of carrots were being ordered and called in the hands who had access to quiz them about the use of so many bags. They noticed it but couldn't account for it. It was felt that someone was coming into the stables during the night and helping themselves to the carrots but the hands didn't know who would do that.

I suggested we fashion a strap similar to a luggage strap and place it around the refrigerators to keep the contents from being stolen, and so we thought the problem of the disappearing carrots was solved. Not so. On the second morning the hands found the straps removed, the refrigerator door open, and the entire sack of carrots gone missing again. I had to go out of town on business and while I was gone, my two hands decided to keep watch in the stables. What they told me they saw defies anything I've ever heard. The side door to the stable was opened around three in the morning, interrupting the all-night gin rummy game my hands were involved in. They looked up from the stall and down towards the end of the promenade was a ghastly looking red-haired monster gingerly making its way to the refrigerators where it made short work of the belt securing it, and when he opened the door he found there were no carrots. Apparently, this angered the monster because it began systematically destroying the surroundings, as was evident when I returned home. The side room containing the refrigerators was left a shambles. Cupboards were down and a wash sink was pulled from the wall. Insurance adjustors came and said it was the work of vandals. To answer your questions, the door into the stables has a normal knob that requires turning to enter; the belt around the refrigerator was torn apart by pressure, we figured. The refrigerator opens up like any refrigerator and the monster knew how to operate all of them in order to gain access. This was not this monster's first rodeo. I guessed he'd been in the stables many times before.

It did no good to lock the outside door; I figured it would only be torn off its hinges. The ranch hands used a dolly to unplug the refrigerators and place both outside the door with their doors wide open. I fully expected the fridge doors to be torn off their hinges, but so far, that hasn't happened.[*]

---

[*] J. Broland, 1996.

Mount Shasta Legend

California's majestic 14,200-foot Mount Shasta has quite a record of strange sightings and a history of mummified 10-foot tall giants discovered in a cave that sloped downward for eleven miles under Mount Shasta's prestigious peak. Shasta is second tallest to Mount Whitney at 14,505 in elevation, located in the Inyo National Forest, east of California's Sequoia. Shasta's neighboring Mount Lassen is approximately ten thousand feet plus. All of them have long histories of giants and hairy man sightings.

According to legend, J.C. Brown, a British gold prospector, located a series of tunnels under Mount Shasta in 1904. The Lord Cowdray Mining Company hired him to prospect the potential for Shasta's gold and, in the process, discovered the entrance to the lava tubing that made up the 11-miles to the underground graveyard. Thirty years later and curious about the 10-foot tall mummies, Brown told John Root about the giants. Together, they gathered a team of 80 people who met at a pre-planned staging area in Stockton, California; it was scheduled before the trip began. Oddly, Brown and Root never showed. A search party on Shasta was formed, but no trace of either man was ever found. The men are still missing more than 100 years later.[183]

Mount Shasta Annotated Bibliography | Legends of Mount Shasta

There are many stories and legends of California's Mount Shasta that include tunneled cities that snake through the giant mountain's fourteen thousand feet. Some of the stories include extraterrestrial overtones, but a few are from conventional flesh and blood thinkers like me, including tribes of hairy wild men who lived in the lava tubes under Mount Shasta and nearby Mount Lassen.

Stories of the hair giants at war with various local tribes are many. Way back when, I vaguely recall a story that supposedly took place on Mount Shasta. A group of prospectors-turned-miners were so harassed by a group of rock-throwing hairy men that they decided to load the cave's entrance with dynamite. Allegedly, it closed the entrance alright and ended the nuisance of the nightly rock-throwing, but the explosion killed a miner when one of the iron ore buckets sailed through the air, decapitating the man. I guess you can't fix stupid. An idiot story like that must have a grain of truth to it. As I've often said, you can't begin to make this stuff up.

Bigfoot and Little People of Mount Shasta

Timothy Green Beckley, in his narrative, *Underground Dwellers and Ancient Gods*, mentions incredible stories that occurred on Mount Shasta, California, and the unusual residents who supposedly dwell on and inside the mountain. For example, Beckley wrote, "...there are some awfully large beings that have been sighted on the slopes of Mount Shasta. My friend, Blue Ocean," Beckley continued, "..who is a Native American, says that as a child growing up there, he and his friends and family heard the sounds of Bigfoot and often there were reports of a little race of beings who would throw stones at the natives.[*] There is even said to be an entrance to a major underground city there, and the Native Americans consider the area to be sacred ground."[184]

The late Rich Grumley told a few stories that involved horses. Initially, Rich wrote to ask the next time I drove north if I would shop for a larger bed pillow for him; he was pretty much housebound by that

------

[*] Little People.

time. Rich was Sasquatch size himself at 6'6", weighing 240 pounds. By the time I finally dropped by Rich's place in Stockton, California, in late October 1999, he was showing the residual effects of a stroke. He spoke easily, but his writing was almost illegible. Still, his ground mail got through, which is great testimony to the dogged determination of the U.S. Postal Service to deliver the mail with barely legible addresses.

Rich, in his overpowering appearance, was quite clear in his memories of an acquaintance who ran a "trail horses for rent stable" high in the California Sierras. He described a few nights when the corralled horses were disturbed by something, enough that they were found well-lathered and quite panicky, snorting and still wild-eyed early next morning.

Two of the mares had plaited manes—not braided like human hair, but twisted in a circular motion into dreadlock-looking spirals that were gathered into a messy knot. Nothing further was learned from the stable owner; he was just as baffled as the next man. It only happened once, and the man was sure it was a mountain lion except for the woven sections in the manes of the two mares, and that part he could not explain. Rich, of course, had his own ideas, concluding it was a Bigfoot entertaining itself and thought the two woven loops on either side of the neck were hand-holds for the juvenile Sasquatch to hang onto during a brisk midnight ride.

Rich told the story to a Sheriff friend who lived near Clearlake, California. The Sheriff reasoned the situation a bit differently. He thought the mares may have been restrained so that the young Sasquatch could suckle the milk rich in nutrients and fat content. I'm not sure what to make of that idea, it was a new one for me. But time passed and sure enough, other stories of plaited manes eventually began to surface.

Here is the kicker – both instances only happened to brood mares, lactating mares. I don't know the reasons for plaiting horse manes, but the behavior has been observed on range stock, domestic riding stock, and wild mustangs. Apparently, the plaiting occurs on what I call fresh mares and only once with a stock wagon-pulling draft horse.

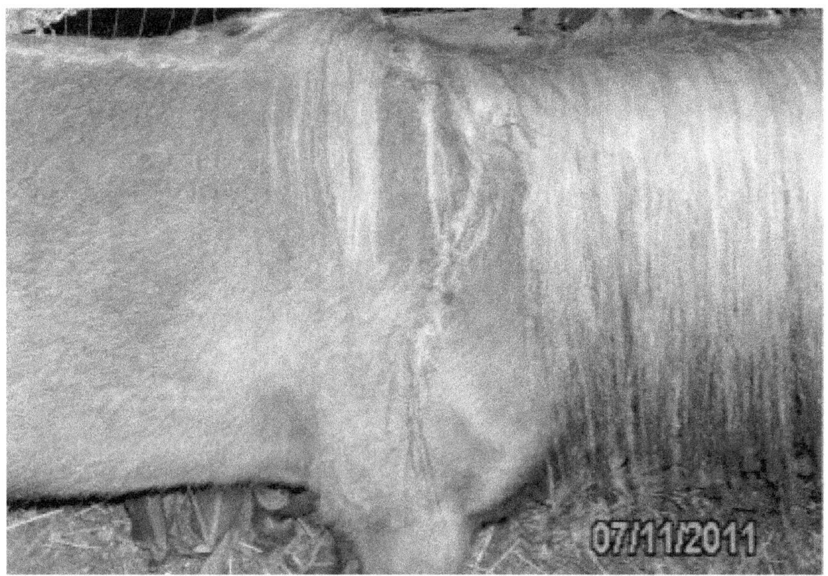

Photo © Jeri Erickson-Flatland, 2011.

I checked back on the old draft horse story, and I spent months tracking down contact information for the Kentucky rancher. Sure enough, the draft horse was a lactating mare. The owner indicated that it was a single incident and that perhaps draft horses were too hard to handle bulk-wise. Her draft horse was 18hh (72-inches at the withers) and weighed nearly 2,300 pounds. Not an easy horse to control if a Sasquatch holding it still by the braided loops while its youngster suckled was the listed behavior. The rancher also mentioned in the course of conversation that the draft horse was in no way stressed from the incident; a baffling remark. At any rate, the Kentucky horsewoman is becoming quite the Sasquatch enthusiast; we've become fast friends.

Mustangs are smaller horses, generally only 12 to 14hh, and presumably easier to control by a large Sasquatch. The idea is that the braided loops on the left and right side of the horse's neck are placed there to control the horse and in some cases hold the horse's neck down on the ground while young Sasquatch suckle under the hindquarters. Sounds fantastic, doesn't it?

If this behavior is common, it leaves me to wonder why horse's milk and not cow's milk? Why do we prefer cow's milk to horse milk? Historically, over 700 years ago, Mongolian warriors made a dried-out concentrated paste from horse milk. When the Mongols were on the march, they added it to water and drank it. Horses produce less milk than cows.

In southeastern Russia, people use fermented horse milk to make a slightly alcoholic drink called kumiss. Where there is a shortage of vodka, there is always kumiss. Individuals who cannot tolerate milk produced by their own kind often exercise great creativity in using the milk of domesticated ungulates, cattle, sheep, goats, yaks, water buffalo, horses, reindeer, and camels. If there is an intolerance to Sasquatch breast milk, it is then not so surprising to hear these stories of mares being milked or suckled. It's an interesting concept and entirely plausible, but is it true?

Don Monroe chronicled several cases from Montana along with photos of similar braiding techniques. Few cases are reported and I think that may be because no association with the Sasquatch is apparent for the horse owner when they discover the braiding.

One case Monroe investigated occurred on a ranch that handled 138 stock horses. Of that number, 40 were found to have plaited or braided manes at one time or another. Woven into some of the strands were longer horse hairs from the coarser strands taken off or pulled from the tail; perhaps to strengthen the loop?

In one of these cases, the mane hairs were originally 14 inches long but became 24-inch long with the addition of longer tail hairs. The extended loops were of equal size on either side of the neck and so tightly woven together, and so erratically, that it was impossible to undo. Removing the braiding required cutting with scissors, and all of these incidents occurred at night during full moon phases. That would make sense because you can't braid very well in the dark. With something like 13 full moon phases a year, the braiding seemingly becomes a moon-phase ritual.

In 2004, when Don Monroe was living in Spencer, Idaho, a horse rancher friend knocked at his door during a horrible blizzard. His name was Ron and he was just back from a trip to Mongolia. Don invited him in for a hot drink and the two hit it off; story-swapping began. The well-traveled Monroe showed his visitor Dmitri Bayanov's book, *On the Trail of the Russian Snowman*, and the photos of the Russian horses with plaited manes and asked, "have you ever seen anything like this happening in your horse stock, Ron?" Ron replied that he had indeed seen this phenomenon occur a few times with his own horses, but neither he nor his wife could understand the meaning or how it happened. That night, the stockman and Monroe brainstormed the reason for the braids, but no reasonable explanation was determined.

It has been speculated that the looped braiding, coupled with the strength of an adult Sasquatch, made restraining the horses easy— perhaps even a source of entertainment. I cannot imagine any horse of mine standing still for such foolishness - unless the horse was accustomed to having the Sasquatch around.

The Mysteries of Mount Shasta: Home of the Underground
Dwellers and Ancient Gods

With looped braids on either side of a horse's neck, a young Sasquatch could hang onto the loops while riding, steer the horse using the braided reins, or an adult could lead the horse by holding the loops. There are reports of trail riders being watched or shadowed by Bigfoot. The simpler explanation is probably that they've observed us riding and perhaps enjoy horseback rides themselves—the young ones, that is, since I cannot imagine a full-grown Sasquatch astride a common mare or gelding. Perhaps a Clydesdale could support an adult, but I have no such reports from breeders of those Budweiser-sized horses. Whatever the reason for the plaiting, it adds to the growing mystery surrounding Sasquatch behavior.

Thick Sasquatch Tracks

Before I forget entirely about Rich Grumley—he proudly showed me a pair of Sasquatch plaster track casts that he made in 1972. Not so amazing in itself but these casts measured out at 18 inches by 9 inches...HUGE! From the casts themselves, it was apparent that the hairy man sunk up to 3.5 inches into the substrate. We speculated what the creature must have weighed. Both left and right tracks clearly showed five digits with an enormous big toe. Rich recalled that the stride was six feet long and persisted for more miles than he was willing to hike.

As if the imagined massiveness of such a life form with feet that length wasn't enough to contemplate, the kicker was that his tracks were not found in deeply forested terrain, but in the open desert sand 90 miles from Lancaster, California. My discussion with Rich was in 1999, October to be exact. I mention this because in 2010, some eleven years later, Peter Guttilla scanned and sent me a copy of the Antelope Valley Ledger Gazette dated April 11, 1973. As if to further authenticate Grumley's track-find in the desert, they were mentioned in the article. We don't usually see tracks set that deep or as wide as 9 inches.[185]

Rich recalled a story involving a shooting of a Bigfoot somewhere near the South Carolina border with Georgia. He said a farmer gunned the creature down because it was literally tearing the legs off his sheep. The corpse of the reddish/brown Bigfoot was taller than the bed of the farmer's truck. With the help of a backhoe, the body was buried under a pile of rocks on the outskirts of town. I regret I did not get a source for that story from Rich. He was full of great stories, talkative, amiable, good-humored, and had many people he called friends. I enjoyed my time with Rich; even in poor health, he was positive and had an infectious laugh I could still hear when I thought long and hard.

Lancaster, California

More Desert Tracks

During a trip to North America, Evan Samuels, a UK wildlife photographer, was walking the desert in Borrego Springs, California, seeking to photograph a trail of Mojave (Mow-haw-vee) sidewinder (rattlesnake) tracks. He was in the company of a local herpetologist. Instead of finding sidewinder imprints, the men told me they found barefooted tracks that came off an incline to the west near Hellhole Palms and traveled north through the roughest part of the cactus-infested desert, trailing off in the distance toward Coachella, California, an area known for its date growers; a delicious desert fruit the Sasquatch might enjoy. The find occurred in September of 2007, and the temperature that day was in excess of 110 degrees; the desert floor was scorching hot. For me, the credibility of his claim was cinched when he described the left foot. "It was crescent-shaped and only the outside of that foot was impressed into the sand along with the two smaller digits. The other foot appeared normal but no arch, appeared to be flat as a pancake."

The data shows that cripple tracks are often seen and cast but rarely in my data in a desert setting; very unusual. I asked if he happened to photograph the tracks, and he said, "no." Odd for a photographer, I thought. The men didn't measure either, and he wouldn't venture a guess only to say they were "broad and flat." Samuels stated that once he figured out what must have made the tracks, he felt "uncomfortable" and wanted to get as far away from the desert as he could and as fast as he could due to the heat, snakes, cactus and now Bigfoot tracks. He called it a "hellish day." Many people underestimate the desert in summer.

Throwing People?

Not since Lake Worth, Texas, resident Charlie Buchanan's claim that he was picked up out of the flatbed of his truck and thrown to the ground by a Sasquatch in November of 1969 have I heard another "throwing people" report quite like his.[186] However, in October of 2011, veteran Bigfoot researcher Al Hakanson sent me an email stating he was contacted by a Native American woman who saw a man being thrown nearly 25-feet by an angry Bigfoot in Montana.

Hakanson said the informant refused to talk about it in much detail, saying only that it was the absolute truth and that he could take it or leave it.

The Graceful Way It Ran; A Beautiful Lope

Julie Davis, a former instructor at the University of Colorado Law School in Boulder, came forward and filed a report describing an 8-foot tall chestnut-colored Sasquatch she observed up close less than 12 feet away. Besides the general description, Davis described the expression on its face as, "...the graceful way it ran off, it was a beautiful lope. I could see the muscles move under the hair." Davis was a volunteer with the Great Bear Foundation in Montana for five years and knows well what a bear looks like; "...this was no bear, I don't care if anybody else believes me or not - there is nothing more persuasive than staring something straight in the face."[187]

San Juan County, Colorado

No Upper Body Hair

An unusual behavior was mentioned in Mike S.'s 1998 case in California's Shasta National Forest at the dead end of Castle Lake Road. Not only was the behavior interesting, but the description was also one of a kind, at least in my data. The informant said the Sasquatch was only haired heavily from the waist down and a little on the arms, describing the hair on the lower body like a pair of flowing brown leather chaps; little hair to none on the upper body. It had a full-length beard and a long head of hair. The informant said the 8-foot tall Bigfoot strolled out onto the road, and instead of ducking for cover like we assume most of them do, this one stayed out on the road and walked several hundred yards with people on the road yelling "hey, hey, hey" as it strolled on by "like a deaf zombie." It was very strange behavior and apparently it was witnessed by many people parked on the dead-end road. I spoke to several of the witnesses who told pretty much the same story as the informant. Some said they didn't think it was a Bigfoot, and others immediately labeled it as such. This is a case where many saw it, but not one of them photographed it. Very strange.[188]

Castle Lake, California, 1998

Swaying Back and Forth

The sight of a Sasquatch swaying back and forth is not an uncommon behavior, but reports in my data are few - no more than four and all of them describe the same rocking side to side. A retired couple described such behavior out using their metal detectors. Separated from her husband on an old wagon trail by a few feet, the woman encountered a curious male Sasquatch who stepped out from the trees and started swaying back and forth. She called to her husband who took his time responding. Meanwhile, the strange behavior continued, and there was a bit of glaring. The informant wrote:

> I went back and picked up the metal detectors and started to move rapidly toward my wife to protect her. The why and how hadn't occurred to me yet. When I got to Mary's side, I could see the wild man's frightened eyes, by God, the face was like any ordinary man's unshaven face but the rest of him was larger around than most men his size. He saw the metal detectors and kept looking down at them, like shifting his eyes from us to the metal detectors and then he took one step backwards into the shaded area and was less visible. His hair was thick, long black and looked well groomed, you know, it was long tresses and one side was pulled back, tucked behind his ear revealing his strange looking face.

The hair was straight but the beard he had was curly. His face was young, I would say, and his features distinct but distorted. He continued to sway back and forth nervously but I'm sure the metal detectors looked like weapons, because he looked quite worried and then this wild man turned and took one giant step towards the trees and was gone; he made no noise. I am sorry to say we never saw him again but at the time he departed, we were relieved![189]

Siskiyou County, California, 2006

Sasquatch Wears a Silver Belt?

A highly unusual Sasquatch mannerism was reported by Annette B. in Jefferson County, New York. She wrote:

My husband and I were coming back from Margaretville, New York, about thirty miles from Perch Lake; this was in 2002. My husband was driving and I was looking out the window. We passed this clearing on the river's bank and there is where we both saw a very LARGE FIGURE. My husband and I saw it clearly but he blew it off telling me it was a large man in a fur coat!? The surprising part was there was something around its waist that had a silver look to it, and a knife. It was like a silver chain of some kind around the waist with a knife attached on its side. It stood about 8-9 feet tall and was covered in hair from head to toes.[190]

Delaware County, New York, 2002

Kidnappings, Rape

I would think it reasonable to believe that abduction, kidnapping and rape are not behaviors the Sasquatch people indulge in very often, but I could be very wrong! If attempted rape, kidnapping, and such are universal traits, the data does not reflect that. It is quite possible that the Sasquatch does not accept these acts as evil or unlawful in their primitive and limited social structure. The Sasquatch is, by our standards, a wild living, primitive-looking human being.

According to the testimony Ostman gave to Rene Dahinden regarding the "talking down" the kidnapper received from his Sasquatch family; what the big kidnapper did was perceived as a really stupid move by his female partner. Rene interviewed Ostman a dozen times; Ostman's testimony never deviated.

We judge the frightful kidnapping behavior because our social structure regards kidnapping and abduction as an unlawful act, an acting out by mentally unstable persons and serial killers. Are there such laws among the Sasquatch? What does the Bigfoot book of rules say about kidnapping? Do they even have social standards? The truth is, we don't know anything about the way they think or if they have a moral code.

The Native Americans and First Nation Canadians used to speak freely about such things. Today, we don't hear much about kidnapping. Does it still happen? I think kidnapping most probably is alive and well, and

I think the process is covered up from the top by the Department of the Interior and those branches and agencies of government service that are extensions of the DOI.

What is generally leaked about campers that go missing is that they wandered off and are generally never seen again. In cases where foul play is suspected, the bear is purported to be the culprit. How do we in general research reconcile the many cases of trail-worn hikers and savvy campers that are never seen again, even in areas where there are no bears?

Newspaper accounts usually write these off as falls, disorientation, or some other logical explanation besides people having encountered a rogue Sasquatch. All societies have rebellious members, some dangerous for sure, but the Sasquatch, oblivious to our social standards, may not be aware that the act of kidnapping women from reservations, hikers, and small children at play is forbidden by civilized man.

In May 1909, a local resident of a First Nation Community was chased by a Sasquatch into his home, where the beast pushed against the exterior walls of the wooden house to abduct the local; it was a close call. Women are not the only potential abductees as we learned from the *Story of Albert Ostman* and Peter Byrne's *Muchalat Harry* stories. These were cases where adult human males were captured. One could gather from those abductions that remote living primitives understand little about civilized man and our rules for living. That probably should be expected.

Certainly, the Albert Ostman account presented a case for the total acceptance of an adult male human being brought into the Sasquatch family group, or so it seemed. Ostman felt the reason for his abduction was that he was a potential mate for the daughter of the hairy hostage taker. How reasonable is it to think a grown male Sasquatch would bring another grown adult male into his family circle? The notion is curious, and the behavior is odd, at least by my standards. If not repulsed by the idea of intercourse with a hair-covered bride, surely

Ostman's performance would be hindered by the stress of a captive situation. The idea also occurs to me that the Sasquatch apparently thought Ostman one of his own species; a man of his own kind, otherwise why did the dominant Sasquatch bring Ostman back to camp as a potential husband for his daughter? In this situation, we had a well-investigated event where there was no discussion of paralytic infrasound or telepathic messaging between the Sasquatch family and Albert Ostman; they spoke in a chatter.

For those who do not know the Ostman story, Albert Ostman lived in Chilliwack, British Columbia. He claimed to have been kidnapped and held for six days by a family of Sasquatch near Toba Inlet on the Strait of Georgia on the mainland opposite Vancouver Island. He escaped unharmed when the hairy captor became violently ill, having chewed and swallowed Ostman's can of tobacco.

Rene Dahinden sent me this photo in 1998 and told me he interviewed Ostman no less than twelve times and that Ostman's story never varied:

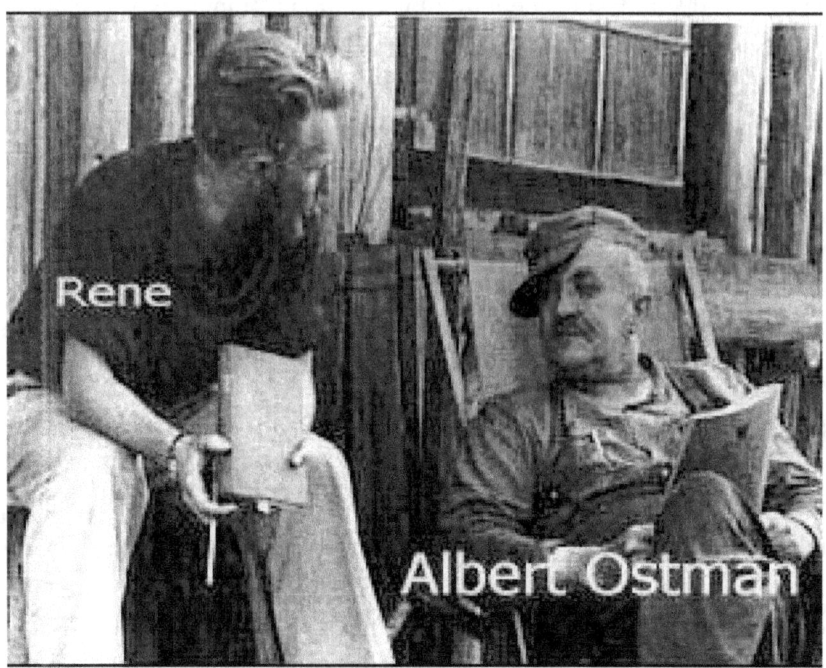

"Albert never wavered." Dahinden found the Ostman case a real head-scratcher but Rene said the story was the same each time he spoke with him. Ostman lived at the time of Rene's interviews in Chilliwack, British Columbia, Canada. In those days, Rene said he thought it was too impossible to make up a story simply to fabricate. Still, Rene was baffled by Ostman's claim.

Albert Ostman, however, a capable male in his own right, used brain-power to make his escape, which doesn't speak well for the Sasquatch being very street smart...in a manner of speaking. If there is a moral compass in the Sasquatch culture, I don't see it demonstrated in the Ostman kidnap story or the case of Peter Byrne's *Muchalat Harry*, a similar kidnapping drama.

One of the Indians of the Nootka Tribe, who lived at Nootka on Vancouver Island in 1928, claims to have been carried off by a Sasquatch and held captive for some time. The story, told to Peter Byrne by Father Anthony Terhaar of Mount Angel Abbey in Oregon, is curious.

> Father Anthony, a much-loved missionary priest who traveled the west coast of Vancouver Island for many years, was living at Nootka at the time of the story and he knew Muchalat Harry very well. Muchalat Harry was a trapper and something of a rarity among his fellow tribes-men. He was, according to Father Anthony, a tough, fearless man of excellent physique.
>
> In the course of his trapping, he was wont to spend long weeks in the forest alone, something that the average Indian did not do in those days. The Indians of the coast were apparently a rather timid people and seemed to regard the deep forest as the home and territory of the Bigfoot. When they went into the deep inland forest for any reason, they never went alone. Muchalat Harry was different from other Indi-ans. He went in the forest alone and feared nothing.
>
> Late one autumn, Muchalat Harry set off for the woods with his traps and camping gear. His plan was to set out a trap line and stay in the

woods for several months. He headed for his favorite hunting area, the Conuma River, at the head of Tlupana Inlet. From Nootka he paddled his own canoe to the mouth of the Conuma. There he cached the canoe and headed upstream on foot. Approximately twelve miles upstream he made his base camp and, after building himself a lean-to, started to put out his trap line.

One night, while wrapped in his blankets and clad only in his underwear, he was suddenly picked up by a huge male Bigfoot and carried off into the hills. He was not carried very far, probably a distance of about two or three miles, at the most. When daylight came he was able to see that he was in a sort of camp, under a high rock shelf and surrounded by some twenty Bigfoot of all sexes and sizes. For some time, they stood around him and stared. The males were in the front of the curious group, the females behind and young ones to the rear. Muchalat Harry was frightened at first and his fear grew to terror when he noticed, he said, the large number of bones lying around the campsite. When he saw these, he was convinced that the Bigfeet were going to eat him.

The Bigfeet did not harm him in any way. Occasionally, one came forward and touched him, as if feeling him, and when they discovered that his "skin" was loose — it was in fact his woolen underwear — several came forward and pulled at it gently.

While they looked at him and examined him, Muchalat Harry sat with his back to the rock wall and did not move. He was cold and hungry, but his thoughts were only on escape. Sometime in the late afternoon, curiosity on the part of the Bigfeet seemed to slacken and with most of the Bigfeet out of camp, probably food-gathering he thought, there came the opportunity that he needed. He leapt to his feet and ran for his life, never looking back. He ran downhill, toward where he guessed the river to be and sure enough, he soon came to his campsite. In what must have been blind panic he bypassed his camp and ran for twelve miles to where his canoe was cached at the mouth of the Conuma.

Father Anthony describes the story of Muchalat Harry's arrival at Nootka as follows. It was probably three in the morning. He and his brother Benedictines were asleep and the village was quiet. Suddenly there was a series of wild cries from the waters of the inlet. Lights were lit and he and others hurried down to the water's edge. There, near frozen and exhausted in his canoe, lay Muchalat Harry. He was barefoot, clad only in his wet and torn underwear, and had paddled his canoe through the winter night 45 miles from the mouth of the Conuma River.

Father Anthony and his companions carried the almost lifeless form up from the water's edge. It took three weeks to nurse Muchalat Harry back to sanity and good health. Father Anthony, who took him into his own care, did the nursing and he told Peter Byrne that during the course of these three weeks, Muchalat Harry's hair turned to pure white.

Byrne spent time at the site, thoroughly investigated the region, but after forty or more years only the forest remained the same as it was in Muchalat Harry's time. It's an excellent story and obviously captured my interest, especially for the mention of Sasquatch behavior and their surroundings.[191]

The Story of Muchalat Harry

Women captives are not usually as lucky as Muchalat Harry or Albert Ostman were. Women kidnapping cases are listed in the Indian Reservations Sightings & Legends Chapter. Let's take a look at these issues and some of the cases to consider. Here is a story I fielded in the early days and practically forgot about it until I began this book.

Author Angus Hall in his book, "Monsters and Mythic Beasts" cited a Miss Helen Westring who a ferocious Sasquatch viciously raped in the forest near Bemidji, Beltrami County, Minnesota. In his book, however, Hall calls the creature a snowman.194a Apparently, rape does happen – that may have been the impetus for this next capture of a young woman gathering berries.

The Sasquatch and the Hat-Pin

Abduction foiled:

I stopped for breakfast one cold winter morning at the Blackberry Patch Restaurant in Burney, California. As small restaurants go, I could hear a conversation going on at the next table. I introduced myself as we exited the restaurant and asked if I could hear the story again.

They were more than willing to accommodate. The couple was from out of state; Collingsworth was his name, the woman I presumed was his wife, but I was careless and didn't get her name…which may have more to do with how good-looking he was than any carelessness I may have had in forgetting to make a note of her name. This man made Brad Pitt look like chopped liver!

The abducted woman they called "Granny Evarts" was described to me as a fair-faced blonde woman in her youth who picked wild berries every spring and jarred them up to sell later at local fairs and flea markets during summer months, a way of supplementing the family income. Her jams and jellies were famous in her hometown, Collingsworth said.

The sequence of events Granny Evarts related to her family was picking a wash-pail full of wild berries in the early morning hours when suddenly she was surprised from behind by a very large hair-covered man with huge shoulders; his height even more surprising. She told the Collingsworth family that the hairy man picked her up and carried her off, scattering her berries about the road. She was carried "under his smelly right arm pit like a sack of potatoes." She said he smelled "foul" and breathed loudly as he walked with her kicking and screaming down a country dirt road, up and over a barbed-wire fence, and through the alfalfa field that backed up directly behind their small one-bedroom farmhouse. Shortening this story up a bit, the ladies of that day wore sun bonnets that were secured on the tops of their heads with long hat pins, and that 5-inch needle-sharp weapon was the means by which the little lady escaped. Dangling upside down, she removed the hat pin and stabbed the hair man in his buttocks. Granny Evarts told her family she was "dropped unceremoniously on the ground" according to the story, and the "Bigfoot moved away swiftly screaming like a squeezed puppy."

The Collingsworth family generally regarded this as "another one of Granny's tales," so the family paid little attention to the story, but it piqued my interest and I never forgot it. Granny Evarts was a lucky woman, and I think it probably happened after I recognized some of the behaviors attributed to the male Sasquatch. This case sent me running to the Goodwill store to find one of those old-fashioned wagon-train type hat pins. I found one with a pearl end stuck proudly in the front of my Buffalo hat...just in case! Who knows, if not for a Sasquatch with romance on his mind then maybe for a mountain lion's backside. A woman never knows!

Everything Went Quiet, Then a Scream

File by David Bray and recorded on Henry Franzoni's old IVBC discussion list:

> My son and I heard a howl or scream in the deep woods of the Colville National Forest in N.W. Washington on 8/24/96 @ 1:00 a.m. The sound was more like the recording found by the Western Bigfoot Society. Actually, it was exactly like that one. It sent shivers down your

back. We were a measured 6 miles North of State Road #20 on Rocky Creek Rd. The sound came from approximately .5 to 1-mile northwest of our campsite. We noticed for the past couple of hours prior to this that the forest was absolutely quiet. No noise at all. The name of the county was Pend O'Reille County (pronounced "pond o'ray") and the closest town was Ione (pronounced "eye-own") about 10 miles by road or 5 miles by air.[*]

Four Men Went Missing in Montana

Seeley Lake, Glacier Creek area, Montana, October 1959. Roy W. Rye, a university-educated and experienced bear hunter from Billings, Montana, was hunting grizzly in the early afternoon. Upon seeing large tracks in the snow, he noticed a creature resting its head and arms on a fallen tree, 5-6 feet above the snow. It had a large flat head, wide shoulders, stubby ears, a short neck, and it was brownish gray-haired.

Older Reports of of Montana From the 1970s

Realizing it had been discovered, the creature looked up and "screamed, rocked from side to side and slobbered." According to a published report in Montana Sports Outdoors, four men disappeared in this same area within a two-year period. Not a trace of them was ever found with the exception of a broken rifle. The disappearance of these men could be attributed to a grizzly, but generally, a grizzly will return

---

[*]   David Bray.

to a kill or will drag off body pieces where clothing, shoes, hats etc. are generally found scattered. This wasn't the case with these disappearances; no clothing or personal items were ever found, only a rifle. This report was published in Montana Sports Outdoors in December 1960 and again in Saga Magazine in January 1961.[192]

The Abduction and Rape of a Railroad Lineman

This next file, I thought, was a highly unusual story, but Lewis repeated it exactly as he had heard it.

In 2007, San Francisco resident John Lewis related a truly bizarre, if not hard-to-believe Bigfoot kidnapping-rape story his grandfather handed down to his mother. Given the time range that the Lewis story occurred, I wasn't all that surprised because the California-Oregon border had a long history of attacks and aggressive behavior patterns noticed by miners, prospectors, loggers, surveyors, and railroad workers; in fact, there was even a gruesome story of a Sasquatch killing a prospector while he was working at his sluice box, allegedly from a Bigfoot bashing the man's head in with a large boulder.

The story that comes to mind for this purpose was one of the kidnapping and rape of a railroad lineman by a female Sasquatch; a most unusual occurrence as these stories go, and it's a wild tale. It read like this:

My grandpa was working for Southern Pacific Railroad building railroad-track in the northern California-Oregon border during the 1900s. I do not know the exact year but during this project, he was dispatched to work on a line camp in the woods. They had a base camp that the crew worked from and each week they would split into two-man teams that would work an area clearing logs and ground, then at the end of one week they would go back to the base camp to check in and replenish their supplies and then set out after the weekend for another week in the woods. During this time, one of the two-man teams came back to base camp with only one man; they were told that the other man had disappeared and was missing. The group at the base camp apparently gave a brief search to no avail. The following week they went out in two-man crews and continued the work on the railroad line clearing. Some weeks later, the group of railroad workers came upon the missing man; he was naked and hysterical/crazed and apparently died soon after he was found. He told of being abducted by a female ape that kept him in a large open pit. During the time he was in the pit the man told of being forced to have sexual contact with the ape many times and said that the ape kept him in the hole by licking his hands and feet raw, so he was not able to escape from it. Apparently, my grandfather saw this man's hands and feet and related that they were indeed completely raw.[*]

Child Abduction Thwarted

The only recorded reference I've read regarding the attempted kidnapping of a young child dates way back to Flintville, Tennessee, in April of 1976; at this writing some 37 years ago. The story itself read something like this:

A most frightening incident occurred in Flintville on April 26, 1976. Mrs. Jennie Robertson nearly lost her 4-year-old son, Gary, to the hands of a Bigfoot. Little Gary was playing outside in the evening hours when his mother heard her little boy cry out. The alert mother rushed outside and saw a huge figure coming around the corner of the house. It was seven or eight feet tall and seemed to be covered with hair. It reached out its long, hairy arm toward little Gary and came within inches of him before Mrs. Robertson could grab him up and pull him to safety. Mr. Robertson ran to the door when he realized what had happened and was just in time to see the backside of a big black shaped figure disappearing into the woods. It was a VERY close call for that youngster. Six heavily armed men tracked the Bigfoot and got close enough to repeatedly fire at it. The Bigfoot screamed

---

[*] John Lewis.

violently and threw rocks at the posse before disappearing into the thickness of the woods. The next day 16-inch tracks were found, alongside hair, blood and mucus. The evidence was analyzed but early-day lab technicians were unable to identify the material.[193]

Gargles and Whistles

Harold Nelson will always remember those few minutes. "I was frozen with terror," he said, still shaken by the experience. "I was face to face with a yeti, a snowman or whatever you want to call those things!" Later, Nelson described the creature:

It had an apelike face but it was definitely not a gorilla. The head was slightly pointed, sloping down like the sketches of cavemen. The whole body was covered with a reddish-brown hair. There were a few spots of white hair along the edge of the enormous shoulders. It stood erect, like a man, and must have weighed 600 or 800 pounds. He was big, real big. My mind just short-circuited. I couldn't think. My flashlight was shining on the beast and I remember very distinctly that the eyes were like those of a wild animal. It made a funny noise sort of like a gargle and whistle at the same time. The thing reached toward me. That's when I screamed. He stepped back, looked puzzled and then frowned. I raced back to my bed and got a .22 caliber pistol from beneath my pillow. I expected the beast to come tearing into the camper. It moved forward, peered curiously into the doorway, then turned and shuffled off into the darkness.[194]

Strange Story

In 1944, Sgt. Charles Reed reported a woman stopped him on the road to Pembroke and claimed she was trying to find her way back to the Lumbee Indian Reserve in North Carolina. She was somewhat inarticulate in her speech but was able to tell Sgt. Reed that she had been taken by a hair-covered hoo-doo man* and had been living in his cave with a woman also covered in dark-colored hair. The sergeant reported that the woman "…smelled to high Heaven but appeared in good health, although gaunt-looking." After saying her ordeal lasted about 6 months or more she refused to comment further. Reed delivered her to the address she had given him and he never saw the woman again. The stench in his vehicle took several days to dissipate.[195]

The Kidnapping of Cherie Darvell

Humboldt County, California – Regarding the Cherie Darvell aka Cherie Nelson story – on May 26, 1976, the Baltimore Sun article on page A-3:

> A young woman, Cherie Darvell, who was reported abducted in rugged mountains by a hairy creature showed up screaming outside a rural resort, but Sheriff's Department officials say they don't believe her story.

The St. Petersburg Times and The Milwaukee Journal also ran similar stories indicating that Darvell, who was Bigfoot enthusiast Ron Olson's girlfriend, walked out from the woods unharmed and in one account said that "…she was relatively unmussed."

The inimitable veteran Bigfoot investigator, Peter Guttilla, remembered the incident this way:

> Sheri, a lovely little tart with too much eye shadow and Dolly Parton hair claimed to have been abducted by Bigfoot someplace near Willow Creek. Of course, it was a hoax. I personally spoke with the Sheriff up there (he was really pissed off about it), who said she was employed by the Olson brothers who were making a Bigfoot movie at the time.

---

* Hoo doo = voo doo-witchcraft.

The last I heard the county was trying to get reimbursed for the expense of searching for Sheri.

Eureka, California - A Del Norte County Superior Court judge who obviously doesn't believe Bigfoot exists has ruled that Humboldt County must pay the $11,613 cost of a 1976 search for an alleged Bigfoot "kidnap victim" by the name of Cherie Darvell.[196]

Miss Darvell was, at the time, girlfriend of Ron Olson, son of Frank Olson of the ANE film distributing company owned by Russell Neihart, Bishop of the Mormon Church in Salt Lake City, Utah. Russell Neihart's best friend, Jerry Romney, originally claimed to be the "man-in-the-suit" in the Roger Patterson film. Romney is, of course, a cousin of Mit Romney, a Republican candidate for President of the USA in 2012.

According to ANE executive Clyde Reinke, he personally signed the payroll checks for Roger Patterson from July to October 1, 1967, for the express purpose of making a film to be circulated by ANE film distributors.

Judge Frank Peterson commented in making the ruling that the search for Bigfoot is "at least an exercise in futility" and said he had "hiked the hills and mountains of Northern California for almost 50 years and the biggest footprint I ever saw was my brother Bob's."

Humboldt County officials sued Shasta County for the costs of the May 22 to 24 aerial and ground search for Cherie Darvell, 25, of Redding. She reportedly had been abducted by a Bigfoot in the Bluff Creek area of Humboldt County. Bigfoot is a legendary hairy, smelly humanoid monster reported seen in Northern California and the Pacific Northwest. Humboldt County Counsel Raymond Schneider argued before Peterson that state law required Shasta County reimburse to Humboldt County because the case involved search and rescue for a Shasta County resident.

> Shasta County Counsel Robert Rehberg countered that Miss Darvell's disappearance was at best a real kidnapping and even the Humboldt County officers' reports indicated they were skeptical about the abduction reports. The girl disappeared while she was with a group searching for Bigfoot. She later walked into the nearby Bluff Creek Resort and, according to the officers' report, "she was remarkably unmussed."[197]

Later, her friends, Ed Bush of Adin, California, and Terry Gaston of Redding, released a movie through ANE film distributors purporting to show a Bigfoot carrying Miss Darvell up a distant mountain slope. Reinke later claimed that the Bigfoot suit for that movie was kept in Russell Neihart's office in Salt Lake City. Later, Judge Peterson ruled that a county is entitled to reimbursement by another county only for the SAR (search and rescue) operations for lost persons or persons "in danger of their lives," and not for investigations of crimes. The judge ruled that the term "in danger of their lives" applies to natural causes, such as floods, heavy snows or other calamities not caused by human beings.

Rehberg said he was "pleased" with the judge's decision but that he sympathized with the dilemmas faced by Humboldt County officials, ranging from whether to begin the search for Miss Darvell to trying to determine who should pay the costs of the search. Rehberg said that if Humboldt County authorities had been willing to stipulate that Bigfoot is a Shasta County resident, negotiations over the costs might have been possible.

Other than the questionable kidnapping of Cherie Darvell in 1976, nothing in recent times has been added to my data that was even close to that story. Still, there may be instances like this in other manuscripts.

The Kidnapping That Didn't Happen

Salmon River, Idaho County, Idaho, during the 1940s:

When I was growing up in Idaho during the 1940s, my father had a ranch in the Salmon River Region. We did not live there, but we went up to the ranch every week flying into the Salmon River Airport in dad's airplane. He had a man named Hiram with a horse and a German Shepard who cared for the ranch and livestock. While business was being taken care of by the men, I was very bored. I would explore the ranch area all day. I found a place where a spring ran through. The trees were tall and there was a lot of brush. It was my little haven, a secret place. One day while there, I heard a noise in the brush and was scared when I saw a huge creature venture out toward me. At first I was frightened, thinking it is was a bear. As the creature came closer, I felt it was trying to calm and reassure me that I was not in any danger.

The creature acted like a female with a motherly attitude. I felt comfortable with her. We sat on a log and she held my hand placing her gentle hand on my knee. I talked to her and she responded with low deep tones and nods of understanding. After about thirty minutes or so, another creature appeared and seemed angry. My new friend stood up and sneered at the other one and put him in his place. He must have been a male; I assumed he was her mate. He would always be there after that, but would stay back and sort of brood. I went back to my haven every time we visited the ranch and always met both of them there. One time the female brought a young creature for me to meet. It must have been her offspring.

My parents sold the ranch in the 1950s and I have never been back. I never did have a chance to say goodbye to my friends, which I would like to have done. I told my mother about my friends, but she did not believe a word of my story. She marveled at my imagination and suggested I stop making up stories like that. I never mentioned the subject again. My friends stood about seven to eight feet tall and the younger one about five feet. The male seemed a bit taller than the female. They had long stringy looking hair over their whole bodies. Their color was a dirty off white with darker hair on the more exposed areas. They both had flat faces with dark squinty eyes. When the male acted irate, his eyes burned black and larger. He actually would strut around trying to show that he was tough and in charge but the female always kept him under control and made him act more gently toward me. I had never heard of Bigfoot as a child, but now I know who my friends were. They will always be a part of my childhood and remembered clearly. They were not the imagination of a child, because I talked and visited with them on a regular basis. I'm sure their offspring may still be in the primitive areas of Idaho, living as nature intended.[198]

ABOUT THE AUTHOR

For nearly thirty years, Bobbie Short has tracked and chronicled newspaper articles and stories, and investigated first-hand reports of sightings and near-sightings of the elusive Sasquatch. Sparked by a 1985 close-up encounter of her own, she has been driven to find out what they are and why they behave the way they do. In this effort, she combines hands-on acquired knowledge with reports both  from her 18-year-old website, Bigfootencounters.com, and nine old computers worth of reports never before published. Mixing the old with the new, she pares away the extraneous information to reveal only that pertaining to Sasquatch conduct and behavioral patterns. DNA may reveal the Sasquatch genome, but it won't tell us how they live, their rules for life, culture and health, or how they manage to survive winters in Yukon, Northwest Territories, or Alaska.

In *The de Facto Sasquatch*, the author documents a list of reported Sasquatch behaviors and their associations with Military Base Installations, Native American and First Nation Reservations in the United States and Canada, taking a hard look at every facet of conduct mentioned in informant testimonies. The book includes shocking reports, both passive encounters and attacks of aggression, and puts to rest rumors about Mt. St. Helens Sasquatch bodies and related false reports about Hollywood suit maker, John Chambers, and claims that he was involved in the making of an ape suit. Hundreds of never-before-seen behavioral traits associated with the Sasquatch are reviewed in this newly released limited edition narrative.

BOOKS BY BOBBIE SHORT

The de Facto Sasquatch

Cultural Legacies and Military Encounters (Book 1)

Behavioral Patterns and Witness Accounts (Book 2)

Controversial Cases and Expert Analyses (Book 3)

AFTERWORD

Go to hangar1publishing.com to learn more about our authors and stay up to date with their newest releases.

NOTES

Sasquatch Behavior

1. www.bigfootencounters.com/sbs/siskiyou.htm
2. www.bigfootencounters.com/sbs/hudspethcounty.htm
3. http://bigfoothistory.wordpress.com/2011/05/24/1975-joplin-missouri-momo-bigfoot-creature
4. www.bigfootencounters.com/sbs/sullivan-cntyTN04.htm
5. https://web.archive.org/web/20120617191945/http://www.examiner.com/article/weird-new-mexico-bigfoot-sightings
6. Richard Gray, Science Correspondence, The London Telegraph.
7. Personal correspondence A.J.R. (1996).
8. Unsealed Conspiracy Files: Bigfoot www.dailymotion.com/video/xxo9l1_unsealed-conspiracy-files-bigfoot_shortfilms#.UTbLYlfNg49
9. Michael Shermer, *The Pattern of Self-Deception*: www.youtube.com/watch?v=b_6-iVz1R0o
10. *What did they really see?* (2011). New York Times editorial.
11. www.burnslakelakesdistrictnews.com/community/sasquatch-sighting-6262139
12. Coon, Carleton S. *Origins of the Races* (1966). Anthropologist Wakefield, Massachusetts. www.bigfootencounters.com/articles/coon.htm
13. D. Trull, Enigma Editor © (1997) ParaScope, Inc. News item published in *The Times* and *The Democrat*, Neeses, South Carolina. www.bigfootencounters.com/stories/south_carolina.htm
14. Personal Correspondence with Wm. Bill Tate, Canon City, Colorado.
15. Hines, Donald M. *Ghost Voices* (1992). Great Eagle Publishing, pp. 327-328.
16. Correspondence with a wheat harvester, Kansas, 2006.
17. Personal correspondence with "Rafter-man", October 25, 2010, Kentucky. www.bigfootencounters.com/stories/clucking.htm
18. Patterson, Roger (1966). *Do Abominable Snowmen of America Really Exist?*
19. The Thomas Byers Story (2011). Paraphrased: *The Shelby Star* Newspaper, North Carolina.
20. Otero County, New Mexico; www.bigfootencounters.com/sbs/otero.htm
21. Story courtesy Peter Byrne, Oregon. www.bigfootencounters.com/stories/paradise.htm
22. Andrews, Edith (May 30, 2008). References from *The Journal Science* on DNA from eastern Asia, Siberia, the Aleutians and over the Bering Sea to the Alaskan shore. www.npr.org/templates/story/story.php?storyId=90960697
23. http://naturalplane.blogspot.com/2011/11/possible-juvenile-bigfoot-sightings.html
24. Mike Acton, Oklahoma. www.bigfootencounters.com/sbs/mcintosh.htm
25. Paraphrased from letters by Edna Walking Horse, 2001. Johnson City, Kansas.
26. Pacific Northwest Magazine (now owned by Seattle Times), 1983.
27. City Monthly, N. Maine articles by Marlene Trask.

28. The Oklahoman. www.bigfootencounters.com/articles/honobia2005.htm

29. The Sasquatch Report, Issue #84 (1997). Report provided by researcher and editor Tim Olson. www.bigfootencounters.com/sbs/iowahappens.htm

30. Bill Dranginis, primary investigator in Virginia (Tommy Davis, March 13, 2012).

31. Buffalo Wilderness, Marion, County, Arkansas. www.bigfootencounters.com/stories/buffalo.htm

32. Marion T. Place, *On the Track of Bigfoot* and Ivan Sanderson's ABSM.

33. *Albuquerque Journal* (1968). Source: Ron Schaffner, *Creature Chronicles*. www.bigfootencounters.com/articles/albuquerque2.htm

34. www.bigfootencounters.com/stories/kezarfallsME.htm

35. www.bigfootencounters.com/films/extended-vocalization.htm

36. The *Akron Beacon*, Union County Ohio: source Ron Schaffner, *Creature Chronicles* (1980).

37. Ibid.

38. Sanderson, Ivan. Abominable Snowman Legend Come to Life, pp. 153, 157. www.sacred-texts.com/lcr/abs/abs12.htm#page_148

39. www.bigfootencounters.com/biology/patty-head-shape.htm

40. Jan Sundberg at GUST website. https://web.archive.org/web/20131111183331/http://sasquatch-pg.net/sasquatch-recovered-fromfire.html

41. Photo is © Jordan Williams, Nevada, April 2012. Paraphrased from Jordan Williams own account on Chuck Prahl and Stacy Hostetler's radio program (2012). https://web.archive.org/web/20121025230954/www.blogtalkradio.com/bigfoottonightshow/2012/04/30/bigfoot-encounters-jordon-willliams-mike-richburg

42. L.R. Traficant (1996). River Forest Park in Cayuga County, New York.

43. www.bigfootencounters.com/stories/bemis.htm

44. The Study of Animals; D.C. Heath & Company, Boston (1911). www.booksshouldbefree.com/book/Guide-for-the-Study-of-Animals-by-Frederic-Lucas and J.E Steele http://answers.yahoo.com/question/index?qid=20070611003939AApRz8c

45. Huffington Post (2012). Chinese boy can see in the dark. www.huffingtonpost.com/2012/01/31/cat-eyes-boy_n_1244543.html

46. Beck, Fred (1924). *I Fought the Ape Men of Mt. St. Helens, Washington.* Written by his son, Ronald A. Beck, 1967.

47. www.bigfootencounters.com/stories/madisoncntyNC.htm

48. https://web.archive.org/web/20110427054441/www.bigfootreferenceguide.com/showthread.php?t=690

49. www.bigfootencounters.com/stories/mottet.htm

50. Hand-written notes in a box from Vance Orchard (2005). Author of Bigfoot of the Blues, (1993), and The Walla Walla Bigfoot, (2001), Walla Walla, Washington.

51. Park County, Montana (2007). www.bigfootencounters.com/sbs/crow-mtn.htm

52. Sean Fries Story. www.bigfootencounters.com/sbs/yuba.htm

53. Mizokami, Kyle (1997). www.bigfootencounters.com/stories/fort.htm Author/writer in San Francisco of such articles as *Bigfoot Ruined by Sex Life* (2001) for Salon dot com. www.salon.com/2001/06/08/scarlet_b/ In the late 1990s, Mizokami created one of the first Bigfoot websites, which contained some of the first and more interesting Native American Legends ever uploaded on the web.

54. The Willits News. www.bigfootencounters.com/articles/willitsCA08.htm

55. Personal correspondence, Heather Gonzales (2009).

56. U.S. Department of Agriculture Research Services. www.ars.usda.gov/Services/docs.htm?docid=9975
57. *Victoria Times* (1975). Article courtesy of Rene Dahinden.
58. Conversations with Rene Dahinden (1999).
59. The Ontario Standard. www.bigfootencounters.com/articles/ontariostandard.htm
60. Conversations with Rene Dahinden (1999).
61. Solunac, Alex (2005). *Too Bizarre for Science.* www.martlet.ca/archives/040916/feature.html
62. http://bigfoothistory.wordpress.com/2011/05/25/1953-riverside-state-park-washington-bigfoot-done-take-my-keds
63. www.blogtalkradio.com/bigfoottonightshow/2013/03/18/david-weverka
64. Brian (2001). Email. www.bigfootencounters.com/sbs/ninebc.htm
65. Mary S. (2000). Masset Inlet, Port Clements, QCI, Canada.
66. http://science.howstuffworks.com/science-vs-myth/strange-creatures/bigfoot.htm
67. Ed Parsons for *The Conway Daily Sun,* New Hampshire. www.bigfootencounters.com/stories/ossipee_rangeNH.htm
68. Older Missouri filings. www.bigfootencounters.com/sbs/oldermissouri.htm
69. Ralph Duff. www.bigfootencounters.com/articles/boonville.htm
70. *The Humboldt Times* (1958), and eight years later published by Roger Patterson in his book *Do Abominable Snowmen of America Really Exist?* (1966), p. 40.
71. Kjeldsen, Maggie (2002). Coos County, New Hampshire. Personal correspondence.
72. *CyberWest Magazine* (1976). www.bigfootencounters.com/stories/sanluisvalley.htm
73. Tim Peeler story. www.bigfootencounters.com/films/tim-peeler.htm
74. J.S. Mendocino, California. www.bigfootencounters.com/stories/bragg.htm
75. Tye Mayer (1999). www.bigfootencounters.com/sbs/mendocino88.htm
76. The Maggie Mae Morgan Story.
77. *Curry Coastal Pilot Newspaper* (2005). Brookings, Oregon.
78. Patterson, Roger (1966). *Do Abominable Snowmen of America Really Exist?*
79. Alissa (2002). Vancouver Island, BC. www.bigfootencounters.com/sbs/boqs.htm
80. www.bigfootencounters.com/stories/pueblocounty.htm
81. www.bigfootencounters.com/articles/clackamas-cntyOR08.htm
82. Recorded by the late Vance Orchard as told by his longtime friend, Bill Laughery.
83. www.bigfootencounters.com/images/patty-hair.htm
84. Sizemore, Edward (2002). Personal correspondence.
85. Mionczynski, John (2010, 2012). Interviews. www.blogtalkradio.com/bigfoottonightshow/2012/09/10/special-guest-john-mionczynski, www.blogtalkradio.com/mnbrt/2012/01/24/mnbrt-radio-with-john-mionczynski and http://wyofile.com/2011/09/john-mionczynski/
86. Wenatchee Valley College Historian, John Brown. www.bigfootencounters.com/legends/spokanes.htm
87. Sanderson, Ivan Terrance (1963). *Abominable Snowmen Legend Come to Life.*
88. *Bigfoot Prowls the Midwest.* www.associatedcontent.com/article/405235/bigfoot_prowls_in_the_midwest.html?cat=37 and *Fortean Times* (2000), FT135. www.bigfootencounters.com/articles/fortean2.htm
89. Lyttle, Rip and the Bigfoot Co-op Newsletter (1994); the IVBC (1996).

90. Wildlife Educator Larry Battson to Short (2005). www.bigfootencounters.com/stories/wabashcountyIN.htm

91. Keno Hill Story: Leonard Jack Thomas. www.bigfootencounters.com/stories/keno hill.htm

92. Fusch, Ed Dr. (2002). *They Walk Among us: S'cwene'y'ti and the Stick Indians of the Colvilles,* second edition, self-published, pp. 32-37. Booklet courtesy Kirk Casey.

93. Pallab Ghosh Science Correspondence for the BBC, *Neanderthals Cooked and Ate Vegetables* (use of fire), BBC Science: *Early Reports Gave the Impression That the Neanderthals Ate Raw Meat.* www.bbc.co.uk/news/science-environment-12071424

94. Joe Beelart's coverage of the Glen Thomas Story http://bfjournal.tripod.com/pages/thomas.html and Jim Hewkin's field report: www.bigfootencounters.com/biology/hewkin92.htm

95. www.bigfootencounters.com/articles/winnipeg.htm

96. Zoologist doubts BF Claim. www.canadaka.net/news/683-zoologist-doubts-bigfoot-claim

97. WHF personal correspondence (2001), and it's also uploaded here: www.bfro.net/GDB/show_report.asp?ID=1226&PrinterFriendly=True

98. Fick, Cory and Wendy (2011). Paraphrased from private correspondence.

99. The Kentucky Post (1980).

100. Sgt. Ken Cooper, Lummi Nation, Washington State. www.bigfootencounters.com/articles/lummi1.htm

101. E. L. MacElwretyh, Greensburg, Pennsylvania. www.bigfootencounters.com/sbs/ligonier.htm

102. Jackson County, West Virginia. www.bigfootencounters.com/sbs/jackson.html

103. *Sasquatch*, Don Hunter and Rene Dahinden. www.bigfootencounters.com/articles/bossburg.htm

104. Story from Michael Lowery. https://web.archive.org/web/20110626115302/www.associatedcontent.com/article/8153577/sasquatch_family_group_footprints_reported_pg2.html?cat=16

105. Vance Orchard, Walla Walla, Washington. www.bigfootencounters.com/stories/bluemtnsWA.htm

106. Al Hodgson's story (2000). www.bigfootencounters.com/sbs/hodgson.htm

107. www.bigfootencounters.com/stories/sharp-cnty.htm

108. *Idaho Falls Post-Register* (1980). Credit John Moore, Ron Schaffner and Peter Guttilla. www.bigfootencounters.com/articles/jacksonwyoming.htm

109. *The Porter Stories* (2006), Meddybemps, Maine. www.bigfootencounters.com/stories/meddybemps.htm

110. *Capital Journal* (1977). Salem, Oregon. www.bigfootencounters.com/articles/ogden123.htm

111. WM. Brann. www.bigfootencounters.com/sbs/chemungcntyNY.htm

112. Nichols, Jon (2009). Vancouver Washington. www.bigfootencounters.com/stories/chenagocntyNY.htm

113. Ken Joholske. www.bigfootencounters.com/sbs/chautauqua.htm

114. Mike Quast. www.bigfootencounters.com/articles/quast.htm

115. Colp, Harry D. (1900). *The Strangest Story Ever Told.* Thomas Bay, Alaska. Published by Virginia Colp. www.bigfootencounters.com/stories/harrycolp.htm

116. www.bigfootencounters.com/sbs/blackgiants.htm

117. *Anchorage Daily News* (1973). www.bigfootencounters.com/sbs/oldalaska.htm

118. Roger Patterson. *Abominable Snowmen*, page 122.

119. Annabel, Russell, authored the Alaskan '*gilyuk* killing', published in *Sports Afield* in the 1930s.

120. Patterson, Roger (1966). *Do Abominable Snowmen of America Really Exist?* Book courtesy Jon Nichols, Vancouver, Washington.

121. Larry Kaniut (unverified story). www.bigfootencounters.com/stories/nome_pilot.htm

122. Larry Battson, Wildlife Educator. www.bigfootencounters.com/sbs/parkecountyIN.htm

123. Hamilton, C. (2011). Inland Empire Website. www.insidetheie.com/bigfoot

124. February 8, 2010. www.damnedct.com/bigfoot-in-connecticut

125. www.bigfootencounters.com/stories/moulton.htm

126. www.bigfootencounters.com/stories/sonomacounty.htm

127. Keith Foster. www.bigfootencounters.com/articles/bugle.htm

128. Foster, Keith (2002). Veteran bow-hunter. *Bugle Magazine,* Volume 19, Issue 6. www.bigfootencounters.com/articles/bugle.htm

129. www.bigfootencounters.com/stories/adamscntyID09.htm

130. Joel White. www.bigfootencounters.com/stories/ansel.htm

131. George, Dan (2004). Taney County, Missouri. www.bigfootencounters.com/stories/taney-cntyMO.htm

132. McKenzie Knight Blog Talk Radio Show (2011). https://web.archive.org/web/20110719024103/www.blogtalkradio.com/mackenzie1/2011/07/17/kris-allen-country-music-star-and-bigfoot-hunter

133. www.bigfootencounters.com/articles/bugle.htm

134. Phil B. (2011).

135. Scott McClean. https://web.archive.org/web/20050130084938/http://mcclean.org/

136. Sanderson, Ivan (1961). *Abominable Snowman*, pp. 34-35; Solunac, Alex (2005). *Too Bizarre for Science.* www.martlet.ca/archives/040916/feature.html

137. Solunac, Alex (2005). *Too Bizarre for Science.* www.martlet.ca/archives/040916/feature.html

138. Seltzer, Leo (2011). Private correspondence.

139. The skyship site has no citations and few sources to lend credibility to them. www.skyshipsovercashiers.com/bigfootet.htm

140. Bord, Colin and Janet (1982). *Bigfoot Casebook.*

141. Vance Orchard's research. www.bigfootencounters.com/articles/vo.htm

142. *The Detroit News-Sunday Edition.* Article provided by Ron Schaffner, Ohio. www.bigfootencounters.com/articles/stclair.htm

143. The story was filed in John Green, B.C., archive index cards and listed in his ape book in 1978, *Sasquatch the Apes Among Us.*

144. *Stag Magazine* (1956). Credit: Jack Kewaunee Lapseritis by way of Dmitri Bayanov. www.bigfootencounters.com/articles/stag_mag1956.htm

145. Correspondence with Keith Foster, Kansas, investigator in Colorado (1990s).

146. Bearman, Joshuah (2002). *Los Angeles Weekly.* www.bigfootencounters.com/articles/labigfoot.htm

147. Witnesses were interviewed by the late Los Angeles County Sheriff's Department

Captain Tom Akren at some point in the 1990s, and forwarded to me. Date unknown.

148. Captain Tom Akren, investigator. www.bigfootencounters.com/sbs/bonners.htm
149. www.bigfootencounters.com/articles/bonner-countyID2012.htm
150. Worley, Don (1977). *Argosy UFO Magazine.*
151. Berry, Rick (1993). *Bigfoot on the East Coast,* p. 51.
152. The Iowa corn farmer (1989). Private correspondence.
153. Dr. Joy Halverson, DVM, www.questgen.biz/cv.htm.050607, Karl A. Breheim, http://bigfootabcs.org/pdf/Karlsjournal.pdf, http://bigfootabcs.org/national.asp, and www.bigfootencounters.com/articles/toolbox.htm
154. Filbey touring map (1989). www.bigfootencounters.com/sightings.htm
155. www.bigfootencounters.com/sightings.htm
156. Glencross, Sandy. *The Sandy Glencross Story.* Personal correspondence.
157. Brock, Ted (2007).
158. www.bigfootencounters.com/stories/wild-man.htm
159. Datus Perry. www.bigfootencounters.com/stories/datus-perry.htm
160. Dahinden, Rene (1999-2000). Conversations.
161. Ibid.
162. www.bigfootencounters.com/stories/delawarecountyNY.htm
163. Schaffner, Ron (1996). Creature Chronicles article. *Cleveland Plain Dealer,* Cincinnati, Ohio.
164. Davis, Marlon K. Mississippi. Correspondence.
165. News article, Peter Guttilla. www.bigfootencounters.com/articles/sierraville.htm
166. Coconino County, Arizona. www.bigfootencounters.com/stories/mogollon.htm
167. Paul Graves. www.inlander.com/spokane/article-16669-hairy-beings-and-nothing ness.html
168. Nathan Graves, MD. www.bigfootencounters.com/sbs/arbuckle.htm
169. Personal correspondence with the late Leo Seltzer, British Columbia, Canada.
170. *Bigfoot roaming the wilds with a human child?* (2000). News article. www.bigfoo tencounters.com/articles/BFbaby.htm
171. Ibid.
172. Ken Kristian, Stuart Island, B.C. www.bigfootencounters.com/articles/hairybeast .htm
173. Larry Battson. www.bigfootencounters.com/stories/putnamcntyIN.htm
174. Larry Battson Stories. www.bigfootencounters.com/stories/putnamcnty2IN.htm
175. Gordon McKoop. www.wawataynews.ca/archive/all/2012/9/6/wunnumin-lake-s-mysterious-bigfoot-family_23409
176. Todd Strong. www.bfro.net/gdb/show_report.asp?id=28709
177. Vance Orchard. www.bigfootencounters.com/stories/marioncnty.htm
178. Martinez, Arturo "Homie" (2006). Story as told to Jerry A. Padilla, Taos, New Mexico. www.bigfootencounters.com/articles/sangre_de_cristo.htm
179. Russ Spence, Tom Hernandez. www.bigfootencounters.com/articles/wyoming.htm
180. Stocking, Diane (1974). Horse/Bigfoot Encounter Report, Douglasville, Georgia.
181. Orchard, Vance (1993, 2001). *Bigfoot of the Blues* and *The Walla Walla Bigfoot.*
182. Sheryl Jenkins. www.bigfootencounters.com/stories/horses.htm
183. J.C. Brown. www.siskiyous.edu/Shasta/bib/B19.htm and *Legends of Mount Shasta* http://en.wikipedia.org/wiki/Legends_of_Mount_Shasta

184. www.ufodigest.com/article/mysteries-mount-shasta-home-underground-dwellers-and-ancient-gods
185. Rich Grumley. www.bigfootencounters.com/articles/grumley.htm
186. Green, John. *Sasquatch the Apes Among Us,* p. 186.
187. Cameron, Connie Dr. (2003). *Bigfoot Co-op Newsletter.* Editor Anthropologist, previously published by Theo Stein in the *Denver Post.* www.bigfootencounters.com/stories/san-juanCO.htm
188. Mike S. www.bigfootencounters.com/sbs/castlelake.htm
189. Private Correspondence. www.bigfootencounters.com/stories/siskiyou2006.htm
190. Annette B. Jefferson County, NY. www.bigfootencounters.com/sbs/perchlake.htm
191. Byrne, Peter (1975). *The Search for Bigfoot.* The story of Muchalat Harry is an outtake from Mr. Byrne's book with his permission (1999). www.bigfootencounters.com/classics/muchalat.htm
192. Montana Sports Outdoors. www.bigfootencounters.com/sbs/oldermontana.htm
193. Bord, Janet and Colin (1982). *The Bigfoot Casebook,* pp. 125-126.
194. Smith, Warren (1969). *SAGA Magazine.*
195. Saturday Evening Post *(*1944).
196. *The California Record-Searchlight.* Clyde Reineke, Peter Guttilla personal correspondence.
197. Ibid.
198. Fate Magazine (2004).

"These are not just animals, these are a type of people...they don't want to be seen, they don't want to be found…"

~ Dr. Melba Ketchum DVM
November 29, 2012
ABC News on Good Morning America